A New Introduction
to American Studies

A New Introduction to American Studies

Edited by Howard Temperley
and Christopher Bigsby

Harlow, England • London • New York • Boston • San Francisco • Toronto
Sydney • Tokyo • Singapore • Hong Kong • Seoul • Taipei • New Delhi
Cape Town • Madrid • Mexico City • Amsterdam • Munich • Paris • Milan

PEARSON EDUCATION LIMITED

Edinburgh Gate
Harlow CM20 2JE
United Kingdom
Tel: +44 (0)1279 623623
Fax: +44 (0)1279 431059
Website: www.pearsoned.co.uk

First edition published in Great Britain in 2006

© Howard Temperley and Christopher Bigsby 2006

ISBN-13: 978-0-582-89437-2
ISBN-10: 0-582-89437-9

British Library Cataloguing in Publication Data
A CIP catalogue record for this book can be obtained from the British Library

Library of Congress Cataloging in Publication Data
A new introduction to American studies / edited by Howard Temperley and Christopher Bigsby.
    p. cm.
  Includes bibliographical references and index.
  ISBN-13: 978-0-582-89437-2
  ISBN-10: 0-582-89437-9
    1. United States--Study and teaching. 2. United States--Civilization. I. Bigsby, C. W. E.
II. Temperley, Howard.

E175.8.N355 2005
973--dc22   2005050429

10 9 8 7 6 5 4 3 2 1
10 09 08 07 06 05

Set by 71 in 9/13.5 pt Stone Serif
Printed and bound in Malaysia

The Publisher's policy is to use paper manufactured from sustainable forests.

In memory of Malcolm Bradbury 1932–2000

Contents

Publisher's acknowledgements   viii

Chronology   ix

Introduction   1

1   The human and natural environment *Peter Coates*   7

2   From settlement to independence *Colin Bonwick*   29

3   American political culture *Adam I. P. Smith*   50

4   Slavery and secession *Howard Temperley*   75

5   Native Americans *Gail D. MacLeitch*   98

6   Revisiting the American West *Margaret Walsh*   123

7   American immigration *Axel R. Schäfer*   147

8   Nineteenth-century American literature
Allan Lloyd Smith   170

9   Industry and technology *Christopher Clark*   198

10   The twentieth-century American novel *John Whitley*   220

11   Twentieth-century American poetry *Daniel Kane*   240

12   Twentieth-century American drama *Christopher Bigsby*   273

13   America and war *Brian Holden Reid*   302

14   American women *Elizabeth J. Clapp*   326

15   Popular culture *Nick Heffernan*   352

16   America at the millennium *Richard Crockatt*   376

Maps   397

Notes on the contributors   403

Index   407

Publisher's acknowledgements

The publishers are grateful to the following for permission to reproduce copyright material:

Excerpt from "Mending Wall" from THE POETRY OF ROBERT FROST edited by Edward Connery Lathem. Copyright 1958 by Robert Frost, copyright 1967 by Lesley Frost Ballantine, copyright 1915, 1930, 1939, 1969 by Henry Holt and Company. Reprinted by permission of Henry Holt and Company, LLC. Carcanet Press Limited for excerpt from "The Picture of Little J.A. in a Prospect of Flowers", featured in NEW YORK POETS: AN ANTHOLOGY, edited by Mark Ford, Carcanet Press Limited, 2004. Carcanet Press Limited for excerpt from "How Much Longer Will I Be Able to Inhabit the Divine Sepulcher", featured in THE MOORING OF STARTING OUT, Carcanet Press Limited, 1997.

In some instances we may have been unable to trace the owners of copyright material, and we would appreciate any information that would enable us to do so.

Chronology

1492	Columbus's first voyage to New World
1519–21	Conquest of Mexico
1531–3	Conquest of Peru
1549	Portugal establishes colonial rule in Brazil
1585–90	Unsuccessful attempt to establish an English colony on Roanoke Island (now North Carolina)
1607	Settlement of Jamestown, Virginia
1608–27	French settlement of St Lawrence Valley
1620	Pilgrim Fathers establish Plymouth Colony
1630	Puritan settlement of Massachusetts Bay
1634	Settlement of Maryland
1636	Harvard College founded
1640	*Bay Psalm Book*
1650	Ann Bradstreet, *The Tenth Muse Lately Sprung up in America*
1661–4	British conquest of New Netherland (New York)
1662	Michael Wigglesworth, *The Day of Doom*
1669–80	Founding of Charleston
1675–6	King Philip's War breaks Indian resistance in New England
1680–2	Founding of Pennsylvania
c.1680–1725	Edward Taylor's poetry written (unpublished until twentieth century)
1689–97	King William's War against French
1698–1702	French settlement of Louisiana
1702	Cotton Mather, *Magnalia Christi Americana*
1702–13	Queen Anne's War against French
1732–57	Benjamin Franklin, *Poor Richard's Almanack*
1733	Founding of Georgia
1736–56	Great Awakening
1744–8	King George's War against French
1754	Beginning of French and Indian War

1760	French surrender Canada to British
1763	Peace of Paris
1765	Stamp Act
1767	Townshend Duties
1773	Boston Tea Party
1774	Coercive Acts
1775	Fighting at Lexington and Concord; Second Continental Congress assembles
1776	Thomas Paine, *Common Sense*; Declaration of Independence
1778	Franco–American alliance
1781	Articles of Confederation proclaimed; defeat of British at Yorktown
1782	J. H. St John de Crèvecoeur, *Letters from an American Farmer*
1783	Articles of Peace ratified (Treaty of Paris); Noah Webster, *American Spelling Book*
1785	Ordinance passed for sale of western lands
1787	Constitutional Convention meets in Philadelphia; Northwest Ordinance provides for government of national domain
1787–8	Alexander Hamilton *et al.*, *The Federalist*
1788	Constitution ratified
1789	George Washington elected first US president
1790	First US census shows population of 3.9 million
1791–6	Hamilton–Jefferson feud leads to emergence of first American party system (Federalists versus Democratic-Republicans)
1793	Eli Whitney invents cotton gin
1800	Thomas Jefferson (Democratic-Republican) elected third US president
1803	Louisiana Purchase extends US border to Rockies
1807	African slave trade to United States abolished; Joel Barlow, *The Columbiad*
1812–14	War of 1812
1815–17	Collapse of Federalist Party
1819	Washington Irving, *Sketch Book of Geoffrey Crayon, Gent.*
1820	Missouri Compromise exludes slavery from Louisiana Purchase Lands north of 36° 319'
1823	Monroe Doctrine; James Fenimore Cooper, *The Pioneers*
1824	Election of John Quincy Adam as sixth US president heralds break-up of Republican Party

1825	Erie Canal links Hudson River and Great Lakes
1826	James Fenimore Cooper, *The Last of the Mohicans*
1828	Noah Webster, *An American Dictionary of the English Language*; Andrew Jackson elected seventh US president
1831	Nat Turner uprising in Virginia; Edgar Allan Poe, *Poems*
1832–3	Nullification Crisis leads to scaling-down of tariffs on imported goods
1833	American Antislavery Society founded
1835–40	Alexis de Tocqueville, *Democracy in America*
1836	Colt pistol patented; Texas achieves independence from Mexico and becomes a sovereign republic
1837	Ralph Waldo Emerson, 'The American Scholar'
1840	Abolitionists launch Liberty Party; William Harrison (Whig) defeats Martin Van Buren (Democrat) in contest for US presidency; Edgar Allan Poe, *Tales of the Grotesque*
1841	Horace Greeley launches *New York Tribune*
1843	W. H. Prescott, *History of the Conquest of Mexico*
1845	Annexation of Texas
1846	Introduction of McCormick reaper; by agreement with Britain, United States acquired control of Pacific Northwest up to the 49th parallel (Oregon Settlement)
1846–8	War with Mexico leads to acquisition of California and Pacific Southwest
1849	California gold rush; Francis Parkman, *Oregon Trail*
1850	Nathaniel Hawthorne, *The Scarlet Letter*; Compromise of 1850; seventh US census shows a population of 23 million
1850–3	Collapse of Whig Party
1851	Herman Melville, *Moby-Dick*; *New York Times* launched
1852	Harriet Beecher Stowe, *Uncle Tom's Cabin*
1854	Kansas–Nebraska Act repeals Missouri Compromise; emergence of Republican Party; Henry David Thoreau, *Walden*
1855	First edition of Walt Whitman's *Leaves of Grass*
1857	Supreme Court's Dred Scott decision denies citizenship to US blacks and right of Congress to exclude slavery from territories
1859	John Brown's raid on arsenal at Harper's Ferry, Virginia
1860	Abraham Lincoln (Republican) elected sixteenth US president

1861	Secession of Southern states leads to outbreak of Civil War; Morrill Tariff inaugurates new high-tariff policy
1862	Homestead Act
1863	Emancipation Proclamation frees slaves in areas under rebel control
1865	Surrender of Confederate forces; slavery abolished by Thirteenth Amendment; assassination of President Lincoln
1867	First Reconstruction Act; purchase of Alaska from Russia; Horatio Alger, *Ragged Dick*
1869	Mark Twain, *Innocents Abroad*; completion of first transcontinental railroad
1870	Bret Harte, *The Luck of Roaring Camp*
1875	Mary Baker Eddy, *Science and Health*
1875–6	Second Sioux War; defeat of Custer's cavalry in Battle of the Little Big Horn
1876	Invention of the telephone by Alexander Graham Bell
1877	Withdrawal of Federal troops from the South marks end of Reconstruction
1881	John D. Rockefeller's Standard Oil Trust established; Henry James, *Portrait of a Lady*
1885	Mark Twain, *The Adventures of Huckleberry Finn*; William Dean Howells, *The Rise of Silas Lapham*
1887	Dawes Severalty Act provides for the settlement of Indians on homesteads
1888	Edward Bellamy, *Looking Backward*
1890	Sherman Antitrust Act; eleventh US census declares frontier closed
1891	Formation of the People's (Populist) Party
1893	Chicago World's Columbian Exposition
1895	J. P. Morgan and Co. established; Stephen Crane, *The Red Badge of Courage*
1896	Supreme Court upholds legality of 'separate but equal' facilities for blacks
1898	Spanish–American War; annexation of Hawaii and Philippines
1899	Thornstein Verblen, *The Theory of the Leisure Class*; Frank Norris, *McTeague*
1900	Theodore Dreiser, *Sister Carrie*; twelfth US census shows population of 76 million
1901	US Steel Corporation established

1903	Henry James, *The Ambassadors*; Jack London, *Call of the Wild*; W. E. B. Du Bois, *The Souls of Black Folk*
1906	Upton Sinclair, *The Jungle*
1907	Peak immigration year: 1,285,000 immigrants enter United States; Henry Adams, *Education of Henry Adams*; William James, *Pragmatism*
1909	First Model T Ford; Gertrude Stein, *Three Lives*
1913	Armory Show exhibits modern art
1914	Eight-hour day with five-dollar minimum wage introduced in all Ford plants; President Wilson proclaims US neutrality
1915	British steamer *Lusitania* torpedoed with loss of over a hundred American lives; Germany restricts submarine warfare; D. W. Griffiths, *The Birth of a Nation*; Edgar Lee Masters, *Spoon River Anthology*
1917	German resumption of unrestricted submarine warfare; US declaration of war; T. S. Eliot, 'The Love Song of J. Alfred Prufrock'
1918	Wilson outlines his Fourteen Points to Congress; Armistice ends war in Europe
1919	Prohibition Amendment ratified; Sherwood Anderson, *Winesburg, Ohio*; Senate votes down US membership of League of Nations
1920	Red Scare leads to mass arrests of labour agitators; Sinclair Lewis, *Main Street*; Ezra Pound, *Hugh Selwyn Mauberley*; fourteenth US census shows urban population exceeds rural
1921	Quota laws restrict immigration
1922	T. S. Eliot, *The Waste Land*; Eugene O'Neill, *Anna Christie*
1923	Henry R. Luce launches *Time*; D. H. Lawrence, *Studies in Classic American Literature*; Wallace Stevens, *Harmonium*
1925	F. Scott Fitzgerald, *The Great Gatsby*; Gertrude Stein, *The Making of Americans*; Scopes (evolution) trial in Dayton, Tennessee; Harold Ross launches *The New Yorker*
1926	Ernest Hemingway, *The Sun Also Rises*
1927	Execution of Sacco and Vanzetti; Charles Lindbergh flies Atlantic
1928	First full-length sound film; 26 million cars and 13 million radios in use in United States
1929	William Faulkner, *The Sound and the Fury*; Ernest Hemingway, *A Farewell to Arms*; stock-market crash

1930	Hart Crane, *The Bridge*; Ezra Pound, *A Draft of XXX Cantos*
1932	William Faulkner, *Light in August*
1933	Inauguration of Franklin D. Roosevelt; beginning of New Deal; end of prohibition
1934	Scott Fitzgerald, *Tender is the Night*; William Carlos Williams, *Collected Poems, 1921–31*
1935–7	Neutrality legislation passed in order to prevent United States being drawn into future foreign wars
1936	John Dos Passos, *U.S.A.*
1939	John Steinbeck, *The Grapes of Wrath*; Nathanael West, *The Day of the Locust*; Britain and France declare war on Germany
1940	Richard Wright, *Native Son*
1941	Lend-Lease Act; Orson Welles's *Citizen Kane*; Japanese attack on Pearl Harbor leads to American entry into war
1942	American troops fighting in Pacific and North Africa; UN Declaration signed in Washington
1943	Rodgers and Hammerstein, *Oklahoma!*
1944	Allied invasion of Normandy; advance of Russian forces into Czechoslovakia, Hungary and Poland
1945	German capitulation; surrender of Japan following dropping of atomic bombs on Hiroshima and Nagasaki; UN Conference in San Francisco
1946	Robert Penn Warren, *All the King's Men*; William Carlos Williams, *Paterson, Book One*
1947	Truman Doctrine and Marshall Plan designed to counteract Soviet expansionism and provide for European reconstruction; Taft-Hartley Act restricts trade union power; Tennessee Williams, *A Streetcar Named Desire*
1948	Norman Mailer, *The Naked and the Dead*
1948–9	Berlin blockade and airlift
1949	NATO established; Arthur Miller, *Death of a Salesman*
1950–3	Korean War
1950	Alger Hiss convicted of perjury; McCarthy launches anticommunist crusade; seventeenth US census shows population of 151 million
1950–60	Advent of mass television
1951	J. D. Salinger, *The Catcher in the Rye*
1952	Ralph Ellison, *Invisible Man*
1953	James Baldwin, *Go Tell it on the Mountain*; execution of Rosenbergs for atomic espionage

1954	J. Robert Oppenheimer denied security clearance; Senate censures McCarthy; Supreme Court rules against school segregation; Wallace Stevens, *Collected Poems*
1956	Suez crisis; Soviet invasion of Hungary; Eugene O'Neill, *Long Day's Journey into Night*
1957	Jack Kerouac, *On the Road*; federal troops enforce school desegregation in Little Rock, Arkansas
1958	John Kenneth Galbraith, *The Affluent Society*
1959	Saul Bellow, *Henderson the Rain King*; Robert Lowell, *Life Studies*
1961	Inauguration of President Kennedy who calls for a 'New Frontier'; Bay of Pigs (Cuban invasion) fiasco
1961–8	Birth control pill comes into general use
1962	Cuban missile crisis; international live telecasts by satellite; Rachel Carson, *Silent Spring*; Edward Albee, *Who's Afraid of Virginia Woolf?*
1963	Assassination of President Kennedy; Betty Friedan, *The Feminine Mystique*
1964	President Johnson calls for a Great Society; Saul Bellow, *Herzog*; Gulf of Tonkin Resolution leads to build-up of US ground forces in South Vietnam
1965–7	Race riots in Los Angeles, Cleveland, Chicago, Newark, Detroit and other major cities
1968–72	Student protest on US campuses
1968	Assassination of Robert Kennedy and Martin Luther King; Norman Mailer, *Armies of the Night*; John Updike, *Couples*
1969	US astronauts land on the Moon
1970	US forces invade Cambodia; National Guard fire on students at Kent State University, Ohio; Saul Bellow, *Mr Sammler's Planet*
1971	Severing of historic link between the dollar and gold marks the end of the post-war international monetary system
1972	President Nixon visits China; SALT I agreement with Soviet Union
1973	US ground troops withdraw from Vietnam; Allende Government of Chile overthrown; OPEC quadruples price of oil; Thomas Pynchon, *Gravity's Rainbow*; *Roe* v. *Wade* gives women right to abortion
1974	Watergate scandals lead to resignation of President Nixon
1975	South Vietnam and Cambodia surrender to communist forces

1976	Saul Bellow awarded Nobel Prize for Literature
1979	Egypt and Israel sign peace agreement at Camp David; President Carter launches national campaign to conserve energy; Shah of Iran overthrown; Soviet invasion of Afghanistan; Congress refuses to ratify SALT II
1980	Hostage crisis in Iran; Ronald Reagan elected president
1981	Reagan calls for massive increases in defence spending
1982	Accumulating evidence of AIDS epidemic in United States; administration adopts tax-cutting policies to promote economic growth
1983	Reagan describes Soviet Union as an 'empire of evil'; announces Strategic Defense (Star Wars) Initiative
1986	Iran-Contra revelations embarrass administration; US planes bomb Libya
1988	Tom Wolfe, *The Bonfire of the Vanities*
1989	Fall of Berlin Wall
1991	Soviet troops begin withdrawal from Eastern Europe
1991	Collapse of Soviet Union; Russian Communist Party disbanded; American-led UN force drives Iraq out of Kuwait in First Gulf War:
1992	Acquittal of police photographed beating Rodney King sparks riots in Los Angeles
1993	Treaty links United States, Canada, Mexico in free trade area; Toni Morrison wins Nobel Prize for Literature
1995	Home-grown terrorists bomb federal building in Oklahoma City; black and white opinion divided over O. J. Simpson acquittal
1999	Poland, Hungary and Czech Republic join NATO
2000	Philip Roth, *The Human Stain*, Supreme Court hands presidency to George W. Bush in disputed election
2001	Al-Qaeda suicide teams fly passenger jets into World Trade Center and Pentagon; President Bush declares global war on terror
2002	UN force led by United States overthrows Taliban régime in Afghanistan
2003	US–UK force invades Iraq without UN approval; public opinion in both countries divided; France, Germany and other former allies accuse United States of high-handedness

2004 President Bush is re-elected despite failure to find weapons of mass destruction and continuing conflict in Iraq

2005 President proclaims intention to promote 'liberty throughout the whole world'

Introduction

When the American Studies movement was founded in the 1930s there was a confidence that America could be explained in terms of its exceptional circumstances and nature. The existence of 'free' land, an abundance of natural resources, the nature of a frontier experience, the fact of immigration and its racial admixture all seemed keys to a society that asserted its unique nature and function. Admittedly that movement was constituted by scholars who were at that moment liable to be in contention with a capitalist ethos that had also seemed definitional until the Depression stopped the American clock. Nonetheless, just as authors of what came to be called the Great American Novel seemed to believe that they could capture the society whole and entire, so it seemed possible for scholars drawing on the techniques of history, literature and the new social sciences to do likewise.

In the Second World War, but more particularly with the advent of the Cold War, American identity became the concern of some who set themselves up as judges of its purity, excluding and persecuting those they regarded as un-American. As Alexis de Tocqueville had observed a century earlier, American patriotism could be oppressively aggressive. So, too, could American notions of equality, democracy and liberty. Some have even compared Americans' commitment to these values as a form of secular religion, noting that what Americans mean by them is not always what other people mean. For example, when Americans talk of liberty it is the right not to be arbitrarily bossed around by the likes of George III rather than the right not to conform to what Tocqueville aptly called 'the tyranny of the majority'. It was reflections such as these that led Henry David Thoreau in 1849 to insist on the need for occasional civil disobedience, by which he meant the absolute right of individuals to follow the dictates of their own conscience rather than conform to the beliefs of their fellow citizens.

Eighty years later there were those who insisted that the American Studies project was flawed precisely because it too readily accepted assumptions about the homogeneity of America and its unique qualities. The familiar metaphor of a melting pot seemed suddenly neither accurate nor desirable. American identity, apparently so self-evident, so aggressively asserted and celebrated daily by the country's children in pledges of allegiance, was revealed as deeply problematic. Confidence in the American Studies idea, at least as originally formulated, was dented. Perhaps, it was suggested, it should defer to studies of those constituent elements that had once seemed no more than fragments in a national mosaic. Maybe gender, race, ethnicity, national origin and sexual preference were something more than local accents, minor variations on a national theme. The task was now to track transnational identities, to see in difference not withdrawal or exclusion from a national consensus but entirely coherent and self-contained assertions of being. National identity depended on a series of negotiations rather than a proposition requiring only assent.

Yet when America was assaulted from without, as it was on 11 September 2001, it was not difference that was celebrated, but shared values, shared apprehension, shared pain and the notion of a shared fate. It was as Americans that they stood stunned and as Americans that they responded. When the President reached back to a Manichean language and insisted that people were either with us or against us there was no doubting, at least at first, as to who that 'us' might be. Answers depend on the question asked. Later, fissures began to open, but in truth these had less to do with any of those sub-groups, resisting such a description of themselves as they may, than with political differences of a kind that characterise any democracy and which certainly characterised the United States. In the first two elections of the twenty-first century the country divided over moral issues as much as over economic strategy and foreign policy. It seemingly divided, too, geographically, with the Democrats commanding East and West Coasts, along with the upper Midwest, and the Republicans all the rest, though such a division was more apparent than real since the electoral college system assigns states to the parties on the basis of a simple majority, thereby concealing the dynamics of party loyalty at the local level. Nonetheless, even at times of stress, when those virtues offered to the world as definitional of the American experience are most frequently invoked even as they are unceremoniously abandoned (as they were in the Red Scare of 1919, the internment of Japanese-Americans in 1942, the McCarthyite period of the

1950s and the Patriot Act of 2002), there is still uncertainty as to what America and Americans might be.

Few if any countries in the world are as concerned with defining a national identity as Americans. Yet at the same time they remain oddly uncertain. In 2004 a book was published entitled *Who Are We?* You would have thought that well over two hundred years after the Declaration of Independence they would have known. Does not the nation's currency celebrate its unity (*E pluribus unum*, 'from many, one')? Do its children not speak of an indivisible nation with liberty and justice for all? Do Americans not salute the flag, fly it, become indignant at its misuse as if it were, indeed, emblematic of an agreed and uncontested nationhood? America offers itself to the world as the model of virtue, the template for political faith, the repository of freedom and opportunity. Why, then, beneath such an apparent assurance, does there evidently remain sufficient doubt to make identity problematic?

When the framers of the Constitution met in Philadelphia to debate priorities they committed those who followed them to an odd objective. Americans, it seemed, were to pursue happiness, not something it is possible to imagine the Germans, say, or the British signing up to. Nor was everyone at Philadelphia satisfied. There were those who preferred the phrase 'the possession of property', and that does appear in a number of state constitutions. For some, then, happiness was an abstract and undefined virtue; for others it was a matter of material possessions, a seeming paradox investigated by F. Scott Fitzgerald in *The Great Gatsby*. This, after all, is a country with a national dream paradoxically committed to its materialisation, but a dream realised is no longer a dream. Happiness possessed is no longer happiness pursued. The dilemma left even Gatsby, the great believer, confused. Indeed, it left him dead, floating in that symbol of achieved wealth, a swimming pool, to the end failing to understand that he had wedded his dreams of transcendence to a perishable materiality.

If that was one contradiction, there were others. One, in particular, was striking. If all men were created equal, what was to be made of slavery? Thomas Jefferson sought to address this in his draft of the Constitution, but the relevant sentences were struck out by representatives from the southern states, while he himself not only kept slaves but produced children by one of them, a fact attested to centuries later by an unmistakable DNA signature. In another context, Walt Whitman asked whether he contradicted himself, only to assert, not with shame but confident assurance that he did, indeed. In so saying perhaps he identified a characteristic of a culture whose contradictions, paradoxically, may prove definitional.

So, was the American to pursue abstractions or embrace the material, to celebrate freedom or insist that freedom did not extend to those whose skin was of a different colour? And since this new country was based on the idea of history restarting itself, the promise of re-invention, how could a fixed identity be either logical or desirable? Was flux to be feared or celebrated as a defining quality?

America's writers in the nineteenth century seemed clear enough on the subject. They wrote books about the impossibility of definition (James Fenimore Cooper's Leatherstocking series, Nathaniel Hawthorne's *The Scarlet Letter*, Herman Melville's *Moby-Dick*, Mark Twain's *Huckleberry Finn*). Their protagonists had problematic names. If, until late in the nineteenth century, America was an undiscovered country, its citizens were about the business of inventing and re-inventing themselves, as Jay Gatz, rooted in a frontier myth, would transform himself into the exploitative but romantic Jay Gatsby.

The truth was that America was built on a series of contradictions, acknowledged or denied. It was simultaneously the embodiment of Rousseauesque ideas about the innocence of the primitive, with echoes of a biblical Eden, and an expression of Enlightenment values, a rational society with defining rules. It apotheosised both the individual and the community, freedom and equality, a utopian future and a mythical past. Its identity would be forged on the frontier or in the city, as the latter became synonymous with a modernity that many would later mistake for Americanism. In the twenty-first century America planned a journey to Mars even as its citizens reached back to a model of community based on fundamentalist religion. A country that boasted a cascade of Nobel scientists saw a revival of Creationism. Declaring its commitment to peace, it waged a series of wars. How, then, to define a culture changing moment by moment as immigrants continue to enter, bringing with them values, traditions, languages and dreams of their own? With a population rising towards 300 million, occupying a land mass so large that it separates governed from governors by thousands of miles, a country of deserts and mountains, open plains and coastal settlements, rural communities and cities that sprawl over tens of miles and in certain places begin to merge into megalopolises stretching for hundreds of miles, how could identity and national purpose be anything but fluid and problematic? A homogenising American dream has to make space for millions of other dreams. A master story has to concede space to multiple narratives, a complex of histories and futures, even as it proposes consensus – a containing endeavour that will resist potentially centrifugal forces. The fear is always of division and entropy (the latter a popular trope in the work of a number of twentieth-century novelists).

The response is always an insistence on the centripetal logic of a nation whose divisions must be denied.

America existed as an idea long before the first Spanish explorer, Dutch sailor or English Puritan set foot on the land, and that idea informed its unfolding history. It was utopian in origin and in expectation, yet it stained its supposed Eden with a withering violence that itself would become definitional. But, of course, identity must remain provisional in a country that declares the irrelevance of history. To those who went there to escape what they had been, it was and is a Protean culture that celebrates those who reinvented themselves.

How, one might ask, could a nation that began with acts of genocide and that practised slavery, that established its frontiers in part by war, present itself as a city on a hill, offer itself as a paradigm, declare itself the source of redemption and liberation? The answer in part lay in an attitude towards history that made it seem irrelevant to a society committed to the future, and in part in choosing to believe that those it subordinated had no real claim on full humanity and were an impediment to the perfection of mankind. In place of history there was a preference for myth, the myth of black incapacity and the Native Americans' destiny to fulfil the function of characters in a morality play by in the end disappearing.

The first European observers, particularly Crèvecoeur and Tocqueville, proved remarkably prescient in their observations, quickly identifying characteristics that would, indeed, prove definitional even in their contrarities. But, then, the outside observer sometimes sees with a keener eye, and for all the changing nature of a society – in which more than one-tenth of the population would, at the beginning of the twenty-first century as at the beginning of the twentieth, be born outside the country – there have been certain defining qualities even as there was a failure to resolve seeming paradoxes.

America might not be one country, indivisible – its fault lines being clear enough – but it clearly differs in certain crucial respects from those countries that now find themselves part of a Pax Americana. Does it make sense, then, to embrace ideas of American exceptionalism? Did many countries – Australia, Canada, Russia among them – not have a frontier? Were there not other countries with indigenous populations whose ill-treatment left a centuries-long stain on the myths of progress and adventure? Are other countries not shaped in part by immigration, technological innovation, a wealth of natural resources, religion, democratic values, dreams of spiritual and material advance? Perhaps a comparative study would help to tease out those nuances that distinguish one culture, one nation, even one empire from another, for, despite resistance to the very word, America's history has in many ways been an imperial one. The settlement of the country offered a classic example of imperial hubris. The policy of creating a world in which America can function, laid out in the 1990s by those who formulated the Project for a New American Century, and who in 2000 came to power, is not without its precedent. For Oswald Spengler, influential in the early years of the twentieth century – not least with F. Scott Fitzgerald who read his work, and, later with Edward Albee who refers to it in *Who's Afraid of Virginia Woolf?* – America was the new Rome.

Today, America is the world's only superpower. It is impossible to ignore. As President George W. Bush declared in his second Inaugural Address on 21 January 2005, 'America, in this young century, proclaims liberty throughout the whole world, and to all the people thereof'. Some may see this as a demonstration of America's overwhelming hubris and a threat to their interests; for others, it represents what the United States, the last, great hope of mankind, truly stands for. As a nation, America uses a disproportionate amount of the world's energy resources. Its corporations reach out across the globe. Its cultural products are omnipresent and, for the most part, eagerly embraced. Its literature, theatre, dance, music, art, popular culture, food, technology and science help shape and define the world and hence what we, who wish to believe ourselves disinterested observers, are. How can we not engage and seek to understand it, if only in the process the better to understand ourselves? One of the most vibrant of academic organisations is the European Association for American Studies. It exists, as its name implies, to facilitate the study of America, but in the process of doing so its members inevitably come to ask the question of what a European might be. Seen from the vantage point of the United States Europe seems more homogeneous than it is. That does not mean that it does not exist. The contrary is also true. Those who feel the impact of the United States, for good or ill, do not perceive it primarily as a divided and problematic state, uncertain of its identity, unsure as to its direction. Its political, economic, scientific and cultural policies seem clear enough, as do the consequences of such policies. The United States is a single country, as Europe manifestly is not. For those studying it, however, the rhetoric of unity, of indivisibility, should not inhibit our exploration of a culture and a society whose distinctiveness may be available for interrogation and challenge but which remains a central fact of the modern experience.

CHAPTER 1

The human and natural environment

Peter Coates

Rediscovering nature in American Studies

The 'fresh green breast of the new world' that F. Scott Fitzgerald conjured up at the end of *The Great Gatsby* (1925) – a lost world that 'once pandered to the last and greatest of human dreams' – is more than a vision of innocence, promise and yearning. America is a physical and biological place – a material place – consisting not just of the trees superseded by lavish mansions like Gatsby's but also of rocks, soil and water and creatures great and small. America the place is more than a setting for the real action of American life. American history and culture are profoundly shaped by the interplay between people and the non-human world of nature.

As Alfred J. Crosby reminded us in *The Columbian Exchange: Biological and Cultural Consequences of 1492* (1972), 'Man is a biological entity before he is a Roman Catholic or a capitalist or anything else'. As well as situating human affairs within a wider biological context – which embraces the human impact on the rest of nature as well as environmental influences on humanity – we need to examine the cultural history of ideas about nature and representations of nature. The third aspect of the dialogue between Americans and their environment covered in this chapter is the phenomenon of conservation and environmentalism, which has constituted one of the most influential social movements and vibrant areas of reformist activity in the United States over the past century and a half.

By studying American relations with the natural environment, we can deepen our understanding of many central ingredients of the American experience: colonisation; material abundance; the perils of prosperity; notions of property; the tension between individual rights and social responsibilities; the impact of technological innovation, industrialisation and urbanisation; popular protest; the regulatory state; and the nature of national identity. Not least, the study of nature and environment reconnects the American experience with that of other 'new' worlds. For Walter Prescott Webb, the United States belonged to a 'Great Frontier' of British/European expansion that also embraced Canada, Australia, New Zealand and the southern parts of Africa and South America. In *The Great Frontier* (1951), the Texan historian highlighted the common features of processes that operated wherever European settlers invaded so-called empty regions stuffed with natural resources.

Creating America: ecological imperialism and biological exchange

Examining interactions between Americans and non-human nature properly begins with the nation's core experience. In British India and the late nineteenth-century European empires of sub-Saharan Africa, a European minority ruled over a native majority. In what became the United States – and other settler colonies planted across the world's temperate zones – the ratio of rulers and aboriginals was reversed. The intrusive society took over demographically as well as politically and economically. Appreciating the character of colonialism in North America thus requires a biological perspective.

Sheer force of numbers and superior firepower (not to mention qualities such as avarice and brutality) are insufficient to explain the speed and extent of takeover. Europeanisation was also facilitated by a phenomenon that Crosby dubbed ecological imperialism. In Asia, despite centuries of contact, Europeans had to deal on fairly equal terms with peoples enjoying comparable military, political, technological and commercial skills. Moreover, Asians – and Africans – already shared Europe's epidemics and it was usually the Europeans who succumbed in a tropical environment. In the Americas, however, Europeans encountered peoples that had developed in almost total isolation since their ancestors migrated across the Bering Land Bridge at the tail end of the last ice age. In fact, Native Americans had been more cut off from the rest of humankind – and for longer – than any other group. Most of the main communicable killer diseases – such as smallpox, measles, chicken pox, bubonic plague, typhoid and scarlet fever – were endemic to Europe and regularly contributed between 3 and 10 per cent of all deaths. But most Europeans contracting them survived. Few of these diseases, however, are native to the Americas. Besides, the frigid cold of Siberia and Alaska killed off any germs that may have accompanied the first Americans.

According to Plymouth Colony's governor, William Bradford, Indians died 'like rotten sheep'. A single European could infect entire villages. By far the worst disease was smallpox, which cut some tribal populations by half and claimed up to 95 per cent mortality in certain villages. During the nineteenth century, further west, repeated assaults crippled the Kiowa of the Great Plains, who developed a story recounted in Alice Marriott and Carol Rachlin's *American Indian Mythology* (1968). The tribe's legendary hero, Saynday, meets a stranger in missionary garb, who opens the conversation:

'Who are you?'
'I'm Saynday . . . Who are you?'
'I'm smallpox.'
'Where do you come from and what do you do and why are you here?'
'I come from far away, across the Eastern Ocean. I am one with the white man – they are my people.as the Kiowa are yours. Sometimes I travel ahead of them, and sometimes I lurk behind. But I am always their companion and you will find me in their camps and in their houses.'
'What do you do?'
'I bring death. My breath causes children to wither like young plants in the spring snow. I bring destruction. No matter how beautiful a woman is, once she has looked at me she becomes as ugly as death . . . The strongest warriors go down before me.'

Initially, Europeans may not have understood what was killing them off, but interpreted mass die-offs as a providential sign.

Survivors were weakened by hunger and the entire socio-economic edifice of villages collapsed. Squanto, who helped the Pilgrim Fathers survive their first winter, was the sole survivor of his ravaged community. Pathogens also eroded the credibility of religious beliefs and practices. It came as a profound shock to Indians that even their medicine men were struck down, and, for many, was an affirmation of the English God's superior spiritual power. Depopulation cleared the way for the English appropriation of Indian lands. Most early Puritan settlements occupied abandoned village sites and fields: Plymouth Colony was rooted where Indians had raised corn (maize) just four years earlier, on the eve of the smallpox epidemic of 1616. (So much for settler claims that they were rehabilitating an unimproved wilderness. The notion of a 'virgin' land undisturbed prior to European arrival is a romantic conceit: all cultures are dynamic and modify their physical habitats.) The impact is even more staggering given that the pre-contact population was bigger than once thought. Southern Africa's demographic profile and history would have been very different if its native peoples – whose technological capacities were not that dissimilar to Native Americans – had fallen to 'virgin soil' epidemics in like style.

Diseases arrived inadvertently, but a familiar floral world was deliberately transplanted. The first Spaniards were horrified by the absence of grapes, olives and wheat. For civilised existence was unimaginable without wine, olive oil and bread. Columbus brought various seeds, cuttings and fruit stones to the Caribbean island of Hispaniola on his second voyage (1493), and American agricultural development has revolved around the acclimatisation of exotic plants. When Thomas Jefferson listed his contributions to his nation, his horticultural achievements overshadowed his better-known political accomplishments. 'The greatest service which can be rendered any country', he announced, 'is to add a useful plant to its culture'. Today, the only significant commercial crops native to the territory that became the United States are cranberry, pecan nut, sugar maple, sunflower and tobacco.

Meanwhile, unwanted plants (weeds) slipped in. Some entered mixed with straw used for packing crockery that was then recycled as livestock bedding and eventually tossed out on to fields. In 1870 Russian Mennonites brought Russian thistle seeds to South Dakota in hand-threshed flax. The flax never flourished but the thorny plant better known as tumbleweed – that rolling emblem of Western movies – spread across the entire region by the 1930s, clogging railroad tracks and forcing homesteaders to move out. Capitalising on the absence of their customary checks and balances, nonnative weeds directly displaced native flora.

Of all the animals commercially raised in the United States today, only the turkey is indisputably native. With the exception of the dog, there were no domesticated animals in pre-Columbian North America. So, on his second voyage, Columbus also brought chicken, sheep, goats, cattle, horses and pigs. They all prospered in an environment comparatively free from pathogens and predators. Pigs, like European people, proved particularly adaptable to a wide range of climates and environments. Proliferating spectacularly, they ran amok among settlers' crops. One solution was to banish swine to the coast, where they devastated Indian shellfish gathering sites. As such, the pig was an unwitting ally in the conquest. The horse, a useful instrument of warfare as well as a beast of burden, quickly made itself at home too. European people, microbes, plants and animals thus moved into new areas together, as part of what Crosby calls a 'mutually supportive' biotic 'team'. Sometimes, however, the new biotic order also empowered certain natives. Acquisition of feral horses (mustangs) facilitated occupation of the continent's grassy heartlands by the early eighteenth century, allowing these tribes to exploit buffalo more extensively and intensively. Moreover, the interior's horse-powered Indians could resist white incursion more effectively than their earlier counterparts back east.

Ecological imperialism, though, was part of a wider biotic exchange. People who remained in Europe benefited as much from the export of American food staples as those who left gained from the transplantation of their regular dietary staples (cheap and abundant animal protein was a considerable inducement to emigration). Rising population pressure in Europe that fuelled emigration partly reflected advances in medical science and hygiene. The most important single factor, however, was superior nutrition thanks to the availability of New World crops (chiefly maize, potatoes and beans) that supplemented their familiar wheat, barley and oats. Maize was a tremendous success throughout Europe's warmer regions, becoming a basic foodstuff comparable to its status in parts of the Americas. By the late eighteenth century, polenta (maize mush) dominated the northern Italian peasant's diet. The potato, originating in the Andes, was even better suited to a diversity of climates and altitudes, as well as a range of tools and land plots. In Ireland, the peasantry's dependence became almost total within a century of the plant's arrival in the late 1500s. (Ironically, when an American parasitic blight finally caught up with its original American host, devastating the Irish crops of the 1840s, millions fled to the potato's ancestral continent.)

The wealth of nature

Even without introductions like livestock and wheat, North America would still have been a peerless land of plenty. In a *New Yorker* cartoon, a Pilgrim explains to an Indian at a Thanksgiving feast: 'Actually, the attraction wasn't freedom from religious persecution but, rather, the all-you-can-eat buffet'. Despite images of a beckoning cornucopia, however, nature's bounty did not always fall into the colonist's mouth like a ripe plum. Hard work was usually required and – especially in the early phases of colonization – settlers were frequently at nature's mercy. Some were poisoned by unfamiliar plants, and deer might raze their painstakingly cultivated crops. Meanwhile, wolves could snatch their lambs. Settlers were tough on nature because nature was tough on them.

Practical threats were complemented by other menaces. The forest primeval that early nineteenth-century poets such as Henry Wadsworth

Longfellow would celebrate was the arch-enemy of social order and morality, a place of regression into brutish savagery. The wilderness, a cursed land
of thorns, thistles and drought, was where Adam and Eve were banished
from Eden. So clearing the forest for cultivation was partly a redemptive
spiritual act. Puritan settlers strove to bring everything wild – be it wolves,
Indians or their own passions – under firm control. Triumphal accounts of
paradise regained trumpet the blessed transformation of 'the close, clouded
woods into goodly cornfields' (though these forests were often less dense
than accounts of impenetrable wastes would suggest – even modest tree cover
would have impressed settlers from East Anglia). Two basic methods prepared woodland for cropping. Girdling – the Indian practice of stripping
off a ring of bark – prevented leaf formation and, eventually, killed the tree.
Meanwhile, settlers planted corn underneath to absorb the sun and light
that now reached the ground. As they rotted, trees were hauled out. This
process was too drawn out, however. By the early 1700s, felling by axe in
late summer was standard. The following spring, the toppled tree was burnt
and corn planted in the ash-enriched soil.

Most things made of stone in timber-scarce Britain were fashioned from
wood in colonial America. In addition, the white pine, the tallest tree in
the New England forest, supplied the Royal Navy's masts. Deforestation had
various environmental repercussions. Trees reduced wind force and mois-
ture loss through evaporation. Forming a canopy, they also moderated the
climate. Bare soil became drier and, unprotected by tree cover, warmer in
summer and colder in winter. Snow melted faster on bare ground, but the
loss of snow's insulating quality meant that soil froze to a greater depth
than in the forest. Roots and leaf litter also retained water; their absence
aggravated spring run-off, resulting in more flooding and stream desicca-
tion. As topsoil washed away, watercourses silted up. Soil depletion was exac-
erbated by demanding mono-cropping. For British observers, the failure to
extend soil fertility by applying manure typified American agriculture's waste-
fulness. But, as Jefferson explained (1793), 'we can buy an acre of new land
cheaper than we can manure an old one'.

So settlers cleared more forest and turned spent land over to pasture.
Cattle provided the basis for a flourishing trade in fresh meat with growing urban areas (also in salted meat with Caribbean sugar islands). Yet grazing prevented seedling regeneration. Large herds and flocks also sealed the
fate of the wolf, bear and lynx, which resorted to calves and lambs as deer
and elk were appropriated by market hunters who supplied white settlements.
A bounty was slapped on the wolf's head and swamps drained to eliminate
their habitat. The beaver's demise at the hands of the fur trade provided

additional agricultural opportunities. The collapse of disused beaver dams drained ponds, exposing acres of silt, leaves and other organic debris. These old pond bottoms provided an ideal seed bed for hay meadows.

Subduing the savage wild was such a deeply ingrained American ethos by the mid-nineteenth century that free blacks readily exported it to West Africa, where they created their own frontier in Liberia. A budding African-American frontiersman from Massachusetts, Augustus Washington, regarded Africa as a potentially valuable wilderness yearning for consummation. As he explained to a friend in a letter (1851), subsequently published in the *Journal of Negro History* (1925), Liberia was:

> Lying waste for want of the hand of science and industry. A land whose bowels are filled with mineral and agricultural wealth . . . The providence of God will not permit a land so rich . . . to remain much longer without civilized inhabitants.

In fact, a future-oriented ethos that sought to remould strange lands imbued all colonisation enterprises at this time, regardless of whether the settler's destination was a brash young nation going it alone, its clone in Africa or one content to maintain ties with the motherland. In *Tutira: The Story of a New Zealand Sheep Station* (1921), Herbert Guthrie-Smith – a Scotsman who emigrated to New Zealand's North Island in the 1880s – where he devoted his adult life to improving the pasturage of a vast sheep station, insisted that:

> There is no fascination in life like that of the amelioration of the surface of the earth . . . to make a fortune by the delightful labour of your hands – to drain your swamps, to cut tracks over your hills, to fence, to split, to build, to sow seed, to watch your flock increase – to note a countryside change under your hands from a wilderness . . . How pastoral! How Arcadian! – the emerald sward that was to paint the alluvial flats, the graded tracks up which the pack team was to climb easily, the spurs over which the fencing was to run . . . the glory of the grass that was to be.

On emerging from the forested regions of western Missouri after the Civil War, the American farming frontier encountered its most arduous environment to date. The 98th meridian separates lands with adequate rainfall from the standpoint of temperate zone farming from those with insufficient precipitation. West of this divide, water, wood and rivers were in short supply. So the onward march depended on railroads, barbed wire, windmills, a dogged refusal to accept natural restraints and a capacity to recover from a bevy of natural hazards, including hail storms, late autumn and early spring blizzards, withering summer winds, wild fire, tornadoes and insect plagues of biblical proportions. In one of her 'Little House on the Prairie' novels, *On the Banks of Plum Creek* (1937), Laura Ingalls Wilder recalled the hordes of sunlight-obscuring grasshoppers (locusts) that descended on ripening wheat in Minnesota in the early 1870s. These traumas were overshadowed, however, by events on the Great Plains in the 1930s. As the Great Depression hit the region, drought combined with relentless winds to blow topsoil on to the decks of ships far out in the Atlantic. Newborn calves suffocated and adults wore their teeth down to the gums attempting to eat dust-encrusted grass. 'Grass no good upside down' was a Plains Indian's verdict on the sodbuster's ploughing under of the thickly matted sod that – carefully maintained by an Indian fire régime that boosted fertility and inhibited tree growth along the eastern margins – had accumulated and protected rich prairie soils over centuries. In *The Grapes of Wrath* (1939), John Steinbeck lashed out at the corporate mentality he believed was responsible for the 'dust bowl'. The tractor man who seizes bankrupt tenant farms and evicts hapless families like the Joads

> could not see the land as it was, he could not smell the land as it smelled . . . He loved the land no more than the bank loved the land . . . Behind the tractor rolled the shining disks, cutting the earth with blades – not plowing but surgery. Behind the harrows, the long seeders – twelve curved iron penes erected in the foundry, orgasms set by gears, raping methodically, raping without passion

But advances in well-drilling technology and centre-pivot irrigation systems allowed farmers to overcome the vagaries of rainfall by tapping deep into underground aquifers. Technological innovation also facilitated a desert-defying urban frontier. A network of dams, reservoirs and aqueducts supplies the improbable 'oasis' cities of the Southwest – the nation's fastest growing region – with their lifeblood. Snowmelt from the Sierra Nevada and Rocky Mountains keeps swimming pools brimming and golf courses lush in what the California novelist and nature writer Mary Austin dubbed the 'land of little rain' (in a 1903 book of that title).

From plenitude to scarcity: the buffalo's tale

During the conquest of North America entire animal species were wiped out and others driven to the brink of extinction. The passenger pigeon population in the early seventeenth century probably numbered between

3 and 5 billion. Flocks were so dense they blocked out the sun, and might take 12 hours to pass overhead. Yet the bird was extinct by 1914, when the last representative, Martha, died in Cincinnati Zoo. Europe's sparrows and starlings replaced them. An estimated 60–75 million buffalo roamed North America in 1492. On the plains in the early 1870s migrating herds held up trains for hours. Yet, by 1900, only about 500 remained. Market hunters like Buffalo Bill Cody, who killed thousands to feed railroad construction crews, were partly to blame. Then, in 1870, tanners worked out how to convert the soft skin into serviceable leather, notably for transmission belts. Hide-hunting outfits systematically butchered herds round the clock with industrial efficiency in an abattoir *al fresco*.

In Kevin Costner's revisionist Western, *Dances with Wolves* (1991), a seminal moment in Lieutenant Dunbar's process of going native at his lonely army outpost in western Kansas is his discovery of 27 pink carcasses left by a party of hide hunters, from which the only meat taken is the tongue. Yet the Comanche Indians Dunbar joins were heavily involved in the earlier robe trade – and hunting for robes (and subsistence) targeted cows in peak breeding condition. Horses (domestic and feral) contributed further to the substantial reduction prior to the notorious killing spree of the 1870s. They not only transmitted exotic diseases but, by competing for water and forage, reduced the range's carrying capacity for buffalo. Feeding the huge herds of horses that Indians maintained was an enormous challenge during drought and winter. Wolf predation, drought and wild fire slashed buffalo numbers further. Moreover, Indian beliefs were sometimes inimical to the wise husbandry of natural resources implicit in the seductive notion of the 'ecological Indian'. The Oglala Sioux were convinced that any buffalo they had lured into an enclosure that they did not kill went off to warn others. Some Plains Indians were also convinced that when buffalo left as part of their seasonal migrations, they had retreated to the bottom of a lake or other underground place. Here, they proliferated wildly, spilling out of cave-like apertures each spring in an endless fresh supply. A full understanding of the buffalo's demise goes beyond restless, money-grubbing Euro-Americans manipulating a static environment and aboriginal bystanders incapable of environmental degradation.

Nature's nation

One of the founding fathers of American Studies, Leo Marx, recently commented (2003) that 'the idea of nature is one of the defining American ideas – as definitive in its way as the ideas of freedom and equality'. This notion of a special relationship between nature and American identity was captured half a century ago in Perry Miller's pithy phrase, 'nature's nation' (1953). The countryside has been a key ingredient in the construction of English and French national identities, but nature in its wilder forms has been a particularly potent force in shaping the United States' sense of itself. Americans, Miller explained, were convinced that theirs was 'a nation that was, above all other nations, embedded in Nature'. New World nature inspired the first distinctively American genre of painting. Prior to the 1830s, most American artists, like their literary counterparts, aspired to nothing higher than the sincere imitation of European styles and subject matter. The Hudson River School broke free from this derivative straitjacket by looking directly to apparently unmodified scenery. Exemplifying the new romantic taste, its artists located truth and beauty in the untamed rivers, lakes, mountains and forests of the Northeast, which they invested with a sacred quality. The founder of this wilderness worshipping school was Thomas Cole, an English immigrant, whose canvases were distinguished by the absence of people. Human figures, even when included, were invariably dwarfed by their surroundings. Likewise, Asher Durand celebrated scenes that had escaped 'the pollutions of civilization', with no apologies for the absence of the picturesque features – castles, church spires and ivy-clad cottages – that Anglophiles cherished. Nonetheless, the prelapsarian wilderness the Hudson River School immortalised was sometimes just as contrived as the 'natural' look of Capability Brown's landscaped gardens in eighteenth-century England. By the 1830s civilisation's less picturesque pollutants had already infiltrated the Hudson Valley and artists consciously deleted the contaminating wharves, mills, shacks and quarries.

To do justice to the more grandiose western landscapes grafted on to the nation in the 1840s, artists chose massive canvases; dimensions of 10 by 15 feet were not unusual. Exaggeration, strictly avoided by the Hudson River School, and though hardly necessary in the superlative Rockies and Sierra Nevada, was nevertheless the rule among Rocky Mountain School artists, whose leading members were Albert Bierstadt and Thomas Moran (both immigrants). By the 1860s Bierstadt's paintings of California's Yosemite Valley were commanding the highest sums ever paid for American art. Many of these paintings – enshrining ground no less sacred than Gettysburg – became national icons. Congress immediately bought two of Moran's paintings and hung them prominently in the Capitol.

The natural monuments that Europe lacked – scientist and explorer Clarence King dubbed them America's 'green old age' – provided a source of identity and self-esteem that more than compensated for any perceived cultural inferiority. (The California coastal redwood and giant sequoia are, respectively, the world's oldest and tallest, and oldest and biggest trees.) Certain creatures have also been embraced as ingredients of patrimony. For the cultural nationalist, the superiority of native birds over imported avifauna was an article of faith. Alexander Wilson, a Scottish immigrant, was in the vanguard of the post-revolutionary generation's eco-jingoists. With reference to the bluebird, Wilson regretted that 'no pastoral muse has yet risen in this western, woody world, to do justice to his name, and endear him to us still more by the tenderness of verse, as has been done to his representative in Britain, the Robin Redbreast'. Nature poet William Cullen Bryant rebuked his brother (1832) for enthusing over the skylark because it was 'an English bird, and an American who has never visited Europe has no right to be in raptures about it'.

The peerless embodiment of nature's nation, though, is the national park. The popular TV series, *The West Wing*, confirms its position at the core of national consciousness. President Bartlett (played by Martin Sheen) frequently exasperates his staff with his intimate knowledge of his beloved national parks. And, in 2004, from 8,000 entries, California's governor, Arnold Schwarzenegger, selected a design showing pioneering conservationist John Muir in Yosemite Valley as the motif for the state's new quarter dollar coin.

'Is it right and best that this should be for the few, the very few of us?', inquired Central Park's designer, Frederick Law Olmsted, when visiting the lovely countryside cordoned off within private estates during his walking tour of England and Wales in 1850: 'Thus without means . . . by government to withhold them from the grasp of individuals', he warned, 'all places favorable in scenery to the recreation of the mind and body will be closed against the great body of the people'. The United States was supposed to offer an alternative to old world patterns of landownership. As well as serving as America's 'crown jewels', national parks were thus a democratic reaction against the exclusivity of Europe's great estates and the growing appropriation of prime scenic land at home by a new feudal class of industrialists. They were designed, to quote the Yellowstone Park Act, as 'pleasuring ground(s) for the benefit and enjoyment of the people'.

Not that the United States was the only settler country to establish national parks. Though the reserve in question was a provincial initiative and more akin to a British urban park, the term 'national park' was first used in the protocol establishing Royal National Park near the burgeoning city of Sydney, New South Wales (1879). Canada and New Zealand had also established national parks before the term was first used in the United States (1899). ('National' may have been previously avoided due to the unsavoury connotations of government ownership in an age of intemperate dedication to private landownership.) These technicalities aside, the national park as an idea and institution is rightly associated with the United States, many other countries being inspired directly by Yellowstone – the world's first national park in all but name (1872) and still the most famous.

Novelist Wallace Stegner once described the national park idea as 'the best we ever had'. And parks have traditionally been viewed as places that display the American spirit at its finest, saying with conviction, for once, that the buck stops here. Yet, though the main aim was to protect spectacular scenery from private acquisition or exploitation by extractive industries, not all forms of economic development were proscribed. Railroad companies were leading proponents, running their tracks into the heart of parks where resort facilities sprang up, lending many the air of a rural (and more refined) Coney Island. What has been saved has also been changed. The nature on display has been sanitised. As Joni Mitchell observed in her song 'Big Yellow Taxi' (1970):

> They took all the trees
> And put them in a tree museum
> And they charged the people
> A dollar and a half just to see them.

Prior to the 1930s the only serious contender for park status was dramatic topography or a geothermal wonder like Old Faithful. Everglades National Park in Florida's swamplands marked a dramatic departure: biodiversity took precedence over 'chocolate box' scenery. Nonetheless, its flora and fauna were at the mercy of drainage and other agricultural activities beyond park boundaries. Meanwhile, air pollution from nearby coal-fired power plants and automobile emissions in southern California compromises the Grand Canyon's air quality (and the views). Park policy no longer routinely subordinates ecological considerations to recreational provision, but a 'nature first' approach remains controversial: witness the public outcry over the 'let it burn' policy adopted toward wild fire at the height of Yellowstone's tourist season. Complicating matters further is the growing realisation that parks like Yosemite and Glacier are emptied rather than empty spaces, representing former Indian hunting grounds. National parks are increasingly accommodating of indigenous peoples' interests as descendants campaign for restoration of subsistence rights. The ten Alaskan parks, preserves and monuments created in 1980 (nearly doubling the size of the US park system) aim to protect natural values *and* traditional cultures.

Other activities further illustrate the racial specificity of many perceptions of the natural world. A walk on the wild side was by no means the
same thing for a runaway slave as it was for the middle-class aesthete who
sought to escape from the cities that suffocated the spirit and confined the
body (or today's weekend hiker on Yosemite's trails). African Americans
tramped north to an uncertain freedom off the beaten track, under cover
of night, through woods, swamps and mountains. Haunted at every turn
by the threat of recapture, there would have been little opportunity for tran-
scendental reverie. For the enslaved, an imposing tree represented a lynch-
ing post rather than an object of beauty or source of national pride.
Nonetheless, encounters with plants and animals provided welcome com-
panionship, sustenance, and, not least, inspiring emblems of independence. 'The happy birds – I envied them', recalled one runaway, 'I wished
for wings like them, that I might cleave the air to . . . the cooler region of
the North'. For the antebellum slave, the city represented a place to escape
to. Yet African Americans also developed profound ties with the fields, gardens and forests they knew through daily work. These feelings, though rarely
expressed in the familiar form of the natural history essay, suffuse the accounts
of fugitive slaves, such as the *Narrative of the Adventures and Escape of Moses
Roper* (1837).

Leaving aside considerations of race, in so far as national traits tran-
scending class and gender exist, how exceptional is the Euro-American relationship with nature in its wilder forms? How often is Canada hailed as
'nature's nation'? The beaver and maple leaf are peerless symbols of
Canadian nationhood. And plenty of Canadian national parks were established for much the same reasons as their counterparts south of the border. Moreover, far more of Canada remains wild country. Yet Canadians of
European extraction have not had the same rapport with wilderness as their
Euro-American cousins, who have placed much more under statutory protection. Some believe that the equation of too much wilderness and too
few people explains the lower appeal of wilderness preservation in Canada
(the scarcity theory of value that Mitchell articulated in 'Big Yellow Taxi':
'Don't it always seem to go, that you don't know what you've got till it's
gone'). For others, the higher cachet of wilderness in the United States
is explicable only by reference to deep-seated cultural-historical factors,
notably the myth of the frontier and its association with a state of nature,
themselves inseparable from the much-vaunted American pursuit of freedom.
Nonetheless, other 'New World' countries, if not quite so self-consciously,
also became nature's nations. In the late nineteenth and early twentieth centuries, from Australia to South Africa, after centuries of avid acclimatisation

of flora and fauna from the motherland, indigenous landscapes, plants and animals were enthroned as national symbols. The Hudson River and Rocky Mountain Schools had their Australian counterpart in the Heidelberg School that emerged in 1880s Melbourne to celebrate the Outback. Its work quickly gained national esteem and the best known paintings retain pride of place in Australia's major galleries. Canada's equivalent was the Group of Seven that enshrined the vast and awesome if thoroughly inhospitable Canadian Shield. The eucalyptus is such a familiar feature of California that many Californians assume it is native. 'Say', an American serviceman from Californian reportedly drawled in Sydney during the Second World War, 'you got some of our eucalypts here'. Though widely exported, the euca-lyptus is as Australian as its resident koala.

Towards a greener America

A literary tradition of mixed feelings about the conquest of the natural world stretches back to James Fenimore Cooper's novel, *The Prairie* (1827). The lead-ing protagonist, confronted with a pigeon massacre, criticises the pioneer's 'wasty ways'. Yet, on balance, Cooper believed the price was worth paying. The most overt disapproval was expressed by visiting Europeans like Alexis de Tocqueville, who brought with them their romantic sensibilities, unencum-bered by the requirement to carve a living out of the wilderness. One of the few antebellum Americans who shared these sentiments was Henry David Thoreau. During his short life, and for a long time after his death at age 45 in 1862, he was largely dismissed as an eccentric drop-out, a Yankee St Francis. Today, his fame has eclipsed that of his erstwhile mentor, Ralph Waldo Emerson, and his account of his two-year sojourn in a primitive cabin on the shores of a small lake, *Walden* (1854) – which sold very modestly in his lifetime – is the most frequently reprinted American book published before the Civil War. The site of his cabin on this rather ordinary lake on the out-skirts of greater Boston, marked by a stone cairn since 1872, is now almost on a par with the Memphis motel where Martin Luther King was shot and Elvis Presley's Graceland mansion as an American place of pilgrimage. Proposals in the early 1990s to erect a three-storey office building with park-ing for 500 vehicles and a 139-unit condominium along part of the shoreline mobilised a high profile campaign. Rock musician Don   ley spearheaded the all-star crusade. A book published as part of the successful bid to save 'the cradle of the American environmental movement' (Henley) – the liter-ary equivalent of a charity rock concert – featured accolades from the worlds of politics and entertainment (in addition to various prominent literary figures). Contributing Thoreau aficionados included Jesse Jackson, Jimmy Carter, Edward Kennedy, John Kerry, César Chávez, Robert Redford, Tom Cruise, Whoopi Goldberg, Tom Hanks, Meryl Streep and Janet Jackson.

Thoreau was largely out of tune with the go-getting spirit of the antebullum North. While he was building a hut at Walden for his lifestyle experiment, legions of his compatriots were trooping west and raising cabins (or sod houses) in far wilder settings. Later in the nineteenth century, however, his unease became more widely shared and various organisations bemoaned the nature that was being lost as a new nation was forged. The pioneering generation of wildlife preservationists sought to protect beleaguered 'good' species from market hunting's depredations – mostly game species but also birds that milliners prized. The aesthetic conservationists fought to preserve remnant patches of wild and imposing scenery by creating national parks. Their utilitarian counterparts within the conservation movement of the Progressive era challenged reckless exploitation by short-sighted robber barons by emphasising the planned and efficient use of natural resources and their more equitable allocation. This technocratic form of conservation, which remained dominant during the New Deal, was exemplified by dams like Grand Coulee on the Columbia River. Celebrated by the folk singer Woody Guthrie, they delivered flood control, rural electrification, irrigation and industrialisation.

These concerns with the 'scientific management' of resources in the long-term public interest, monumental landscapes and iconic creatures that symbolised the old frontier (notably buffalo) have since been supplemented by a range of new preoccupations and fresh ideas about the right relationship between humans and the rest of the natural world. Americans have increasingly counted the ecological costs of an advanced industrial-urban/suburban society and worked to replace facile notions of 'good' and 'bad' animals with a more holistic and dispassionate understanding of the role of individual species within ecological communities. In his posthumously published book, *A Sand County Almanac* (1949), which served as the bible of a stirring environmentalism, the wildlife biologist, Aldo Leopold, regretted that

> twenty centuries of 'progress' have brought the average citizen a vote, a national anthem, a Ford, a bank account, and a high opinion of himself, but not the capacity to live in high density without befouling and denuding his environment, nor a conviction that such capacity, rather than such density, is the true test of whether he is civilized.

The befouling of the earth – increasingly dubbed pollution – was the new environmentalism's leitmotif. In *The Affluent Society* (1958), the economist,

John Kenneth Galbraith, warned of the effluence of affluence and the artificiality of the 'good life':

> The family which takes its mauve and cerise, air-conditioned, power-steered, and power-braked automobile out for a tour passes through cities that are badly paved, made hideous by litter . . . [and] billboards . . . They pass into a countryside that has been rendered largely invisible by commercial art . . . They picnic on exquisitely packaged food from a portable icebox by a polluted stream . . . Just before dozing off on an air mattress, beneath a nylon tent, amid the stench of decaying refuse, they may reflect vaguely on the curious unevenness of their blessings. Is this, indeed, the American genius?

A novel, also published in 1958, popularised the nascent counterculture's advocacy of communion with wild nature as a liberating alternative to the stultifying regimentation of corporate non-identity and routine existence in the comfortable concentration camps of suburbia. In *The Dharma Bums*, the Beat writer, Jack Kerouac, serenaded free spirits imbued with eco-friendly Buddhist beliefs running wild in California's Sierra Nevada. The main character, Japhy Ryder (modelled on the Zen poet and future environmental activist, Gary Snyder), welcomes the prospect of 'thousands or even millions of young Americans wandering around with rucksacks, going up to the mountains to pray . . . all of 'em Zen lunatics who . . . by strange unexpected acts keep giving visions of eternal freedom to everybody and to all living creatures'.

There have been few stranger and more unexpected acts than the successful testing of the first atomic bomb at Alamogordo in the New Mexico desert in July 1945. The dawn of the atomic age brought an unprecedented new order of environmental threat. For the first time, humankind possessed the power to wipe out all forms of planetary life. Witnessing the blast, J. Robert Oppenheimer, the Manhattan Project's chief scientist, recalled a line spoken by Vishnu in the Hindu scripture, the *Bhagavad-Gita*: 'I am become death, the destroyer of worlds'. Simultaneously, though, this apocalyptic act precipitated a revolution in consciousness. Between 1952 and 1963 radioactive nuclides from atmospheric testing in Nevada drifted eastward. The St Louis Citizens' Committee on Nuclear Information delivered an ecology lesson when it launched the famous Baby Tooth Survey to measure levels of Strontium-90 in milk. Mothers across the nation sent in nearly 160,000 milk teeth between 1959 and 1964. In 'The Clan of the One-Breasted Women', the epilogue to her book *Refuge: An Unnatural History of Family and Place* (1991), Terry Tempest Williams, a novelist and nature writer from Utah, related how her mother and eight other women in her immediate family who lived 'downwind' of the 'bombs in the backyard' were smitten by breast cancer.

The book hailed as the *Uncle Tom's Cabin* of the environmental movement – a reference to the pivotal role of Harriet Beecher Stowe's anti-slavery novel in advancing abolitionism – was Rachel Carson's *Silent Spring* (1962). This unlikely bestseller thrust the dangers of over-reliance on chemical pesticides (particularly DDT) for the sake of unblemished, bumper crops to the forefront of public and governmental awareness. President Kennedy read it and set up an investigatory commission. 'Hey farmer, farmer, put away that DDT now. Give me the spots on my apples but leave me the birds and the bees', urged Mitchell in 'Big Yellow Taxi'. Particularly enthusiastic devotees of DDT were the agri-businessmen of California's Central Valley, which produces many of the nation's fruits and vegetables. Exposure to pesticides was a key grievance among Hispanic farm labourers and the Delano Grape Strike of 1964–6, led by César Chávez, was a seminal event in the assertion of Chicano civil rights. (Cherrié Moraga's play, *Heroes and Saints* (1989), was inspired by the high incidence of cancer deaths and birth defects among the children of farm workers in the Central Valley town of McFarland.) Gardeners were avid pesticide users too. A cartoon showed a suburban couple relaxing in their lounge with a swarm of insects buzzing around their heads. They explain to a nonplussed guest: 'Since we read *Silent Spring*, we decided to live and let live'. Others were less impressed. Carson's exposé precipitated a fierce backlash from the agro-chemical industry which warned that following Carson's advice would return humanity to the dark ages of hunger and starvation. Playing on Lincoln's famous remark on meeting the author of *Uncle Tom's Cabin*, Senator Abraham Ribicoff, calling Senate hearings on pesticides to order in June 1963, introduced the prime witness as follows: 'Miss Carson, we welcome you here. You are the lady that started all of this'.

The photographs of the Earth that the Apollo space missions beamed back played a vital role in driving home ecology's basic insights. 'Earthrise' (1968), which showed a blue Earth rising over a silvery Moon, vividly embodied the finiteness, singularity and fragility of our common planetary home, a small, delicate egg afloat in an enormity of lifeless space. Though neglected by historians of 1960s radicalism, environmentalism was a potent force during that turbulent decade. Rallies reverberated with the slogan 'Give Earth a Chance' and those who planned the first Earth Day (April 1970) – when 20 million Americans turned out to protest – were also active in the anti-war, civil rights and women's movements. During the late 1960s and early 1970s, established groups like the Sierra Club (1892), the

Audubon Society (1890s) and the Wilderness Society (1935) were revitalised. Joining them were new groups with a global agenda and more confrontational style, notably Friends of the Earth (1969) and Greenpeace (1970). The latter was the brainchild of a handful of American draft dodgers living in British Columbia who sailed a fishing boat into the nuclear testing zone around a remote Aleutian island selected for the biggest and most expensive underground test in US history. Meanwhile, the ecological side-effects of American military involvement in Indo-China were publicised in anti-war circles: aerial spraying of napalm and chemical defoliants contaminated vast swathes of jungle and rice paddies.

Environmentalism emerged from a mood that not only assailed the prevailing liberal democratic political system and its underpinning capitalist ethos but also questioned the philosophical assumptions of Western industrial civilisation. 'Flower power' was more than a slogan. In his bestseller, *The Greening of America* (1970), Charles Reich, a Yale law professor, contended that a new consciousness stressing human values and a rediscovered respect for a re-enchanted natural world was dissolving not only racism and imperialism but also materialism, rationalism and technocracy. He saw the promise of rebirth rising out of 'the wasteland of the Corporate State, like flowers pushing up through the concrete pavement'. That Grand Coulee's construction might have been prevented or delayed by those concerned about migrating salmon and the loss of wild rivers was unthinkable. By the late 1960s, though, some of the gloss of the technological sublime had worn off. The completion of the $116 million Tellico Dam on the Little Tennessee River fell foul of the Endangered Species Act (1973), invoked on behalf of the snail darter. A Supreme Court ruling (1978) backed the 3-inch minnow but the dam was finally finished after political manoeuvrings.

Environmentalism's arrival as a compelling social concern and pressing political issue coincided with a sustained period of economic growth that furnished a receptive climate. President Johnson's vision of the Great Society placed clean air and water, wildlife protection and more national parks on a par with health, education and civil rights (the pet project of the First Lady, Lady Bird, was to eliminate the blight of billboards along highways). By 1970 environmental protection was a widely acknowledged societal good. Some of the most important environmental legislation in American history was enacted during the Nixon administration, which, though not particularly interested in advancing a green agenda, was obliged to respond to powerful societal and political impulses.

This high degree of consensus and bipartisan support broke down under economic malaise in the later 1970s and with the rise of the 'new' right. Since Ronald Reagan ran for president in 1980, Republicans have been overwhelmingly hostile to environmental protection (one of Reagan's most notorious remarks while governor of California in the mid-1960s was 'if you've seen one redwood tree, you've seen them all'). Republicans regarded environmentalism as inimical to economic well-being and business interests and closely allied to the beast of big government. In the vanguard of Reagan's 'anti-environmental revolution' was Secretary of the Interior James Watt, a Wyoming lawyer, whose firm represented a string of corporate mining, logging, grazing and oil interests eager to circumvent environmental regulations. Watt was also a born-again Christian who adhered closely to the Judeo-Christian belief that God gave humans dominion over the Earth and its creatures. While a fox was in charge of the hen house, environmental organizations enjoyed another surge in membership and their cause became firmly associated with the Democrats and various left-of-centre groups.

A host of outfits propounding a biocentric philosophy that promotes the 'rights' and interests of nature (animate and inanimate) – sometimes placing them on a par with human rights and interests – have gathered on the left wing of the green spectrum since the late 1970s. Taking their cue from the radical abolitionist William Lloyd Garrison, the mantra of those who speak of land slavery is 'No compromise in defense of Mother Earth!' Edward Abbey's novel, *The Monkey Wrench Gang* (1975), inspired direct action groups like Earth First! (1980). Abbey recounts the neo-Luddite adventures of a motley crew of eco-saboteurs (monkey wrenchers) whose goal is to throw a spanner into the works of the techno-industrialism that is desecrating his beloved southwest desert. As Abbey later explained in *Ecodefense: A Field Guide to Monkeywrenching* (1987), 'An Englishman's home is his castle; an American's home is his favorite mountain range, his favorite desert canyon'.

Most Americans, though, do not go to such lengths. By the early 1990s, Hal Rothman reflected in *The Greening of a Nation?* (1998), 'environmentalists had succeeded in persuading the majority of Americans of the value of protecting the environment. They had not resolved the fundamental tension between the cultural and individual restraint that this ethic of protection requires and the acquisitiveness and individualism that has been the hallmark of the nation during most of its first two hundred years'. One of the most divisive domestic issues in the United States since 1980 has been the Republican attempt to open the coastal plain of Alaska's Arctic National Wildlife Refuge to oil development. Yet many Americans who want to keep the oilmen out drive large distances to their treasured national parks in their equally treasured gas-guzzling sport utility vehicles (SUVs).

Environmentalism is sometimes dismissed as a luxury that only affluent whites can afford – a 'full stomach' concern that fails to address the more basic needs of those – often 'people of colour' – whose primary concerns are jobs, crime and education. More often, though, it is a case of 'minorities' being concerned with different types of environments and environmental issues. A survey of opinion in Detroit (1998) suggested that blacks are more exercised than whites about air and water pollution. This finding correlates with the lower environmental quality of black neighbourhoods. African Americans today are much more likely than whites to be living near a hazardous waste dump or source of industrial pollution. Since the early 1980s a series of local (often southern) 'environmental justice' campaigns – frequently spearheaded by women – have protested against the installation of toxic facilities in or near 'minority' districts. In fact, the state of the environment affects all Americans, and, though not as crucial as economic issues in determining voter behaviour, can exert a critical influence. The presidential contest in 2000 pitted 'Mr Ozone' (Vice-President Al Gore, on whose office wall a portrait of Rachel Carson hung) against the 'Toxic Texan' (George W. Bush), and the dark green credentials of third party candidate Ralph Nader may have swung the election to Bush by splitting the environmentalist vote in Florida.

The return of the natives (or, nature bats last)

Paeans to nature's scenic glories abound in Meriwether Lewis's journal of his transcontinental odyssey with William Clark to the mouth of the Columbia two centuries ago. Yet he had an even sharper eye for what nature could become in American hands. Lewis typified a deep American ambivalence between admiration for untouched nature and the desire to improve on it. Thus nature has often been loved and subjugated without any sense of contradiction. The rock band, The Eagles, captured this equivocal mentality in a bittersweet ballad about what happened to the big, wild and beautiful land that was America. 'The Last Resort' (1976) concludes:

> They called it Paradise
> I don't know why
> Call someplace Paradise
> Kiss it goodbye.

Still, the death of nature is sometimes announced prematurely. Given the opportunity, nature can often heal itself. The early twentieth-century switch from wood to gas and electricity as fuel sources, the advent of reinforced concrete, steel beams and girders for construction after 1914, and the replacement of wooden carriages and wagons by automobiles lifted pressure on declining timber supplies. Today's New England is more heavily wooded than at any time since the 1700s. In fact, recovery here began in the early nineteenth century, when the opening up of the Midwest's rich prairie soils and the growing availability to eastern industrial consumers of cheap western grain encouraged the abandonment of hardscrabble northeast farms. Trees as well as towns and factories grew up in their stead (if not necessarily the same species as before). Tumbledown stone walls that streak through thick regrowth suggest the impermanence of the human imprint on the land. And along the banks of Oil Creek in western Pennsylvania, abandoned for oil fields further west in Oklahoma and Texas, new growth obscures the naked stumps that serve as reminders of America's first oil boom in the 1860s.

Meanwhile, wildlife comeback stories abound. The arrival of 14 Canadian wolves in Yellowstone National Park in January 1995 after nearly 70 wolf-less years was accompanied by the ceremonial and security trappings associated with a presidential visit: Bill Clinton visiting the park's hottest new attraction while they were in their acclimation pens. Wolves are also welcome on the vast eco-ranches in Montana that Hollywood celebrities have stocked with buffalo. The buffalo's return is being assisted by the growing plight of the Great Plains. Battered by prolonged drought, depleted aquifers, rising irrigation costs, falling commodity prices and evaporating federal subsidies, residents are deserting the nation's troubled rural heartland in droves. The most dramatic recovery plan has provoked heated debate within the region. The 'Buffalo Commons' (1994), a proposal closely associated with two New Jersey-based urban geographers, Deborah and Frank Popper, argues for the replacement of cattle and crops with a sustainable, buffalo-based economy that will also yield eco-tourist dividends for an 'American Serengeti'. Though the Poppers have received death threats, ranchers are gradually realising that buffalo make more economic sense than Herefords. They are better at surviving drought and blizzards, using their huge foreheads as snow-ploughs to access the grass they crop more efficiently than cattle. In addition, increasingly health-conscious consumers represent a growing market for low-cholesterol buffalo steaks.

The story of American relations with their natural environment has often been told as a linear narrative of remorseless, accelerating decline predicated on the lamentable loss of Eden. Before white people showed up, the natural world was pristine and bountiful. After that, it was all downhill. A more nuanced, less moralistic tale sees a more complex set of changes at work, including gains for nature as well as losses. Wild nature can flourish in the most inauspicious places. Witness the metamorphosis of one of the nation's most blighted nuclear sites. The central core of Colorado's Rocky Mountain Arsenal remains seriously contaminated (not least with bombs containing the deadly nerve agent, liquid sarin). But national security dictated the appropriation of a far larger chunk of land than the business of bomb making required. Some 5,000 acres of the chemical-free buffer zone has now been designated the nation's newest national wildlife refuge. The splendid isolation of this people-free and farm-free zone created hospitable conditions for wildlife increasingly marginalised as suburban sprawl consumes habitat north of Denver. All empires are vulnerable – not least the American dominion over the American earth.

Further reading

Bak, Hans and Walter W. Hölbling (eds), 'Nature's Nation' Revisited: American Concepts of Nature from Wonder to Ecological Crisis (2003).

Cronon, William, Changes in the Land: Indians, Colonists, and the Ecology of New England (1983).

Crosby, Alfred W., Ecological Imperialism: The Biological Expansion of Europe, 900–1900 (2nd edn, 2004).

Dunlap, Thomas R., Nature and the English Diaspora: Environment and History in the United States, Canada, Australia, and New Zealand (1999).

Merchant, Carolyn, The Columbia Guide to North American Environmental History (2002).

Nash, Roderick, Wilderness and the American Mind (rev. edn, 2001).

Opie, John, Nature's Nation: An Environmental History of the United States (1998).

Rothman, Hal, The Greening of a Nation? Environmentalism in the United States since 1945 (1998).

Runte, Alfred, National Parks: The American Experience (1979).

Steinberg, Theodore, Down to Earth: Nature's Role in American History (2002).

Warren, Louis (ed.), American Environmental History (2003).

CHAPTER 2

From settlement to independence

Colin Bonwick

The great temptation facing students of colonial America is to interpret it in the context of the Revolution. From this perspective its development was a natural progression from the founding of English colonies in the seventeenth century to the emergence of the United States late in the next century. Some illumination can of course be found from this perspective. Carl Bridenbaugh in *The Spirit of '76* (1975) declared that the act of planting new colonies was an unconscious act of independence. He brilliantly argued that as the colonies developed, became richer, more populated and increasingly sophisticated, their sense of being different from Britain grew stronger. The Declaration of Independence was the grand climax of a long process: 'In every way the Spirit of '76 was the culmination of the 169 years that compose nearly all of the first half of our history'. In one sense this was correct. Looking backwards there can be little doubt that sooner or later the colonies would separate from the British Empire and that seeds of separation were sown at the moments of first settlements. But, as J. M. Bumsted in 'Things in the Womb of Time', *William and Mary Quarterly* (1974) acknowledges, predictions of independence and much of the discussion before 1760 came from British officials and writers, not Americans. Yet every garden contains the seeds of many flowers. Every economic, political, cultural and ideological argument adduced to explain the eighteenth-century Revolution has an obverse capable of sustaining the survival of the Anglo-American community well into the next century. Patriots as well as Loyalists were enthusiastic members of the British Empire until the final crisis. Better, then, to examine colonial America in its own terms rather than using its future to explain its past; better to consider it as it reached maturity in mid-eighteenth century, without skewing analysis by reference to the causes and character of the Revolution. Such an approach will also illuminate the path to separation.

Patterns of settlement

Britain came late to colonising the Western hemisphere. By the end of the sixteenth century Spain already controlled Central America and the Pacific coast of South America. Its colonies had become sophisticated societies and cultures: their cathedrals projected a grandeur unmatched in British America. Moreover, by the mid-eighteenth century Spanish borderlands included Florida and missionary bridgeheads in what became the southwestern United States. Portuguese colonisation of Brazil, though slower, was also well advanced by 1600. In contrast the first successful British colony, at Jamestown on Chesapeake Bay in Virginia, was not founded until 1607. Even then, only one in five settlers survived the brutal disease régime during the early years, and their colony's existence was exiguous; initially they relied on supplies from England and depended on the Indians to teach them how to survive. Not until they began cultivating tobacco for sale abroad could they finance their activities and develop their colony. By the middle of the seventeenth century, however, Virginia had been joined by several more northerly colonies in New England as well as adjacent Maryland, a colony similar to Virginia but founded primarily as a haven for Roman Catholics. From this point on it was clear that a permanent British bridgehead had been established. Before the end of the century New York had been captured from the Dutch, and New Jersey, Pennsylvania and North and South Carolina had been founded; Georgia, the final colony among those that later formed the United States, was founded in 1732.

By this time there were three major nodes for future expansion: the New England colonies of New Hampshire, Massachusetts, Rhode Island and Connecticut; second the Middle colonies of New York, New Jersey, Pennsylvania and Delaware (often brigaded with New England as the North); and lastly the South, which included Maryland, Virginia, the two Carolinas and Georgia. As late as the mid-eighteenth century, however, all areas densely inhabited by whites lay close to the Atlantic coast, and settlement extended only 350 miles inland; most of the continent's wealth lay west of the Appalachian Mountains. Even so, the British colonies had already outpaced French Canada (founded in 1609) in population and economic prosperity, though French explorers had penetrated far deeper into the continent and small settlements ran along the Mississippi River. Two other points are worthy of note. The mainland British colonies were only a part – and in some ways not the most attractive part – of a chain of British colonies that extended from Nova Scotia (acquired from France in 1713) and Newfoundland through the sugar islands of the Caribbean to central America. Second, North America remained a region where European nations played out their imperial rivalries. But this is to define the human structure solely in European terms. In actuality three races – Native Americans and Africans as well as Europeans – populated the continent in the mid-eighteenth century.

First to arrive and probably still greatest in number were Native Americans, known to Europeans as 'Red Indians'. Estimates of their numbers before Europeans arrived in the area that became the United States are highly contentious. Some scholars argue that there were scarcely more than one million or so, but bearing in mind the intensity of their relations with incoming whites, this estimate seems unduly low. Archaeological evidence and modern demographic analysis suggest that there may have been up to 10 million, of whom perhaps 300,000 lived within 150 miles of the Atlantic seaboard. By the middle of the eighteenth century their numbers along the coast had diminished drastically, though some still lived everywhere in the white settled zone. Often culturally complex and sophisticated – though not according to criteria applied by whites – their efforts to resist European expansion were handicapped by a great diversity of languages and interests. Stone Age technology, divisions among themselves, and a debilitating incapacity to resist European diseases made it impossible for tribes east of the Appalachian Mountains to prevent the expropriation of much of their land. Things were somewhat different in the zone of contact beyond the current limit of white settlement, for Europeans needed Indians as trading partners, principally in the fur trade. This was particularly true in French Canada: its agricultural settlements along the St Lawrence River were limited in economic value, and fur trading became its principal economic activity. Nevertheless, the mutual benefits of reciprocal relations with whites in what has been called the 'middle ground' only postponed the Indians' forced withdrawal. By 1776 their numbers east of the Appalachians had shrunk by two-thirds, and they had lost control almost everywhere. West of the mountains, a vast area that they continued to control, their numbers remained high.

It was altogether different for Europeans and Africans. Rapid population growth was central to colonial development throughout the eighteenth century. Benjamin Franklin estimated that numbers doubled every 25 years – a very high rate of increase by global standards. By 1775 the total non-Indian population had risen from about 275,000 in 1700 to roughly 2,500,000. Growth was fastest in newly developing areas just behind the leading edge of white settlement, and lowest in long-established coastal counties. The rate varied considerably from region to region. It was highest in the Middle colonies and lowest in New England. A coastal strip from southern New England to Pennsylvania and around Chesapeake Bay was the most thickly settled area, partly because it contained most of the larger towns. Natural increase accounted for most of this rise, and the family provided its essential framework. As Walter Nugent observes in *Structures of American Social History* (1981), Americans lived longer, married younger, had more children and saw more of them grow to maturity than Europeans did. With a median age of 16 for whites, every productive worker was obliged to support two or perhaps three other persons. In the particular environment of eighteenth-century America this imperative was stimulating rather than onerous.

Immigration raised this already high natural increase in the white population. The continuing influx was a significant part of the great transatlantic migration that brought 50 million people to the Western hemisphere from 1500 onwards. Before 1690 some 90 per cent of the immigrants were English, but improved employment opportunities at home reduced the flow of British migrants; thereafter the proportion dropped to only 25 per cent. In their place, the British government encouraged continental European immigration as a means of increasing national power *vis-à-vis* its rivals. The policy was highly successful and the colonies' ethnic structure was substantially modified. Calculations based on the first federal census of 1790 record that people of English stock formed only 61 per cent of the white population (or 47 per cent of total non-Indian population). Even when the Welsh, Scots, Scots-Irish and southern Irish are included, the proportion of Americans originating from the British Isles was still only 67 per cent of the total European and African settler population. A further 7.2 per cent of this total was made up of Germans, 2.1 per cent of Dutch, 1.7 per cent of French, and 0.2 per cent of Swedes. Altogether, allowing for a few Swiss and Finns, together with about 250 Jewish families, Europeans accounted for roughly four fifths of the settler population, the remaining fifth being of African origin. Native Americans living in settled areas are not included in these figures, although had they been it would have made little difference for by 1790, partly as a result of warfare but principally to the introduction of European and African diseases, they were not numerous.

As might be expected, there was considerable regional variation in the distribution of these groups. Among whites, New England was the most homogeneous area, since four-fifths of its inhabitants were English in origin. Moreover, it was the only region to receive almost no significant immigration after the initial wave ended in 1640; its population grew only as a product of very low rates of mortality. By contrast, the Middle colonies, especially Pennsylvania, were ethnically by far the most heterogeneous, with substantial numbers of Dutch, Scotch Irish and Germans, among others. Further south, more than half the white population was English in origin, except in South Carolina whose white population was more mixed. This diversity of the white population contrasted with that of the Spanish, Portuguese and French colonies, whose settlers came overwhelmingly from their respective home countries.

The third race present in colonial America came from Africa as slaves. Captured from virtually every tribe south of the Sahara but principally from the immediate hinterland of the West Coast, all had been forcibly transported. Their numbers ran to about 350,000, of whom the great majority arrived during the eighteenth century as the colonial economy expanded. Natural increase, especially when the sex ratio approached parity, augmented continued importation of so-called 'saltwater' slaves to produce a black rate of increase higher than that among whites during the 60 years before 1770. One ironic consequence was that by the time of the Revolution the vast majority of Chesapeake slaves were native-born and often the children of native-born parents.

Africans were distributed unequally across the colonies, in accordance with white requirements for their labour. Few were imported into New England, which was unique in that nearly all the physical work was performed by free native-born whites, but the number of slaves increased steadily in some parts of the Middle colonies. The proportion of Africans in the total population rose to 10 per cent in New York and New Jersey as a whole, and to 18 per cent around New York City; the effect was especially evident in Philadelphia. Even so, these northern slaves formed only a small element in the African population, for 89 per cent of all blacks lived in the South. The effect of this concentration on the ethnic structure of the South was striking. Blacks formed between 32 and 45 per cent of the populations of Maryland, Virginia, North Carolina and Georgia and a massive 61 per cent of the coastal parishes of South Carolina. Unlike the native Indians, Africans formed an important component of American society during the colonial era.

Economic activity

Long-term economic trends in eighteenth-century America were highly favourable, in spite of cyclical fluctuations. By comparison with contemporary British standards, American growth was rapid. Between 1650 and 1770 the colonial gross product grew annually by 3.2 per cent on average, though growth rates varied from region to region. The rate of economic growth was perhaps double that of Britain, and per capita gross domestic product was higher than any other country. Incomes per capita rose by at least 0.3 per cent per year for much of the colonial period, and by 0.5 per cent after 1750. In other words, the population was becoming richer as well as more numerous. By 1774, Americans possessed non-human wealth (that is, counting servants and slaves as potential consumers not as property) that gave the large majority higher real incomes than those enjoyed by any European country. If slaves and indentured servants are considered as property and discounted as consumers, the increase for free whites becomes even higher.

This expansion was powered by two interactive motors. The first was the rapid population growth; the second was increasing overseas demand for staple products such as tobacco, grain, flour and bread, rice and indigo, and forest products. Both motors were essential, but their consequences were different.

As yet the colonial economy was overwhelmingly agricultural in character. Ownership of land was the most promising route to wealth and power, especially on the frontier. Between 75 and 80 per cent of colonial men and women worked the land as landowners, tenants, servants, labourers or slaves. Much of what they produced was for domestic use or local sale, and this agricultural production amply kept up with the demands of a rising population for food. Moreover, a high-quality diet provided the strength necessary for child-bearing and hard physical work. Rapid population growth encouraged cultivation of fresh land within existing areas of occupation, extension of settlement on the frontier, and formation of new communities. When added to the output of previously settled areas, the new production accounted for the bulk of American growth. Yet this expansion merely replicated existing economic activity.

The key to greater development, that is to say economic and social change as well as simple growth, was generation of a substantial surplus of agricultural and other goods for export. Production of these staples had far more dynamic effects, even though only 9–12 per cent of gross output was directly engaged in overseas commerce. The trade was highly beneficial. Thus in every year from 1768 to 1772 the colonists paid on average £3,920,000 for imported goods, £280,000 for slaves and indentured white servants, and £40,000 in taxes and duties to Britain. New England and the Middle colonies in particular ran a large commodity deficit. On the credit side, however, they earned almost enough to meet the entire cost. Exports of commodities brought in an average of £2,800,000 each year to meet the bulk of the import bill. Additionally, Americans sold ships valued at £140,000 and earned £600,000 from the carrying trade and £220,000 from commission. When British military and civilian expenditure is added to the credit side a manageable deficit of only £40,000 on current account was left.

As the eighteenth century progressed, those areas most directly engaged in overseas trade became increasingly sophisticated and more self-reliant. The most obvious physical evidence of this economic development was urban growth. Although land was the prime source of wealth and agriculture engaged almost all the workforce, it is arguable that the towns were the most dynamic sector in the colonial economy. Five towns with more than 10,000 inhabitants developed by 1775; all were ports. Philadelphia, with at least 24,000 and perhaps more than 30,000 inhabitants, and New York with about 22,000, were the largest. Boston and Newport, Rhode Island, were handicapped by New England's lack of agricultural exports, but their populations had reached 16,000 and 11,000 respectively. The only substantial town in the South was Charleston, South Carolina, but in spite of the area's great wealth its population was no more than 14,000. Most manufacturing was still conducted in the home, and extensive industrialisation, which was developing rapidly in Britain, was still far in the future, and unlike the Iberian colonies there was no large-scale mining for precious metals. Nevertheless, specialised activities such as iron-making, shipbuilding, and small-scale workshop activities become increasingly important. For their part, traders were merchants in the fullest sense. They engaged in the import and export trade, bought and sold in many different markets, and owned and managed ships. Although remaining heavily dependent on European capital for much of their business, they increasingly provided banking and insurance services, and financed local industry. This process was also evident in the growth of the financial system. In spite of frequent complaints, the colonies' monetary system was adequate to support their economic growth. Improvements in commercial organisation, cheaper and more efficient transport and slowly rising productivity strengthened the trend to greater efficiency and profitability; in comparison, improvements in agricultural productivity were limited. Towns also provided entry-points for immigrants and served as centres of government and cultural activity.

Within this general pattern the colonial economy can be better described as a collection of local economies than as a single continental system. Rural New England grew more slowly than other regions because it had few agricultural products suited to export markets, and the South grew faster, especially for slaveholders who appropriated the surplus wealth generated by their black slaves. The Middle colonies both diversified most, as their exports of grain, iron and ships demonstrated, and grew fast. Regional differences in exports are especially revealing. The Upper South colonies around Chesapeake Bay were most productive. Over five years from 1768 they earned £1,046,883 per annum from commodity exports; in contrast the Lower South earned £551,949, the Middle colonies £526,545 and New England only £439,101. Differences in the ratio of exports to population are also striking. In 1774 the Upper South exported goods to the value of £1.82 per capita, compared with £1.78 from the Lower South and £1.03 from the Middle colonies; New England managed to export only £0.84 per capita.

Variations in economic activity such as these both influenced the distribution of wealth and structure of society in each region. They also interacted with broader cultural and ideological imperatives to create regional and local communities possessing distinctive characteristics and interests as well as shared common qualities. New England was poorer than the other regions; with a quarter of the population it possessed only one-fifth of the wealth. Lacking extensive rich soils, it was populated largely by small farmers whose engagement with a trading economy through a chain of small towns was limited. Boston, however, was a well-established commercial centre, and evidence suggests a high level of domestic comfort. The region's most substantial exports came from the sea. They included fish exported to the West Indies and Southern Europe; whale oil, which together with potash was its only major export to Britain; and (particularly in the case of Newport) the slave trade.

To move into the Middle colonies was to enter another country. Agriculture was more advanced, more commercial and more prosperous than in New England, and the towns were more substantial than in either New England or the South. The developed area of Pennsylvania contained perhaps the richest soils in the North, as well as a milder climate. It quickly became a major area for family farmers (both as landowners and large-scale tenants), and exported large quantities of flour, bread and wheat. Two other elements also benefited the region's economy. Pennsylvania virtually ignored British imperial legislation to become a major producer of bar and pig iron, and Philadelphia and New York became major entrepôts by profiting from the development of their respective hinterlands. What enabled the northern colonies to finance their trade deficits was profit earned from providing shipping, insurance and financial services in North Atlantic trade. This diversity also had importance for the scale and distribution of wealth. The inhabitants of the Middle colonies were richer than those in New England and their wealth was more evenly distributed. They formed 27 per cent of the population, and possessed 25 per cent of the colonies' net wealth.

The South was different again. It was geographically more extensive and even more rural and agricultural than other regions. Development was most advanced in the tobacco-growing Upper South colonies of Maryland and Virginia around Chesapeake Bay, where population was densest and overall wealth at its greatest. Tobacco was profitable, though not greatly so. It required relatively little start-up capital and was best grown in small plots with no more than ten workers on each, thus giving opportunities to small producers. However, ownership of several plots and many workers brought advantages of scale, so that slave labour became the key to greater individual prosperity. A likely reason for the absence of large towns is that the tobacco trade could be easily organised and controlled from Britain. Yet as tobacco culture expanded into the Piedmont and took slavery with it, so the older-established areas diversified into grain; this in turn stimulated growth of small milling towns like Baltimore and Norfolk. The Lower South of South Carolina and Georgia formed a second centre of southern society. Here the principal cash crops were rice and indigo. Rice was especially profitable. Start-up costs were high, particularly since at least 30 working slaves were required, but the rewards were far greater than in the Chesapeake. A voracious appetite for slave labour made South Carolina unique as the only colony with a black majority. It was also the richest province per free person, had the highest standards of living among whites and the greatest concentration of wealth.

Social structures

Contemporary Europeans were mistaken in believing that America was socially more-or-less homogeneous. Unquestionably there was no counterpart for whites to the stark contrast between the degradation of the poor and the great wealth, privileges and prescriptive power of the aristocracy evident in Britain and especially continental Europe. Yet substantial differences in wealth and income were clearly visible everywhere. The richest tenth of the population owned more than half the total physical wealth of the community, and within that fortunate group the richest 1 per cent owned almost 15 per cent. At the other end of the scale, the bottom fifth of the population (being slaves) were themselves a species of property, and the next 30 per cent above owned less than 3 per cent of the total. Within this general picture there were further significant variations. Although its richest citizens were not as rich as those elsewhere, the distribution of New England's wealth was notably unequal. In the Middle colonies, agricultural conditions better suited

to large-scale family farming and the cultivation of commercial crops produced more equally distributed wealth than in either of the other regions.
The South as a whole possessed half the total population but only about
one-third of the white population. This minority owned 55 per cent of the
colonies' total wealth, including half the land and 95 per cent of the slaves.
On this basis the region was almost three times richer than New England
and more than twice as rich as the Middle colonies; its white inhabitants
enjoyed the highest standard of living in colonial America. This economic
inequality was probably increasing in the older settled areas (particularly
in the towns) during the mid-eighteenth century. At the same time, new
frontier settlements created more economic opportunities for younger and
poorer people – thus probably counterbalancing the growing inequality in
older communities. Although social bands were narrower, and relationships
between the classes more fluid than in Britain, colonial society was clearly
stratified. The consequent existence of a social hierarchy of wealth, status
and authority was generally acknowledged by all, if frequently resented
by the less fortunate. In some areas the social fault lines were blurred, in
others sharp and steep.

Starting at the bottom, there was one point at which the dividing line
between social strata was crisp and clear. By the mid-eighteenth century
slavery existed in every colony (as in every other European empire). Race
provided the crucial determinant of status: all slaves were blacks or in rare
instances Native Indians. However, there was an important distinction
between North and South. Using the definition employed by Ira Berlin in
Many Thousands Gone (1998), the northern colonies can be described as 'societies with slaves'. That is to say, they were societies where slavery was one
among several forms of labour and was marginal to the principal productive process. In contrast, the southern colonies were 'slave societies' in which
slavery was at the centre of production, the master–slave relationship was
the model for all social relationships, and slaveholders were the ruling élite.
Slaves were given limited legal protection against maltreatment but no rights.
Just as whites decided where slaves should be directed, so they determined
the employment to which they would be put. In the 'slave societies' of the
South, where the demand for labour was greatest, slaves were deployed in
large numbers as agricultural labourers. In northern 'societies with slaves'
they were used as agricultural workers in parts of Rhode Island and lower
New York, but also formed an important component of the urban labour
force. By the 1760s one-fifth of all workers in Philadelphia were slaves – 40
per cent of whom were owned by tradesmen and artisans. Their numbers
in these areas were so great that Berlin has argued that they were taking on

the trappings of a slave society. They were also used in the workshops and distilleries of small towns. Everywhere, from south to north, slaves were employed as domestic servants.

Slave life consisted of many variations on a common theme. In spite of everything, African Americans sustained a measure of social and cultural life not controlled by their masters, though its character varied according to particular circumstances. But the universal fact for almost all blacks was the dependent insecurity of their enslavement: their circumstances could change in an instant at the whim of their owner. Malingering, indiscipline, sullen insubordination and running away were common expressions of protest against this uncontrollable predicament. Counterpart fears of a black uprising constantly haunted white minds, but a careful policy of frustrating the growth of African solidarity by mingling members of different tribes, coupled to ruthless coercion and calculated rewards prevented the outbreak of many rebellions. Revolts in New York in 1739 and South Carolina during the 1740s were notable for their rarity – and the brutality with which they were suppressed. Fewer than 5 per cent of blacks, mostly in the North, were free. Nevertheless, the existence of a body of free blacks demonstrated to whites as well as blacks that African Americans were capable of conducting their own lives successfully, and in that respect posed a challenge to the legitimacy of slavery. It did not substantively threaten white authority.

Unlike blacks, all whites were either free or enjoyed the prospect of freedom. Nevertheless, there was a steeply graded hierarchy of wealth and status. Charles County, Maryland, provides a microcosm of rural society in the South: above the slaves came convicts and indentured servants, then free labourers, tenants, and smaller and middling planters; at its apex were the gentry. The large number of landless labourers, servants and convicts included perhaps one-fifth of adult males. Close proximity to blacks in the South encouraged some poor whites to associate with slaves, but the general trend was in the opposite direction. In Virginia a reciprocal deep contempt developed between slaves and poorer whites. Encouraged by the gentry, the whites increasingly felt a sense of racial solidarity that overcame other social and economic differences of interest; similarly, in Charleston white artisans complained about black competition. Many landless whites lived in the major towns. Mechanics such as merchant seamen, day labourers and other unskilled workers were about one-quarter of the total; many were poor.

Further social stratification was clearly visible in town and country alike. In towns the critical distinction was between those who worked with their hands and formed up to two-thirds of the population (including the poor), and those who did not. Artisans, mostly self-employed craftsmen, formed the remainder of the mechanic community. They, too, had their hierarchy. At the bottom were coopers, weavers and shoemakers who possessed limited and easily learned skills and needed little capital. At the top were highly skilled artisans who included shipwrights, house-builders, printers and iron-masters. Many of these men, and occasionally women, employed up to two dozen workers, including slaves, and owned substantial property. Above the artisans in status (though not necessarily wealth) were those who did not work with their hands, including ministers of religion, doctors, lawyers and particularly traders. Here, too, there were hierarchies. Among professional men, schoolmasters were lowest in status and poorest, receiving salaries as little as £20 a year. At the opposite end of the scale, the practice of law gave access to political influence as well as income (in rural areas as well as towns). Traders ranged from small shopkeepers engaged in local retail markets to wealthy merchants with sufficient resources to take financial risks and sustain trade with Europe. The great merchants had incomes that probably averaged £500 per annum; shopkeepers earned half that amount or less.

But about two-thirds of all white men were farmers. Most owned their land, although tenancy was common in some areas, notably the Hudson Valley, developed areas of Pennsylvania, and the Chesapeake. Throughout the colonies as little as 50 or even 25 acres could provide a minimal living for a family, though much would depend on the location, quality and tenure of the land. All but about 10–15 per cent of landholders farmed between 50 and 500 acres – a large size by British standards. Ordinary farms in New England were seldom more that 100 acres in extent, but those in the Middle colonies were generally larger; small freehold farmers owned 50–500 acres in Virginia. Even in the South, small farmers preponderated numerically, though the social effects of staple crops and slavery were profound. Possession of slaves raised their owners' status as well as increased profitability. Not surprisingly, the great planters and their families, who formed no more than about 5 per cent of the white population, dominated Chesapeake society. The consequences of commercial agriculture were even more pronounced in South Carolina. Since efficient production of the primary staple crop, rice, required substantial capital investment and large numbers of slaves, it was known as the aristocratic crop.

The relative social equality that had distinguished the seventeenth-century colonies from Britain diminished over time. In its place the unequal distribution of property generated powerful and self-conscious élites. Their character varied considerably. At the lowest level of a small New England township, the élite often consisted of no more than prosperous farmers and storekeepers. In contrast, the richest planters in old-established southern areas usually controlled their local communities. A similar situation existed in large towns where rich merchants exercised political as well as commercial power. The supremacy of the rich was particularly evident in colonial government. It was common for a local 'court' consisting of great planters, merchants and officials to revolve around the royal governor, especially in the South. These élites expected to exercise authority in accordance with their own assessment of the public interest – which, happily for them, always coincided with their own group interests – and were convinced of their entitlement to the deference of their social inferiors.

Yet colonial élites were by no means wholly secure or totally self-confident. None were aristocratic in the British or continental European sense. Their wealth was relatively new, they lacked the titles, privileges and above all the possession of high family status over many generations that gave prescriptive social prestige and political authority across the Atlantic. In Virginia they were forced to compete for the votes of their social inferiors; George Washington found the process distasteful but inescapable. Even if the deference of inferiors had previously existed to the extent that they persuaded themselves that it had done, cracks were beginning to appear by the mid-eighteenth century. From 1770 onward, Alfred F. Young argues in *Beyond the American Revolution* (1993), there was a democratic element in American politics, and the old élites began to wonder whether they could take their chances with the new men. Beneath the surface there was a recognition that these élites depended on their inferiors and a lurking fear that the lower orders might not always acquiesce in their supremacy.

Communal life

Hierarchies of a different type existed among communities. The lowest stratum of political organisation were townships (frequently little more than villages) in the North, Anglican parish vestries in the Upper South, and parishes in South Carolina. Counties were a stage up. Their responsibilities were to maintain law and order, arrange for poor relief when necessary, and provide limited local services such as highway maintenance. These local communities were the most important sphere of social and political activity as far as day-to-day life was concerned. Above them were two higher levels of community. First came the 13 individual and separate colonies whose governments dealt with broader issues. In the absence of any continent-wide union, the British Empire was the highest level of community.

Religious denominationalism provided another form of community of the greatest importance. Church membership among whites was high, ranging from about 56 per cent of the population in the South to as high as 80 per cent in parts of the North. Religion in the British colonies was diverse but overwhelmingly Protestant – in sharp contrast to the uniformly Roman Catholic French, Spanish and Portuguese empires. Maryland alone possessed a substantial Roman Catholic minority. Apart from a few Jewish families, all other white Americans belonged to one or another of the principal Protestant churches: Anglican, Baptist, Congregationalist, Lutheran, Presbyterian, Dutch Reformed, Mennonites, or the Society of Friends, known as Quakers. But every colony – even those known for their religious tolerance such as Rhode Island and Pennsylvania – used the law to promote Christianity in general, and frequently Protestantism in particular. Two churches, the Congregational church in Massachusetts, Connecticut and New Hampshire, and the Anglican church around New York city and throughout the South, enjoyed the legal privileges of establishment, though these were not as extensive as those of the Roman Catholic church elsewhere in the Americas or the Church of England in England itself; even the Anglican church lacked a bishop and the apparatus of ecclesiastical law. During the mid-eighteenth century the non-established sects were galloping ahead in numbers, particularly in the more recently settled areas. By comparison, enslavement and transportation had all but destroyed African religion in America. Nevertheless, some African practices survived, and there is evidence of the secret practice of African rituals in the Chesapeake. Whites made increasing efforts to Christianise their slaves, but the number of converts remained small. Most Christian denominations attempted to convert Indians east of the Mississippi River to Christianity; for their part, the Indians were remarkably resistant to white evangelism.

Political structures

The institutions of colonial government superficially replicated their British counterparts. Unlike the French and Iberian colonies, each colony possessed a representative body as well as a governor representing imperial authority in London. Traditional functional divisions between executive (the governor), legislature and judiciary, and distinctions between governor, upper house (except in Pennsylvania and Georgia) and lower house mimicked the British balance of king, lords and commons. But these similarities were misleading, for American politics operated differently from British practice. There was no counterpart to the social balance between monarchy, aristocracy and people because there was no comparably sharp division between estates. The disparity between institutional structure and actual practice was especially acute in the case of the governors. Formally they represented the dignity and authority of the Crown. But, as Bernard Bailyn argues in *The Origins of American Politics* (1968), the reality was different. In practice they seldom possessed the patronage that enabled British prime ministers to control the House of Commons; rather they depended on lower houses of assembly answerable to their local communities for political support, revenue and even their own salaries. Prudent governors occasionally found it necessary to turn a blind eye to their instructions if they wished to achieve anything in their colonies; in this respect they had something in common with Spanish governors whose powers were nominally greater than those of their British counterparts. By comparison the lower houses were in some respects more powerful in their respective spheres than was the House of Commons.

The franchise for elections to the lower house of assembly, while much broader than in Britain (and with no counterpart in the other European empires), was nevertheless restricted. Two principal criteria determined eligibility: the degree to which potential voters were deemed to display commitment to the interests of the community, and the extent to which they possessed an independent political will and were capable of exercising impartial judgements on public matters. It was also implicitly argued that good government depended on a measure of ethnic, religious and social homogeneity. Doubts concerning their allegiance to the community were sufficient to exclude Jews in seven colonies and Roman Catholics in five, including Maryland. Even rich Catholics such as Charles Carroll of Carrollton could not be as influential as they might have been because they were legally excluded from voting and holding office. The requirement to possess the capacity for independent judgement was automatically deemed to exclude all women, young men not living independently, servants and slaves – though not necessarily free black men. In practice the possession of property was the principal criterion for the franchise. Between 50 and 80 per cent of free white adult males were qualified, but they generally chose from among members of the élite rather than their equals. Whether the colonial political system was democratic in any more recent sense has been vigorously debated.

Intellectual life

By the mid-eighteenth century colonial culture was maturing rapidly. If its arts and literature were still relatively unsophisticated by comparison with British high culture, in other respects it was notably more advanced. Literacy was high and schooling widespread, if erratic. Two-thirds of American white men were literate, ranging from about a quarter in the South to almost universal literacy in New England. Public education for boys was usual in New England. Elsewhere education was largely left to the churches or to individual families. By 1775 there were also nine colleges, though rich southern planters like the Lees of Virginia often sent their sons abroad. Little care was taken over women's education and none over that of black slaves. Rising levels of education had extensive ramifications. Printing presses and booksellers were common, especially in major towns. The American Philosophical Society was founded in 1743 to promote scientific enquiry, several towns had chartered libraries, and by 1775 there were 36 newspapers. The physical barrier of the Atlantic Ocean was easily surmountable, and Americans became corresponding members of the European Enlightenment, sharing its spirit of enquiry and many of its more liberal values.

The colonial mind's principal concerns were rational Christianity and the exploration of the natural universe. No single intellectual system reigned supreme, for important elements were in competition with each other: the belief of some in the power of human reason and the possibility of progress was matched by the pessimism of others and an awareness of the frailty of human nature. Already the colonies had produced two men of substantial intellectual achievement. Benjamin Franklin made important contributions to electrical theory and had been elected to the Royal Society in London, and Jonathan Edwards, a Massachusetts minister, incorporated Calvinist theology, Newtonian physics and Lockean psychology to develop a powerful theology. At a deeper, cultural rather than intellectual level there was the élite notion of gentility, which required conformity to acceptable standards of behaviour that were generally drawn from British models. To some degree this was matched by a plebeian culture that at its best was a manifestation of the propriety of fairness, and at its worst gave way to outbursts of crude anti-Catholicism.

Many colonists devoted great attention to exploring and comprehending the natural world. Recorders in Rhode Island and Pennsylvania joined the worldwide campaign to observe the transit of Venus across the Sun in 1769. David Rittenhouse constructed a clockwork model to demonstrate the planetary system, and John Bartram and many others explored the American continent. Much of their effort was devoted to the recording and classification of flora and fauna, but they went beyond this by attempting to identify and interpret the significance of what they observed. They concluded that God had created a logical, orderly universe that functioned according to rational principles, and that His purpose was benevolent. Furthermore, they believed that it was within the capacity of human reason to comprehend the nature of both the universe and God's intentions for mankind. In particular they concluded that the eighteenth century was a period highly favourable for human development and insisted on the possibility of progress, though this belief was increasingly tempered by a pessimistic fear that it might not be achieved.

Most churches and sects rejected the rigours of much early Protestantism in favour of a rational Christianity that had much in common with secular theories of the universe. But although the commanding authority of seventeenth-century Puritanism had diminished in New England as elsewhere, it was by no means dead. The revivals collectively known as the Great Awakening were clearly Puritan in character. Edwards, its greatest preacher, emphasised the depravity of human nature and the supremacy of God. The doctrines of original sin (whereby all humans are considered to have been tainted by Adam's ultimate sin of defying God's will in the Garden of Eden), predestination (whereby God chooses an 'elect' few for salvation, leaving all others to eternal damnation) and God's irresistible grace lay at the centre of their theology. The ramifications of the Awakening rumbled on for more than a generation and were especially influential among settlers filling the southern backcountry during the decades immediately before the war.

Political ideology assumed increasing importance during the mid-eighteenth century. Drawn from many sources, it was neither completely systematic nor always consistent. Besides Puritanism, the rationalism of the Enlightenment and English legalism, it incorporated the putative Anglo-Saxon Ancient Constitution that allegedly had provided a model system of representative government before 1066. Other major elements were republicanism and to a much lesser extent economic individualism. There were also deeply rooted values such as mutuality and a sense of fairness that underpinned day-to-day behaviour. Together they provided a general theory of citizenship, social behaviour and authority. Before the Anglo-American crisis it was latent rather than active, and initially it was neither inherently anti-monarchical nor totally inconsistent with loyal membership of the British Empire.

American republicanism was especially concerned with the moral integrity of the people, since it was considered vital to every community's welfare and prosperity. At its core was concern over the private integrity of individual citizens: their honesty, frugality, self-control and moral self-responsibility. Here it came close to and was reinforced by the still-living Puritan doctrine of 'calling': the duty of every person to serve God by serving the community and conforming to the ethical canons of moral behaviour. Both placed great emphasis on the duty of all citizens to put public welfare above private interest.

The concept of the relationship between citizens and their government was contractual. The ideal citizen was the yeoman farmer possessing his land as a freeholder rather than a tenant; as such he was beholden to no one and capable of exercising a free and independent political judgement. In this rationally ordered universe within which government derived its authority from contract, it was essential that the citizens should be in certain crucial respects equal. Since colonial America was a socially differentiated society, the concept of equality caused particular difficulty. Essentially it meant equality by virtue of creation, equality of moral responsibility, equality of rights such as liberty and entitlement of equal consideration of legitimate interests. Enjoyment of liberty was of prime importance.

Another strain of liberalism flowed from the Hobbesian and especially Lockean theory that people had formed governments for convenience. In exchange for abandoning certain natural rights they enjoyed the benefits of policing and order but had added no fresh rights. In this sense liberty was essentially a negative right: the freedom from interference by others, especially government. The function of government was only to protect its citizens' lives, liberty and property. It rested on the assumption that the public interest was best achieved by the consequences of citizens pursuing their individual private interests. By the eve of Revolution, this individualist social theory matched the experience, sense of self-worth and aspirations of many white Americans, particularly independent male landowners.

British Americans

It is tempting to insist that the 13 colonies were becoming distinctively American as they moved, at first unknowingly, towards independence. In some respects this was, of course, true. But in other respects, Jack Greene argues in *Pursuits of Happiness* (1988), they were converging and becoming more, not less, anglicised as the eighteenth century wore on. Economic, political and cultural connections tied them increasingly into British metropolitan culture, and British standards became the primary model for colonial behaviour. Élites deliberately attempted to imitate metropolitan culture and values. In spite of the ethnic variety of the population, the English heritage dominated the colonies, and although those outside the élite were perhaps less enthusiastic than their social superiors, English culture also played a major role in the development of American popular culture. The colonists thought of themselves as being primarily British, albeit Britons living overseas. Colonial patriotism was British patriotism. Americans frequently protested their loyalty to the Crown and joined together in celebrating the birthdays of the King, Queen and other members of the royal family. This was the case even in Boston right up to the eve of the Tea Party in 1773. They also applauded British victories in wars against France and Spain, contributed troops to a British expedition to Central America and participated in the capture of Louisburg in 1745 and Québec in 1759. Nor was personal commitment to British royal authority confined to those who later became Loyalists. George Washington served as a provincial officer attached to the British Army and was deeply disappointed not to be offered a royal commission. Even Thomas Jefferson, who came to hate Britain, started in certain respects as the apotheosis of an English country gentleman. As a young man he was an active member of Governor Francis Fauquier's court at Williamsburg, accepted a royal commission from Governor Baron de Botetourt as 'Lieutenant and Chief Commander of All his Majesty's Militia in Albemarle County', and in 1771 sought a family coat of arms in London. The conflict between those elements of society that were distinctively American and the growing aspirations to anglicisation added to colonial stress as the imperial crisis worsened.

Several features of mid-eighteenth-century America were undoubtedly conducive to unity. The topography of eastern North America emphasised the geographic coherence of the 13 colonies in relation to the British settlements in Canada (which faced the northern Atlantic rather than southwards), the Spanish Empire west and south of the Mississippi, and both the British and French colonies in the Caribbean. Cultural dependence on Britain and shared Protestantism bound the colonies to each other, and there were increasing numbers of inter-colonial connections and associations. Sects such as the Quakers and Presbyterians held regional meetings, and the evangelical Great Awakening extended across many of the colonies. Scientific enquiry attracted interest from north to south, and the American Philosophical Society had members in every colony except North Carolina. Similarly, the *Pennsylvania Journal* had numerous subscribers throughout the Middle colonies and Chesapeake and a few in every other colony. Gradual improvement of roads supplemented seaborne communications, and inter-colonial commerce increased considerably – between 1734 and 1772 the number of ships trading between major colonial ports quadrupled. This increase had significant political consequences during a period in which the number of American newspapers published rose from 9 to 38. By 1775 not only was there six times more news of other provinces' affairs in each colony's newspapers but, according to Richard L. Merritt in *Symbols of American Community* (1966), the papers contained far more words such as 'American', 'continental' and 'united colonies' – than symbols implying membership of the Empire. Separation from Britain was anticipated for many years on both sides of the Atlantic, but at mid-century disunion was still presumed to be several generations in the future. And as yet the colonies had not developed the degree of political cohesion necessary for a lasting union.

In particular, there was no 'American nation' before the imperial crisis exploded. Continental unity was much more a product than a precursor of the Revolution. Before the eve of the imperial crisis the colonies were still only 13 links in a long chain of settlements. Each had formal political ties with Britain, but none with its sister colonies. Many customary features of nationhood were missing: the army, customs service and post office were British, and there was no single established church, legal system or monetary system, neither was there a unified continent-wide élite. The highest level of community for pre-Revolutionary Americans was not the continent. Their commonality consisted largely of shared experience as subordinate members of a wider imperial society. They shared the Protestantism and relative political liberty that distinguished Britain from the continental empires, and enjoyed protected access to the most rapidly developing economic system on the North Atlantic. At most there was some regional unity, but it was defined more by differences from other regions than by internal cohesion. Feuding among neighbouring colonies was almost constant. Much revolved around political boundaries, but some was more serious and led to violence. New York and New Hampshire each laid claim to the area that became the separate state of Vermont during the Revolution. Most serious of all was rivalry between Connecticut and Pennsylvania over settlements in the Wyoming Valley of interior Pennsylvania. Andrew Burnaby, an English clergyman who visited America in 1759, judged that the colonies were so different from each other that 'were they left to themselves, there would soon be civil war, from one end of the continent to the other'.

By the third quarter of the eighteenth century the 13 British colonies were well set. Their population was increasing rapidly without overreaching the capacity of the land to sustain it. Similarly, their economy was growing and developing, and provided a sturdy infrastructure of social growth. Cultural development was keeping pace and, as later events conclusively proved, the colonies had developed the capacity for self-government. Like other communities they were susceptible to disruption, but their long-term prospects were highly favourable – whether they remained members of the British Empire or became an independent nation.

Further reading

There is an extensive and often contentious literature on colonial America. Fourteen scholars discuss the state of scholarship as it stood at the beginning of the 1980s in J. P. Greene and J. R. Pole (eds), *Colonial British America* (1984); each essay contains extensive bibliographic notes. Much has been published since then. R. C. Simmons, *The American Colonies* (1976) is a masterpiece of comprehensive, concise and detailed exposition. Native Americans are discussed in G. B. Nash, *Red, White and Black* (1974); see also C. G. Calloway, *The American Revolution in Indian Country* (1995), a fine general study based on eight case studies. J. P. Greene, *Pursuits of Happiness* (1988) is a brilliant interpretation of social development, as is J. A. Henretta and G. H. Nobles, *Evolution and Revolution: American Society, 1600–1820* (1987). A general description of late colonial society is J. Butler, *Becoming America* (2000). Economic development is covered in S. L. Engerman and R. E. Gallman (eds), *The Cambridge Economic History of the United States*, Vol. I, *The Colonial Era* (1996), and urban society in G. B. Nash, *Urban Crucible* (1979). Ira Berlin, *Many Thousands Gone* (1998) discusses the development of the slave system, while P. D. Morgan, *Slave Counterpoint: Black Culture in the Eighteenth-Century Chesapeake and Low Country* (1998) is a wide-ranging masterpiece of comparative analysis. Women are treated in C. Berkin, *First Generations: Women in Colonial America* (1996). Religion is discussed both comprehensively and sympathetically by P. V. Bonomi in *Under the Cope of Heaven* (1986) and by J. Butler in *Awash in a Sea of Faith* (1990). Broad cultural issues are examined in R. L. Bushman, *The Refinement of America* (1993), which covers the growth of gentility. B. Bailyn, *The Origins of American Politics* (1968) is a major analysis of the difference between constitutional theory and actual political behaviour. H. S. Commager, *The Empire of Reason* (1978) discusses various aspects of the Enlightenment. Regional studies are legion. Outstanding examples are R. L. Bushman, *From Puritan to Yankee* [on Connecticut] (1967), J. T. Lemon, *The Best Poor Man's Country* (1972) and A. Kulikoff, *Tobacco and Slaves* (1986).

CHAPTER 3

American political culture

Adam I. P. Smith

American exceptionalism

With a sense of timing that all successful authors require, a book was published in London in 1782 that posed a famous question: 'what is the American, this new man?' This was the issue of the hour for many Britons, stung by the humiliating defeat of the greatest military superpower on Earth by a rabble of colonists with pretensions of national destiny. How should this upstart new nation be explained and understood? The book, *Letters from an American Farmer*, was written by an upstate New Yorker of French ancestry, J. Hector St John de Crèvecoeur. It was a classic formulation of the argument that America was a truly exceptional place, severed from the rules that determined the historical development of the Old World. In America, Crèvecoeur insisted, 'individuals of all nations are melted into a new race of men'. The richness and abundance of the land, he explained, offered opportunities for even the lowliest settler, creating a more egalitarian society than Europeans could ever imagine in their homelands. More than that, Crèvecoeur argued that becoming an American was an act of faith, a declaration of a commitment to a new set of egalitarian assumptions about society. 'He is an American', wrote Crèvecoeur, 'who, leaving behind him all his antient prejudices and manners, receives new ones from the new mode of life he has embraced, the new government he obeys and the new rank he holds'. Making a claim that would find many an echo in subsequent efforts to explain America, Crèvecoeur told his readers that the passage across the Atlantic was as much an ideological journey as a geographical one.

Forty years after *Letters from an American Farmer* appeared, another Frenchman, this time a minor aristocrat with pronounced liberal sympathies, Alexis de Tocqueville, went to America – not as an immigrant but as a curious visitor – and produced what remains to this day by far the single most influential analysis of American political culture: *Democracy in America* (1835). In two large volumes, full of stunning insight, telling anecdote and occasional inconsistency, Tocqueville offered a vision of the United States as the exemplar of a liberal, democratic society. Founded on the principle of equal rights for all and government by the consent of the governed, the overwhelming 'basic fact' about American society was, he argued, the (relative) equality of conditions. Tocqueville sought to explain why the United States was at the vanguard of a democratic revolution. His explanation for its being ahead of Europe in this respect rested on two central observations. First, like Crèvecoeur, Tocqueville pointed to the availability of land 'inhabited only by wondering tribes who had not thought of exploiting' it, which enabled white Americans to spread out and make their fortune. The second point was that American settlers, coming overwhelmingly from England where they had 'unusual acquaintance with notions of rights and principles of true liberty' had a fierce attachment to democratic ideas. Never having had to struggle against feudalism, Americans possessed a kind of democratic innocence. 'The great advantage of the American', Tocqueville had written, 'is that he has arrived at a state of democracy without having to endure a democratic revolution and that he is born free without having to become so'. A 'middle class and democratic freedom' flourished almost from the outset, obscuring alternative political traditions. American national identity, according to the Tocquevillian story, is thus bound up with a set of commitments to certain liberal or democratic values.

Many hundreds of efforts have been made to 'explain America'. There have been very few that have not, at root, interpreted US history in the light of the rejection of Old World hierarchy. Very few of America's many analysts have dissented from the proposition that it is a nation in some sense 'dedicated' to equality and freedom. Over the last 200 years the idea that the United States has been shaped from its founding by an unusual and pervasive commitment to liberal values has been used by analysts to explain almost every aspect of American history from the early expansion of the suffrage and the process by which immigrants are assimilated to the high crime rates and the perennial old chestnut of a question: why was there no socialism in the United States? The Tocquevillian analysis – that America was good for equality and freedom – is rooted in important truths. It offers a compelling and putatively comprehensive paradigm for understanding the history of the United States. The purpose of this essay is to examine this powerful 'consensus' theory, to explain its continuing appeal, to identify its limitations and to consider some alternative ways of understanding American political values and social relations.

Tocqueville's heirs

The persistence of the Tocquevillian orthodoxy owes much to two highly influential books published in the mid-twentieth century: *An American Dilemma* (1944) by the Swedish sociologist Gunnar Myrdal and *The Liberal Tradition in America* (1955) by the Harvard political scientist Louis Hartz. Although they are very different kinds of book, each in its own way reaffirmed the idea of a distinctive American liberal consensus.

In Myrdal's view, Americans were committed to the tenets of what he called 'the American creed': beliefs rooted in the 'humanistic liberalism' of the Enlightenment, embodied in the nation's founding documents, and serving as the ideological cement that held the nation together. The creed, with its democratic commitment to the moral equality of all human beings and their 'inalienable rights to freedom, justice, and a fair opportunity', was what gave Americans their common identity. With this as the basis of his understanding of American nationality, he set out to explore the 'dilemma' of race. Here was an apparent paradox: why in this land of liberal and democratic values was racial discrimination so deeply entrenched? Myrdal did not think that the failure of Americans to live up to their creed invalidated the existence of the ideals in the first place. Racism was a mere 'prejudice', most characteristic of the 'poor and uneducated white' people of the South and which most Americans knew was not on the same moral plane as their national commitment to equality and freedom. Myrdal was sweeping in his condemnation of the Jim Crow segregation laws, but his analysis was ultimately optimistic; the American creed had triumphed in the past and would do so in the future.

Twenty years later, Myrdal's analysis seemed vindicated by events. Martin Luther King's 'I have a dream' speech from the steps of the Lincoln Memorial in 1963 was a seemingly successful appeal to what Abraham Lincoln had once called 'the better angels of our nature'. King argued that African Americans wanted to 'cash the check' promised in the Declaration of Independence. They did not want special privileges; they wanted to be treated as Americans. In overwhelming numbers, white Americans joined blacks in revulsion at the continued hypocrisy of millions of American citizens being denied basic democratic rights. Huge majorities supported the Civil Rights Act and the Voting Rights Act and elected Lyndon Johnson with his vision of a multiracial 'Great Society' by a generous margin in 1964. Subsequent historians have largely accepted the analysis of contemporaries who described America in the early 1960s – before the conflicts created by Vietnam and the counterculture – as a period dominated by a 'liberal consensus'. This was a moment when, it has been argued, civil rights were widely accepted by all except white southerners, who in any case did not truly represent American values. In the post-war world, a faith in American capitalism and its capacity to spread affluence had rendered class conflict meaningless and racial discrimination a legacy from a less enlightened era. For many, the struggles of the 1960s were about confronting entrenched double standards and righting the nation with its own ideals. The essential 'goodness' of American society was affirmed by the way in which injustice could seemingly be overcome by an appeal to the values on which the nation was founded.

If Myrdal popularised the notion of an American creed, Louis Hartz's *The Liberal Tradition in America*, proceeding from very similar assumptions, offered a more wary analysis. Echoing Tocqueville both in the comprehensiveness of his interpretation and in the conclusions he reached, Hartz argued that at the soul of American politics there was a deep commitment to liberalism. Like Tocqueville, Hartz believed that the starting point for understanding American history was to grasp the fact that Americans had never had to struggle to overcome feudalism. In this fundamental sense, America was an exceptional place. Having missed this crucial stage of historical development, the explanation for what America was, and who Americans were, lay in America.

In Hartz's vision, this virgin America was dedicated to the ideas of the radical English philosopher, John Locke (1632–1704), a highly influential writer whose ideas about individual liberty and the rational pursuit of truth resonated in the anti-authoritarian climate of the British American colonies. As Hartz reminded his readers, the Declaration of Independence (1776) was only the most well-known of a number of essentially Lockean documents written by the Founding Fathers. Locke was certainly responsible for popularising among eighteenth-century pamphleteers and men of letters in both Britain and the colonies the idea of the natural rights of man and the notion that legitimate government arose from a 'social contract' among free individuals. The 'truths' elaborated by Thomas Jefferson in the Declaration of Independence – that all men were created equal and endowed with 'unalienable' rights including 'life, liberty, and the pursuit of happiness' – were 'self-evident' to those who had read and internalised Locke. The resonance of Locke in America was not surprising. After all, unlike in the Old World, the process of forming governments from a 'state of nature' had taken place in the course of recent generations. 'In the beginning', Locke wrote, 'all the world was America.' Unlike in Europe, written constitutions or covenants defined the powers of colonial governments and appeared to be something close to 'social contracts' in action. Locke saw in the New World the opportunity to create a model civic society. He even put theory into practice by contributing a section on religious toleration to the 'The Fundamental Constitutions of Carolina' (1669), the document that gave form to the government of that new colony.

In Hartz's view, Locke – or at least a selective interpretation of Locke – has loomed so large in the American imagination that he has become 'a massive national cliché'. So deeply ingrained has the image of Locke been in American culture that few even know it by its name: 'there has never been a "liberal movement" or a real "liberal party" in America', argued Hartz, 'we have only had the American Way of Life'. Who is the American? Hartz's answer to Crèvecoeur's question is that Lockean liberalism defines what America is and who Americans are.

This notion, embodied in the work of Myrdal and Hartz, that the United States is an essentially creedal society – a nation dedicated to a set of beliefs and defined by its efforts to live up to its own ideals – is the most familiar and certainly the most powerful interpretation of American national identity. In recent years, scholars have become familiar with the idea that nations are more than just political entities with borders drawn on a map. They are also 'imagined communities', in Benedict Anderson's famous phrase, that are continually made and re-made in people's minds. Nationalism is an unstable construct. Scholars have emphasised how malleable and historically contingent ideas of nationhood are. Traditionally, analysts have distinguished between 'ethnic nationalism', where the nation is defined by real or imagined ties of ancestry, and 'civic nationalism', in which membership is based on allegiance to a set of political institutions or values. Ethnic nationalism tends to look to the past for legitimacy, civic nationalism, while it will require a founding moment of some kind, ultimately looks to a vision of the future for its rationale. Germany is often cited as the exemplar of an exclusive ethnically based nation. In contrast, the United States is usually seen as the ultimate civic nation. From its founding, scholars argue, American nationhood was identified with universal values. As Crèvecoeur suggested, an American was one who signed up to certain beliefs, and from the eighteenth century to the present day it has been commonplace to remark that the United States is, above all else, a political construct.

This view has been summed up most recently by Seymour M. Lipset: 'Being an American', he has written, 'is an ideological commitment. It is not a matter of birth. Those who reject American values are un-American'. The salience of this American creed has even been invoked to explain 'exceptional' aspects of American society. It has been suggested, for example, that the unusually high crime rate in America – especially of violent crime – can be explained with reference to the underlying political culture. According to Lipset, 'In a country that stresses success above all, people are led to feel that the most important thing is to win fame regardless of the methods employed in doing so'. Acknowledging his debt to Hartz, the historian Richard Hofstadter famously remarked that it was America's fate, 'not to have ideologies but to be one', by which he meant that commitment to American ideas was an 'ism' as salient and as coherent as other powerful world-views like socialism or communism. Indeed, perhaps only the Soviet Union in recent times has so closely intertwined national identity and political belief.

In this respect, as in many others, Hartz's book had such a big impact because it was a powerful articulation of ideas that were already widely held. Since the mid-nineteenth century, those who lamented, or celebrated, the apparent absence in the United States of a mass working-class movement dedicated to socialist ideas had often turned to an essentially ideological explanation. The lack of a genuine 'revolutionary tradition', and a political culture that celebrated individualism and saw government as a threat to individual liberty, denied socialists any ideological space. Hartz's emphasis on the implications of the absence of feudalism fitted neatly with this view. Hartz, who himself came out of a Marxist tradition, explained that 'socialism is an ideological phenomenon, arising out of the principles of class and the revolutionary liberal revolt against them which the old European order inspired'. It followed that 'it is not accidental that America, which has uniquely lacked a feudal tradition, has uniquely lacked also a socialist tradition'. Hartz was not the first – and nor would he be the last – to point out that conservatism has had a different meaning in America than elsewhere. Since the Revolution, there has never been a proper 'Tory' tradition, in the sense of aristocratic disdain for bourgeois values and the upholding of a hierarchical social order and an established church.

The purpose of Hartz's book was not just to document the supposed pervasiveness of this liberal creed – which he called Americans' 'irrational attachment' to Locke, but to emphasise its implication: if to be American meant to be a Lockean liberal, then where did that leave the quality of intellectual debate in America? In thrall to the nostrums of individual and property rights and to a fear of governmental power, the range of ideological choices open to Americans was severely impoverished. Whereas Tocqueville worried about the 'tyranny of a majority' in a democratic system, Hartz went a step further and suggested that 'the basic ethical problem of a liberal society' is the 'danger of unanimity', or the 'massive pressure to conform'. A close reading of Hartz makes clear that he basically favoured the liberal values that he saw all around him. Yet he still found the unanimity and intellectual rigidity stifling. Ironically, even while making a powerful intellectual-historical case for the exceptionalism of American culture, he deplored American parochialism and self-obsession.

The 'liberal consensus' Hartz described has more often been celebrated than condemned. Like Myrdal, who saw the American creed as a source of inspiration that would enable Americans to overcome their more base prejudices, many writers have argued that a consensus on basic liberal values has been a blessing for the United States, just as they have understood American exceptionalism to mean American superiority. At the height of the Cold War, most historians stressed what Americans had in common rather than what divided them. In books with titles like *The Genius of American Politics*, the historian Daniel Boorstin, for example, unashamedly celebrated what he saw as the absence of class conflict and pernicious foreign ideologies.

It is true, of course, that despite a discourse that stresses its newness, the United States has one of the oldest continually functioning constitutions in the world. This remarkable stability in its governing institutions seemed even more astonishing in the era of the world wars, when the rest of the world seemed so vulnerable to catastrophe. In such circumstances it was not surprising that a historical theory that saw the defining feature of America as its continuity and coherence should be so resonant.

The Puritan legacy

Since Hartz argued that the 'escape from Europe' and the absence of feudalism are the keys to understanding America, it was important for him – even more than for Tocqueville – to present the origins of America as a kind of immaculate conception. Untainted by Old World influences, Lockeanism could flourish in the exceptional climate of America as nowhere else. Oddly, though, for a scholar whose thesis depended on establishing the unique origins of American society as the continuing explanation for its exceptional culture, Louis Hartz slighted the colonial phase of American development. As a consequence, he ignored entirely an alternative 'key' to American political culture: the Puritanism of the first settlers. Just like Hartz, recent proponents of the importance of the Puritan origins of American history are believers in American exceptionalism. For these scholars, though, the dominant culture owes its distinctive features not to Lockean liberalism, or to the effect of the Wild West on the American character, but to the Pilgrim Fathers, the men who sought to found what Lincoln would later call the 'last, best hope of earth', a nation with a mission to save mankind.

In this respect, as in so many others, Tocqueville got there first. 'Puritanism was almost as much a political theory as a religious doctrine', he wrote. 'No sooner had the immigrants landed than they made it their first care to organize themselves as a society'. Therefore, he concluded, 'the whole destiny of America was contained in the first Puritan who landed on these shores, as that of the whole human race in the first man'. This is the starting point for the analysis of American culture offered by Sacvan Bercovitch, the scholar who, since Hartz, has offered the most forceful argument for the existence of an 'ideological consensus'. In the introduction to his book *The American Jeremiad* (1978), Bercovitch, in the tradition of Tocqueville, Myrdal and Hartz, described his astonishment, as a Canadian, at encountering the all-pervasiveness of the American creed. Here was a country that,

> despite its bewildering mixture of race and creed, could believe in something called an American mission, and could invest that patent fiction with all the emotional, spiritual, and intellectual appeal of a religious quest. Here was . . . the civil rights leader Martin Luther King, descendent of slaves, denouncing segregation as a violation of the American dream; here, an endless debate about national identity, full of rage and faith . . . conservative politicians hunting out socialists as conspirators against the dream, left-wing polemics proving that capitalism was a betrayal of the country's sacred origins.

In no other country, Bercovitch thought, was there such a powerful sense that the nation was dedicated to a purpose, nor such unanimity about the mission they had collectively undertaken. Like many other analysts before him he argued that the 'American dream' was a device that convinced Americans – of whatever class or race, and whether they were victims or beneficiaries of existing power structures – that competitive individualism, free enterprise, and faith in social mobility and *laissez-faire* was the only true American Way. For Bercovitch, the explanation for the 'astonishing cultural hegemony' of these values had to be traced back to the Puritan settlers. His approach was indebted to the German sociologist Max Weber, who brilliantly argued in the early twentieth century that the cultural values propagated by

Protestantism stimulated the rise of capitalist development. For Weber, the influence of the Puritans on American development was a key piece of evidence. 'The spirit of capitalism' in America, Weber wrote, 'was present before the capitalistic order'. There was what Weber called an 'elective affinity' between, on the one hand, the Protestant values of hard work, individualism and an inner-directed pursuit of perfection, and the culture of capitalism on the other.

Any argument that credits the religious practices of a group of seventeenth-century settlers with having created the template for an entire national culture needs to do more than simply point out similarities across time; it needs to demonstrate a mechanism whereby Puritan cultural values could be transmitted through the generations. For Bercovitch, a literary scholar, the answer to this problem of cultural transmission lies in what he regards as a distinctively American literary form: a type of sermon known as a Jeremiad. Originally the Jeremiad was a ritualised warning by Puritan preachers, reminiscent of the lamentations of the Old Testament prophet Jeremiah, of the wrath of God that would be incurred by the declension from the high principles and ambition of their society. In its classic form it was a denunciation of deviant behaviour and an injunction to strive for improvement. Bercovitch sees it as a recurring impulse behind Americans' search for national identity. 'Their church-state was to be at once a model to the world of Reformed Christianity and a prefiguration of the New Jerusalem to come', Bercovitch wrote of the early Puritans. So whereas in other societies fundamentalist religion was used to condemn waywardness and induce feelings of guilt and remorse, in America it was, besides being a warning of present-day deficiencies, a vision of a perfect society to come. 'God's punishments were *corrective* not destructive', wrote Bercovitch. 'Here, as no where else, His vengeance was a sign of love, a father's rod used to improve the errant child. In short their punishments confirmed their promise'.

At the heart of what is distinctive about the American national experience, Bercovitch suggests, is its ability to co-opt the powerful religious ideas of redemption and salvation. 'Of all symbols of identity', he writes, 'only *America* has united nationality and universality, civic past and paradise to be, in a single synthetic ideal'. In his emphasis on the way in which the tropes of American national identity invoke and replicate religious ideas, Bercovitch's analysis captures an important truth about the nature of American national identity, one frequently commented on by foreign observers. The United States has often been described as having a 'civic religion'. The cult of the flag in American society, to cite only one of the more obvious pieces of evidence, is very reminiscent of the status accorded to the cross in the Christian tradition. Similarly, the public ceremonies of the nation – from the recitation of the 'pledge of allegiance' in schools to the readings of 'sacred texts' like Lincoln's Gettysburg Address on public occasions, to the veneration of the Founding Fathers and the obsessive textual analysis of the intentions of the framers of the Constitution – are quasi-religious in their aura and their social function.

These fundamental aspects of American political culture are neglected by Hartz. Yet although their versions of the American 'creation myth' are very different, Hartz and Bercovitch ultimately reach similar conclusions. One sees America in entirely secular terms, the other as having bestowed on itself a Providential mission, yet both see America as enveloped in a stultifying consensus that precludes the emergence of alternative ideologies. Both see individualism, democracy and capitalism as synonymous with each other and with American nationhood. As Daniel Walker Howe notes in an article appearing in the 1982 issue of *American Quarterly*, 'Bercovitch has, in effect, restated the thesis of Louis Hartz's *The Liberal Tradition in America*, substituting Puritanism for the Enlightenment . . . "The Jeremiad" seems to become a code-word for American bourgeois culture in general, much as Hartz used Locke as a shorthand for the same thing'.

Conflict and consensus

The 'consensus theory' was developed in the 1950s as a necessary corrective to the tendency of a previous generation of historians to stress socio-economic conflict as the engine of American historical development. By pointing to the basic level of agreement on fundamental issues, Hartz and his followers sought to make a contribution essential to any useful historical theory: they outlined the boundaries of conflict. Yet it remains unclear whether an interpretation of American history based on the idea of a fundamental consensus is viable given the depths of the conflict that has so often rent American society. The United States is now, and always has been, starkly divided. At different times and to different degrees issues of race, culture, religion, gender, ethnicity, geographical location, wealth and class have set Americans against each other. Northerners have fought southerners, rural dwellers have felt alienated from urbanites, cosmopolitan 'moderns' have been pitched against evangelical traditionalists. How can these very obvious conflicts and structured inequalities be integrated into a consensual view of American history?

Hartz explains away the most obvious conflict – the Civil War – by arguing that the antebellum South was the one great example of deviance. In similar language to that deployed by Myrdal to explain away southern racism in the twentieth century, Hartz sees the antebellum South as 'an alien child in a liberal family, tortured and confused, driven to a fantasy life which, instead of disproving the power of Locke in America, portrays more poignantly than anything else the tyranny he has had'. (This is an ingenious but ultimately circular argument: if even large-scale dissension from the 'consensus' is yet more evidence of the power of the consensus, what, it may be asked, could possibly *disprove* the consensus theory, in Hartz's judgement?) As Richard Hofstadter, a sympathetic critic of Hartz, trenchantly remarks in *The Progressive Historians* (1983), 'consensus, to be effective, must be a matter of behavior as well as thought, of institutions as well as theories'. Patently this has often not been the case.

One way of explaining conflict while not jettisoning the idea of a basic consensus has been to argue, as Myrdal did, that American struggles have been caused by the tension between the promise of the American creed – equality, freedom, democracy – and the reality. In his book *American Politics: The Promise of Disharmony* (1981), the political scientist Samuel P. Huntington concludes that conflict arises because, although everyone agrees with the creed, some seek to pursue its logic more vigorously than others. When values are so widely held, any deviation from them is bound to be criticised, so consensus is in itself a cause of conflict. Huntington opens his book by quoting from a student speech at Harvard's 1969 commencement. With America convulsed by riots, anti-war protests and the shock of the counterculture, the spokesman for the graduating class of that year sought to explain what these conflicts meant. The protests, he said, were not 'an effort to subvert institutions or an attempt to challenge values which have been affirmed for centuries'. Rather than 'conspiring to destroy America' the student told the assembled parents and faculty, 'we are attempting to do precisely the reverse: we are affirming the values which you have instilled in us and which you have taught us to expect'. For Huntington, this sums up the fundamental unity of American culture: even its most vigorous dissidents dissent in the name of the same values held by the rest.

Other scholars have suggested that the key problem with Hartz was his failure to distinguish clearly enough between different strands of the 'liberal tradition'. Acknowledging his debt to Hartz, the historian Arthur J. Schlesinger Jr in *The Politics of Hope* (1962) has argued that there is a long-standing division between a liberal and conservative version of the liberal tradition. Not that, as he concedes, liberals or conservatives have held consistent positions over time, even on such fundamental questions as the role of government or the rights of minorities. Invoking the New England poet and essayist Ralph Waldo Emerson, Schlesinger argued that the basic difference was between 'the party of memory and the party of hope'. No deep differences of principle separated conservatives and liberals. 'Each is a great half but an impossible whole. Each exposes the abuses of the other but in a true society, in a true man, both must combine.' A similar argument has been made by Seymour M. Lipset, who also recognises conflict over values without accepting that this means there is more than one overarching political-cultural system. The reason why there is conflict within a culture of consensus, Lipset contends, is that some of the consensual values – equality and freedom are the two most important – if pushed hard, are impossible to reconcile:

> Liberals and conservatives typically do not take alternative positions on issues of equality and freedom. Instead, each side appeals to one or the other core values, as liberals stress egalitarianism's primacy and the social injustice that flows from unfettered individualism, while conservatives enshrine individual freedom and the social need for mobility and achievement as values 'endangered' by the collectivism inherent in liberal nostrums.

For Lipset, a fully-fledged believer in 'national character', this tension is a psychological one within each American, as much as a cause of political tension.

The philosopher J. David Greenstone offered a more complex view of liberty. While agreeing with Hartz that all Americans share a liberal commitment to freedom, individualism and pluralism, Greenstone made the case that 'American liberalism is divided between two liberal outlooks, one of which is Lockean as Hartz maintains, while the other stems from a Protestant mode of thought and social action that [Hartz] largely ignores'. American political culture thus juxtaposes a moral, benevolent aspiration to create a more perfect society with a rights-based, utilitarian conception of law and politics. Two different conceptions of freedom underlie this difference, Greenstone maintains. When they speak of freedom, 'Lockean liberals' generally mean 'negative liberty' (freedom *from* something, usually government) whereas Protestant liberals tend to favour 'positive liberty' (freedom *to* do something). Greenstone's contribution is important because he reminds us that liberalism does not have to be Lockean (in the sense of embracing a belief in the unfettered market, privileging private desires over public interest or collective moral choices over individual desires.)

The philosopher James P. Young (*Reconsidering American Liberalism*, 1995) has also developed an argument which, while reasserting the idea that all Americans are in some sense liberal, has suggested that liberalism can mean several, often contradictory, things. He has identified three, ultimately irreconcilable, different liberal traditions in America: the pursuit of constitutional limitations on government power; free market or *laissez-faire* liberalism; and 'reform liberalism', which seeks to use government to secure equality. The common liberal values in each of these strands are 'an image of human beings as essentially equal, rights-bearing, interest-oriented individuals – individuals who are entitled to have those rights defended, particularly against governmental intrusion'. While all Americans can sign up to this common denominator, they have been divided according to which of the three liberal strands they most identify with.

To these scholars, then, the consensus idea might still hold water so long as differences of emphasis within the consensual liberal tradition are recognised. The important question begged by their analysis, of course, is how big do these differences of emphasis need to be before the notion of a single tradition ceases to have any analytical value?

Race, gender and class: hierarchy and inequality in America

The real problem with the theory of liberal consensus, however, is that it confuses the dominant national discourse with the underlying reality. Generations of Americans – mostly white, male and of the kind who write the histories and make the speeches – have celebrated the dominance of the values of individualism and democracy. But that does not mean that we should take them at their word. Maybe the different constructions given to the 'key words' of liberty, equality and democracy distract us from the reality of deep and enduring political and cultural conflicts within America, conflicts rooted in dramatically different social experiences and which, on closer examination, seem remarkably similar to political and social divisions in other societies. Indeed the concept of American exceptionalism itself surely results from mistaking rhetoric for reality. Only by exaggerating differences between the United States and other nations can the argument be made that American society is distinctively egalitarian. The much-touted absence in America of specifically European forms of class division masks the presence in the United States of forms of oppression at least as pernicious as those the Old World.

Hartz and his followers have overlooked the deep ideological structures of inequality and hierarchy in American history. It may have been true that, relative to European countries, the young United States developed without a rigid class structure. The majority of young white men in the nineteenth century and through much of the twentieth century may well have had a better chance in what Lincoln called 'the race of life' in America than they would have done in Europe. It is certainly the case that one of the most distinctive features of the American Revolution was its complete rejection of titles of rank and the hereditary principle. But it was also true that this egalitarianism was sharply circumscribed by race, ethnicity and gender. As Rogers M. Smith has argued in an article appearing in the *American Political Science Review* (1993), the 'Tocquvillian story is thus deceptive because it is too narrow. It is centered on relationships among a minority of Americans (white men, largely of northern European ancestry)'. Myrdal argued that equality was the natural state of American life, to which discrimination and hierarchy were the exception.

Recent scholarship, however, has emphasised the elaborate justifications formulated by élites to explain the inequality they sanctioned, and suggested that it has been the norm rather than the aberration for Americans to adhere to justifications for inequality and hierarchy. 'True Americanism', historically speaking, has always been equated with distinctions associated with race, ethnicity and religion. For most of American history women and non-white men have been considered biologically unsuited to equal status either in the domestic or the public spheres. Even religious denomination has been used as a reason to exclude whole sections of the population from equal status. In the late nineteenth century the discrimination faced by Catholic and Jewish immigrants was defended by élites on the grounds that these new arrivals did not conform to the Protestant values that were regarded as essential attributes of American identity. For the first century or more of US history, free women, while always having a designated role in the republican community, were not regarded as possessing the essential attributes required for full political participation. The American creed, in other words, had gendered, ethnic and racial assumptions built into it.

Most analysts may have described American nationalism as 'civic' and 'voluntary', but in truth it has always combined both civic and ethnic definitions. As Eric Foner in an essay entitled 'Who is an American?' (1996) has put it: 'for most of our history, American citizenship has been defined by blood as well as allegiance'. While American identity has certainly been defined by a set of universal claims about human nature, it has simultaneously, for most of the last 200 years, limited membership to people of particular races and ethnicities. Crèvecoeur presented the American as a man who had chosen to adopt a new way of life and who adhered to new values, but he also defined the American as 'a mixture of English, Scotch, Irish, French, Dutch,

Germans, and Swedes'. Foner points out that this was at a time when 'fully one-fifth of the population (the highest proportion in our history) consisted of Africans and their descendents'. Those Africans were mostly slaves of course. Slavery's presence in the land of liberty had the paradoxical effect of making the liberties of American citizenship seem even more precious. (Samuel Johnson famously exclaimed at the time of the American Revolution: 'How is it we hear the loudest yelps for liberty among the drivers of negroes?' The answer was that the two were bound up together: the denial of freedom to others made freedom an even more valuable possession, and the sight of actual chattel slavery gave a powerful charge to the fear of being reduced to metaphorical slavery in the rhetoric of the Revolutionaries.)

The orthodox narrative of American history assumes the incremental triumph of liberal values as barriers to inclusion fell one after the other. First, the Revolution ended monarchical subjugation, then slavery was abolished, women were enfranchised, immigrant rights recognised and eventually African-American equality guaranteed by the civil rights movement. New work in the fields of social and political history has challenged this Hartzian assumption of Whiggish progress. In the late nineteenth and early twentieth centuries, for example, the boundaries determining who were to be included in American citizenship were restricted in some areas just at the moment when they were expanded in others. Thus, while blacks were formally recognised as citizens by the Fourteenth Amendment, new forms of racial discrimination were being imposed. For the first century of US history any free, white person could arrive and claim citizenship (the only exception being those who proved themselves to lack republican credentials by claiming titles of hereditary nobility), but by the 1920s it was virtually impossible for anyone not of white European heritage to do so. No sooner was one form of discrimination destroyed than another form of hierarchy arose to take its place. This overwhelming evidence of the depth and persistence of discrimination and hierarchy in America needs to be kept in mind when considering the idea that the United States was 'born free' and baptised in liberal, individualist, democratic values. As Rogers M. Smith concludes in the article already quoted, Americans' commitment to 'hierarchy' represents a rival political tradition that has battled with 'liberalism' throughout American history. It certainly seems clear that freedom for some has flourished in a society that discriminates against others and that most Americans, just like people everywhere, have never had any trouble holding logically inconsistent views.

The case can also be made that as more political rights have been gained by greater numbers of people, the quality of democratic participation has declined. In the antebellum period, the vote was restricted to white men, but the active participation of those entitled to play a part within the body politic was much greater than it was later to become. Not only did a far higher proportion of them turn out to vote in elections in that period, but as (white, male) citizens they were also far more likely to hold office, attend public meetings and argue the finer points of political issues with their fellow citizens than is the case today. The political historian Walter Dean Burnham has even described a 'lost Atlantis' of participatory democracy. Although some recent scholarship has warned us against this kind of romanticism, there is a basis of truth in the claim. Certainly, subsequent generations of democratic reformers have been disappointed that each new expansion in the size of the political community – be it through the enfranchisement of women in the 1920s, of African Americans in the 1960s, or of under-21s in the 1970s – has failed to be matched by a corresponding increase in democratic participation.

The 'republican synthesis'

If this evidence of systematised exclusion and hierarchy gives modern-day Tocquevillians pause for thought, the idea of a liberal consensus has also been challenged from a different direction, namely by students of eighteenth and early nineteenth-century political culture. Historians studying the ideological origins of the American Revolution, for example, have dissented from the idea that Locke was the intellectual godfather that Hartz claimed. A generation of historians, following Bernard Bailyn's *Ideological Origins of the American Revolution* (1967), probed the heart of American political culture and instead of liberalism came up with the ideology of classical republicanism. Whereas Hartz argued, following Tocqueville, that America was 'born liberal', republican revisionists counter that America *became* liberal. Bailyn stressed the republican worldview through which colonists articulated their disagreements with the Mother Country in the run up to the Revolution. In *The Creation of the American Republic* (1969), Gordon Wood extended the republican theme into the 1770s and 1780s by explaining how republican ideals of consensus and community, and of the opposition between liberty and power, shaped the debates about the form the new republic should take. The work of these historians was bolstered a few years later by the publication of an influential work on the history of political thought, J. G. A. Pocock's, *The Machiavellian Moment: Florentine Political Thought and the Atlantic Republican Tradition* (1975), which saw eighteenth-century Americans as the last standard bearers of a tradition of early modern republican thought.

In the view of the proponents of this 'republican synthesis' the engine of American politics was driven not by the pursuit of private gain, as Hartz had argued, but by a shared public life of civic duty. As the political scientist James Morone has explained, 'natural leaders were expected to rise up among the people; others would acknowledge their place within the natural order and contribute their own talents to the common good'. Far from distancing citizens from government, republicans in early America fostered participation in government at all levels. Rather than capitalists bent on the creation of a modern industrial economy, Americans wanted to preserve the homogeneity and relative egalitarianism of agrarian communities. In recent years the republican theme has been extended well into the nineteenth century. Labour historians, in particular, have found that the republican ideal of a harmonious community inspired working men's organisations, while political historians have turned to the republican yearning for unity and emphasis on civic virtue to explain the persistence of anti-partisanship and distrust of professional politicians in the nineteenth century. Even the coming of the Civil War has been fitted into a republican paradigm, with northerners and southerners each becoming convinced that the other side was corrupt (in the sense of lacking in civic virtue) and engaged in a vast conspiracy to destroy republican liberty.

For some years debate has raged among historians of the early Republic about the timing of the transition from a society structured by republican beliefs to a 'modern' liberal society. Other scholars have suggested that, rather than battling it out like two opposing faiths, republicanism and liberalism were fused in a peculiarly American mix. The political philosopher Benjamin Barber, for example, has argued that the Founding Fathers recognised that they could not simply import a classical republican formula and apply it to the creation of a government that covered such a large area and a diverse population. Compromises were needed to create a bold experiment: not a solution that replicated ancient republics (because it couldn't) but one that retained some of their advantages in a new context. 'The goal', explains Benjamin Barber, 'was unity (the republican ideal and the national imperative) through diversity (the democratic ideal and the sectional imperative)'. James Kloppenberg has argued that political discourse in the nineteenth century combined elements of liberal individualism (anti-hierarchy) and classical republicanism (emphasis on public significance of private acts, need for collective good, strong group loyalties, virtue, etc.). Furthermore, republican language was adapted to fit liberal individualist needs. The key word 'virtue', for example, came to denote less about the self-less pursuit of the common good, and more about industry and self-discipline – in other words, an inner-directed and individualist rather than outer-directed and communitarian ideal.

Whether liberalism eventually 'triumphed' or whether it 'assimilated' republican rhetoric, the displacement of Locke from the pivotal ideological role Hartz accorded him seriously undermines the plausibility of Hartz's thesis. As Eric Foner in 'Why is there no Socialism in the United States?' (*History Workshop*, 1984) has pointed out, if the 'liberal consensus did not characterize all of American history, then other elements of his argument, such as the absence of a feudal past, lose much of their explanatory power'. If liberal values cannot be regarded as elements of a sacred covenant made at the nation's founding, neither can they be taken for granted as forming the ethical standard governing its public life.

Liberalism versus egalitarianism

The debate about whether the 'soul' of American politics is liberal or republican obscures the possibility that a polarity between these two impulses is itself what characterises American political values and social relations. Several recent analysts of American political culture have argued that the key values associated with the republican tradition form the basis of an alternative political culture, which has been locked in a continual struggle with the tenets of liberalism. In *The Democratic Wish* (1998), Morone makes a powerful case that 'much though not all of the republican world view discovered in the 1770s has resurfaced (in a narrower form) throughout American history'. Far from being part of a common consensual culture, these two impulses – a democratic and egalitarian tradition versus a liberal, individualist tradition – are 'almost mirror opposites', although Morone stresses the ways in which liberal individualism co-opts and thus defeats the 'democratic wish'. What is especially interesting about Morone's interpretation of American political culture is that he argues that far from being synonymous as Hartz assumed, the 'democratic wish' and the 'liberal tradition' exist in a state of tension.

Other contemporary scholars have formulated similar arguments. Russell Hanson, for example, has argued that economic liberalism creates such inequalities of wealth and power that the democratic ideal is undermined. What Morone calls the 'democratic wish', other scholars label an egalitarian or communitarian tradition, but all are basically describing an indigenous radical tradition based on republican notions of the equal citizen and the independent small producer. As Morone has emphasised, this radical tradition has been infused with a conception of Protestant ethics requiring the pursuit of social justice and emphasising equality of conditions and the importance of community. It has taken the form of movements to 'redeem' American society by ridding it of sin – whether the sin be slavery or liquor – as well as 'populist' crusades against big business and the increasing powerlessness of the 'little man'.

If proponents of a liberal consensus interpretation of American political culture have failed to see the richness of this egalitarian tradition it may be because, as the political philosopher Richard Ellis argues, they have been working with an impoverished understanding of the concept of individualism. Most observers of American political culture comment on the pervasive individualism of American society, yet the term 'individualism', as Ellis rightly points out, is fraught with ambiguity. Most scholars have assumed that individualism exists on a single dimension: from the hierarchical society of the Old World at one extreme, to the democratic and individualistic New World at the other. Hartz implied that there were only two alternatives – traditional hierarchy at one end of the spectrum and competitive individualism at the other. In contrast Richard Ellis, following the argument put forward by the influential anthropologist Mary Douglas, in *Essays in the Sociology of Perception* (1982), has pointed out that individual autonomy can be restricted either by external regulation or by group membership. External prescriptions include the apparatus of the state that so many commentators have seen as being unusually lacking in America, whether it be laws, taxes, police or a standing army. Group restrictions, on the other hand, arise out of the obligations imposed by the social group or groups to which an individual belongs, whether it is a family, a church, or a village. At the furthest end of the spectrum, the rules of admission to the group are strict and members of a group become sharply distinguished from non-members. 'The extreme case of a strong group', explains Douglas, citing a military regiment as a possible example, 'will be one in which members gain their whole life-support from the group as such'. By drawing attention to the group dimension of individuation, Ellis (and Douglas) conclude that 'in addition to the familiar categories of competitive individualism (where group involvement and external prescription are low) and hierarchical collectivism (in which group allegiance and external proscriptions are high)' it is also possible to have an atomised, subordinate society in which group involvement is low but external prescription is high, or an egalitarian or communitarian society in which external prescriptions are minimal but group commitment is high. It is this last category – a society in which individuals are free from external restraint, but in which their autonomy is compromised by group expectations – that Ellis sees as most pertinent to an analysis of American political culture. Not only is it, he suggests, an accurate description of the Puritan legacy and the social relations of many American communities through history, but the model of society it offers has been the inspiration for an alternative egalitarian political culture that has provided a powerful counterpoint to classical individualism (low group involvement and low external restrictions). A culture that resists government control and regulation – as many people in the United States have done – might still require the individual to conform to community-enforced norms.

The advantage of Ellis's approach is that it can take full account of the egalitarian tradition – the many voices throughout American history who have condemned liberal individualism for isolating the individual from the community and advocated a restoration of collective purpose, civic virtue and greater equality, but who have never sought to strengthen state power. As Ellis observes, this egalitarian tradition 'resembles individualism in its aspiration to free the individual from the structured differences of hierarchy'. It differs from the Hartzian liberal tradition in 'its effort to integrate the individual into a caring collectivity'.

These different visions of the relationship between the individual and the community parallel ideological divides in other countries, but, as Hartz always recognised, both liberals and egalitarians share a dread of government. The distinctiveness of the egalitarian tradition in America is that, unlike in Europe, believers in equality did not need, for most of American history at least, advocate state intervention. Indeed the reverse was true: as the historian Gordon Wood points out in *The Creation of the American Republic* (1990), at the time of the American Revolution 'it was widely believed that equality of opportunity would necessarily result in a rough equality of station . . . As long as the channels of ascent and descent were kept open it would be impossible for artificial aristocrats or overgrown rich men to maintain themselves for long'. That great English radical Thomas Paine – as Eric Foner has shown – was a believer in 'the self-regulating market – in labor as well as goods – as an instrument of progress'. Supporters of President Andrew Jackson in the 1820s and 1830s also believed that the free market would provide equal conditions and that the cause of inequality of wealth in society was not the self-regulating free market but interfering government and the concentrations of wealth that state power and aristocratic privilege created.

If, at least in America, a radical egalitarianism was possible to reconcile with individualistic doctrine of self-regulation, perhaps that explains the limited appeal of socialism. If the path to equality and liberty for Americans lay in avoiding the European vices – big government, big business, overweaning aristocrats – then socialism would gain no ground, not because radicals rejected the ideal of equality of condition but because the path to achieving it lay in enlisting markets rather than government. As the radical writer Henry George set out to show in his book *Progress and Poverty* (1879): '*laissez-faire* (in its full true meaning) opens that way to a realization of the noble dreams of socialism'. Indeed Eric Foner has gone so far as to argue that socialism in America was inhibited not by the power of capitalist ideas but by the remarkable persistence of a 'radical vision resting on small property'. Radical egalitarians in American history have, unlike in Europe, often been the defenders of an old order rather than the proponents of revolution. To late nineteenth-century socialists and agrarians, capitalism, not socialism, was the truly revolutionary force in American life. According to Foner in 'Why is there no Socialism in the United States?' (1984), capitalism was the intruder that old-style radical republicans saw 'disrupting local communities, undermining the ideal of the independent citizen, and introducing class divisions into a previously homogenous social order'. It can be argued that the New Left of the 1960s were heirs to this distinctively American radical vision which clung to a faith that freedom and equality could be reconciled. Students for a Democratic Society (SDS) condemned capitalism *and* bureaucracy (big government), and sought to build uncorrupted 'counter-institutions' or 'moral communities within an amoral society'.

There is an irony here. Scholars who have portrayed American political culture divided between very different conceptions of individualism (an atomised liberal vision and a communitarian vision) may have set out to provide an alternative to a mono-cultural vision of American politics but they end up, like Tocqueville and Hartz, recognising some striking common denominators, of which anti-statism is the most prominent. If, only in America, radicals have often believed that equality and liberty could be reconciled, and that the 'beloved community' could be realised through collective will rather than through state intervention, we are led back to the idea of American exceptionalism. In recent years, historians who have acknowledged this problem – especially those, like Sacvan Bercovitch for example, who are influenced by the work of the Italian Marxist Antonio Gramsci – have tended to describe a liberal 'hegemony' rather than a 'consensus'. Such interpretations suffer from the same weakness as the consensus theory: they homogenise the past, imposing a coherence and continuity where none may have existed and slighting exceptions to their generalisations.

A nation divided by a common language

The Tocquevillian view of American history – what might be called the old orthodoxy – contained three basic claims. First, America was characterised by an all-pervasive liberal, democratic consensus – a belief in individual rights, equality before the law, the pursuit of material enrichment and limited government – which has impoverished (for good or ill) alternative strands of thought. Second, this culture emerged in reaction to the hierarchies of Europe, and thus America is an exceptional place – not simply different, but completely immune from the rules of historical development that govern the rest of the world. Third, while social realities may sometimes have failed to live up to the high principles of the creed, there is an unfolding Whiggish pattern that imbues American history with an aura of optimism and progress: an endless pursuit of a noble ideal.

The notion of an all-embracing liberal consensus is hard to sustain in the face of the evidence of the existence of multiple political traditions. More than simply variants of the liberal idea, dramatically opposing visions of the meaning of key contested concepts like equality and liberty – or the extent of popular participation needed in order for democracy to be meaningful – makes the concept of consensus inadequate to describe the stormy reality. Even more important, slavery and many other forms of discrimination that have been legally sanctioned or embedded in social reality, provide more than a mere caveat to the idea that America was 'born free'. The historical evidence also undermines a confident notion of progress towards liberal ideas; there is no simple balance sheet that charts increasing progress.

The Tocquevillian tradition too often assumed that a common political vocabulary represents a consensus over values. In fact, very different visions of the ideal community, of the meaning of democracy, liberty and individualism can be imposed on the same words. The New Left of the 1960s, for example, may have explained that it was simply trying to realise timeless American ideals, and its rhetoric, appealing in the Port Huron Statement (1962) to the individual's right to 'share in those social decisions affecting the quality and direction of his life', may have sounded like the platitudes of all American politicians. But for New Leftists, the implications led in a direction that radically challenged conventional assumptions. Richard Ellis explains that:

> Beneath the vague rhetoric of participatory democracy lay the New Left's deep
> distrust of those mechanisms that most Americans took to be the essence of
> the democratic ideal: voting in competitive elections, representative
> government, accountable leadership, and the freedom to pursue one's own
> private interests. On each of these issues, the New Left offered a vision of
> democracy that conflicted fundamentally with the democratic ideals of much
> of the rest of American society.

Ellis points out that the SDS motto 'Let the people decide' expressed a sentiment with which few Americans at any point in history would disagree. But while for New Leftists freedom meant the power to participate equally in the decisions taken that affected one's life, for other Americans democracy was simply a matter of process: the people would decide by exercising their vote in the choice between two competing alternatives.

But in stressing the existence of multiple political traditions, rather than one consensual culture, we would be unwise to reject entirely the Hartzian – Tocquevillian insight that the particular circumstances in which the United States was created and has developed have profoundly influenced its political values and social relations. After all, while a common language obscures deep value divides, a shared vocabulary is itself indicative of a distinctive pattern of development. Suffused in Enlightenment rationalism, influenced by their Protestant heritage, by the English radical republican tradition, and by a desire to create in America a free community safe from the corruption of government that they saw in England, the Founding Fathers created a discursive template that has proved impressively durable. We should reject the distracting idea of American exceptionalism, if only because it exaggerates and caricatures what the rest of the world has in common, but that does not mean that we should overlook the very obvious ways in which the United States is distinctive. Deep political battles over who should be included in the American polity, and over substantial issues like the meaning of democracy and the relationship between the individual and the rest of society, may have analogies in the political conflicts in other countries, but they have no exact parallels. The American Republic was founded by men who wanted to create a distinctive and different kind of political community, one that reflected the redemptive hopes that had been invested in the idea of America for three centuries before the American Revolution. Successive generations have endorsed these aims.

Understanding the cultural framework in which politics happens is vital, as Hartz recognised very well. So, too, is understanding the way in which cultural norms are transmitted through the generations. This is the most neglected dimension in the voluminous literature on American political culture. The problem with so much work that tries to explain America is that it assumes an immutable process from the start, or somewhere near the start. For Hartz, the consensual liberal culture, established at the moment of origin, grimly precluded the emergence of alternatives. Exactly how and why it did so is less clear. Part of the problem is that the political scientists and philosophers who have addressed the issue of American political culture have too often been insufficiently sensitive to change over time and the complexity of the issue of how formative influences – be they Puritanism or Lockean liberalism – continue to influence. Meanwhile, historians, hampered by their profession's obsession with highlighting the exception to every rule, have too often been reluctant to make the generalisations necessary in order to capture important distinctive truths about the United States.

Culture does not, and has not, predetermined the patterns of American politics, but it has provided the unavoidable context in which it has taken place, and – as Hartz recognised – the dominance of certain concepts can preclude, or at least hamper, the adoption of others. Certainly the 'civic' dimension of American nationalism has dramatically limited the range of political possibilities for those wanting to remain inside the boundaries of mainstream political discourse. Institutions are also a crucial element in the story of how values are transmitted. The US Constitution has not only provided a sacred text – one that has been constantly looked to and constantly fought over – it has also configured the way in which debate over such apparently unconnected issues as abortion and gun control are conducted. If the Declaration of Independence's universalist claims about the equality of Man have provided a touchstone for more than 200 years of political debate, the Constitution, or more precisely the reverence with which the Constitution has been treated, has often given American political discourse the character of biblical exegesis: rather than debate issues on their own terms, they are discussed with reference to the intentions of the Founding Fathers. Only in the United States of America has the world-view of a self-appointed group of enlightenment gentry farmers been reified into dogma that proscribes the limits of political debate.

Political conflict in the United States has often been intensely felt. Divisions over cultural issues have often intertwined with political, racial or ethnic divisions. Perhaps some of this intensity comes from a conviction, held by partisans of very different political traditions, that somehow their political and social visions are validated by the historical mission and the founding documents of their country. In other countries, political divisions rarely touch on fundamental issues about national identity and purpose.

In the United States they almost always do. Both liberal individualists and radical egalitarians can validate their appeals in terms of the American mission. They do this not necessarily because they both share the same basic values, as the Tocquevillian paradigm would have it, but because they operate in a political culture in which the symbols of the nation are so readily adaptable to this kind of use. The two most important key words – liberty and equality – have been the foundations of very different political traditions, but in America, unlike elsewhere, their use evokes the nation. By appealing to what all protagonists claim is the one true meaning of their national creed – the 'real' American values – a common language has polarised politics at least as much as it has provided the basis for consensus.

Further reading

Barber, Benjamin E., *A Passion for Democracy* (1998).

Bercovitch, Sacvan, *The American Jeremiad* (1978).

Diggins, John Patrick, *The Lost Soul of American Politics: Virtue, Self-interest and the Foundations of American Liberalism* (1984).

Ellis, Richard, *American Political Cultures* (1993).

Greenstone, J., David *The Lincoln Persuasion: Remaking American Liberalism* (1993).

Hanson, Russell, *The Democratic Imagination in America* (1985).

Hartz, Louis, *The Liberal Tradition in America* (1955).

Huntington, Samuel P., *American Politics: The Promise of Disharmony* (1981).

Lipset, Seymour M., *American Exceptionalism: A Double Edged Sword* (1998).

Morone, James, *The Democratic Wish: Popular Participation and the Limits of American Government* (1998).

Myrdal, Gunnar, *An American Dilemma: The Negro Problem and American Democracy* (1944).

Tocqueville, Alexis de, *Democracy in America*, ed. J. P. Meyer (1969).

Young, James P., *Reconsidering American Liberalism* (1995).

CHAPTER 4

Slavery and secession

Howard Temperley

The peculiar institution

When southerners referred to their 'peculiar institution', as in the course of sectional debates they frequently did, they meant no more than that slavery was peculiar to the southern states of the Union. However, 'peculiar' can equally well mean strange, aberrant, or anomalous, and that was precisely how it appeared to a growing number of their fellow countrymen. There was, after all, something very peculiar indeed about a nation supposedly founded on libertarian principles holding upwards of a sixth of its population in bondage. Of course, excuses could be made as excuses always can, but numerous and sophisticated though these came to be they could not conceal the oddity of the situation.

At the time of America's first settlement the situation had been quite otherwise. Although chattel slavery had virtually died out in England by the thirteenth century and serfdom by Tudor times, that had not been the case elsewhere. In Spain, Portugal and other parts of Southern Europe it had remained very much a fact of life, servitude being the common fate of Europeans taken captive in the course of wars with the Ottoman Empire and of North Africans captured by European powers. Plantation agriculture, too, was no innovation, Europeans having introduced sugar plantations into Cyprus and Sicily by the late Middle Ages, from whence it had in due course spread to Spain, Portugal, Madeira and the Canaries, eventually reaching the New World. As readers of Daniel Defoe's *Robinson Crusoe* (1719) discover at the outset, the enslavement of Africans by Europeans and vice-versa was very much an integral part of the world of the seventeenth-century mariner. So when the British introduced slavery, first into Barbados and then into Virginia, they were simply adopting practices that had long been familiar elsewhere.

Thus, from the start, New World settlement was very much bound up with African slavery. In fact, prior to 1820, African settlers in the New World as a whole outnumbered Europeans by a ratio of some five to one. In that part of the Americas that later became the United States, however, the proportions were almost reversed, the number of Africans imported being somewhat under half a million. Nevertheless, their numbers grew by natural increase, with the result that by the time of the early Republic there were actually more slaves in the United States than anywhere else. So, although English-speaking North America was not important in the history of the slave trade, the slave trade was important in its history. It was also the case that a disproportionate amount of the arduous work involved in settlement – clearing land, planting crops and producing the exports on which the prosperity of the enterprise as a whole depended – was performed by Africans. Even those British colonies not directly involved in employing slave labour on any scale, as was the case with New England, benefited from it indirectly in that much of their trade consisted of providing the colonies to the south, including the West Indies, with dried fish and timber for use on the plantations. In return, besides acting as carriers, they received sugar and molasses, which they turned into rum for export to Europe and Africa. Much is made of Americans' quest for liberty, but it is no exaggeration to say that the principal driving force behind the entire Atlantic economy, of which the British settlement of North America was part, was Europe's demand for slave-produced products.

The first Africans to set foot in English-speaking America were 'twenty Negars' purchased by John Rolf from a Dutch man-o'-war in 1619. Rolf had lately begun experimenting with tobacco production, but the off-hand reference he makes to the transaction in his journal suggest he failed to foresee the key role Africans were destined to play in its production. Most likely he made no clear distinction between the white indentured servants on whom he had hitherto relied and these African newcomers.

The fact is that in 1619 Virginians were more intent on surviving than on pondering the long-term implications of their actions. So appalling was the mortality rate, half or more of the settlers dying in some years, that in 1624 the Crown felt obliged to revoke the Virginia Company's charter. Thereafter conditions gradually improved, Virginia becoming less like a labour camp and more like a community of farmers. Practically all the early settlers had been men, but in time women began arriving, a development that distinguished not only Virginia but North America generally from the Caribbean colonies.

The arrival of white women, by virtue of encouraging the establishment of family farms, helps explain the peculiar virulence of North American racial attitudes. In the all-male European societies of the Caribbean, racial mixing was not only tolerated but regarded as normal, the result being the emergence of a mulatto class, some of whose members rose to become wealthy planters in their own right. This is not to say that slaves were better treated in the sugar colonies. On the contrary, such evidence as we have suggests just the opposite, tropical disease and the physical demands of sugar production taking a heavy toll. Nevertheless, whether for good or ill, sexual relations were far less inhibited there than they were on the American mainland.

Quite what the status of blacks was in early Virginia no one knows, part of difficulty being the fact that there were so few of them. Even as late as 1649, 42 years after the settlement of Jamestown, they constituted only some 2 per cent of the total population. What is clear is that their situation was very different from that of later generations. Most of the founding generation of black settlers had come, not directly from Africa, but by a more circuitous route involving periods of residence either on the African coast or in the Caribbean, acquiring a familiarity with one or more European languages along the way. Nor were they all slaves at the time of arrival, some being mariners or traders who simply came to Virginia to settle. In time, a number of the more successful acquired land, embraced Christianity, learned how to employ the colony's laws to their benefit, and even married into prominent settler families.

Which came first, slavery or racism, is a chicken-and-egg question. Saying that the first arrivals did not encounter virulent racial prejudice does not mean that prejudice did not exist. Whether John Rolf's new acquisitions were released after a number of years in the same way his British indentured servants were his journals do not reveal. But whatever their fate, it was very different from that of their successors. These, arriving later in the century, found themselves consigned to large plantations, cut off from the rest of society and allowed little opportunity to acquire even the rudiments of European culture. Most came from deep in the African interior – traumatised individuals who had seen family and friends slaughtered, endured the march to the coast and the weeks of incarceration in the stinking holds of slave ships, and finally been deposited in a land where almost everything they encountered was totally alien. Coming from different parts of Africa and speaking different languages they had arrived lacking even the means of communicating with one another. Many bore tribal scars and seemed, at least to Europeans, altogether outlandish. In short, they were simply African captives, abruptly wrenched from their families and cultures, their pasts obliterated, and now compelled to work long hours and with nothing to look forward to but years of unremitting toil.

The so-called 'plantation revolution' transformed what had been societies with slaves into slave societies. That is to say it turned what had been communities of small farmers where blacks and whites worked side by side into societies where the bulk of the labour, or at least that part of it directed towards producing the exports on which the prosperity of the whole depended, was performed by slaves working on plantations. Wherever it occurred – first in the tobacco region around the Chesapeake, then in the rice fields of the Lower South – a new dominant class of white employers and landholders arose, while other whites, less fortunate, found themselves pushed, socially and economically, to the margin. Like the industrial revolution, which in many ways it resembled, it carried all before it. Small farmers could not compete in terms of price and efficiency with the plantation any more than village shoemakers and handloom weavers could compete with the factory. In later years, challenged by the rise of northern industry, southerners would make much of their agrarian roots. But in the sense that plantations brought together labour and capital for the purpose of mass-producing products for sale on the world's markets they were, in effect, factories.

Like the industrial revolution, the plantation revolution laid the basis for the rise of a dominant new group, the planter class. Through their control of labour, the planters acquired the power to influence the politics of the region and thereby shape its laws to their advantage. From their estates their authority radiated out to the colonies' churches, counting houses, clubs, legislatures and judiciaries. Like the English aristocracy, on whom they modelled their lifestyles, they regarded it as their natural right to rule. This was the world of George Washington, Thomas Jefferson and other principal leaders of the American Revolution.

The Founding Fathers and slavery

When Dr Samuel Johnson famously enquired in 1775, 'How is it we hear the loudest yelps for liberty among the drivers of negroes?' he touched on an issue that embarrassed America's founders and was destined to bedevil American politics for the next 90 years. For what made the American War of Independence historically significant was not simply its demonstration that a colonial people could throw off European rule, important though that was, but the principles Americans invoked as their justification for doing so. In framing their case in terms of universal human rights they endowed it with a significance quite out of proportion to the wrongs they had suffered and the position they then occupied in the world.

Americans had not, of course, invented the notion of universal human rights. They had simply seized on them as an appropriate response to what they regarded as British high-handedness. The arguments they used were the product of eighteenth-century Enlightenment thinking. Philosophers had bandied them about for years. Nevertheless, Americans were the first to put them into practice by making them the basis on which to erect a whole new system of government. By basing their claim to self-rule on universal abstract rights they made their War of Independence, by implication, a crusade for the rights of all people everywhere. It was an inspired move but one fraught with unforeseen consequences. For by linking their cause to a libertarian ideology at odds with their social practices Americans created problems that in time would come close to destroying the nation they had founded.

That they were creating difficulties for themselves was evident right from the start. In his original draft of the Declaration of Independence Jefferson attempted to lay the blame for slavery on George III. This was so obviously self-serving nonsense that the passage was struck out. Others adopted different tactics. The Virginia Assembly resolved that the principles contained in its Bill of Rights, which virtually paraphrased the Declaration, could never be applied to slaves on account of their 'not being constituent members of our society'. In other words, universal principles were not universal; they applied only to citizens, which the slaves plainly were not.

Democratic countries have always found ways of justifying slavery when it has been in their interests to do so. Examples can be cited from the days of Periclean Athens onwards. All the same, it requires no small amount of ingenuity, and the arguments used have not always succeeded in convincing even those using them. To Americans of the Revolutionary generation the equality referred to in the Declaration might mean anything from not being bossed around by the likes of George III to the abolition of hereditary privileges or the opening up of opportunities for self-advancement. What it most emphatically did not mean was offering equal status to people of African descent.

Yet, even granting that Americans of all sections harboured racist attitudes, it was obviously much easier for northerners than for southerners to abolish slavery. Having relatively few slaves, the economic impact would be correspondingly less severe. Those employed as domestics could be relied on to continue working much as before, as could those working as agricultural labourers. They would, of course, still be regarded as belonging to a lower caste and as such denied the opportunities for self-advancement available to whites. All the same, slavery could be got rid of, little social disruption would be involved, and if it were done gradually, as in most cases it was – freedom being granted to new-born slaves only after they had attained a certain age – their unrequited labour during that period would help compensate owners for financial loss. In short, northerners were in a much better position to adjust their behaviour in accordance with their principles than were southerners.

In the plantation societies of the South, the situation was quite different. In some the slaves accounted for half or more of the population. In such circumstances there was no question of using the law to abolish slavery. Quite apart from the financial loss, which would have been enormous, the impact on society and work practices was seen as being simply too great. Nevertheless, in the Upper South, where tobacco production was proving less profitable than formerly, some owners did begin manumitting their slaves. George Washington did so, setting aside money for their resettlement and specifying that they should be set free immediately upon his death. In the Lower South manumission was much less common, southern legislatures citing the loss of labour consequent upon the War of Independence as justification for their beginning once again to import slaves directly from Africa.

The war itself, of course, had caused immense disruption, particularly in the Lower South. Encouraged by the British, hordes of slaves had fled the plantations. Some were later recaptured, but a good number were not, one consequence of the war being a four-fold increase in the number of free blacks, many of whom gravitated towards the nation's towns and cities in search of work.

Thus by 1787, when the Founding Fathers met to draft a new constitution, some degree of stability had been established, at least so far as slavery was concerned. But with 13 former colonies, now sovereign states, linked together by no more than the slender provisions outlined in the Articles of Confederation, the future of the American nation, if it could be called a nation, remained very much in doubt. That was why, rather than simply doing as the Continental Congress had requested and amending the Articles, the delegates determined to draft a proposal providing for an entirely new system of government.

One notable feature of the draft they prepared was the omission of any specific mention of slavery, although it was referred to obliquely in a number of key passages. For example, in Article I, Section 2, it is stated that, in addition to those specifically mentioned, 'all other persons' would count as three-fifths of a person for purposes of representation. No one doubted that the 'persons' referred to were slaves, the purpose of the article being to grant southern states additional representation (the so-called 'slave vote') in order to protect their special interests, in spite of the fact that slaves, being categorised as personal property, could not vote. Similarly, the reference in Article IV to persons 'held to labor in one State, under the laws thereof, escaping to another' obviously referred to runaway slaves. There was even a 20-year guarantee forbidding the federal government from interfering with the importation of further slaves from Africa.

It can be argued, as Lincoln was later to do, that the Founders' refusal to mention slavery by name shows that they not only disapproved of it but were hoping for its early demise. On the other hand, there is no denying that, taken as a whole, the Constitution is a pro-slavery document. In the circumstances it could hardly have been otherwise. Slavery still existed in all the states, six of which were slave states in the full sense of depending on it for a large part of their economic production. Why should they or any of the other states for that matter cede authority to a new federal government to deal with a question they were perfectly well equipped to deal with themselves, had they wished to do so? The basic issue confronting the nation's founders was not slavery but how much power states were willing to cede to the federal authority. In order for the new constitution to take effect, 9 of the 13 states would have to ratify. Without a cast-iron guarantee that slavery would be protected there was no hope that southern states would agree to sign up. In other words, it was not a question of whether to have a constitution with or without slavery, but whether to have a constitution with slavery or no constitution at all.

Yet, for all that, there was no question that the struggle for independence had challenged prevailing attitudes. Who could doubt that slavery contradicted the universal principles for which Americans had allegedly fought? The practical implications of this were most clearly evident in the North where, between 1777 and 1810, one state after another adopted measures for slavery's eradication. In the Upper South, too, where tobacco cultivation was giving way to wheat, slavery was increasingly viewed as at best a necessary evil. In the Deep South, where until 1808 slaves continued to be legally imported, attitudes were different. All the same, taking the country as a whole, it looked as though libertarian ideas were in the ascendant.

Westward expansion

Nevertheless, developments were already in train that would reverse this process. One was the invention of the cotton gin ('gin' is simply short for 'engine') and the introduction into Britain of new methods of spinning and weaving that greatly increased the demand for cotton. During their struggle for independence Americans had looked forward to being free of the restrictions Britain had placed on their commerce. What they had not foreseen was that, being no longer British, they would find themselves shut out of many of their former markets, still less that demand for their traditional exports – tobacco, rice and indigo – would languish. The introduction of the cotton gin in 1793, however, gave slavery a new lease of life by allowing the plantation system to expand from South Carolina and Georgia westwards to Louisiana and Texas.

Cotton had been grown before, but largely for use within the household. This was because of the tedious labour involved in separating out the lint from the seed. Done by hand it might take a whole day to produce enough for a single garment. But thanks to Eli Whitney's simple device, a revolving drum armed with wires that tore the lint through the slats of the hamper containing the cotton bolls, separating lint from seed ceased to be a problem. Combined with the application of steam power to spinning and weaving in Britain, the demand for southern cotton seemed almost limitless, setting off a boom that led to the rapid settlement of vast tracts of land that had previously appeared unsuitable for staple production.

Thus the cotton economy advanced westward with giant strides, transforming the landscape as it went. In every decade from the 1790s to the Civil War output doubled and the centre of production moved further west. By the 1830s Alabama and Mississippi, virtually uninhabited a generation earlier, were producing more cotton than South Carolina and Georgia where the boom started. And as cotton moved west, so too did the slaves responsible for its cultivation, whether as individuals sold away from their families, as was the fate of Uncle Tom in Harriet Beecher Stowe's *Uncle Tom's Cabin*, or in the form of entire workforces that upped sticks and moved from Virginia and Maryland to Mississippi or Louisiana. So whereas upwards of two-thirds of the South's slave population had previously been engaged in tobacco growing up around the Chesapeake, by the 1850s the situation had been reversed, with the largest concentrations being found along the lower stretches of the Mississippi and around the Gulf coast.

To understand what was going on it is necessary to peel away the thick crust of *Gone with the Wind* romance that pictures the Old South as consisting largely of great landed estates occupied by southern belles and leisured gentlemen. The fact is that the greater part of the regions just described, and of what later became the Confederacy, was still frontier territory, having been settled for less than two generations. Far from life there being like that on the long-established plantations of the Virginia tidewater, some of which went back to the seventeenth century, along the Gulf coast it was still raw and new.

Saying that cotton gave slavery a new lease of life is not, of course, to say that without it slavery would have disappeared. There were social as well as economic reasons why whites wanted slavery preserved, if only as a means of containing what many saw as a potential danger. Uniquely among New World slave populations, the black population of the South increased at approximately the same rate as the free population, doubling every generation, a distinction commonly attributed to the relative lack of tropical diseases in North America and the more strenuous demands of sugar cultivation, which was the principal occupation of slaves elsewhere. The idea of letting such a population loose or, even more unthinkable, of attempting to incorporate it into white society, quite apart from the economic and financial losses entailed, was a proposition southerners did not like to contemplate.

Counterfactual history – saying what might have happened if circumstances had been different – is necessarily a matter of guesswork. Nevertheless, such evidence as there is suggests that had cotton not come along, other ways of employing slaves would have been found. During the 1840s, when cotton prices fell, there were signs of something of the sort happening. But what is clear is that cotton gave a boost to the South's geopolitical ambitions in a way that it is unlikely that industry would have done. In short, it made the South expansive, prosperous and economically formidable, while at the same time ensuring that it remained shackled to plantation agriculture, a form of economic production that had changed little since it was first introduced in the late seventeenth century.

A nation divided

In spite of the ending of the slave trade in 1808, the slave population of the South continued to grow at approximately the same rate as the free population. From 500,000 in 1776 it had grown to almost a million by the start of the century and to 2 million by 1830. Yet in spite of this and the westward extension of the plantation economy, hopes lingered that slavery was a problem to which a solution would eventually be found. And for a time, with gradual emancipation occurring in the North and some individual slaveholders manumitting their slaves in the Upper South, it was possible to believe that something of the sort was happening.

In 1819 these hopes were abruptly shattered. Up to that time slave and free territories had been admitted to the Union alternately, so that there were now 11 of each. As the Northwest and Southwest Ordinances of 1787 and 1790 had divided the area east of the Mississippi into roughly equal free-soil and slave territories, and as westward migration was largely along lateral lines, this had hitherto caused few problems. However, Missouri's application to Congress for admission as a slave state was different, Missouri being north of the line specified in the two ordinances. More important, being west of the Mississippi – it was part of the 1803 Louisiana Purchase and thus acquired after the two ordinances were drafted – its acceptance might be taken as implying that slavery would be allowed to expand into the whole of that vast area extending west to the Rocky Mountains, north to Canada, and south to the Gulf of Mexico. In other words, instead of slavery being confined to one section – arguably an embarrassing legacy left over from colonial times – the prospect suddenly loomed of its becoming the dominant form of labour across the greater part of the nation's land area.

Not surprisingly, this brought cries of protest from northerners, New Englanders especially. What was principally at stake, as they saw it, was not the suffering of the slaves but the future character of the nation and its politics. After all, there was no reason to suppose that the slaves would suffer more if they were widely distributed than if they were confined to the area east of the Mississippi. No one, at least at that stage, was contemplating reopening the African slave trade. But if the plantation system were to spread at large throughout the West, northern farmers would be discouraged from going there. Hating blacks and slaveholders alike, they would not want to live within what they regarded as an alien system. For slavery was not just a marginal issue that others could ignore. It affected every aspect of the societies in which it occurred, boosting the wealth and influence of those who owned slaves and devaluing the status and efforts of those who did not. From the point of view of western farmers slavery was, quite simply, un-American.

Americans were no strangers to sectional politics. There had been earlier disputes over such issues as tariff policies and the War of 1812, showing, incidentally, that southerners were not the only ones prepared to invoke state rights when their interests were threatened. Nevertheless, this was the first time that slavery had been the primary issue. 'This momentous question', declared Thomas Jefferson, 'like a fire bell in the night, awakened and filled me with terror'. What Jefferson was one of the first to realise was that slavery was a problem that would not go away. Regardless of what happened to Missouri, the country would remain divided for, as Jefferson perceived, it raised issues to which the American system of government was incapable of providing a solution.

The Constitution was, to be sure, quite clear on one point, namely that slavery as it existed within the individual states was a state matter. Regardless of issues of morality, the laws and practices of southern states were no concern of the federal government. However, no such restriction applied to slavery in the territories – that is to say in those areas where, as in the case of Missouri, statehood had yet to be granted – nor did it apply to the nation's capital, Washington DC. These were the main bones of contention, although there were other questions relating to slavery that also fell within the federal government's purview, such as the obligation to return runaways, suppress slave insurrections, regulate interstate commerce and, in the case of antislavery literature, determine what it was or was not legitimate to send through the mails. Thus there was no basis for claiming, as for a time south-erners were to do, that any discussion of slavery in Congress was out of bounds. Plainly there were legitimate issues to discuss, although any final solution to the slavery question in the form of abolition could only be achieved by means of a constitutional amendment, which was effectively ruled out by virtue of requiring the assent of three-quarters of the states, which there was never any prospect of achieving.

The Missouri Crisis of 1820 gave Americans a foretaste of what lay ahead. On this occasion, however, an agreement was cobbled together. Missouri, it was agreed, would become a slave state, its admission into the Union being counterbalanced by the admission of Maine as a free state, the remainder of the Louisiana Purchase being divided into free and slave segments by a line at 36° 30' that ran from the southern border of Missouri to the Rocky Mountains. Although this meant that the North got the lion's share of the disputed area, it was widely regarded at the time as a southern victory, much of the area allocated to the North being thought unsuitable for settlement.

Slave culture

Because the majority of slaves were illiterate they have left relatively few accounts of how they viewed their experiences; such accounts they have left being in many cases written as antislavery tracts and therefore needing to be treated with caution. This is not to say that they were deliberately falsified, but rather that the details selected were chosen with an ulterior purpose in view. The same cannot be said of the interviews conducted by the Federal Writers' Project in the 1930s, but, as everyone knows, old people's memo-ries are prone to distortion. To complicate the issue further, much of what has latterly been written about slave life has been in answer to questions arising out of current debates on cultural and racial questions rather than as an objective attempt to reconstruct the thinking of people in the past.

Nevertheless, attempts to look at slavery from the slaves' rather than the masters' point of view has greatly increased our understanding of the institution. The key factor has been the belated acceptance of the view that racial differences are superficial and that all human beings are otherwise similarly endowed. The result has been a redefinition of the moral problems involved. Until relatively recently writers began with the assumption that there was a hierarchy of ability, with Europeans at the top and Africans at the bottom. Latterly, however, scholars have sought not only to look at the minutiae of slave life through the eyes of the slaves themselves but, on the assumption that blacks responded in precisely the same way as whites would have done in like circumstances, to enquire into the ways in which slaves sought to cope mentally with their experiences.

The result has been the discovery of a whole new world that previous writers on slavery had ignored. Among the discoveries was the fact that slaves were deeply devoted to their families, that most households were headed by two parents, that fathers exercised a much stronger role within the household than had previously been supposed, and that most slave children were raised in such households. There were also, it transpired, limits to the power of masters, who could punish and reward slaves at will but could not control was said about them in their absence or what was thought about them in their presence.

It furthermore emerged that it made little sense to talk about 'the slave experience' since, although subject to obvious limitations, the experiences of slaves were scarcely less varied than those of free people. Quite apart from the differences arising out of the characters of individual owners and overseers there were those associated with time, place, type of unit, specific occupation, extent of contact with whites and innumerable other variables. Some slaves, as in the Georgia Sea Islands, lived out their lives in an almost entirely black world; others, such as domestic servants, had more contact with whites than with fellow slaves. Many, perhaps most, had a variety of experiences, working at a mixture of tasks under a succession of different owners and overseers.

One startling discovery was the existence of an independent slave economy within the plantation régime. The fact that slaves, at least in theory, were debarred from having possessions did not prevent them using their spare time to grow and sell crops, and generally act as small-scale entrepreneurs, even acquiring capital to pass down to their children. Slaves, it turns out, far from being simply the oppressed victims or loyal servants pictured in earlier writings, were active agents in seeking to protect their families and interests, achieving thereby a measure of independence and dignity in spite of the inauspicious circumstances in which they lived.

The American abolitionists

Thanks to the Missouri Compromise, it was possible, at least for a time, to suppose that an equitable arrangement had been reached as regards the territories. The nation was prosperous, its population was expanding, no enemies menaced its borders, and vast new areas had been opened up to settlement. Never before, it seemed, had a nation been so blessed. But if God had given Americans the wherewithal to create a new Eden, the Devil had placed a snake in the garden, and that snake was, or so an increasing number of northerners were beginning to believe, slavery. The suffering of the slaves was only one aspect of the problem, and for most abolitionists by no means the most important. As they saw it, slavery affected whites as much as blacks, being a source of corruption that, like a virulent infection, permeated society as a whole. There was not a single one of the deadly sins – pride, lust, gluttony, covetousness, anger, envy and sloth – that slavery did not in some way encourage. As abolitionists saw it, slavery was not, like say poverty, a problem to be dealt with over time; it was a sin in the eyes of God and as such required instant remedy.

The idea that a divine purpose lay behind the opening up of America to settlement was not new. It had been vividly present in the minds of the seventeenth-century settlers of New England and had lurked in the consciousness of Americans ever since. So, too, had the idea of their misdeeds incurring God's wrath – the subject of countless jeremiads. Why, then, did they surface in this particular form in the 1830s? In part the answer lies in the utopianism arising out of the uniquely fortunate situation in which Americans believed they now found themselves, but in part too it arose out of more recent events, among them the realisation that the gradual emancipation previously hoped for was not occurring, and the new emphasis that the evangelical reformers of the 1820s placed on practical benevolence as evidence of God's grace. Important too was the fact of Britain's having abolished slavery in the West Indies.

Although the American Antislavery Society, founded in 1833 in the wake of Parliament's Emancipation Act, was modelled on its rather staid British counterpart, the techniques it employed had more than a little in common with the camp meeting methods used by revivalists. In fact the abolitionist crusade of the 1830s was in large part a carry over from the so-called Great Revival of the 1820s, adopting a highly moralistic approach and drawing in many of the same people. Its leaders had initially hoped to win converts in the South, but when this proved wildly over-optimistic they turned instead to winning the hearts and minds of northerners. Because little in the way of action was required on their part, northerners were not unreceptive to the message. On the other hand, satisfying though it is to condemn the sinfulness of others, its effects can be counterproductive, in this case hardening southerners' determination to defend what they saw as their interests. The result was a remarkably sophisticated literature that questioned not only the libertarian beliefs on which the nation was supposedly founded but the values of industrial capitalism as exemplified by the 'wage slavery' practised in northern factories. At least, it was argued, slaves had owners whose interests required them to provide cradle-to-grave care, which was more than could be said of northern employers who simply hired labour by the hour. Whatever the validity of such arguments, there is no question but that the abolitionists had helped polarise opinion in ways that threatened the future viability of the Union.

The basic issues

One notion that Americans had cherished, at least up to the 1830s, was a belief that their Constitution was based on the principle of divided sovereignty. As if to dispel any doubts on the matter, it was spelled out in the tenth article of the Bill of Rights, which provided that 'The powers not delegated to the United States by the Constitution, nor prohibited by it to the States, are reserved to the States respectively, or to the people'. From this it followed that certain issues, like slavery within individual states, were state matters, and other issues, like the importation of slaves from Africa, were matters for the federal government. What most Americans had also assumed was that when the preamble to the Constitution said 'We the People of the United States . . .' it actually meant the people of the United States as a whole.

Under the pressure of sectional conflict, however, these apparently straightforward statements acquired new meanings. After all, it had not been the American people *as a whole* who had endorsed the Constitution but the citizens of the individual states, each state acting in its sovereign and independent capacity. In other words, the Constitution was an agreement between states rather than individuals. More to the point, it had never been said at the time the 1787 draft was ratified that those states agreeing to join were giving up the sovereignty they enjoyed under the terms of the Articles of Confederation. In other words, looking to the way the Constitution was created, there was a strong case for arguing that it should be looked on as being analogous to a treaty between states rather than a guarantee of nationhood. Conversely, if attention were directed towards what had happened since ratification, most notably to the way in which territories had subsequently been incorporated into the Union as states, the United States appeared very much a nation.

Which view is correct it is impossible to say. What can be said is that each appeared plausible to its adherents. The Founding Fathers, anxious to create a stronger union, but not one so strong that states would refuse to ratify, had left the question of sovereignty for time to resolve, which in due course it did, but in different ways so far as the North and South were concerned. Unlike sovereignty, however, power is readily divisible. On that basis northern and southern states continued to work together, but with rapidly diverging views as to whether the power being exercised came from the people of the United States collectively or from a confederation of sovereign states bound together by treaty.

This is not to suggest that such abstract concerns were the principal motivating force behind the growing sectional controversy. Uppermost in most people's minds were more immediate issues, such as maintaining the value of slave property, securing the return of runaways or, in the case of northerners, preventing the 'slave power' from extending its control into new areas. Nevertheless, the issue of whether the United States was a single nation, as northerners had come to believe, or a collection of sovereign states, as southerners were increasingly persuaded, provided a context into which the arguments used by the two sides could be readily fitted.

The increasing use of such terms as 'slave power' and 'abolitionist conspiracy' bore testimony to the growing estrangement of the two sides. By way of defining their own peculiar virtues Americans had traditionally looked to Britain, the United States being seen as liberal, democratic and forward-looking, as opposed to illiberal, hierarchical and reactionary. Now, however, northerners and southerners took to using one another in much the same way, southerners being charged with a propensity for idleness, improvidence, drunkenness and violence, northerners with religious scepticism, dollar-worship and a lack of respect for the fair sex. It was even claimed that the two populations were descended from different ancestors, northerners being descended from Britain's Roundheads and southerners from the Cavaliers.

This was, needless to say, historical nonsense, but that there actually was a slave power in the sense that slaveholders exercised far more influence over the nation's affairs than their numbers warranted was plain for all to see. Prior to the Civil War a majority of the presidents, Supreme Court justices, speakers of the House, and presidents of the Senate came from the South. Their dominance can be explained partly in terms of southern tradition – plantation ownership providing the kind of wealth and leisure that encouraged engagement in politics – and partly in terms of southerners' determination to use their disproportionate hold on office in the three branches of government to defend their peculiar interests. Similarly, the abolitionist conspiracy, although hardly a conspiracy in the sense of involving secret machinations, quite plainly was an attempt by well-organised groups to undermine a cherished southern institution, thereby threatening to strip southerners of several billion dollars worth of capital.

Whether the wealth tied up in slavery was 'real' may, of course, be disputed. If the slaves were freed, they would not disappear. When comparisons were made between the wealth of the sections, the 'personal wealth' of southerners was listed as being double that of the North and West combined, slaves being counted as capital. Northern workers, on the other hand, being free, had no capital value, even though the wealth of the section was largely the product of their labour. A more meaningful comparison would be one like that currently used by the United Nations, which takes account of levels of education and availability for skilled employment. Nevertheless, slaves did have a capital value in that they could be, and routinely were, sold. Indeed, the sums people were willing to pay for slaves went on increasing decade by decade right up to the Civil War, by which time they had risen to such a level that some had even begun demanding a reopening of the African slave trade. Plainly slaves were seen as a good investment in much the same way land, houses and livestock were and, like them, could readily be bought, sold, rented, or used as collateral in raising loans. In short, when southerners spoke of an abolitionist conspiracy they were referring not merely to a quarrelsome group of northern do-gooders but to what they saw as a concerted attempt to deprive them of assets with an exchangeable value that amounted, by the late 1850s, to some $4,000,000,000.

The road to secession

At the time of the adoption of the American Constitution approximately half the US population lived in the six southern states. By 1860 the population of the slaveholding states was less than a third that of the free states.

In other respects the contrast was more striking still. Nine-tenths of the nation's factory production was in the North, along with 97 per cent of its coal production, 93 per cent of its textile production, and practically all its banking capital. Nearly all the nation's insurance societies, railroad companies and shipping firms were also in the North. In short, the North was already what would now be called a 'developed' society, in contrast to the South which, although it had expanded mightily, remained 'undeveloped' to the extent that it was still largely agricultural, depending for its prosperity on the production of cotton, tobacco and other export staples. Moreover, 4 million of its 11 million inhabitants were slaves, whose subservience required that they remain illiterate, ignorant and segregated from mainstream society.

These demographic and economic changes had political consequences. As the northern population increased, so, too, did its representation in Congress. By 1850 the Northeast was already returning more members to the House of Representatives than the South and West together. Power in the Senate was more equally balanced, thanks to each state having two senators. In 1845, when Texas joined the Union, there were 15 slave and 15 free states, but with the admission of Iowa, Wisconsin, California, Minnesota and Oregon it was becoming plain that any semblance of political parity could no longer be maintained.

Finding themselves thus overshadowed by the North, it is hardly surprising that southerners felt threatened. It can be argued that, given the impossibility of forcing through a constitutional amendment abolishing slavery, their fundamental interests were never in serious danger. As Lincoln was to explain in his First Inaugural, the Founding Fathers had so arranged things as to greatly limit the powers exercised by the federal government. Such assurances, however, failed to allay southern fears. Slavery might be secure, but other southern interests, like maintaining low import tariffs, were not. And looming over the entire scene was the question of the territories.

Had the United States not been expanding westward, slavery would hardly have been a political issue. Moral questions would still have arisen. Doubtless there would still have been abolitionists and presumably controversies over what went on in the nation's capital, freedom of the mails and returning runaways. But it was the status of slavery in the territories that made the situation perilous, for it was a question on which, according to how it was resolved, the entire future shape and character of the nation depended. Playing for such high stakes it is hardly surprising that a growing sense of paranoia pervaded American politics.

To understand Americans' anxiety on the subject it is also worth bearing in mind that up to the Civil War, and even beyond, Americans had no clear idea of what the eventual geographical limits of their nation would be. Thanks to the Louisiana Purchase of 1803 they knew it would extend at least to the Rocky Mountains. Other acquisitions followed. In 1845 the Jacksonian journalist John L. O'Sullivan coined the term 'manifest destiny', by which he meant that, as if by providential right, the United States would occupy the whole of North America, a prophesy that seemed destined to be achieved when, over the next five years, Texas, Oregon and the Pacific Southwest were added to the Union. Many, probably most, Americans believed Canada would eventually become part of the United States. Efforts were also made to acquire Cuba and Nicaragua. Might the United States take over parts of Latin America too? No one could know for certain where it would all end.

It was against this backdrop, therefore, that the sectional struggle unfolded. The first crisis arose over the question of annexing Texas, something south-erners fervently wanted because it opened up the prospect of new land on which to grow cotton and additional seats in Congress. Many northerners, however, opposed the 1845 annexation for precisely those reasons. Texans themselves, having already fought one war with Mexico and fearing another, enthusiastically supported annexation. A further argument for not annexing Texas was the likelihood of its provoking a war between Mexico and the United States which, in 1846, it duly did.

As there were already slaves in Texas there never had been any doubt as to its becoming a slave state. The situation with regard to California and the other territories acquired as a result of the Mexican War was less clear. So, too, was the question of whether anyone would actually *want* to take slaves into areas like New Mexico, much of which was desert. But such was the intensity of sectional rivalry that practicalities were brushed aside. As one witty Congressman remarked, it seemed to him as if the whole debate related to an imaginary slave in an impossible place. Nevertheless, the prob-lem of determining where slavery could or couldn't go largely dominated the national politics of the late 1840s. Eventually a solution of sorts was cobbled together in the form of the Compromise of 1850, the principal fea-ture of which was an agreement that California be admitted to the Union as a free state and that elsewhere in the newly acquired territories the settlers themselves be left to decide what should be done about slavery.

This latter arrangement, which came to be known as 'popular sovereignty', appealed particularly to the Democratic Party. Not the least of its attractions was that it offered a way of taking the issue out of the hands of Washington politicians and gave it to those most immediately affected, namely the settlers themselves. That, at least, was the theory. In less fraught times it might have worked. In the 1850s, however, it proved a disaster, most notably in Kansas where, having ill-advisedly revoked the Missouri Compromise, a mini civil war developed between proslavery and antislavery settlers, complicated by the intervention of outsiders who swarmed into the territory to lend their support to one or other of the factions. So desperate did the situation become that for a time Kansas Territory had two capitals, each with its own legislature and constitution.

Subjected to these strains, the nation's institutions began falling apart. The churches were the first to go – the major denominations transforming themselves into warring factions – shortly followed by the political parties. In the presidential election of 1852 the Whigs put up a respectable fight, but by 1856 they had virtually disappeared from the political map. The Democrats, although they carried both elections, had trouble too in agreeing on candidates for president, so much so that in 1860 they nominated two, with fatal results. It was out of all this confusion that there arose, in the form of the Republican Party, something that southerners had all along feared, namely a purely northern party owing no allegiance to southern interests or support.

Up to that time, the nation's parties had had an important role to play in keeping the nation together. This was because, to elect a president, they had had to sink their differences sufficiently to agree on a candidate and platform capable of appealing to voters of all sections. With the rise of the Republicans, and thanks to the demographic changes that had been occurring, this was no longer necessary. Henceforward Republicans would be free to say and do what they liked with regard to the South and still expect to get re-elected. Lincoln was not, as many southerners supposed, an abolitionist. Nevertheless, his party was committed to preventing the further expansion of slavery. So far as southern radicals were concerned, that was enough to merit action. Whatever Lincoln did or didn't do, they faced the prospect of having to deal with a federal government hostile to their interests. However far they looked into the future that would continue to be the case. Given that the Union was, or so they had come to believe, a voluntary compact, the time had come to leave.

The Civil War and emancipation

In retrospect, the developments leading up to the American Civil War appear to follow one another with all the inevitability of a Greek tragedy. Did the deadly process begin with the Constitution? Already in 1787 one can see the forces at work that 80 years later were to tear the Union apart. Did it begin with the Declaration of Independence, that document whose high-flown libertarian notions Jefferson's fellow Virginians found so perturbing? Yet even in 1776 opinion over slavery was divided. In fact, however far one goes back the fatal ingredients were present.

That, however, was not how the situation appeared to Lincoln and his Republican contemporaries. Even after South Carolina had begun the seces-sion process it was still not absolutely clear that there would be a civil war, let alone one as long drawn out and destructive as the one that ensued. After all, there had been talk of secession before, but it had never come to anything. Mostly it had been a matter of political blackmail. Someone always backed down, usually the North, leaving the blackmailers to walk away with their gains. So why should it be different this time? Wouldn't the Republicans retreat from their demand that slavery cease expanding? The Republicans, for their part, remained convinced that the secessionists were bluffing. Not even the secessionists themselves could be sure that secession would go ahead, still less that, if it did so, there would be a war. In other words, what seems obvious in retrospect appeared far from obvious to people at the time.

It is easy to see what the South's motives were for wanting to leave a Union whose future policies promised to work to its disadvantage. What is less easy to see are the North's motives for preventing it from doing so. Why not, to use the phrase then current, 'let the erring sisters depart in peace?' Other federations have broken up without blood being shed. Plainly the wish to abolish slavery was not the primary motive. Northerners might dislike slavery and oppose its extension, but by and large they were no less racist than southerners. So why should northern farm boys, or factory work-ers for that matter, lay down their lives in order to perpetuate what had long been an unhappy relationship?

The answer is to be found in Lincoln's Gettysburg Address, conjuring up as it does an almost mystical sense that it was America's destiny to per-petuate the ideals set out in the Declaration of Independence, not only on its own behalf, but so 'that government of the people, by the people, for the people, shall not perish from the earth'. No other president has equalled Lincoln in terms of eloquence or single-mindedness. As a war leader, Lincoln's strength lay in his ability to evoke the latent patriotism of the northern population, something his Confederate counterpart, Jefferson Davis, signally failed to do with respect to the South.

Lincoln had hated slavery ever since he was a young man. When run-ning for president, however, he made a firm distinction between his personal feelings and what the Constitution required him to do. In his First Inaugural he undertook, among other things, to return runaways, a policy he struggled to adhere to even after the war had broken out. In response to questions about his aims, he argued that his primary purpose was to restore the Union and that everything else, including what he did regarding slavery, was dedicated to the achievement of that objective.

In ordinary times, as already indicated, there was relatively little he could have done. Secession and his assumption of special war powers changed that, enabling him to declare that, as of 1 January 1863, all slaves within the areas currently in rebel hands were free. The Emancipation Proclamation did not, therefore, apply to slaves in areas under northern control who, technically at least, remained slaves until the Thirteenth Amendment was ratified on 18 December 1865, by which time Lincoln was dead and the war over.

Contrary to what many supposed, Lincoln's Emancipation Proclamation did not inspire Nat Turner-type uprisings. Blacks did not go on the rampage; masters and their families were not murdered in their beds. On the other hand, slaves did run away in great numbers, showing that they were not the devoted bondsmen southerners had believed. In the first year of the war, before there was an agreed policy, owners were entitled to reclaim their slaves from the Union army, but as the numbers grew this became less and less feasible. Many of those who fled became camp followers, carrying equipment, cooking meals, putting up tents and digging latrines in return for food and shelter. Once the abolition of slavery became an official policy, however, it obviously made more sense to have the men properly inducted into the military, which was largely what happened.

By the time the war ended there were some 200,000 blacks serving in the Union army, accounting for approximately one-tenth of its total strength. The vast majority served in segregated units. One such, the famous Fifty-fourth Massachusetts Infantry Regiment, lost half of its strength in an attack on Fort Wagner in Charleston Harbour in 1863. Most former slaves, however, were assigned to garrison or labour duty, suffering fewer battle casualties than those in combatant units but a higher overall mortality rate due to poorer pay and living conditions.

The majority of southern slaves remained on their plantations under the nominal authority of their owners. To say that they staged a 'general strike' would be an exaggeration, but with their masters away at the war, the women and boys who remained found them increasingly difficult to handle. Even at the best of times, switching from cotton, sugar, rice and tobacco to producing foodstuffs would have been difficult, but under wartime conditions it led to a progressive weakening of white authority. With so many slaves running away punishment naturally became problematical. Increasingly slaves found it convenient to work at their own pace or only when it suited them. The longer the war went on, the more the system fell into disarray.

The memories of events that people cherish seldom accord with what actually happened. Southerners would in time create a 'lost cause' myth according to which the real issue was states rights, which is to say their freedom to choose their own form of government – the self-same right for which Americans had fought in the War for Independence. According to this interpretation, slavery was not the cause of the war, only an incidental aspect, a claim that directly contradicts the statements issued by the individual state secession conventions and what southerners said in their speeches and letters at the time.

For Americans generally, the Civil War became a defining moment in their nation's history – determining once and for all that the United States was a single nation, one and indivisible, rather than a congeries of independent sovereign states. In due course it came to be seen as a sort of Passover, an event to be celebrated in commemoration of all the young men who died, but also as marking the beginning of a new era of reconciliation between North and South. In time Americans also came to cherish the pathos of the war – the songs, uniforms and sepia prints of all the young men who marched off to their deaths.

Largely forgotten in all this nostalgia was the role of all those whose existence had given rise to the conflict and whose freedom it had brought about, namely the slaves. In so far as they were taken account of at all it was as having played an essentially passive role, in spite of the numbers who served in the Union forces. They were not invited to attend veterans' reunions or photographed shaking hands with other combatants at Civil War commemoration sites. Yet they were the ones whose fate was most directly affected by the war. They did have their own celebrations, although when to hold them remained a problem as there was no specific day on which it could be said that slavery ended. Theoretically most were freed on 1 January 1863 by Lincoln's Emancipation Proclamation, but as we have seen that applied only to those living in areas under Confederate control.

Not until 18 December 1865, therefore, could it be legitimately claimed that all the slaves were free, and even then their freedom was often more notional than real. The sacrifices associated with bringing it about had been enormous, but the result was not quite all that might have been hoped. Some 650,000 Americans were dead, slavery had gone, the sectional struggle had been resolved, a huge moral burden had been lifted, and northerners and southerners were actively seeking political reconciliation, but the racial beliefs that had sustained slavery and which slavery, in turn, had engendered remained as virulent as ever.

Further reading

Berlin, Ira, *Generations of Captivity: A History of African American Slaves* (2003).

Fogel, R. W., *Without Consent or Contract: The Rise and Fall of American Slavery* (1989).

Genovese, Eugene D., *Roll Jordan Roll: The World the Slaves Made* (1974).

Johnson, Walter, *Soul by Soul: Life inside the Antebellum Slave Market* (1999).

Kolchin, Peter, *American Slavery, 1619–1877* (1993).

Parish, Peter J., *Slavery: History and Historians* (1989).

Potter, David M., *The Impending Crisis: 1848–1861* (1976).

Stowe, Harriet Beecher, *Uncle Tom's Cabin* (1852).

Wright, Gavin, *The Political Economy of the Cotton South* (1978).

CHAPTER 5

Native Americans

Gail D. MacLeitch

Perhaps no aspect of American Studies has given rise to more misinformation and misunderstanding than the history, culture, and place of Native Americans in American society. It is a subject on which contrasting assumptions have clouded both public consciousness and academia. Most date back to earlier centuries and yet they still have a currency in modern America. European philosophers of the fifteenth and sixteenth centuries popularised the image of the noble savage: brave, stoic and honourable, who lived harmoniously in an Eden-like America untainted by the contaminating influences of civilisation. This European construct served as a foil against which whites could criticise their own society, a strategy that has persisted throughout the centuries. A fear of becoming over-civilised in the 1890s encouraged a renewed love affair with noble savages, as demonstrated, for example, by the formation of the Boy Scouts movement. In the 1970s concern over pollution led white Americans to appropriate the image of the American Indian as the face of environmentalism. Even as late as 1990, coming at the end of the decade associated with the 'me' generation of materialism and greed, MGM studios released the epic *Dances with Wolves*, in which an embittered Civil War veteran finds salvation by immersing himself among the noble La Kota Sioux. While this image of Indian nobility is certainly more favourable than its alter ego – the bloodthirsty ignoble savage – it is still a stereotype representing Euro-American need rather than Indian reality.

A second equally persistent assumption about Indians posits that they are on the verge of vanishing. The discourse of a disappearing race has been employed as part of a broader narrative of American progress. During the era of the early Republic, when Americans were consciously creating a new national culture, the vanishing race myth was used to symbolise the passing of the old order. Popularised in James Fenimore Cooper's Leatherstocking novels of the 1820s (with such titles as *The Last of the Mohicans*, 1826), it became widespread 'knowledge' that Indians were about to become extinct. Maris Pearce, a Seneca activist, expressed his frustration in 1838 against this misconception: 'It has been said and reiterated so frequently as to have obtained the familiarity of household words, that it is the *doom* of the Indian to disappear . . . But *whence* and why are we thus doomed?' The official closing of the frontier in 1890 and publication of Frederick Jackson Turner's frontier thesis three years later reinforced the theme of Indian extinction, a theme propagated in contemporary art, photography and literature.

The myth of the vanishing race is associated with a third fallacy regarding Indians, namely that they represent, as Johannes Fabian notes in *Time and the Other: How Anthropology Makes its Object* (1983), 'other men in another time'. Native Americans have indeed become stuck in time, being often presented as a primitive people of a bygone era, unable to modernise (although, strangely, if they do modernise they are no longer considered 'real' Indians). Popular culture has played a hand in perpetuating this inert image. As a consequence of George Catlin's paintings, Edward Curtis's photography, Buffalo Bill's Wild West Show, and the Hollywood Western, the most recognisable visual image of the American Indian for most Americans is of the war-whooping, feather-headed Plains Indian. But academia, too, is partially responsible for promoting a historically static view. In the late-nineteenth century, guided by the belief that Indians were disappearing, the new discipline of anthropology set about recording and collecting vestiges of traditional native cultures. In the process anthropologists constructed a narrative of Indian primitivism. Influenced by Darwinist thought, they embraced a progressive linear view of history in which Indians were situated at the lower stages of evolution. Such academic 'knowledge' found visual expression in the numerous museums and expositions of turn-of-the-century America in which displays of primitive Indians were juxtaposed against exhibits of white American technology and progress.

A final prevalent assumption about Indians concerns their status as tragic victims. In the nineteenth century the tragedy was seen as being of their own making. They were too racially inept or culturally stubborn to evolve and assimilate into white society. Their inability to keep up with the forces of change led to their unfortunate but, nonetheless, inevitable demise. Twentieth-century Americans have been far more willing to see the Indian's tragedy as deriving from US government Indian policy and white racism, a combination that led inexorably to a history of military violence, dispossession and impoverishment. While this later view is more sympathetic to Indians, it still presents them as victims and, as such, powerless. Repeatedly Indians have been depicted as helpless objects, rather than historical subjects in their own right: creatures made by history rather than being themselves makers of history.

Static one-dimensional portrayals of Indians as noble, vanishing, primitive and powerless are not only inaccurate but harmful, creating the impression that Indians exist outside of mainstream society and are consequently peripheral to the study of American culture. Supposedly stuck in time and disappearing, Indians are thus deemed irrelevant. That many live on reservations seems only to reinforce this sense of spatial and conceptual separation from the rest of America, a separation that manifests itself in academia where Native Americans are often seen as an exotic subtopic to be studied on specialist courses or relegated to separate chapters rather than being integrated into a broader national narrative.

Fortunately, a flourishing literature on Native Americans in recent years demonstrates not only the vitality of this field but its relevance to American culture in general. In American Studies in particular the study of native peoples addresses broader themes and debates. First, at the heart of the American experience there is the contact between a medley of different ethnic and racial groups occurring in a variety of contexts. How we conceptualise this contact – whether we emphasise themes of conflict or co-operation, change or resistance, human agency or disempowerment – raises important theoretical concerns. The significance of the story of Indian–white contact is not self-evident, being the subject of continuing scholarly debate and revision. Second, as a direct consequence of this contact, Native Americans were obliged to reorient their subsistence economies toward a capitalist marketplace. While there are peculiarities to the Indian experience, Indians nonetheless shared with other early Americans the need to make what were often painful adjustments. Hence, examining Indians' responses to the market economy provides an important means of bringing them into the mainstream of American history.

Third, in the process of adapting to the forces of colonisation, Indians refashioned cultural identities. Far from being a static category, the term 'Indian' is historically relative and contingent on a variety of factors. Adapting to new market conditions, engaging in high rates of interracial marriage, and imbibing new doctrines of gender and race, Indians have been continually required to reinvent their identity. Along the way, Europeans and Americans, who have attempted to construct and impose notions of 'Indianness', have also influenced Indian self-conception. Thus the study of Indian identity helps to elucidate broader debates in American Studies on the meaning of ethnicity and race. With groups still petitioning the federal government for tribal recognition, this controversy over the nature of identity is not about to go away. Finally, the startling growth of the Indian population in the twentieth century offers a powerful disproof of the vanishing race myth. Moreover, this population growth has been matched by significant political activism, cultural rejuvenation and for some communities, economic renewal. These numerous forms of revitalisation compel us to reconsider the place of Native Americans in the twenty-first century. This essay explores these four areas – contact, economy, identity and revitalisation – to demonstrate the centrality and significance of Native Americans within the broader scope of American Studies.

Contact

Since the 1960s a burgeoning literature on Native Americans in the colonial period has reconceptualised the era of Indian–European contact. Writing in reaction to the gross neglect of native peoples in traditional historiography, a New Indian History emerged determined to put native peoples at the forefront of historical studies. A particular offshoot of this scholarship was ethnohistory, a new form of analysis that combined the tools and perspectives of history and ethnology to produce historical studies that were sensitive to the cultural nuances of native societies. This new scholarship has provided a more complex understanding of Indian–white contact – one that avoids over-simplified narratives of conflict and demise by undermining old metaphors and ways of thinking about this period. Most important, it has provided a more satisfying depiction of Indians, no longer portraying them as tragic victims or timeless primitives but as active agents responding to colonisation and finding new and creative ways of coping with its effects.

One significant way scholars have rewritten the contact narrative has been by adjusting their timeframe to include a consideration of pre-contact native America. American Indian history, after all, did not begin with the arrival of Europeans. Thousands of years before Christopher Columbus landed in San Salvador in 1492, Siberian migrants 'discovered' North America when they travelled across the Bering Strait in search of game. These nomadic Asian tribes, encouraged by abundant natural resources, continued to pass across this land bridge, spreading southwards through the vast continent and eventually pushing down into South America with the result that contact and change far predated European colonisation. As they traded, clashed, resettled, regrouped, adapted to diverse terrains, and gradually shifted from hunter-gatherers to semi-subsistence farmers they evolved into diverse and culturally distinct communities, ranging from the Pueblo Indians of New Mexico to the great mound builders of the Mississippi. Scholars estimate that there were probably more than 7 million Indians in North America by 1500. Across the north and south continents, an estimated total of 2000 languages were spoken, making this one of the most linguistically diverse regions in the world. Thus when Europeans landed in America they did not encounter a 'virgin wilderness'. Native North America comprised diverse, complex and dynamic cultures.

Undeniably, the advent of European colonisation ushered in a new historical epoch for indigenous peoples. Europeans, along with their microbes, religions, trade goods and livestock, transformed the continent, literally creating a 'New World' *for all*. The broad events of colonisation and their effect on Indians are well known. Indians throughout the Americas felt the impact of colonisation in successive waves. First came Old World microbes. Lacking immunity to smallpox, measles, influenza, cholera and the bubonic plague, many thousands of Indians succumbed to these deadly diseases without ever having come into direct contact with Europeans. It was not unusual for villages to lose up to 75 per cent of their population. Then, following on from the pathogens, there came missionaries and traders, bringing with them novel ideas and goods that altered the cultural and material worlds of those they encountered. The final phase of colonisation was made up of settlers who brought livestock and built farms and fences that transformed the natural landscape.

While noting that the colonial era was a time of great change and upheaval for native peoples, historians have disagreed over how exactly to tell this story. Writing in the politically charged atmosphere of the Vietnam War and embracing a critical stance toward the US government, a cohort of scholars in the late 1960s were motivated by a desire to highlight a history of white oppression and racism. Consequently, they tended to focus on the destructive effects of colonisation and by doing so promoted an Indian-as-victims model. Best exemplified by Dee Brown's tragic *Bury My Heart at Wounded Knee* (1970), their narratives emphasised themes of violence and devastation. The frontier – as the principal zone of contact – was presented in very traditional ways: as an unambiguous dividing line between savagery and civilisation, the only difference now being that whites were equated with savagery and Indians with civility. In his brief overall treatment of the colonial period, Brown documented the selfish deeds of greedy Englishmen who 'ravaged and squandered' the earth causing Indian groups to become 'virtually exterminated' or 'utterly obliterated'. By outlining white atrocities, Brown strove to elicit sympathy for Native Americans, but he did so at the expense of reinforcing stereotypes of them as passive, powerless and doomed.

Dissatisfied by such depictions of victimhood, another group of scholars during the 1970s and 1980s posited a more empowering conceptual model that emphasised Indian cultural persistence. Colonisation may have been disruptive and distressing but it did not culminate in the inevitable death and disappearance of Native Americans. These historians paid attention to how Indians creatively forged strategies that enabled them to resist, adapt and endure by playing off imperial rivalries and forming new political confederacies. Not surprisingly this involved adopting aspects of European material culture and behaviour, but internally Native Americans preserved the essence of their ancient heritage. In short, they behaved in precisely the way any thinking, resourceful and imaginative people might have been expected to do in the circumstances. Yet, despite all its strengths, this model runs the danger of overstating Indian agency. By focusing on groups in isolated frontier communities divorced from the broader imperial context, it becomes easier than otherwise to emphasise themes of personal power. Cultural persistence needs to be considered in the context of the corrosive impact of colonisation. Furthermore, Europeans in these studies tended to fade into the background as an undifferentiated mass that Indians had to resist, overcome and survive.

During the 1990s the cultural persistence model gave way to a more nuanced understanding of cross-cultural relations, one that emphasised themes of mutual accommodation and cultural synthesis. In his study of Indian–white relations in the Great Lakes region from 1650 to 1815, Richard White argued that because neither side could initially conquer or control the other and yet was dependent on the other's trade and support, each was compelled to adapt to the other's requirements. Native peoples and Europeans thus carved out a 'mutually comprehensible world' linking their two cultures and so negotiated relationships based on mutual accommodation. This naturally led to an intermingling of European and Indian cultural forms and practices. White, and others who quickly followed suit, reconceptualised the frontier, not as a strict boundary separating essentially alienated peoples, but a porous zone of contact, an ambiguous in-between space where practices and values were swapped, exchanged and reinvented, and where power was contested.

Scholars have applied this middle-ground model to many aspects of Indian–white relations. Indian missionary history, for example, has been revised from a narrative of cultural imperialism to one of cultural mediation. Missionaries did not simply impose their alien religions on unwitting

Indians. Many Indians were drawn to Christianity. The havoc and misery generated by epidemics had made them receptive to missionary teachings, especially as their own shamans appeared so ineffectual. Nor did they embrace these new religious systems in their entirety. Instead they borrowed and blended old with new, taking practices and ideas that fitted in with their pre-existing native world views and rejecting the rest. In New France, native women resisted the subjugating tendencies of patriarchal ideology by selectively appropriated Christianity in ways that brought meaning to their lives, drawing on the iconography of Catholicism, as exemplified by female saints and the Virgin Mary.

Although colonisation was destructive, and in many instances deadly, it did not entail the unequivocal European conquest of native peoples. For over 300 years colonists and Indians were obliged to find ways to co-exist through negotiation and compromise. So the middle-ground model is not peculiar to the colonial period, but can be applied to Indian–white contact wherever and whenever it occurred. Furthermore, how we understand and make sense of what happened during the contact period has a significant bearing on how we regard native peoples in general. Highlighting the hardships Indians endured runs the danger of treating them as mere objects with little agency of their own. Focusing on themes of Indian activity, ability and power, on the other hand, downplays the malign nature of colonisation. It is no longer sufficient or acceptable to talk about Indian victimhood, but nor is it appropriate to romanticise Indians' resistance and the capacity of their cultures to survive the European onslaught. An important challenge facing scholars of Native America is finding ways of exploring Indian agency while making due allowance for the external factors shaping their lives.

Economy

Contact with Europeans generated immense change for American Indians, but more specifically it was contact with a distinct economic order and its attendant value system that determined the nature and direction of that change. Ever since colonisation, the lives of the indigenous peoples of North America have been largely shaped by their involvement in an emergent capitalist market economy. Throughout the past three centuries, activities of the government and ordinary Euro-Americans have promoted the absorption of Indian land, labour and resources into a transatlantic capitalist economy by means of commercialised trade, a diminishing land base and wage labour. As was to be expected, involvement in ever-changing and expanding market relations has generated both opportunity and distress. Never simply victims, Native Americans responded to economic pressures in a variety of ways, drawing on their cultural world to help cope with the forces of material change. Some resisted the encroaching tide of capitalist forces for as long as possible; others became active market participants, merging old practices with new. But if Indians participated in shaping this new economic order, they were, in turn, shaped by it. Because older tribal histories tend to focus on the familiar themes of diplomacy, warfare and US government policy, they often lose sight of the fact that the underlying cause for historical change for Native Americans was economic. The study of Indians and the market economy is important because it removes them from the realm of the exotic and the peripheral and treats them like ordinary human beings caught up in the messy business of capitalist expansion. Examining their economic entanglement brings their history into line with that of other Americans who also had to contend with the rise of global capitalism.

In pre-contact North America, eastern Indians embraced a subsistence economy based on a mixture of horticulture and hunting. Among the east woodland tribes women produced the bulk of their diet through the cultivation of corn, pumpkin and squash, while men supplemented agricultural produce through fishing and hunting. Small-scale trade occurred between tribes but was non-commercial in character. Indians understood trade within the gift-giving complex, whereby trade items were considered to be gifts, and giving was construed as a demonstration of friendship and goodwill – gift-giving being a means of creating a social debt between parties. For native peoples then, the act of giving was just as important, if not more so, than the gift itself.

During the colonial period the Indians' 'moral' economy came into contact with a profit-driven mercantile Atlantic economy, with England, Holland and France seeking to extract commercially valuable commodities from the New World, while at the same exploiting the indigenous and colonial populations of North America as a market for their manufactures. Trade was thus at the cutting edge of change, drawing Native Americans into this emergent market as both consumers and producers. Typically, in exchange for beaver pelts and deerskins, Indians gained access to a bevy of European wares, including guns and ammunition, textiles, utensils and tools and an array of decorative articles including ribbon, mirrors and buckles. For much of the colonial period, as already explained, trade relations were conducted on a cultural middle ground on which Europeans, dependent on Indians as trading partners, were obliged to observe Indian economic protocol. By playing off one imperial power against the other, Indian headmen were able to persuade colonial governors to indulge them with presents and subsidised trade agreements. To deter traders from championing profits over personal ties, Indians encouraged unions between native women and European men, thereby incorporating traders into kinship networks. To minimise the disruptive intrusion of an alien material culture some sought to 'Indianise' European goods, as for example by adorning their bodies with European coins and pieces of copper kettles.

Yet as the power and presence of Europeans grew, the ability of Indians to influence the nature of exchange diminished. Increasingly market forces, centred on profit and the laws of supply and demand, overshadowed the custom of gift-giving and concerns for alliance. Indian complaints against the 'unbrotherlike' behaviour of traders became widespread. In some regions of the United States, particularly around the Great Lakes, the fur trade continued to be mutually advantageous into the early nineteenth century, but in the Southeast the balance of power had tipped in favour of the Americans by the late eighteenth century. As a result of a decline in foreign markets for furs and a depletion of fur-bearing animals, the Choctaws and Chickasaw's dependence on foreign goods, including an unhealthy overreliance on alcohol, left them in a vulnerable position. The US government compounded the problem further when it instructed the federally operated trading posts to phase out the practice of 'gifting' and replace it with 'loans'. By extending credit and abolishing presents, the US government ensured that southern tribes became entrapped in cycles of debt.

Alongside the commercialisation of trade, contact with a burgeoning market economy had a profound affect on Native Americans' relationship to land. Pre-contact Indians believed in the common ownership of land and its resources. Given that land preceded their arrival on Earth and would exist long after they were gone, it seemed nonsensical to them to claim private tenure. So far as people used or occupied land they had a right to it, but this right did not constitute a form of permanent or private possession. In contrast, Europeans embraced a radically different conception, one that held that land was an economic resource that could establish and generate wealth. Legal title guaranteed to the individual an exclusive right to the land that could be passed down through the family line. Land's increasingly commercial value led to a policy of enclosure in England whereby thousands of people were literally pushed off the land to make way for agrarian capitalism, a process which, in turn, prompted immigration to America. Throughout the colonial period, Native Americans experienced even more unrelenting encroachments by successive generations of immigrants determined to acquire land through sale, illegal occupation, fraudulent deed or, if necessary, by violence. Exposed to European ways of thinking, some Indians sought to control the pace and pattern of land transfers by loaning, selling and renting lands. But their efforts to direct European settlement proved futile in the face of the swelling colonial influx. Even attempts by the British Crown, as in 1763, to protect Indian country by erecting a boundary line running the length of the Appalachian Mountains failed.

Pressures on Indian lands intensified following the American Revolution. The invention of the cotton gin in 1793 and the consequent expansion of cotton production in the southern states sealed the fate of the native inhabitants. Cotton production, dependent on access to new lands for planting, proved a lucrative enterprise. In the early 1800s the Creeks, Chickasaws, Cherokees, Choctaws and Catawbas still occupied this fertile and thus commercially valuable territory. The US government, with the assistance of fur-trading merchants, deliberately manipulated Indian commerce to obtain land cessions, extending credit so as to encourage debt, thereby forcing tribes to relinquish land in order to pay back loans. In 1822, for example, the Choctaw nation was obliged to cede nearly 13 million acres of land to pay off debts to the government trading post, but still ended up owing $13,000. Still dissatisfied, the US government raised the possibility of removing tribes west of the Mississippi so as to free up eastern lands for white settlement. Removal, it was claimed, could be justified on benevolent grounds in that it protected Indians from predatory neighbours and would enable them to live as they wished, undisturbed. The Louisiana Purchase of 1803 made removal a possibility, but it took Andrew Jackson's coming to power in 1828 to push through the Indian Removal Act of 1830, in consequence of which tens of thousands of Indians from all along the eastern seaboard and Great Lakes region were dispossessed and forcibly removed to Oklahoma.

As they confronted the commercialisation of trade and land expropriation, Indians throughout the colonial period and early nineteenth century continued to respond creatively to changing economic conditions. In spite of their worsening material circumstances, native peoples survived by discovering new economic roles and diversifying tribal economies. New England Indians, who had experienced significant land loss as early as the seventeenth century, developed alternative livelihoods. Women supplemented subsistence farming with petty commodity production, manufacturing baskets, brooms and pottery, as well as maple sugar and beeswax, which they peddled around local towns. Men likewise found wage-employment in the thriving whaling industry. Native indentured servitude also became commonplace, with local white officials hiring out indigent Indians to labour for families.

In New York, Iroquois men sold their martial skills to the British for wages during the Seven Years' War (1756–63) and by the early 1800s complemented their role as hunters by selling lumber. Among the southern Cherokee an economic élite participated in the plantation economy, relying on slave labour to produce cotton for foreign export. The Choctaws became important cattle ranchers in the region, while southern native women engaged in seasonal labour, picking cotton.

Involvement in wage labour, petty-commodity production and land sales inevitably made inroads on native cultural worldviews. Cultural change was not radical, nor universal, but some segments of the indigenous population had clearly developed commercially tinged attitudes, including an individual ambition to accumulate wealth and an appreciation of land as a form of private property. What is particularly striking by the late eighteenth and early nineteenth centuries is the emergence of class stratification within Indian nations. Among the Mohawks and Creeks, for example, the unequal distribution of wealth – in the form of houses, barns, livestock and farming equipment – has been well documented.

In the second half of the nineteenth century, economic forces continued to shape the Native American experience. The relentless drive by white Americans to accumulate western lands led to a series of military conflicts between the US Army and Plains Indians, resulting in the eventual containment and concentration of these tribes on reservations. Reservation life did not, however, disconnect Indians from the larger market economy. Some Indians arrived on reservations with an already well-developed capitalist outlook. For others, the reservation provided an opportunity to develop one. Traditional activities, such as hunting, were no longer feasible options for reservation Indians, and to rely solely on federal annuity payments was simply unsatisfactory. Furthermore, with the passage of the notorious Dawes Allotment Act and Burke Act, market forces continued to shape government policy towards the reservations, often to the Indians' detriment.

The White Earth reservation, created in northern Minnesota in 1867, for example, attracted Anishinaabe immigrants because its fertile lands, rich abundance of natural resources and proximity to local markets offered a range of economic options. Melissa L. Meyer describes how a large segment of these immigrants were the mixed-race descendants of fur-trading families already well acquainted with the workings of the market economy. Faced with a declining fur trade they had migrated to White Earth determined to create new market-oriented roles. Some found a livelihood cultivating marketable crops, while, as she notes, 'others adapted their entrepreneurial skills to the reservation environment, becoming merchant-traders, real estate agents, and newspaper publishers and filling positions associated with the operation of the Indian Agency'. Among the Menominee Indians of northeastern Wisconsin, reservation life also offered economic opportunity. Brian Hosmer documents how the construction of a saw mill and a lumber finishing plant provided Menominees with a valuable form of wage employment. Reservation prosperity meant that by 1912 only 100 out of the 1700 Menominees relied on government rations.

The late-nineteenth and early-twentieth centuries, however, were not a time of economic innovation and prosperity but of large-scale impoverishment and dispossession. The reservation system was less to blame for this economic nadir than the Dawes Allotment Act passed by Congress in 1887. Created by a group of well-intentioned, but nonetheless misguided Indian reformers, the Act authorised agents to carve up communally held lands into parcels of 160 acres and to allot them to male heads of households. The Act was intended to encourage Indians to become independent yeoman farmers by undermining tribal allegiance, an added advantage being that it allowed for 'surplus' lands (i.e. those not so allotted) to be offered for public sale. To safeguard naïve Indians against greedy and unscrupulous whites, it stipulated that lands allotted to Indians, although privately owned, would be held in trust by the government for 25 years so as to allow enough time for Indians to become acquainted with the mechanics of real estate.

Far from transforming nomadic warriors into individualistic profit-seeking farmers, the Act led to widespread dispossession, as the overpowering drive to accumulate Indian land overcame the paternalistic impulse to shield Indians from market relations. The measures intended to prevent Indians from selling their land were soon dissolved. The Burke Act, passed by Congress in 1906, made it possible for Indians to sell their property so long as the Secretary of the Interior considered them 'competent' enough to manage their affairs, thereby opening up a loophole allowing state politicians to offer Indian lands for sale. In Minnesota, a few months after the passage of the Burke Act, a former lumber baron and now state senator, one Moses A. Clapp, attached a proviso to an Indian bill that declared all 'mixed-blood' Indians to be 'competent' and therefore entitled to sell off their allotments. On the White Earth reservation, hundreds of unknowing Indians were approached, pressured, bribed and tricked into selling their lands. By 1820, as Meyer notes, 'most of the reservation land base had been transferred to Euroamerican hands'.

Identity

Images of Indians as wage labourers, cattle ranchers or plantation owners challenge our preconceived notions of what constitutes 'Indianness'. Far from being a static and one-dimensional category, the term 'Indian' has proven inconstant and multilayered. Examining the historical and cultural construction of Indian identity constitutes a challenging but essential aspect of Native American Studies. The generic label 'Indian', along with all the various tribal designations – Iroquois, Comanche, Navajo and so on – has fostered a false impression that these groups are coherent, organic and timeless, when in fact many of the tribes so designated are simply the by-product of colonisation. Forcing disparate bands to live together on reservations, for example, encouraged the formation of new tribal identities. The Comanche did not identify themselves as a nation until after the 1870s. Furthermore, in reaction to external conditions, Indians have reconstituted the meaning of group membership, focusing sometimes on cultural criteria and at other times on racial precepts. Groups and individuals have reclaimed and disclaimed Indian identity depending on political circumstance. In other words, what it means to be Indian is determined by historical and cultural context.

Historicising Indianness not only provides a way of undermining static views of Indians, but also illuminates debates on identity in the broader field of American Studies. Since the 1960s, academics have radically revised our understanding of race and ethnicity. Race is no longer understood to be a fixed and stable category based on discrete biological differences, but rather a historical construct designed to serve cultural needs. In much the same way, scholars reject the notion of ethnicity as a primordial essence. Ethnicity 'is not a thing but a process', as Werner Sollors has reminded us in his 1989 edited collection, *The Invention of Ethnicity*. In the US context ethnicity has been reinvented as a consequence of the immigration experience. The history of Indian identity throws light on these conceptual debates. Responding to situational needs, Indians have regularly demonstrated that their identity is not rigid and essential but fluid and contingent. Nor have they been alone in their efforts to craft cultural identities. Ever since Columbus mislabelled the indigenous population of the West Indies 'Indian', Europeans and Euro-Americans have attempted to impose their own identity constructs on native peoples. Indians have rejected, negotiated and sometimes incorporated Euro-American definitions. Thus 'Indianness' has often been a co-creation, so we should not lament the passing of 'real' Indians, but acknowledge rather that a central theme of their history has been the refashioning of group identity. Rejecting the notion of Indian as a timeless and objective category we should, as Alexandra Harmon urges us, 'conceive of Indians' history as the history of the meanings of "Indian", "Indian tribe", and their synonyms'.

The arrival of Europeans precipitated the redrawing of ethnic boundaries between native peoples. As warfare, disease, and dispossession took their toll, remnant groups reformed to create new tribal entities. Anthropologists refer to this process as ethnogenesis. In the colonial Southeast disparate groups of Indians, in what James Merrell describes as a 'bewildering round of mergers and migrations', forged the multi-ethnic nation of the Catawbas. Despite cultural dissimilarities, the presence of the warring Iroquois nation to the north and English traders in the vicinity helped solidify their new ethnic identity. The English generally encouraged such group cohesion. Wishing to simplify Indian diplomacy, and unwilling or unable to recognise the diversity of indigenous peoples and their decentralised power formations, colonial officials set about imposing political structures and collective identities on to groups that had never previously possessed them. By the late colonial period the growing dominance of the British, characterised by a history of land thefts, fostered a pan-Indian identity among the Indian populations in the Ohio Valley and Great Lakes region. Historically these diverse Indian groups had never thought of themselves in collective terms. Nevertheless, a series of prophets encouraged the development of a racial identity, espousing doctrines emphasising Indians' separate origins and divergent destinies from 'whites'. By way of driving their message home they denounced aspects of 'white' culture and celebrated a return to native traditions.

Most Indians, however, resisted racialised definitions of identity, preferring to define their Indian status by means of such cultural markers such as dress, economic behaviour, shared folklore beliefs and religious rites. Many saw the communal ownership of land as central to their construction of Indianness. But as Indian communities underwent significant socio-economic change, cultural markers of identity altered. Among New England Indians in the early 1800s involvement in a market economy and a high rate of intermarriage with African Americans and whites gave rise to changes in their physical appearance, along with new commercial values and new ways of organising gender roles and households. The vanishing race myth thus gained ascendancy among white New Englanders, not because it was true, but because local Indians failed to live up to white expectations of what constituted a 'real' Indian. Racially mixed, market-oriented Indians appeared decidedly non-Indian. Local officials removed Indians from the historical record by refusing to recognise them as indigenese in official documents, listing them instead under the generic label of 'Negro' or 'black'.

Changing behaviour and appearance also engendered discord within the Indian communities themselves, as arguments arose over the true meaning of Indianness. It was as a result of widening political and cultural divisions within the Creek confederacy that a group splintered off to form a new ethnic entity called the Seminoles. In Massachusetts the state-proposed Indian Enfranchisement Act gave rise to similar internal dissension. In addition to guaranteeing citizenship, the Act was intended to enable individuals to petition for private landholdings. However, a sizeable segment, seeing communal ownership as essential to the preservation of their identity, opposed the Act on the grounds that it constituted a direct threat to their community.

To fight removal in the 1830s, Indians engaged in an inventive refashioning of individual and group identity. Some groups sought to emphasise their cultural similarity with whites, to demonstrate that they had taken on the requisite hallmarks of 'civilised' life. The Cherokee élite, many of whom were of mixed racial ancestry, pursued plantation slavery, sent their children to school, and ran a government modelled on that provided for by the US Constitution. They also supported a model of human origins based on the notion of monogenesis, claiming to be the descendants of Noah and thus part of the same biblical family as whites. Yet during this period white Americans were increasingly defining Indians in racial terms, some even promoting a view of separate origins. To behave like whites was no longer enough, since Euro-Americans increasingly perceived skin colour and other racial markers as key determinants of human difference. The Indiana Potawatomi Indians, who had long become settled farmers, living in log cabins, dressing in European fashion and even converting to Catholicism, found it necessary to deny their Indian identity further if they wished to hold on to their lands. Susan Sleeper-Smith argues that many communities 'erected "façades of whiteness" to mask their indigenous identity', choosing as community leaders to represent their interests those who most closely resembled members of the local white community. The Miami family of Ma-con-no-qua managed to hold on to their land when in 1837, Ma-con-no-qua publicly announced that she was in fact a white captive, a claim that was soon supported by her long-lost siblings in Pennsylvania. Although Ma-con-no-qua – widowed but with children – had lived as an Indian for almost 65 years, and was unable to speak English, her lawyer carefully reconstructed her as the tragic figure of a fragile white woman, Frances Slocum, in need of white paternal protection. By doing so he won state approval to allow her and indeed her entire village to remain. The Mission Band of Potawatomi and Brotherton Indians of Wisconsin both relinquished their legal status as Indians to become citizens so that they could secure individual shares of property and avoid removal. That groups and individuals have been willing to deny their Indianness in response to government policy is further evidence of the contingent nature of identity.

Throughout the nineteenth century white Americans oscillated between concepts of Indian identity. On the one hand they embraced a racialised perception, which encouraged a static view of Indians as primitive, trapped in the past, unwilling or unable to change and therefore on the verge of extinction. In this scenario 'Indian' was a fixed immutable category. On the other hand, reformers embraced the belief that through education and Christian conversion it was possible to eradicate 'Indianness' and to assimilate acculturated Indians into mainstream society. Thus Indianness was a temporary state of existence that needed to be overcome. This dual impulse to reify Indian otherness and yet wish to dissolve Indians' identity co-existed, sometimes within a single individual.

When Indian reformers and policymakers set about obliterating the category of 'Indian' by implementing the Dawes Allotment Act they inadvertently helped to reinforce this category of difference by imbruing it with a new racial content. Aside from economic motives, reformers implemented the Act principally as a means of substituting individualistic values for tribal allegiances. In short, the hope was to remake Indians by turning them into property owners in the expectation that they would thereby acquire such capitalistic values as thrift and industry. The practical realities of implementing the legislation, however, required that government officials first come up with a system to identify who were Indians and therefore eligible for an allotment, in much the same way that Clapp's proviso had required officials to define who were 'full bloods' and who were 'mixed bloods'. This proved a mammoth project involving not only the drawing up of lengthy roll calls for every reservation but reconstructing family genealogies and creating a new system of blood quantum whereby degrees of Indianness could be measured. If Indians were to be eradicated, it was first necessary to determine who they were.

This is another instance of the way outsider definitions of Indianness have shaped Indian self-conception. The connection between blood, biology and identity was wholly alien to Indian culture, which had traditionally drawn on such cultural attributes as language, behaviour and loyalty. Nevertheless, Indians quite readily adapted to this new system, increasingly perceiving measures of blood as central to their status. By the 1930s they had assumed greater control over defining what quantum of blood was necessary for tribal membership, a measurement that varied from tribe to tribe. Their willingness to adopt blood quantum demonstrates that their attitude toward identity is both flexible and instrumental. Just as the Indian Removal Act encouraged certain groups to deny Indian identity, the Allotment Act worked in the opposite direction, encouraging individuals who did not live on reservations, who did not associate with tribal groups, or even speak a native language, to re-identify as Indian. All they had to do was to prove their blood quantum to become eligible to receive land.

Reformers also sought to eradicate Indian identity through the boarding school system, but instead boarding schools helped foster a bi-cultural or trans-cultural sense of self and allegiance among a new generation of Indians. The boarding school system had been premised on the belief that it was necessary to remove children physically from the corrupting influence of their families. By forbidding them to speak in their native tongues, giving them English names, and teaching them literacy, Christianity and Euro-American gender roles, reformers hoped to eradicate all traces of Indianness. For many children, the boarding school was a harrowing experience, leaving a legacy of psychological trauma. Culturally it represented a vicious assault on native religion, languages and traditions. But many pupils turned this situation to their advantage by using their new gained knowledge and literacy skills to serve their Indian communities as teachers, administrators, doctors and political activists. Nevertheless, the boarding school experience left an indelible mark on their identity, leaving many feeling culturally adrift, separated from their native heritage but without having been fully assimilated into white society. Gertrude Simmons Bonnin (Zitkala-Sa), a Yankton Sioux who was educated in a missionary school before she became a teacher, writer and political activist, lamented in her autobiographical piece 'An Indian Teacher Among Indians', published in 1990: 'Like a slender tender tree, I had been uprooted from my mother, nature, and God'. But being able to maintain connections to both worlds and serving as cultural mediators could also be empowering. Frederick Hoxie in a 1992 article in the *Journal of American History* explains how these individuals inhabited a cultural borderland, possessing as they did hybrid identities. A case in point was Charles Alexander Eastman, a three-quarter Dakota Sioux and the first Indian to become a doctor, who received his MD degree from Boston University in 1890. Expressing his dual identity, in his 1912 autobiography *From the Deep Woods to Civilization* he concluded: 'I am an Indian; and while I have learned much from civilization, for which I am grateful, I have never lost my Indian sense of right and justice . . . Nevertheless, so long as I live, I am an American'. On the verge of the twentieth century, Indians were not disappearing, but creating new ways of experiencing and articulating their Indianness.

Revitalisation

Since the 1990s revitalisation has become something of a buzz word in Native American Studies. One only has to look at the number of recent publications that include, 'revitalisation', 'resurgence', 'renewal' or 'revival' in the title to gauge their pervading sense of optimism. The impact of allotment and boarding schools meant that the twentieth century got off to a painful start for most Native Americans. However, through a series of political, demographic, cultural and economic trends the status and situation of many improved. Refusing to suffer in silence, they engaged in new forms of political protest, developed a renewed pride in their cultural heritage and experimented in new economic enterprises aimed at generating tribal wealth. A series of sympathetic administrations, wishing to right the wrongs of past governments, supported their fight for political and socio-economic renewal. Larger numbers than ever before began identifying themselves as Indian. Yet, as has already been shown in relation to the historical agency debate, themes of resurgence tend to mask broader patterns of continued struggle. All the same, the focus on renewal reminds us that Indians have not disappeared from American society and are still a force to be reckoned with.

A major form of revitalisation during the last hundred years has been political. By the close of the nineteenth century native peoples had been militarily subdued and contained on reservations, but they had not been, to use Thomas Biolsi's expression, 'internally pacified'. Making use of their literary skills and emergent pan-Indian identity they formed new organisations, marched, lobbied, filed lawsuits and generally utilised a range of political and legal channels to fight their cause. In the 1910s a group of so-called 'Red Progressives' founded the first pan-Indian organisation, the Society of American Indians which, among other things, campaigned to improve reservation conditions. In the years that followed political groups periodically formed to fight specific government policies. The American Indian Federation was set up during the 1930s in response to the Indian Reorganization Act (IRA). Many Indians opposed the radical changes this legislation called for, notably the creation of Western-democratic-style tribal governments, which many perceived as an attack on their traditional forms of government based on the notion of consensus rather than majority rule. The National Congress of American Indians formed in 1944 to fight the federal policy of 'termination'. During the 1940s and 1950s, by withdrawing federal recognition from various tribes, the government was seeking to end its obligation to provide them with services. In the 1960s and

1970s Indian activism intensified when predominantly young urban Indians employed militant tactics to express their grievances. The National Indian Youth Council was created in 1961 and the American Indian Movement in 1968. The spirit of urban militancy these groups helped to engender quickly spread to the reservations. Most activists focused on the issue of self-rule, advocating the right of tribes to run their own reservations free from interference from the Bureau of Indian Affairs (BIA). Indian groups also took the government to task for failing to fulfil past treaties, demanding to be compensated for stolen lands and waging 'fish-ins' to demonstrate violation of their historic fishing rights. The 19-month occupation of Alcatraz Island in San Francisco bay, which began in 1969, the 'Trail of Broken Treaties' march from Minneapolis to Washington DC in 1972, which ended in a group of militants seizing the BIA building for six days, and the violence that erupted at Wounded Knee, South Dakota, in 1973, when a group attempted to declare independence from the US, forcefully brought Native Americans and their issues to the forefront of public consciousness.

Indian activism has obliged the federal government to address Indian grievances. The history of US Indian policy in the twentieth century has been uneven, with the government taking two steps forward only to take ten steps back. Nonetheless there has been an admittance of the past errors and injustices and a move towards compensation. New Deal Indian legislation put an end to allotment and the boarding school system. Despite some opposition to the IRA, many others viewed the opportunity of organising their own tribal government as a move in the right direction to self-determination. Following the Second World War, the government stepped up its commitment to compensate Indians for past injuries. Wishing to settle Indian land grievances once and for all, the Indian Claims Commission was created in 1946 to review tribal claims over treaty violations. Although the commission was beset with problems, by 1978, the year it was dismantled, it had settled 285 cases and awarded more than $800 million in compensation.

Even though the heyday of Indian militancy is long over, Indians have not given up the use of political channels to fight on a range of issues. Indians have continued to protest against treaty violations. Most famously, President Jimmy Carter in 1980 paid $81.5 million compensation to the Passamaquoddy and Penobscot tribes of Maine. By means of incessant lobbying Indians have also made gains in repatriation, as in the case of the Native American Grave Protection and Repatriation Act of 1990, according to which federally funded museums are now obliged to return Indian religious artefacts and skeletal remains to their places of origin.

One particularly arresting aspect of twentieth-century Native American experience has been the degree of demographic revitalisation. The 1900 US census recorded the Indian population as being 237,196, thus lending credence to the claim that they were indeed a vanishing race. According to the 2000 census their numbers have subsequently shot up to 2.5 million. The post-Second World War decades saw the biggest rise. From 523,591 in 1960, the number claiming Indian identity had risen to 1,878,285 by 1990. This apparent growth is not attributable to a straightforward rise in birth rates or decline in deaths but rather to an increase in the number of Americans self-identifying as Indians, a trend facilitated by a change in the way the Census Bureau records information. Prior to 1960, the race of a person was based on the enumerator's personal observation. The 1960 census introduced a new method that permitted individual self-identification. Demographic and ethnic renewal has also occurred at a collective level. Throughout the century various groups have petitioned government for federal recognition. In 1978 the government set up a special body to review their cases. Henceforward, groups claiming to be tribes would have to prove, among other things, a historical connection to a particular place and a history of political leadership and community cohesion. Some groups, such as the Lumbees of North Carolina, have failed to attain tribal status, but many others, including the Grand Traverse Band of Ottawa and Chippewa in 1980, the Narragansett in 1983, the Gay Head Wampanoags in 1987, the San Juan Southern Paiutes in 1990 and the Mohegans in 1994, succeeded in their petitions.

A combination of material and cultural factors can explain why a growing number of individuals and groups wish to be identified as Indian. As members of a federally recognised tribe, individuals enjoy access to a host of economic benefits such as educational scholarships, subsidised healthcare, and exemption from state and federal taxes. Hence there are strong material incentives for claiming Indian credentials. But an increase in the number of individuals willing to recognise Indian ancestry also points to renewed ethnic pride. The radical politics of the 1960s and 1970s encouraged ethnic renewal. Joanne Nagel argued that the literate, racially mixed urban Indians who had built new communities and networks were especially 'poised' for ethnic renewal. The civil rights movement along with new government legislation aimed at minority groups revitalised an Indian consciousness among urban dwellers. Participation in the militant red activism of the 1970s further heightened ethnic identity, encouraging many Indians to return to their roots.

The rise in the number of self-identifying Indians again highlights the question of what or who exactly is an Indian. Issues of identity become more ambiguous as we begin the twenty-first century. Russell Thornton in his 1990 study *American Indian Holdcaust and Survival* has shown that Indians, more than any other American ethnicity, marry outside their group. In 1990, 95 per cent of married Indians were married to non-Indians. Thus the number of 'mixed-blood' Indians and, in particular, Indians with less than one-half Indian ancestry continues to rise. If this trend persists, the system of blood quantum as a key determinant of Indian identity will become wholly redundant. In response to this situation, Indians have begun to reassess the way they assign Indian identity. Colin Calloway in *First Peoples: A Documentary Survey of American Indian History* observes that some tribes are creating more exclusive definitions, withdrawing tribal membership from people who marry outside their tribe, or denying admittance to the children of mixed marriages. Alternatively, groups like the Oglalas in South Dakota have cast aside blood quantum, choosing once again to focus on cultural factors to determine community membership.

Not surprisingly, political and demographic renewal has helped fuel cultural revitalisation. After a decades-long assault by the US government on their religion, language and lifestyles, communities throughout Indian country are finding ways to re-enact, preserve and extend their cultural practices and tribal heritage. This process has been aided in part by a more sympathetic government, which has actively sought to reverse past policies of religious and cultural repression. The American Indian Religious Freedom Act of 1978 recognised the right of Indians to 'believe, express, and exercise', their traditional religions. This act was further strengthened by the passage of the Native American Free Exercise of Religion Act in 1994. The Native American Languages Act passed in 1990 paved the way for funding to teach and record tribal languages. In 1978, responding to relentless Indian lobbying, Congress also passed the Tribally Controlled Community Colleges Act, which provided government grants for colleges. Tribes thereby gained the right and means to create a school curriculum that not only prepared children for the modern world, but taught them about their heritage. The enormous popularity of the pow-wow is indicative of this new spirit of cultural revitalisation. As social gatherings that involve singing, dancing and drum beating, pow-wows are usually annual events lasting several days. In the early decades of the nineteenth century pow-wows were made illegal by the US government, but by the 1990s an average of 2,000 were being held annually in the United States, marking a vibrant celebration of Indian tribal culture and attracting huge crowds of both Indians and whites.

Indigenous cultural revitalisation has not been confined to the reservation. Native American authors, artists and scholars have slowly, but steadily, made inroads into popular culture and academia. Although the novels of Leslie Marmon Silko, James Welch, Louise Erdrich and N. Scott Momaday have made only a small dent in mainstream literature, these authors, nonetheless, enjoy a public visibility unheard of a generation or so ago. Furthermore, since the late 1960s there has been a renewed scholarly interest in all things Native American. The creation of Native American Studies as a distinct discipline, the birth of a New Indian History and indeed the establishment of departments and degree programmes devoted entirely to the study of Indian history and culture demonstrate a new sensitivity to the needs of indigenous peoples and a long overdue recognition that this is a topic worthy of study. It is also pleasing to note that a cohort of scholars of Native American descent have played a part in setting up and running these programmes and departments. 'Knowledge' about Indians is no longer an exclusive preserve of white America. Indeed the growing number of Indian authors and scholars is a crucial aspect of cultural revitalisation, precisely because it means that native peoples are enjoying a more prominent role in producing and disseminating information about their cultures and history, and exercise greater control over images of themselves in the public domain. But their success must not be overstated. Indian outrage against the movies *Dances with Wolves* and Walt Disney's *Pocahontas* (1995), as well as their continuing campaign against the use of Indian images as sport mascots, illustrates that they still have a long hard battle to fight. Yet their refusal to accept white stereotypes passively and their continued vocal protests mean that certain cinematic images or historical renditions of the past are no longer acceptable.

Revitalisation in the economic realm is a mixed story. Among some communities economic rejuvenation has been colossal. But success has often come at a cost and not without contention. Taking advantage of special funding available to them during President Lyndon Johnson's War on Poverty in the 1960s, the Mississippi Choctaw invested in a modern industrial park. According to their official website at www.choctaw.org they now operate 'a diversified portfolio of manufacturing, service, retail and tourism enterprises', including a substantial printing press and various electronic plants that produce parts for cars. By the 1990s, according to their official website, the Choctaw tribe had become one of the biggest employers in the state and the average Choctaw family had enjoyed a seven-fold increase in income since the 1980s. Other western tribes have sought to prosper from the substantial reserves of coal, oil, natural gas and uranium found in their reservations. Since the Second World War groups like the Navajo, Hopi and Laguna Pueblo in the Southwest have struggled against the exploitative practices of large energy corporations and have had to deal with problems of pollution. The immediate post-war decades were trying times, but since the 1970s tribal

groups have taken greater control over marketing their resources. By forming intertribal organisations such as the Council of Energy Resource Tribes,
Indians have used collective action to obtain more favourable contracts. Some
tribes now drill their own oil wells and organise and run their own environmental protection agencies. Mining has undeniably generated an
important source of wealth. Calloway writes that, 'as late as 1996, approximately 75 per cent of the Navajo Nation's operating budget depended on
royalties from coal sales'. But the marketing of natural resources has generated conflict. For many it stands in opposition to native spiritual beliefs
of the need to honour planet Earth. For others, given their limited economic
options, mining is a necessary and pragmatic choice.

Because they are exempt from federal anti-gaming laws and taxes, some
Indian communities have been able to establish casinos on their reservations,
so achieving enormous prosperity. Although only a recent development, tribal
gaming has proven a phenomenal success. Fergus Bordewich estimates that
from 1988 to the mid-1990s the collective revenues from Indian casinos rose
to $6 billion. By 1994 more than 160 tribes were reported to have estab-
lished gambling venues, the most famous being Foxwoods Casino, owned
and run by the Mashantucket Pequot of southern Connecticut. Granted federal recognition only in 1983, this tribe was by 1994 in receipt of annual
profits of some $800 million, employing a staff of around 9,000 workers and
thus providing a major source of employment for both Pequots and local
whites. Like mining, gambling has aroused virulent debate within Indian communities. Opponents claim that gambling encourages vice and promotes capitalistic values antithetical to Indian ethics. Proponents, on the other hand,
point to the tremendous economic revitalisation that gaming has generated.
Tribes have used profits to rejuvenate their reservations, providing residents
with better housing, health care, schools and community centres, together
with college scholarships for the more ambitious. The Mashantucket Pequot
have concentrated on using their money to preserve their cultural heritage
and educate non-Indians about their culture, spending $193 million on the
Mashantucket Pequot Museum and Research Center. No one knows yet how
sustainable gambling ventures will prove. More cautious individuals hope that
profits made can and will be channelled into other less divisive economic ventures to ensure the long-term prosperity of native communities.

Economic revitalisation is not, however, universal. Rampant unemployment and poverty remains the hallmarks of many reservations. In 1990,
according to US census figures, almost 50 per cent of all reservation Indian
families had incomes that placed them below the poverty level. Stifled economic opportunity and impoverishment have, in turn, led to alarming rates

of alcoholism, death and despondency. But focusing on extraordinary cases of either prosperity or deprivation diverts attention from the many thousands of Indians who have simply chosen to join urban mainstream society. More Indians today live in urban settings than on reservations, occupying a middle ground between these two extremes, engaging in a variety of jobs and enjoying various levels of economic success. As always, Indians' relationship to the market economy gives rise to a wide variety of outcomes.

Not noble, primitive or powerless – and certainly not about to disappear – Native Americans have demonstrated time and time again over the last three centuries that they are a dynamic ever-changing and diverse people. Although their history has had more than its share of tragedy, hardship and oppression, it has equally demonstrated their capacity for resistance and creative adaptation, leading, in some instances, to outstanding success. Just as Native Americans remain a force to be reckoned with in American society, so Native American Studies remains a vital aspect of American Studies, deserving particular attention because it has hitherto given rise to so many misunderstandings and misconceptions. By moving away from the traditional focuses of Indian history – wars, reservation policies, poverty, victimhood – and exploring new areas of Indians' experience – their involvement in the market economy, their creation of new identities and many acts of agency and revitalisation – it can be shown that the experience of Indians has a relevance to people of all races, which it never seemed to have before. At the forefront of this effort are Native Americans themselves. As David Holahan, the spokesman for the Mashantucket Pequot Museum and Research Center, puts it: 'We want to show that Native peoples are not a static part of history, but are still evolving, vital contributors to modern society'.

Further reading

Biolsi, Thomas, *Organizing the Lakota: The Political Economy of the New Deal on the Pine Ridge and Rosebud Reservations* (1992).

Bordewich, Fergus M., *Killing the White Man's Indian: Reinventing Native Americans at the End of the Twentieth Century* (1996).

Calloway, Colin G., *First Peoples: A Documentary Survey of American Indian History* (1999).

Harmon, Alexandra, *Indians in the Making: Ethnic Relations and Indian Identities around Puget Sound* (1998).

Hosmer, Brian C., *American Indians in the Market Place: Persistence and Innovation among the Menominees and Metlakatlans, 1870–1920* (1999).

Merrell, James H., *The Indians' New World: Catawbas and Their Neighbors from European Contact through the Era of Removal* (1989).

Meyer, Melissa L., *The White Earth Tragedy: Ethnicity and Dispossession at a Minnesota Anishinaabe Reservation, 1889–1920* (1994).

Nagel, Joanne, *American Indian Ethnic Renewal: Red Power and the Resurgence of Identity and Culture* (1996).

Sleeper-Smith, Susan, *Indian Women and French Men: Rethinking Cultural Encounters in the Western Great Lakes* (2001).

White, Richard, *The Middle Ground: Indians, Empires, and Republics in the Great Lakes Regions, 1650–1815* (1991).

CHAPTER 6

Revisiting the American West

Margaret Walsh

T he American West, its context and its connections, continues to be a challenging and exciting theme in American Studies in the twenty-first century. The West also remains perplexing and difficult for those searching for answers to the ever-changing meaning of what it is or was to be western or how the West has contributed to being American. Frederick Jackson Turner thought he knew the answer to these questions when he presented his now legendary essay, 'The significance of the frontier in American History' in 1893. His thesis about the centrality of abundant free land, its imminent ending and the character-forming qualities of the frontier was the product of a confident ethos and a rapidly developing nation. A century of ensuing controversy and academic debate, however, suggests that there remains abundant room for alternative propositions. Such alternatives are likely only to provide suggestions rather than definitive statements. Modern academics are fully aware that they may never know or fully understand the American West. They can only suggest ideas, try to deconstruct texts and artefacts and demystify perceptions.

Revisiting the American West involves a journey into the historiography of the frontier and the West in order to appreciate the diversity of discussions among academics and the issues that they have considered to be important. Having examined the varied sites of contest, the West as a centre of opportunity based on its abundant resources is called into question. For whom was the West a stepping-stone to upward mobility? Migrants other than young white males peopled the West. A multicultural past as well as a multicultural present is gradually emerging. In the process of becoming a culturally as well as an economically diverse region with a long unbroken history, western myths and popular legends are examined. But there are no final answers. There is rather a multiplicity of suggestions.

From American frontier to American West: issues of interpretation

The debate about the nature, extent, development and relevance of the American West has its roots in the nineteenth century. Some observers suggest that literature, migrant and immigrant letters, diaries and official reports both from and about the expanding frontier aroused much contemporary interest as well as stimulating continuing visions. More widespread ideas originated from comic almanacs, dime novels or romantic pulp fiction, cheap print lithographs and the popular Wild West shows. Other commentators suggest that Theodore Roosevelt's epic-style four volumes, *The Winning of the West* (1885–94), was a source of knowledge and appeal. Yet most would start their discussions by looking at the frontier thesis of historian, Frederick Jackson Turner. Whether these academics would dismiss Turner, praise him, qualify or criticise him would depend on their discipline, their training, their location and their socio-political environment. Turner's thesis has been buried, resurrected, reburied, restored to life again, and cremated, but his ashes have not as yet been successfully scattered. Although his presence has become more ghost-like on each reappearance, it continues to influence the way we regard the American West.

So what did Turner say and why has he become so difficult to dismiss? As a product of a midwestern background, a Progressive and nationalistic era, and as an interdisciplinary social scientist, Turner reflected views that were peculiar to himself and his age, but he also pointed to some ideas and processes that had national and international application. Basic to his thesis is the existence of an area of what he called 'free land' and its continuous recession as pioneers moved west and settled. This land provided the material foundation which enabled millions of people to build the United States into the wealthy and democratic nation visible at the end of the nineteenth century. There was, however, more to the frontier thesis than bounteous resources and their potential for growth. The settlement of western lands also involved a socio-cultural developmental process in which migrants and immigrants adapted to new environments by adopting different habits or modifying their patterns of behaviour. Often forced to use their initiative in sparsely populated areas, they considered they were the equals of anyone. In forging a distinctive type of person they took on democratic characteristics. Such frontier traits became American traits because the frontier experience was transmitted both geographically across space and historically through time.

Turner's views originally met with little positive response because they questioned mainstream political history. But he was persistent. He spread his ideas in his teaching – and he had many postgraduate students who went on to academic careers. He wrote in popular journals, gave many public lectures and progressed up the professional ladder to become a well-known historian. By the early twentieth century his thesis was widely accepted in the academic world and there was a reputable Turnerian school of history. Reaction set in during the 1930s when serious economic difficulties produced a criticism based on scarcity and misuse of resources. By this time, however, academics were also asserting that the distinctive western contribution to the United States could never account for the nation's state of being. Other major influences shaped the country, for example, immigration and ethnicity, urbanism and technology, along with various other international intellectual and commercial currents. Too much had been attributed to the settlement of the American West.

Though the frontier thesis faded in significance, it did not die. It was revised in the post-war years of affluence and optimism. Again Americans believed in themselves and in their exceptionalism. Another historian, Ray Allen Billington, re-energised the frontier experience for the academic world and the American people and gave it an international reputation. His classic textbook, *Westward Expansion* (1949), together with his other professional work advanced the idea of the importance of the frontier as a formative experience. Soon historians and social scientists, equipped with early computers capable of quantitatively testing theories, eagerly explored the process of settling the United States. Frontier ideas spread abroad as historians and geographers compared the American West with other grassland areas of the world, and the emerging interdisciplinary area, American Studies, funded in part by American money overseas, added new insights through the use of literary and cultural analysis. Indeed 'frontier' became a trendy word as it moved into American language as a pseudonym for opportunity.

This popularity did not continue long. By the 1970s the study of the West had become dull and tedious because too many micro-studies exploring aspects of Turner's frontier thesis had flooded the market. Those undertaking interesting research had moved into new areas and new methods. The relevance of American western history appeared marginal. Yet some of the new histories and methodologies drawn from other disciplines in turn stimulated interest in the West, not as a formative force in the nation, but as a distinctive regional entity. A group of historians, known as the 'New Western Historians', came to prominence by asserting the downside of the western past and by claiming to offer more realistic views.

Their histories were highly controversial, albeit in tune with the post-Vietnam years of loss of confidence. Patricia Limerick, Richard White and Donald Worster talked about a West that spread from the Missouri River to the Pacific coast and either dismissed or ignored Turner's frontier process of settlement. The West was a place with a long continuous past stretching from 'time immemorial' to the present. There was no turning point at the census of 1890 as the frontier thesis of 1893 had claimed. Indeed, those dates and the concept of West as nation had grossly distorted western history. So too had the positive interpretation of achievement which, in its various retellings, had become a romantic and triumphalist epic. The New West became a colonial area exploited by outside capitalists. European nation states employed a mercantile variety of domination; the federal government clothed its control in more restrained language, as manifest destiny, territorial government or conservation of national resources. The West as region was distinctive for its disappointments and failures. These failures were human as well as economic and physical. Too many peoples of colour suffered when the white pioneers invaded from the East. They were either destroyed or were robbed of their heritage, were made to assimilate and were treated as being vastly inferior. This West was not democratic. It was distinctly inegalitarian.

Such a vigorous interpretation was received with both enthusiasm and dismay. Many who subsequently called themselves western historians and increasingly also specialists in western literature and culture considered that the New West offered a negative but a more realistic assessment of economic development, ecological disasters and political subservience. Living in a multicultural society they also appreciated the acknowledgement of demographic diversity and the traditional dominance of whiteness. Western communities in the past as well as the present were island archipelagos that developed their own styles and identities. There was no assimilation to some American norm. Though dominant by the 1990s, New Western Historians were not unchallenged. Many of the older generation educated in the post-war years, now renamed the Old Western Historians, responded sharply, branding the newer interpreters politically correct pessimists and criticising their output as defective, partial and egotistical. The battle lines were drawn for confrontation.

Though both sides waged academic war for several years, a truce of kinds seems to have emerged. Looking at the state of western history from the European side of the Atlantic, this seems to have arisen partly because frameworks are no longer in vogue. It seems pointless to establish any one structure of analysis when historians are interested in diversities and individual experiences. Perhaps more important, many historians work outside the tenets of either New or Old Western History, and some are trying to reconcile the two schools, suggesting that they can be compatible.

Though it was difficult not to take sides in the heated arguments about the merits of the New Western History during the 1990s, there were many historians, including some of the major protagonists themselves, who simply continued with their research in other styles, taking other approaches. They contributed to many reinterpretations of aspects of the American West which have become vital to a healthy examination of either the region or the nation. These revisions, however, were marginalised in both the popular and academic commotion about the New Western History. Such new western histories included ethnohistory, women's history, ecological or environmental history, Chicano history and borderlands approaches, all of which drew their ideas from other theoretical and methodological areas and brought fresh perspectives. The many western historians, for example, writing environmental histories of water, mining, land use and lumbering continued, with their work throughout the controversy, stimulating new ideas about the western past. There was both an evolutionary approach to re-envisaging the West as well as the abrupt intervention, known as New Western History.

Other western historians and interpreters refused to abandon some of the basic propositions of Turner's thesis, insisting that there was a legacy that was worth preserving. William Cronon, often identified as a New Western Historian and included within the 'gang of four', never accepted that nomenclature. While recognising that the frontier thesis was seriously flawed on several counts, he wanted to understand how a West that changed geographically through time was related to the nation as a whole and how its diverse population interacted with landscape and mixed together through cultural and economic exchanges. It might be better, he suggested, to use a word other than 'frontier', which had been impaired by association with human and environmental exploitation, but the basic concept was still valuable. So too, he argued, is the Turner thesis itself if it is read as a speculative essay, posing questions rather than offering definitive answers.

When asking what the American West is and was and what it is perceived to be and by whom, there are as many answers as questions. The recent historiographical debates, which have spread to disciplines other than history, have not resolved contested issues. They have, however, highlighted themes that are of central importance to understanding the West.

The following four sections address central issues in order to offer some insights into the exciting, but perplexing challenge of discovering the American West, its context and its connections.

The land and its ownership

Land and natural resources in the West have always been abundant regardless of whoever perceived these assets. Native inhabitants occupied and used much land and still plenty remained vacant. European incomers were overwhelmed by the availability of valuable terrain that could potentially yield a decent standard of living, whether to farmers or to those processing other resources. Furthermore the land was often beautiful and attracted the attention of those who wanted to preserve it as a natural wilderness or to conserve its bounty for future generations. Land was certainly available, but there have been tensions between alternative patterns of usage and the desire or need to conserve.

The nature of virgin land in the American West remains unknown. Habitat transformation is a disputed subject, despite the best endeavours of anthropologists, geographers, ethnographers, biologists and historians, who have examined changing patterns of vegetation and animal and mineral exploitation, using scientific techniques, evidence from material culture, oral traditions and more conventional print and pictorial records. Much of the debate focuses on what is meant by plentiful, efficient and wasteful and what is considered exploitation as distinct from management. At the heart of the matter is the issue of who owns the land and whether they have a responsibility to their present community or to future inhabitants.

Traditionally Native Americans were considered to utilise resources inefficiently, gathering fruits, seeds and plants, hunting on foot (until the Europeans introduced horses) and farming irregularly with primitive tools. Newcomers from the Old World thought that they had a right to take land and use it more productively for the benefit of themselves and their rulers. They deemed native peoples to be incompetent because they were ignorant of metal technology and improved agricultural practices. Such a culturally superior interpretation came into disrepute when liberal academics in the second half of the twentieth century became more sensitive to racial-ethnic differences and were concerned about the rapid depletion of resources. Then native peoples were perceived to live in harmony with nature, taking only what they needed for their basic requirements. They could be portrayed as ecological role models.

Since the advent of environmental history and ethnohistory, which draws on social anthropology, ethnology, archaeology and oral traditions to gain knowledge of native peoples, indigenous communities have been examined more intensively. Accepting alternative folkways as valid, academics recognise that what Turner may have called virgin land had already been transformed, and possibly several times. Native groups used such techniques as burning and slashing to alter vegetation cover and cater to their food requirements. They fished the rivers, lakes and oceans, and destroyed trees for shelter, fuel and artefacts. They farmed systematically within their technological knowledge and their labour supply, and often hunted more animals than they could consume for food, clothing or shelter. It appears that like subsequent American settlers they took what they needed within the means that they possessed and accumulated surpluses for trading.

Contact with incoming European nations changed this native use of resources. European demands for fish, fur and lumber, and then for land as mercantile capitalists decided to settle as well as trade, created more intense inter-tribal rivalries in the search to barter. The exchange of furs for iron goods, domestic utensils and alcohol altered native patterns and standards of living as well as depleting some resources. Subsequent European demands for more land promoted early ownership disputes. What is now called the 'middle ground' or years of contact in which natives and incoming Europeans exchanged goods, negotiated for land and fought with each other, using traditional skills, new weapons and differing allies, were transition years in which there was potential for developing neighbourly relationships. In adjusting to European colonial invasions, native communities acquired a desire to collect more goods, which was part of the capitalist ethic, were demoralised by white deceit and greed, and were decimated by white diseases and alcohol. But they retained an integrity, which had positive features. The near-total loss of land and access to resources needed for their traditional mode of livelihood and culture would take place in the nineteenth century. This would be the tragedy of native peoples.

When European peoples became settlers and then resident Americans, attitudes to and utilisation of land became more demanding. Colonists moved gradually inland from the Atlantic, but the major sweep westwards across the Appalachians and on to the central plains followed the official American acquisition of land from other nations, the removal of native peoples and advances in machine technology. Early in the history of the United States, politicians, entrepreneurs and 'grass-roots' settlers turned their attention inland and decided that land was abundant and desirable. Each group in their own way accelerated American occupation until they had used and misused the resources of the area now called the United States. They failed to own the lands that are now called Canada and Mexico, but their influence spread widely across the official borders, so that some observers have called the other North American nations informal empires.

Leading Americans early agreed that the ex-colonies, now states, should form a national entity and they successfully negotiated that the 7 of the original 13 states claiming lands beyond the Appalachian Mountains should yield their titles to the federal government. Initially this area stretched only to the Mississippi River and excluded the Floridas but, concerned about Indian and foreign threats in the unsettled backcountry and on its borderlands, the government made early attempts to negotiate with the British in Canada and the Great Lakes area and with the French and Spanish in Louisiana. President Jefferson (1801–9), sometimes called the intellectual father of expansionism, seized the opportunity to buy Louisiana from the French in 1803, thereby securing the navigation rights to the Mississippi River and stifling any possible western rebellion. Dissident ex-colonists or American settlers, who had moved to foreign-held lands in the Floridas and Texas, actively sought or were encouraged to ask for admission or 're-admission' to the United States in 1810 and 1836. The government further actively pursued boundary adjustments with Britain in Canada in 1818 and Spain in Mexico in 1819 to consolidate early land acquisitions.

What had appeared rapid expansion prior to 1820 was vastly overshadowed by the gains of the mid-nineteenth century. Continental ambitions dominated the 1840s. The lone-star republic of Texas was admitted into the Union in 1845. In the Northwest the Oregon country was 're-annexed' in 1846 following its joint occupation with Britain, and in the Southwest, Mexico ceded much territory after the short war of 1846–8. Settlers had helped the official expansion. Small numbers of pioneers had moved to distant lands hoping to gain a better livelihood. They then wanted to secure their holdings by having the protection of the United States, whether in the form of its army, its legislative authority or its cultural and intellectual ambience. American politicians, increasingly ambitious to establish the nation as a major influence, were only too willing to perceive these settlers as planting the American flag. Subsequent acquisitions in the shape of the Gadsden Purchase of 1853 to ensure a route for a transcontinental railroad, and the purchase of the then 'icebox' of Alaska from Russia in 1867 were easily negotiated. The occupation of Hawaii in 1898 created more opposition, but by then the formalisation of American dominance was only a matter of time. Academics have endlessly discussed whether this process of expansion should be called 'manifest destiny' or continental imperialism. The former

description is associated with Americans' honourable mission to spread democratic ideals in a world where autocratic governments were rife. The latter
is associated with overruling others' sovereignty and imposing new régimes.
In the contemporary world, even while recognising the peculiar ideological flavour of the American version, it is difficult to avoid being cynical about
nineteenth-century expansionism.

The debate about democracy or empire has also been encountered in
the framework of government that was established for the western lands.
The Northwest Ordinance of 1787, which replaced the more liberal 'Jefferson'
Ordinance of 1784, established a three-stage political process enabling
settlers to move from subordinate territory to full statehood. Worried about
security in the face of native responses to aggressive white settlers, the presence of foreign powers on the continent and unknown dangers, Congress
favoured an authoritarian system. This style of government was moderated
by settler protests and by the reduction of belligerent or diplomatic threats
in the early nineteenth century. Moreover, new territories had always enjoyed
a bill of rights ensuring basic liberties. Yet territorial government was never
fully democratic because the final authority remained with Congress in
Washington DC, which decided when territories were ready for statehood
and whether their proposed constitutions were sound. Furthermore, as the
federal government remained in control of the distribution of land, paid
the salaries of territorial officials, was influential in terms of political
patronage, and governed native peoples through its various agencies, territorial residents often felt that they were subjects rather than equals.

Certainly the pessimistic approach of the New Western Historians, contemporary critiques and the sagebrush rebellions of western states desirous
of state control over resources within their boundaries have all stimulated
a dependency mindset when discussing the role of the federal government.
Yet there has always been ambivalence about the experiences of being a
territorial or a western resident. Many settlers gained from federal management when they were pioneers, as they could obtain military protection, labour, land ownership and assistance during disasters. Some residents
also benefited from the delays in gaining statehood in the late nineteenth
century because as opportunists they acquired wealth and influence
through being politically dependent on a distant authority. Much later,
in the twentieth century, federal government expenditure on defence and
conservation brought more income-generating activities to a West that was
politically equal, but considered that it was still supervised by federal
politicians. Western territorial status and its legacies have always been a
double-edged sword.

Land disposal policy has also generated heated debate. The Land Ordinance of 1785 originally governed the disposal of those federally controlled lands known as the public domain. This enacted that Indian titles to land should first be cleared and land itself surveyed before it was sold at an auction to the highest bidder. A minimum price per acre and a minimum size of purchase per unit was established. Market forces would thus be the dominant influence shaping who would have early access to resources. But the government was flexible enough to adapt its policies to changing times and conditions. Ascertaining that its initial attempt to sell land discriminated against pioneers as distinct from entrepreneurs, it lowered both the price and the size of minimum purchases. It did not, however, consider setting maximum prices and acquisitions. Furthermore it only offered credit temporarily and thus exposed pioneers to borrowing from intermediaries who, in negative terminology, have been called speculators. Yet the government also listened to settlers' pleas for cheaper land by pardoning trespass on public domain and allowing them to squat ahead of survey and sale. This official free use of land offered westerners the opportunity to make a living from the land prior to purchase. By the mid-nineteenth century some land could be acquired cheaply while other land was acquired at its market price. Inconsistency prevailed.

It also grew more marked as white settlement accelerated. Westerners continued to agitate for cheaper access to land and they won a landmark victory in the Homestead Act of 1862. This law gave 160 acres or a quarter section to genuine settlers who resided continuously on their land and paid filing and registration fees. Yet for many the act was a hollow victory. Though attracting much publicity, it enabled only a small proportion of land to be distributed free to pioneers. Much of the remaining public domain was not open to homesteading and many would-be settlers had no capital with which to build up a free farm. More land was given away as grants for the construction of transport networks, primarily railroads, and much more was sold cheaply to entrepreneurs who wanted large cattle ranches or lumber holdings. Rapid economic development had become a key issue in industrialising America. Even more land was sold on the open market to whoever had cash. This included many immigrants and transplanted Americans, as well as speculators who then resold the land, often on credit. There were major inequities in land disposal policies. Whether the American government could have established a fairer and more rational system remains a contentious issue. Official intentions and actual results are perceived differently, with descriptions ranging from incompetent, inefficient and corrupt, to liberal, democratic and generous. The adjective that perhaps captures the most nuances of the policies of flexibility is perhaps 'incongruous'.

Developing western resources

If American land disposal was inconsistent, its usage was rapid and productive. Productive, however, has a dual meaning. Defined within the capitalistic framework, productive can mean making a comfortable living by upgrading a self-sufficient unit, usually a farm, by entering the marketplace. Trade and earnings were the mechanisms that drove most farmers into commercial production and encouraged the rapid agricultural development of the United States. Productive can also mean improving land by having a care for the future of soils and for nature. Such an interest in resource use has been redefined as concern over the environment. Neither definition of productive is static. Technology has the capacity to alter resource-use productivity positively and negatively. Improvements in transport, machinery, genetics and chemistry have vastly increased yields from farms. Simultaneously, however, they have helped to 'lay waste' major areas not only in farming but also in mining, trapping and lumbering.

Most newcomers to the American West in the eighteenth and nineteenth century migrated to farm. They frequently came from a rural background and saw western lands as plentiful and fruitful. If they moved in the years before 1820, they frequently found their lives dominated by the struggle to build a family farm. Through arduous labour they could break the soil, plant and harvest crops for their own consumption. To finance purchases of commodities that they could not raise, they needed to sell a surplus crop, whether this was livestock, cereals, maple syrup or potash, and they needed to transport this crop to market by soft-topped roads or by raft on the rivers. In the next half century improvements in transport technology in the shape of steamboats, canals and railroads facilitated access to both local and more distant urban markets. Improvements in agricultural machinery in the shape of reapers, cast iron and steel ploughs and harvesters accelerated production. The extension of agricultural knowledge through farm journals, country fairs and colleges, and scientific experiments in seeds, breeds, hormones and pesticides further stimulated growth. Even before the Civil War many farmers had left self-sufficiency behind and were commercialised. The impact of technology rapidly accelerated in the late nineteenth and early twentieth centuries when railroads, aided by improvements in local roads and wagon freighting, forged a national market. By then most land that was suitable for agricultural use was settled and already many smaller farms were being merged into an early stage of agribusiness in order to rationalise the use of improved machinery.

This process of turning western lands into an agrarian empire has been perceived as either a triumphal and democratic success or as a settlement process fraught with dangers and disasters for both humans and the environment. The positive interpretation lauds the productivity levels of farmers and their ability to supply both the food needs of the growing population of the United States and export markets. Yet there has also been a note of caution. Agricultural historians, who themselves originated in the region, and the new rural historians talk about the families who struggled to make ends meet on their small mixed farms. The margin between success and failure was slight. These families borrowed machinery, used out-of-date equipment or did without, thereby putting themselves at a competitive disadvantage. They were regularly in debt for the mortgage on their farm, their machinery and sometimes their seed and tools. They needed to repay these loans if they were ever to own their farm, but for this they required good harvests. Any natural hazard – for example, hot summers, severe winters, storms, grasshopper plagues and fires, or a human clash between farmers and would-be ranchers – could undercut their precarious position. Furthermore, the market price of cash crops declined overall between 1867 and 1897 and freight rates on the railroads, though also declining, were considered to be too high. There was considerable agrarian discontent and much individual failure that was not recorded in the general assessment of wheat belts, corn belts, feedlots and cattle kingdoms.

Environmental historians examining the American West change the focus from the human struggles of farming families to ecological disasters. In this trajectory, the misuse of the land and wastage of western resources have often been represented as plunder or rape. Water shortages often impeded farm productivity in arid areas, but the construction of irrigation and storage systems encouraged farming in areas that were at best marginal. The infamous dust storms of the 1930s, occurring in areas collectively known as the 'Dust Bowl', were but one example of severe resource devastation in dry lands. The more general over-use of land without crop rotation or composting often resulted in depletion of topsoil, loss of fertility and environmental damage. As for the landscape, the naturalists of the mid-nineteenth century and the tourists and interest groups of subsequent years, like the Sierra Club, called for the protection of scenery and nature, but it was only towards the end of the nineteenth century that the federal government took any lead in conserving resources and in creating natural sanctuaries in the form of what later became national parks. Most westerners and Americans alike thought that resources were infinitely bountiful and gave little consideration to the future.

Western residents have shown the same ambivalence to resources other than land, namely forests, fish, furs and minerals. Some deplore the wastage and the destructive effects of their exploitation on the environment. Others admire and insist on using the wealth-generating capacity provided by any natural resources. Native Americans used these resources well before the Europeans invaded. They fished, hunted animals, destroyed trees and enjoyed wearing gold, but either because they respected the lives of others and nature or because they had limited access to weapons and tools of destruction, their impact on resources, in the overall historical pattern of exploitation, was negligible. European traders, initially interested in the cod banks of the Atlantic coast, soon moved inland in search of furs and precious metals. They also recognised the superior sources of timber for shipbuilding. By the seventeenth century such transient visitors had established trading posts, and soon these became permanent settlements or colonial outposts. Then the pressure on resources increased because Europeans saw that their success involved the destruction of resources. As these appeared to be bountiful, traders and colonists with their enterprising attitudes and more advanced technologies both negotiated with native communities and seized the commodities that they desired.

Their levels of exploitation increased rapidly with the arrival of more newcomers, improved machinery and a rising level of international commerce. The fur trade spread across the continent, moving down the St Lawrence River to and through the Great Lakes, across the Canadian prairies, down the Mississippi River to the Gulf coast and up the Missouri River, long before separate political identities were established in North America in the late eighteenth century. The fur trade subsequently developed as separate American and Canadian enterprises on the Pacific coast, in the Rocky Mountains and in the Great Plains. Europeans and later Americans provided the capital and the markets for beaver fur, otter skins and buffalo robes. They also supplied the weaponry for hunting, and used native, mixed blood and immigrant labour to catch and process animals into an end-product. Such was the intensity of the exploitation that many fur-bearing animals were commercially exhausted in the Great Lakes in the eighteenth century, in the Rockies and on the Pacific coast by the 1830s and on the plains by the 1880s. The fur trade, however, did not die out. Never very important economically to the American West, it shifted emphasis to other animals like the racoon or the seal that were more abundant. Its reputation lives on, both in the romanticism of such western storytelling about 'mountain men' and buffalo hunters, and in providing evidence for conservationists to protect species that have witnessed a comeback in the twentieth century.

Lumber exploitation followed another continental trajectory with a more intensive and longer-lasting impact on the American West. Early activities in northeastern colonies and states supplied shipbuilding and allied industries, regional farmers and growing towns and cities. By the 1830s, however, the extensive forest resources here had been denuded and lumbermen moved west to exploit the pine woods of the Great Lakes region. Bringing their business knowledge and a developing technology they took advantage of natural waterways and railroads. In the years after the Civil War they systemised their business by applying steam power, circular saws and labour-saving devices like the endless chain. Exploitation accelerated as corporations acquired new resources to satisfy the demands of a growing national market. They looked west and south and invested their capital in the pine and redwood forests of the Pacific and Rocky Mountain regions and in the yellow pine areas of the Gulf States. Again they slashed timber rapidly, using ever more sophisticated machinery. There was little incentive to follow any other strategy because forests were perceived to be abundant. That these resources were not exhaustive without remedial action became clear at the turn of the twentieth century. By then pressure groups interested in retaining wilderness beauty and, more important, the federal government, which wanted to administer resources efficiently, combined to restrain the plunder. But they failed to stop it. Only when businesses recognised that management and renewal would sustain high yields and provide a regular supply was conservation achieved.

The long haul to recognising an economic need, if not an environmental benefit, to reclaiming forested lands was not achieved without major loss and wastage. Lumbermen left a trail of 'cut-over' districts and massive debris that scarred the landscape for generations. Though some of this devastation has been cleared and trees have been planted or the land put to other uses, the environmental damage was visible in terms of soil erosion, river pollution, stream flow, burnt-over land and diseased vegetation. Forestry also had a human as well as an ecological cost. Male loggers and mill hands, whether farmers looking for seasonal work or young single immigrants, lived in wretched conditions in crude and unsanitary lumber camps, worked long hours in difficult conditions and faced very dangerous tasks, cutting trees, damming streams, loading logs and processing them. The pressure of work was fast and the industrial accident rate high. The general pattern of lumbering also had a destabilising effect on the western economy, best described in terms of boom and slump.

Lumbering, however, was not the only extractive activity that contributed to the rapid, but erratic growth of the western economy. Mining had the potential to create a more dramatic impact, especially the mining of precious minerals. The Mountain and Pacific West were well endowed with deposits of gold and silver, even though these deposits were not always easily accessible. Early gold strikes in California in the 1840s were followed by major silver strikes in Nevada and Colorado and less rich strikes throughout the Far West. The lure of instant riches mobilised thousands of newcomers to migrate, and the knowledge that both unskilled and skilled work was available in the mines drew in many more. Only a lucky few made their fortune. Initially these were not miners but retailers or haulage contractors. Later entrepreneurs with capital moved in as their money, or their ability to generate investment finance on the stock markets, was necessary for deep-vein mining, which required equipment for drilling and blasting, heavy timbering to prevent cave-ins, pumps to prevent flooding, and crushing and smelting technology. They were able to make profits, but developing silver mines in the mountains was often a high-risk business. Better access to markets through new mountain roads and then railroads stimulated production, but the less precious silver markets could, and often did, collapse, subjecting the local economy to slumps. The rising demand for baser metals like zinc and lead and the more substantial later demand for oil and coal continued the western reliance on extractive industries well into the twentieth century.

As with lumbering, mining left a trail of devastation in its wake and much of this legacy remains to be cleaned up. It is still possible to travel the Mountain and Pacific coast regions and see pockmarked surfaces, mounds of mine tailings and mining equipment, constructed debris of shacks and lean-tos and ghost towns. In some districts the environment became and remains an artificial wasteland. At the time, air pollution caused by milling and smelting and water pollution created by dumping caused further ecological damage and created major occupational hazards. These may not, however, have been as precarious as working deep underground with the dangers of explosions, cave-ins, fires and accidents involving machinery, as well as other longer-term workplace adversities leading to disability and disease. Resentment of such dangerous working conditions was often revealed in miners' hostility to their employers and in the radical nature of their unions.

The American West was a source of abundance to early settlers and has continued to provide a living for millions of residents. Yet the process of providing this living has been neither smooth nor equal. Commentators remark that the development of a vast expanse of land and bountiful resources over the course of centuries unsurprisingly entailed unevenness. What western historians have been discussing recently is whether in telling and examining the process of this development they should paint the picture in bright glowing colours or in shades of grey and black. The debate is never-ending. Currently it seems that the tragic portrait is dominant, but the more vibrant description remains attractive, not only with observers who remain positive about past economic achievements, but with image and myth makers who prefer romance to reality.

Peoples and communities of the American West

Many peoples have occupied western lands and they have developed diverse communities. The American West has both a multicultural past and a multicultural present. Interpreters of both the West as region and the West as nation, whether historians, novelists, artists or residents, have been very active in demonstrating this human and cultural variety by deconstructing the traditional and romantic white male past. There was no monolithic West. Human diversity has become the key to understanding western society.

Native Americans have always been present, but increasingly they are no longer the 'others', but are the lawful inhabitants whose rights have been exploited by invaders. The numbers of native peoples prior to European contact in 1492 remains hard to estimate, despite the volumes that have been devoted to their demography and the impact of disease, warfare, malnutrition, starvation, forced labour and dietary changes. Whatever their numbers, Native Americans were diverse in their settlements and lifestyles. Since the 1960s anthropologists, ethnologists and ethnohistorians have offered ample evidence to demonstrate the presence of language families that differed within and between each other in customs, beliefs, modes of livelihood and location. Groups, traditionally known as tribes, were still evolving before they encountered European newcomers. More changes ensued through interaction with the Spanish in the Southwest, the Russians in the Northwest and the English and French, primarily, but also the Dutch and Swedes moving inland from the East Coast.

Native groups made more adjustments than Europeans because they were pressured into releasing lands as well as adapting their lifestyles to new trading patterns and manufactured goods. In migrating to new homes, often in a westerly direction, they encountered conflicts with other native groups who resisted intrusions into their homelands. New alliances and arrangements were forged with different native neighbours, and new trading patterns were negotiated with Europeans. These exchanges resulted in ethnic diversity, armed instability and an increasing dependency of native peoples on trade goods. European imperial rivalries played out on the North American continent brought major cultural and economic changes and indeterminate destruction to the native inhabitants.

When Americans formed a new nation, the pace of interaction with native communities accelerated and with this went any notion of co-existence. For many Americans, removing natives from western lands became part of the national agenda. Though the federal government considered policies of treating Indians with respect and dignity and recognised prior residence, it had neither the willpower nor the military and administrative presence to prevent white intrusions on and claims to native territories. A pattern of raids, counter raids, wars and treaties ceding lands was established in the early years of the Republic. Indian removal became an official removal policy in the 1830s as one tribe after another was relocated on lands west of the Mississippi River. However, this attempt to separate whites and natives was proved to be of short duration. More invasions and treaties requiring further adjustments to land holdings followed. After the Civil War, the strengthened American army was able to subdue any native resistance. Corralled increasingly on to smaller and smaller areas known as reservations, which were managed inefficiently by white bureaucrats, Native Americans lost both their traditional links to the environment and many of their cultural habits. They became dependent and demoralised. Not until the 1930s was there any faint recognition of their rights and only in the 1960s and 1970s was there any attempt at restitution and restoration of ethno/racial pride.

Discussion of other antecedent residents also took the form of a colonial-style demographic evasion. Little is written about peoples of mixed ancestry like the métis, the mestizo and the mulatto. In the United States, in contrast to Canada, the former have, until very recently, been subsumed into native communities and only during Spanish occupation were mestizos an acknowledged part of western society. Mexicans, however defined, were recognised, and during the short period between Mexican independence in 1821 and the annexation of the southwest territories by the United States in 1848 many lived in what was then the northern province of an independent nation. They were mostly farm workers either on their own smallholdings or on the large rancheros owned by lighter skinned ricos who claimed to have more Spanish blood. Under American government they either remained as peons on the land or became despised 'alien miners'. The ricos were displaced politically and socially by the more savvy and supposedly superior incoming Anglo-Americans. Race was at the root of social and economic discrimination and remained so even when, as the railroads spread through the Southwest, the rural population migrated to the cities. The influx of Mexican immigrants across the Rio Grande border in the twentieth century confirmed rather than alleviated discrimination and subordination, and it was not until the 1960s that Chicanos made any headway towards equal treatment.

Native peoples, mixed native groups and Mexicans were early residents of a multi-ethnic West. Migrants from the East Coast were essentially newcomers, who added to the demographic diversity. The majority of these new arrivals were native-born Americans of European ancestry. They often moved in a leapfrog style from nearby states along similar lines of latitude to the homes they were leaving in the hope of acquiring a more profitable farm. They carried with them not only their farm equipment and livestock, but also a cultural heritage that influenced the make-up of their rural communities. East Coast traditions, however, were diluted into midwestern modifications and these in turn were thinned down as these pioneers moved on to the arid lands west of the ninety-eighth meridian where major environmental adjustments became necessary. Some native-born migrants to areas west of the Mississippi and Missouri Rivers were still called Yankee-Yorkers. Such naming, without recognition of shifting characteristics, contributed to the more general labelling of the westward movement as being white Anglo-American. Certainly this broad grouping had an allegiance to the English language and an attachment to common law traditions, but like its urban counterpart it contained significant economic, social and cultural differences. There was no universal native-born pioneer.

If the migration of native-born Americans cannot be clearly categorised, then immigrants to the American West also need recognition as specific ethnic groups, rather than being seen as Europeans or conflated with native-born Americans into a mainstream category known as Euro-American. Northwestern Europeans moved into the Old Northwest and the Upper Mississippi Valley in the years before the Civil War. They were however, greatly outnumbered by the flood of immigrants who subsequently moved to the Great Plains, Mountain and Far Western regions. Settlers from Central and Southern Europe joined the Scandinavians, Germans, English and Irish in the late nineteenth and early twentieth centuries. A quarter of Nebraska's population of 1870, a third of California's population of 1880 and a third of North Dakota's population of 1900 were foreign-born. If second-generation immigrants are included, the proportion of ethnic population in some rural and urban parts of the Plains and Mountain West was much higher. These ethnic communities were diverse culturally and socially and contributed to creating distinct ethno-cultural enclaves, some of which retained a remarkable degree of persistence despite a rapid adaptation to American patterns of economic behaviour. This variety makes generalisations about European immigrants difficult, if not impossible. The complex nature of white western society itself suggests a cultural pluralism to add to the existing mixture of antecedent settlers.

African Americans added a further ethno-racial component. Whether as slaves or emancipated people, they constituted a distinctive minority group. Sometimes they worked in agriculture either as cowboys and ranch hands, or tried plains farming, as did the Exodusters who migrated to Kansas in the 1870s. More often they worked as laundresses, domestic servants, miners, cleaners and on construction sites. These unskilled black labourers were joined by a handful of small entrepreneurs like barbers, milliners and grocers, or professionals like teachers, lawyers and doctors who catered to black communities. The relatively modest numbers of African Americans in the West suggests that they did not consider that the region offered significantly more opportunities than other parts of the country. Racism was prevalent in many parts of the West and their individual stories commonly reveal difficult struggles against prejudice. Yet, even facing discrimination, black Americans not infrequently found that they were better able to live the kind of lives they wanted in the West than elsewhere.

East Asian immigrants, primarily Chinese in the nineteenth century, had virtually no opportunity to integrate into western life. Initially hoping to be temporary residents, they planned on earning enough in the gold mines to pay off the cost of their return passages and to send back enough for their families to live on. Many, however, found they could not accumulate enough money to achieve their objectives. As a result, they were themselves obliged to struggle on in sexually imbalanced and crowded communities, facing discrimination wherever they worked, with the additional danger of being preyed on by Chinese gangs. Some Chinese men worked on the land, some eventually becoming landholders, but most found work in the mines, in laundries, in the food trade, or building railroads. The few women who migrated to America were apt to become prostitutes. Culturally and politically as well as economically Chinese Americans remained isolated and stigmatised. Because they retained their dress, religion and language they appeared both exotic and alien, giving rise to cultural fears as well as economic resentment. As a result, white hostility built up sufficient momentum to erupt into violence and to be codified in exclusion laws, even though Chinese labour was essential to the western economy. Even as late as the mid-twentieth century the Chinese presence in the West was accepted only on sufferance.

The modern American West is a cosmopolitan region. Many have thus been perplexed as to why its history has been constructed around the mythical upwardly aspiring white male American norm. Surely multiple communities existed side by side in the past as they do in the present? Though there is an element of 'reading the present into the past' in this viewpoint, it is also valid to suggest that traditionally most historians and filmmakers have been primarily concerned with the success of the young white man. The new histories that emerged in the 1960s and 1970s investigated demographic diversity, the female presence and same-sex relationships, while the multiculturalism of subsequent years has fostered a greater awareness of racialism beyond the white/'other' dualism. Though the slow use of sources written in other languages or evidence in artefact format may have retarded research on specific groups, the recognition of a western mosaic of population is now widespread. The American West has never experienced a universal or even a mainstream demography. It has always consisted of a proliferation of small communities that existed like island archipelagos, often with porous boundaries. These communities were both rural and urban, immigrant and native, religious and secular, voluntary and organised. They sometimes co-existed within a defined geographical area, yet remained distinctly separate.

Myths and realities

No recent western history survey can omit a discussion of western myths, though whether these are encountered as dreams, fantasies, images, popular culture, cultural predispositions, erroneous beliefs or storytelling will depend on the disciplinary background, the interdisciplinary connections and the intellectual training of their authors. Academics were slow to study the myriad myths surrounding the American West, even though the area had early become a vast construction site for individual and collective stories. Historians, in particular, considered that knowledge about the West was either myth or reality. For them myth consisted of emotional hazy ideas or beliefs, while history – or the real past – was a rational re-enactment of facts. Not until the mid-twentieth century and the publication of Henry Nash Smith's influential classic, *Virgin Land: The American West as Symbol and Myth* (1950) was this false dichotomy widely discussed. Trained in cultural and literary criticism as well as in history, Smith demonstrated that history was made as well as experienced. It concerned 'what people thought they were doing as much as what they actually did'.

For many years *Virgin Land* influenced American Studies practitioners as well as historians, some of whom wrote cultural histories that integrated commonly held and emotionally charged convictions about the West into their writings. Their approach expanded the impact of *Virgin Land* and for a time it was popular to examine themes like cowboys and violence and ideals like wilderness and heroes. Yet this interdisciplinary approach was itself bypassed, if not overtaken, by the new genre of cultural history or the cultural approach to academic studies. Borrowing from anthropology, literary theory and critical theory, those imbued with philosophical ideas about language asked how different groups of people perceived meaning and communicated ideas. They inquired into the West's signifying systems or its various interpretive mechanisms and value systems. For these observers, imbued with postmodernism, it became essential to 'deconstruct' narratives earlier considered to be factual to uncover the cultural assumptions within which they were created and to reveal the more complicated 'truths' about their context. In what became an almost frenzied attempt to empty language of ideology, the past became fragmented as the collection of stories grew. There was a postmodern proliferation of histories, many of which remain as narratives rather than rational modes of discourse. These two cultural approaches to the West, the classic and the more recent, have helped sustain and rework western history.

Ideas about the West, either as nation or as region, are older than settler experiences, because Europeans invented a New World centuries before they traded or invaded. Once they arrived they still imagined a wilderness, about which they spoke with either dread or confidence. Written or pictorial information brought back by explorers and travellers, sent back by pioneers to their relatives and to the media, or remembered by early settlers, provided a range of stories that encouraged migrants to move into the new country. By the early nineteenth century the American West also featured in such American literature as James Fenimore Cooper's Leatherstocking series (1823–41). Davy Crockett's autobiography (1834) and its many imitations duly became part of the mass production of American cheap fiction. This early commodification of western literature anticipated the explosion of dime novels, starting in 1860. Real westerners like Davy Crockett, William F. Cody, Kit Carson and Calamity Jane merged with apocryphal characters like Deadwood Dick, Rattlesnake Ned, the Black Avenger and *Malaeska: The Indian Wife of the White Hunter* (1860). Here were 'creation stories' in the making.

Pulp literature was not alone in constructing western imagery in the nineteenth century. Artists early travelled west, either with official survey groups or on their own. The canvasses of such diverse painters as George Catlin (1796–1832), Albert Bierstadt (1830–1902) and Frederic Remington (1861–1909) may not have been viewed by many contemporary Americans, yet audiences for western art were widespread thanks to the cheap and popular reproductions sold to millions by Nathaniel Currier and James Merritt Ives.

Among their representations those of the trapper – that solitary Euro-American adventurer who roamed the Rocky Mountains in the 1820s and 1830s – helped spread the romantic vision of the West, while other prints of the railroad suggested the triumph of white technology and civilisation over nature and savagery. Magazines like *Harper's* published Charles M. Russell's illustrations of western scenes, while photographers, first used on official government expeditions, found that they too had an audience that welcomed visual depictions of the West. But perhaps the most enjoyable nineteenth-century depictions were the Wild West Shows produced by Buffalo Bill Cody. Certainly recent commentators have made much of the fact that Buffalo Bill and Frederick Jackson Turner both 'played' Chicago in 1893 and that it is advisable for those seeking to understand the West to recognise that both versions can be considered either authentic or mythical and that they are both part of the *actual* history of the West.

The twentieth century witnessed yet more portrayals of the West, both popular and intellectually respectable. By far the most widespread were Hollywood Westerns. The cowboy, his guns and his herds of cattle, set against magnificent scenery, have featured as the longest-running and most successful filmic dramas of the history of the West. Even before their popularity peaked in the 1950s they had been transferred to the small screen and were joined by many more versions in television mini series. Their attraction faded in the Vietnam War era, but they made a comeback with cable television and then with the introduction of docu-dramas and documentaries, the latter authenticated by commentary from respected scholars.

The classic West of the cattle trails and the ranch wars also featured widely in the popular literature of the twentieth century. Following the publication of Owen Wister's massive best-selling novel, *The Virginian*, in 1902, cowboys became super heroes. *The Virginian* paved the way for a long line of cowboy stories stretching from Zane Grey, through Max Brand to the modern writer Louis L'Amour, who by the end of the twentieth century had sold nearly 250 million copies of his novels. Traditionally such literature has been regarded as the 'pot boilers' of the frontier mentality, separated in style, though not chronologically, from worthwhile regional writers like Mary Austin, Willa Cather and John Steinbeck, who in turn were distinctly different from the culturally diverse and structurally complex post-regional authors like Larry McMurtry, Marilynne Robinson, N. Scott Momaday, Cormac McCarthy and Amy Tan. In such an organisational framework the regional novelists of the inter-war years created a literature of place, while the post-war writings offered an assortment of minority insights that have deconstructed any western canon. But the 'mythic' West of cowboy novels and the inclusive West of recent literature may not be as mutually exclusive as academic writers have suggested, leastwise as a way of understanding the West, what it means, and how it should be classified.

What is real and what is mythical are often difficult, if not impossible to separate, once literary critics, critical theorists and cultural historians have persuaded readers into thinking about the nature of evidence and the status of values. But if all western portrayals are stories based on personal perceptions and accumulations of individual views, then the West has become a series of relative visions that have stimulated learning, enjoyment and fantasy. The endless discussions that continue to surround George Armstrong Custer and his 'last stand' of 25 June 1876, now known as the Battle of Little Bighorn, are but one example of how historical records, native testimony, archaeological evidence, theories, multiple layers of interpretation, artistic and filmic impressions have combined and overlapped to suggest that Custer was either a flamboyant egomaniac or an upstanding hero and the battle was either a catastrophic defeat or a valiant resistance for the Seventh Cavalry and a triumphant victory or a last stand for the Native Americans. What happened was both fact and perception and what the discussion of western icons alongside western history has accomplished is to emphasise selectivity and cultural filtering. Perhaps the last word should be given to the film star Tom Mix, who in 1938 is reputed to have said 'The Old West is not a certain place in a certain time: it's a state of mind. It's whatever you want it to be'.

Further reading

Cronon, William, George Miles and Jay Gitlin (eds), *Under an Open Sky. Rethinking American's Western Past* (1992).

Etulain, Richard W., *Re-Imagining the Modern American West: A Century of Fiction, History, and Art* (1996).

Goetzmann, William H. and William N. Goetzmann, *The West of the Imagination* (1986).

Hine, Robert V. and John Mack Faragher, *The American West: A New Interpretative History* (2000).

Patricia N. Limerick, *The Legacy of Conquest: The Unbroken Past of the American West* (1987).

Limerick, Patricia N., Clyde A. Milner II and Charles E. Rankin (eds), *Trails: Toward a New Western History* (1991).

Robbins, William G., *Colony and Empire: The Capitalist Transformation of the West* (1994).

Walsh, Margaret, *The American West: Visions and Revisions* (2005).

White, Richard, *It's Your Misfortune and None of My Own: A New History of the American West* (1991).

Wrobel, David M., 'Movement and adjustment in twentieth century Western writing', *Pacific Historical Review*, 72:3 (2003), pp. 393–404.

CHAPTER 7

American immigration

Axel R. Schäfer

D erived from Latin origins, the term 'immigration' denotes not only the movement of people, but also the process of change, of crossing boundaries, of overcoming, even of trespassing. While etymological origins are not always useful indicators of current meanings, in the case of immigration they clearly reflect the term's multiple connotations. Immigration means more than physical relocation. It means packing up and leaving, saying good-bye, breaking with the past, starting over again. Implicit in the migratory process is the questioning of all given relations, traditions, practices and positions. This shared experience of displacement, Oscar Handlin wrote in his classic study *The Uprooted* (1951), made immigration a quintessentially American experience. Immigrants, he noted, 'were on their way toward being Americans almost before they stepped off the boat'.

The dual meaning of immigration as changing places and cultural transformation is invoked in the mythical image of the United States as a 'nation of immigrants' celebrated in college textbooks, during pageants, in the media and in public speeches. Not only did the United States witness the continuous influx of millions of people from an ever-growing variety of ethnic and cultural backgrounds, these newcomers also shared the experience of being strangers in a country where everybody came from somewhere else, where 'nothin' is fixed', as a character in E. L. Doctorow's novel *Welcome to Hard Times* exclaims, and where the process of *becoming*, rather than *being*, constituted the essence of one's existence.

Examining immigration and its place in American history thus means more than just chronicling and measuring the migratory patterns of multitudes of individuals. The study of immigration provides insights not only into the peopling of America, but also explains much about the distinctive cultural characteristics and habits of Americans. It means engaging with a fundamental self-conception of American society in which the mythology of movement and liberation, of not being tied down, of coming into your own, of being all you can be, of lighting out for the territories, and of being judged by your ability and character rather than your origins or creed are powerful narrative components.

This is only one side of the coin, however. In addition to the influx of people from places as different as impoverished nineteenth-century Galicia and war-ravaged twentieth-century Vietnam, and in addition to the forging of new mental habits and cultural practices in the process of dislocation and resettlement, immigration is also at the core of the complex process of American nation-building. This process, which culminated in the twentieth century in the emergence of the United States as the most powerful country in the world, was based on the interplay of three main components: a liberal political order, a national identity based on civic ideals rather than on ethnic homogeneity, and the dynamics of industrial capitalism. However, the flourishing of the United States as an immigration-based nation-state was not simply the result of a great feat of assimilation and inclusion based on republican principles, civic nationalism and free enterprise. Instead, the story of the United States as an immigrant nation reveals the tensions and contradictions between the universalistic and democratic impulses of republicanism, the requirements of the nation-state and the economic demands of industrial capitalism.

What America promised was political freedom, civic equality and economic opportunity. Yet the institutional and ideological forms these promises took frequently helped sustain patterns of inequality. All too frequently republican government was for whites only, ethnopolitics prevailed over political inclusiveness, and capitalism's incessant demand for cheap labour destroyed economic independence. The Korean American businessman who saw his livelihood ruined when his corner store was burned down by African American rioters in Los Angeles in 1992 is as much a part of this 'nation of immigrants' as the Jewish American suburban professional whose grandparents owned no more than a pushcart and a sewing machine in the tenements of New York. The Americans of Japanese descent who were deported to the internment camps in the deserts in the 1940s were as much a part of it as the Cuban American refugees who benefited from government resettlement programmes in the 1960s. And the Mexican Americans living in largely Spanish-speaking enclaves in the Southwest are as much part of the story as the Americans of German descent who repudiated all vestiges of their cultural heritage at the height of the anti-German hysteria during the First World War.

To this day, immigration continues to raise unsettling questions not only about how to cope with ethnic and cultural diversity, but also about the socio-economic inequalities, political exclusions and race discrimination that characterise the political fabric of the nation. No matter whether one emphasises integration or ethnic particularity, economic opportunity or discrimination, the study of immigration is central to understanding the dynamics of a society that combines the universalistic democratic promise with a social and political order that functions on the basis of conflict, exclusion and exploitation.

Immigration patterns

It is not simply the number of people who flocked to America's shores that makes American immigration distinctive. After all, immigration to the United States was part and parcel of the global, and sometimes forced, movement of people to a wide variety of destinations. It was one component in the dramatic process of the rapid peopling of vast and resource-rich areas of the world that accelerated in the nineteenth century in the context of colonialism, imperialism and industrialisation. Between 1820 and 1930, 38 million people moved to the United States, but 24 million moved to Canada, Australia, Brazil, Argentina, New Zealand and South Africa. What makes American immigration distinctive is that it involved a much broader variety of immigrants. Other English-speaking countries drew their settlers primarily from linguistically related areas, and Latin American societies received immigrants mainly from Iberian and Italian backgrounds. In the United States, however, significant immigrant streams from Europe, Asia, Latin America and Africa intermingled, and became part of a single cultural-linguistic space and body politic. All in all, out of a total of 64 million immigrants who entered the United States between the 1820s and the 1990s, more than 8 million people came from Asia, 7 million from Germany, close to 6 million from Mexico, around 5 million each from Italy, Great Britain and Ireland, 4.5 million each from Canada and the lands of the Austro-Hungarian Empire, close to 4 million from Russia or the Soviet Union, a further 3.5 million from the Caribbean, close to 3 million from Central and South America, and over 2 million from Norway and Sweden. Both hybridity and multiculturalism are facts of life in a country where a phonebook in any mid-sized city, particularly in the North and the West, lists names such as Rabinowitz, Kirchmeyer, O'Shaughnessy, Chavez, Nguyen, Van Oosterwijk, Olson and Smith, and where the Korean owner of a restaurant in Texas trains Hispanic workers to prepare Chinese-style food for a largely black clientele ordering their food in English.

Immigration to the United States was a continuous process characterised by dramatic shifts in the numbers and the ethnic and social composition of the newcomers. By the time of the first census in 1790, close to 4 million people lived in the 13 original states and the prospective states of Vermont, Kentucky and Tennessee. Over half of them had come from England or Scotland, about 300,000 each from Ireland and Germany, and almost 800,000 were mainly African slaves. In the early period up to the 1830s, most immigrants listing an occupation were either merchants, skilled artisans or farmers. Little is known about immigration patterns between the 1790s and 1819, when the federal government first required the captains of immigrant ships to report the names and numbers of passengers. Between 1820 and the 1880s, however, a period still referred to as the 'old immigration', about 10 million people entered the United States. Around 3 million new Americans each came from German-speaking regions and from Ireland, 2 million from Great Britain, 600,000 from Canada, 350,000 from Norway and Sweden, and about 300,000 from China.

With the advent of mass immigration the social composition of the newcomers also began to change. Beginning in the 1830s, the number of unskilled and semi-skilled labourers began to increase and the overall skills level fell significantly. Prior to the 1830s, around a third of all immigrants had been farmers, domestic servants or labourers. This percentage rose to over 70 per cent by mid-century. Throughout this period around 70 per cent of immigrants were between 14 and 44 years of age, and roughly 60 per cent were mostly single males. The main exception was the Irish, whose arriving cohorts included a high percentage of single women. On average, the population in the United States increased by almost a third in each decade, and overall the population increased fivefold from roughly 10 million in 1820 to 50 million by 1880.

Between the 1880s and the 1920s, frequently called the period of the 'new immigration', another 24 million people entered the United States. In contrast to previous patterns, dominated by Protestant immigrants from Northern and Western Europe, Catholic, Orthodox and Jewish immigrants from Southern, East-Central and Eastern Europe and Russia now constituted the bulk of the newcomers. Over 4 million immigrants each came from mainly southern Italy and the widespread lands of the Austro-Hungarian Empire. More than 3 million came from Russia, close to a million from China and other Asian countries, half a million from Greece, and 300,000 each from Mexico and Finland. Although immigration from Germany (2.4 million),

Ireland (1.5 million), Great Britain (2 million) and Sweden and Norway (1.5 million) continued unabated, in the period between 1900 and 1914 46 per cent of all immigrants came from Central and Eastern Europe and a further 26 per cent from Southern Europe. By 1920 the American population had more than doubled to over 105 million.

The different ethnic composition also intensified the socio-economic and demographic trends that had emerged by mid-century. Over two-thirds of all immigrants came from unskilled or semi-skilled backgrounds, and the figures remained in this region until the 1920s. The percentage of males rose to close to 70 per cent in the period between 1899 and 1914, and over 80 per cent were of 'productive age', i.e. in the age group comprising 14–44-year-olds. The immigrant workforce not only became more proletarian in character, but also more fluid as remigration rates increased. The conditions of transatlantic travel had much to do with this. In the age of sail-boats, paying for an ocean passage was beyond the financial means of most immigrants, and most could only reach America in the hold of cargo vessels returning with manufactured goods from delivering agricultural goods to European ports, such as Antwerp, Le Havre, Bremen or Hamburg. Thus mass immigration was largely from areas that had direct trade ties with America. By the second half of the nineteenth century the rapid expansion of railroads and the advent of steam travel expanded the range of mass immigration to Eastern and Southern Europe. Steamboat travel replaced the wind-driven sailboats that had made journeys across the Atlantic or Pacific an unpredictable five-week ordeal at best and a three-month nightmare at worst. Not only was the journey time shortened but the trip was safer and, though crowded and uncomfortable, much cheaper. By the latter part of the nineteenth century, an immigrant could reach the United States in less than two weeks for less than $15. This was still a good-sized expenditure at the time, but no longer out of reach for most people. Steamship travel also made it easier to return to the home country after a period of work. Increasingly, immigration was not about moving away, but about going back and forth.

In the wake of restrictive legislation in the aftermath of the First World War, the ethnic and socio-economic composition of immigrants began to shift yet again, though the overall number of immigrants remained remarkably stable. While immigration from Asia was completely banned and low quotas for Southern and Eastern Europe effectively reduced immigration from the former Austro-Hungary and Russia to a trickle, large increases of immigrants from the Western hemisphere, which was exempted from nationality quotas and admissions ceilings, kept up the overall numbers. Some 460,000 new entrants came from Mexico, close to a million from Canada, and thousands more from US possessions, such as Puerto Rico and the Philippines. While about 5.7 million new arrivals entered the United States between 1911 and 1920, between 1921 and 1930 there were only some 4.1 million. But it was the Great Depression rather than restrictive legislation that subsequently brought about a large drop in immigration. By the 1930s, for the first time in US history, the number of people leaving the United States exceeded the number entering. A Soviet trading agency, for example, which advertised for 6,000 jobs, received 100,000 applications from unemployed Americans. Nonetheless, as the influential migration of cultural and scientific élites from Nazi Germany indicates, immigration continued to exert an important influence on American society.

During and after the Second World War, a mixture of restriction, wartime exigencies, and Cold War policy reshaped immigration patterns. On the one hand, the war was responsible for easing the immigration ban on China, now an ally of the United States. On the other hand, citizenship was no obstacle to placing more than 100,000 American citizens of Japanese descent in internment camps. When opportunities for entry were offered to immigrants from India and the Philippines the initial annual quotas were set at the ludicrously low level of around 100 persons per year. Moreover, the United States only issued 250,000 visas to Jewish refugees, and after the war the country admitted only about 400,000 of the roughly 5 million 'displaced persons' from Europe. During the Cold War, however, the United States opened its doors to refugees from communist countries such as Hungary after the failure of the 1956 uprising, and Cuba after Castro's 1959 revolution. Legal immigration in the 1940s and 1950s was running at between 250,000 and 300,000 annually. It was also the case that between the 1930s and the 1970s the percentage of professionals and skilled workers again increased among legal immigrants. Altogether, between 1921 and 1960, although the population grew from 105 million to 180 million, only 8 million new immigrants arrived on American shores.

The past few decades have seen another shift in immigration patterns, with the percentage of professionals and skilled workers falling again and the majority of newcomers coming from Asia, Latin America and the Caribbean. Before 1965 90 per cent of immigrants were Europeans. By 1985 this figure had dropped to roughly 10 per cent. In the mid-1960s the Cold War global political involvement of the United States and the abolition of the racially based quotas played a significant role in this transformation. Between 1961 and 1997 almost 7 million people came from Asia. In addition to immigrants from South Korea, China, Taiwan, Korea and the Philippines, many refugees came from Vietnam, Cambodia and Laos in the aftermath of the Vietnam War. Over 5 million newcomers came from Mexico, close to 3 million from the Caribbean and 2.5 million from Central and South America.

Since the 1970s immigrants from Asia have made up a third of all arrivals, while Mexican immigrants have accounted for another 21 per cent. Together they comprised the bulk of the 22 million newcomers. Moreover, between the Second World War and 1990 2.5 million refugees gained access via special legislation. In many large port cities, such as New York and Los Angeles, Americans of European origin are rapidly becoming a minority. With current demographic and immigration trends continuing, Americans tracing their ancestry to Europe will be a minority by 2030. Overall, immigration had doubled to close to 600,000 per year by the 1980s, and if one adds in illegal immigration, which, though difficult to measure, was running at an estimated 300,000, the number of immigrants per year reached approximately one million. Since the 1930s the gender composition has changed somewhat, with males comprising about one-half of all immigrants and the percentage of immigrants over the age of 45 rising to almost 16 per cent. Overall, the population has now increased to over 270 million.

These figures, however, need to be taken with a grain of salt. Immigration records are often spotty. Illegal immigration has run high at all times, particularly since the Second World War. Moreover, immigration was not a one-way street. A sizeable proportion of immigrants were 'birds of passage' who returned to their homelands after working and earning money for a period of time in America. Particularly in the late nineteenth and early twentieth centuries, close to a third of all immigrants went back to their homelands only to return and be counted again. Remigration rates, however, differed significantly across the ethnic spectrum. While Italians and Greeks were among the groups with the highest rates, Eastern European Jews were among those with the lowest. Although the US government stopped collecting data on remigration in 1957, rates for certain countries, particularly in the geographically closer Western hemisphere, are thought to have topped 40 per cent. Estimates of the Immigration and Naturalization Service (INS) show that since the 1960s about one in five immigrants returned home.

Motivations and settlement patterns

Scholars often discuss the complex motivations for immigration in terms of 'push' and 'pull' factors. Population pressure, land shortage, industrialisation and natural disasters figure most prominently among the former. After the mid-1700s, as a result of improved medical care, sanitation and food supplies, European infant mortality rates declined, life expectancy increased and populations grew. The ensuing land shortages – in conjunction with natural disasters such as the potato famine in Ireland, the undercutting of cottage industries by mechanised industrial production, and the enclosure of common lands by landlords – led to a massive displacement of population.

Yet why would people flock to the United States, rather than to, say, Latin America, Australia or Russia? The expectation of higher wages, the availability of inexpensive and abundant land, the lure of political, religious and economic freedom, a reputation for a distant military and government, the clever marketing of promoters, and 'letters from America' which were read out aloud in taverns and public places in the old country were among the main motivations. Particularly among the single young males seeking to make it in the world, who constituted the bulk of immigrants, America embodied the various conceptions of the good life nurtured by European cultural imagery of the age of Enlightenment and Romanticism: the freedom of the emancipated individual; the righteous living of the thrifty and independent farmer; the ease and luxury of the landed gentry; and the larger-than-life experiences of the heroic adventurer.

In contrast to the rhetoric of the 'melting pot', many immigrants clustered around certain regions, frequently retained their ethnic identity, and imprinted their cultural practices and institutions on to their settlement areas. During the colonial period and into the early Republic, New England and the Chesapeake were largely settled by people from the British Isles. While New England was dominated by Puritan migration of more prosperous family groups, the Chesapeake region attracted large numbers of poorer single males, often from Scots-Irish backgrounds. The Middle colonies, particularly the cities, were more ethnically diverse. New York, for example, had a strong Dutch presence, and almost all the German newcomers settled in Pennsylvania.

Immigrants in the nineteenth and early twentieth centuries were not evenly spread across the land. Most settled in a triangular area ranging from New England down the coast to Washington DC and westwards to St Louis. Few ventured to the South with its legacy of racial division and nativist sentiment, and its lack of job opportunities. As a result, the region remained largely untouched by immigration, except for its larger cities. Of the 4 million foreign-born inhabitants in the United States in 1860, only about 500,000 lived in the slave states. This helped shift the demographic balance in favour of the North. By the time of the Civil War, only one out of three Americans lived in the South, and it has been estimated that one-third of northern soldiers and one-half of the workforce in the North were immigrants.

Many of the Irish Catholics who came in mid-century, frequently single men or women, settled in the eastern cities such as Boston and worked in canal and later railroad building and domestic service. The Germans, who frequently arrived in family groups and tended to be well-off farmers, skilled artisans and shopkeepers, often settled in the new cities and rural areas of the Great Lakes, the upper and lower Midwest and the upper South. Cities such as Milwaukee, Cincinnati and St Louis were largely German. Many Scandinavians flocked to the upper Midwest and the Plains region, with Minneapolis-St Paul as their centre. The latter two groups also established a strong presence in the Pacific Northwest and the future states of Oregon and Washington. The Chinese lived almost exclusively in West Coast cities and western railway towns, working in railroad gangs, mines and small urban businesses. Italians and Eastern European Jews showed little inclination to move to the land and become farmers. Most settled in northeastern port cities, working in the garment industry, manufacturing, construction, heavy industry or mining. Many lived in cramped rows of tenements in more or less segregated ethnic neighbourhoods. In the late nineteenth and early twentieth centuries it was they who provided the manpower for America's rise to industrial might.

Three-quarters of the post-Second World War immigrants settled in six states: California, New York, Texas, New Jersey, Florida and Illinois. Most of the Mexicans moved to Californian and Texan cities and provided the main labour force for irrigation agriculture of southern California. Puerto Ricans clustered in the northern cities, and Canadians in mill towns and rural areas of New England, while the Chinese, Koreans and Vietnamese settled mainly in California. Since the 1960s in particular, the West Coast has emerged as a premier settlement area, with more than a third of new-comers planning to live in California.

In short, what made the United States distinctive was not the number of people it attracted, but their ethnic diversity, as millions of people from Europe, Asia, Latin America and Africa intermingled. The periods when the number of immigrants was highest were characterised by a growing percentage of unskilled or semi-skilled male arrivals. Mostly they settled in the Northeast, Midwest and West, largely bypassing the South. Being in their prime of life, they provided the main source of labour for the industries of America's burgeoning capitalist system.

Immigration policies and the liberal state

Numbers and statistics rarely tell the whole story. Mass immigration is part and parcel of the political, social and economic history of the United States, particularly its rise as a unified nation-state and an industrial powerhouse. In the final analysis, immigration helped define the republican form of government, American nationalism, and the capitalist economy in ways that often defy the mythical image of the land of freedom and opportunity.

To many immigrants, one of the fundamental promises of American life was that republican values and institutions would overcome ancient prejudices, feudal dependencies and medieval privileges that had divided, categorised and constrained the peoples of Europe for centuries. In true Enlightenment fashion, those who shaped the new nation believed in universal human rights, the capacity for self-government, political egalitarianism, religious toleration and economic independence, and they declared their aspirations in a public and intelligible constitution.

Though rendered in universal language, the nation's founding documents were nonetheless often bereft of universal intent. In many ways republican ideology was tied to specific ethno-cultural settings and modes of production. It reflected the bourgeois culture, property-based conceptions of political participation, and Protestant beliefs of Anglo-Saxon colonists who frequently used the language and principles of popular sovereignty, constitutional government and natural rights to justify the exclusion of African Americans, women, immigrants and native peoples. They invoked the language of republican virtues and proprietarian individualism to declare excluded groups unfit for self-government due to their alleged lack of moral agency, reason and economic independence.

This historical conjunction of racialism and democracy in the liberal state made the very existence of republican institutions dependent upon racially sanctioned exclusions. Immigration policies were an important, if frequently symbolic, political, economic, legal and cultural strategy for asserting white rule over excluded groups. Although the ringing words of Emma Lazarus's poem inscribed on a tablet in the pedestal of the Statue of Liberty proclaim, 'Give me your tired, your poor/Your huddled masses yearning to breathe free/The wretched refuse of your teeming shore./Send these, the homeless, tempest-tost to me/I lift my lamp beside the golden door!', American immigration policies have never been quite that welcoming. Already during the early Republic they exemplified the tension between universal aspiration and ethno-cultural categorising, confining the rights associated with citizenship largely to free whites.

Throughout the history of the United States, both state and federal immigration policies attempted to regulate and control the influx and movement of people by means of a wide variety of restrictive policies, ranging from laws excluding convicts and paupers to alien registration acts and bans on those with contagious diseases. Nativist fears, economic calculations, humanitarian impulses, ethno-cultural politics and global politics have all at different times shaped the size and composition of the immigrant stream. Not all these laws, however, were formulated with immigrants in mind, and many were often poorly enforced. Nonetheless, the history of restrictive legislation highlights how racial and ethnic categorising formed the ideological sediment of the liberal state under the conditions of industrial capitalism. It also shows that the functioning of republican institutions was predicated upon shifting definitions of 'whiteness' that subsumed European ethnic divisions while at the same time sustaining racial discriminations.

A plethora of colonial and state laws regulating the treatment of criminals and paupers, public health, slavery and racial subordination controlled the cross-border movement of people prior to the advent of a codified federal immigration policy in the 1880s. Since the transportation of convicts from Britain to the American colonies caused widespread outrage, to the extent that Benjamin Franklin suggested sending rattlesnakes to England in return, state laws prohibiting the importation of felons became part and parcel of restrictive policies and were included in the first federal statute restricting European immigration in 1875. These exclusions were closely linked to the notorious poor laws, conflating criminals and paupers and making immigration law a main instrument in limiting the civil rights and free movement of the poor.

Inherited from English poor laws, state statutes gave local communities power to inhibit the settlement of people deemed likely to become public charges. As more and more poor immigrants arrived at American shores, many of them were not entitled to 'settlement' under poor laws and remained permanently subject to deportation and the threat of removal to state workhouses. In 1882 bans on the entry of a 'lunatic, idiot, or any person unable to take care of himself or herself without becoming a public charge' were written into federal statutes regulating immigration and have played an important role in federal law ever since. This also shows the extent to which political and civil rights in the liberal state were tied to a producer-class ideology, which ultimately justified the granting of political rights on the basis of an individual's perceived capacity for productive work.

Public health considerations, while more innocuous on the surface, were often difficult to disentangle from racial and ethnic stereotypes. Health inspectors at Ellis Island, who looked at hands, faces and hair, and snapped back eyelids with button hooks to check for cholera, smallpox, trachoma, syphilis or 'feeble-mindedness', often used health criteria to enforce racial exclusion. By the same token, the concerns of urban reformers about diseases spread by unsanitary conditions were frequently couched in language that denounced the cultural practices of the 'queer conglomerate mass of heterogeneous elements . . . with a taint of whiskey'. Images of Italian mothers giving wine to their babies, Irish juveniles terrorising neighbourhoods, swarthy and bearded immigrants clad in strange dress living in the 'alien enclaves' of the urban slums and practising 'popery and superstition' became code for middle-class fears associated with urban life, industrial capitalism, poverty, crime and overcrowding. Genuine concerns about the welfare of immigrants among reformers were thus difficult to separate from the desire to impose middle-class norms, the urge to create a disciplined industrial workforce, and the impulse to hamper immigrant political organising.

Similarly, politically motivated restrictions, harassments and deportations had been part and parcel of immigration laws since the beginning of the Republic. The 1798 Alien and Sedition Acts, for example, provided the legal justification for arresting and deporting political radicals, imposed an alien registration system, and raised the naturalisation barrier by extending the residency requirements for citizenship to 14 years. Although most of these acts were either ignored or repealed a few years after their passage, similar legislation was frequently invoked during times of war or crises. The First World War was one of the most blatant examples. The Espionage Act (1917) and the Sedition Act (1918) provided the legislative background for imprisonment, internment, withdrawal of citizenship, deportation and press censorship of critics of the war. Likewise, criminal syndicalism acts passed by states were used to break radical labour agitation, limit rights of assembly and free speech, and officially sanctioned mob violence against immigrant radicals.

Race laws designed to restrict the entry or free movement of African Americans had long been inscribed into a wide swathe of state legislation by the time federal legislation used race for the first time as the basis for excluding immigrants. In both the South and the North, exclusions on the basis of poor laws, criminal records and the denial of citizenship continued to inhibit the free movement of African Americans. These slave and bondage laws received a new lease on life in the 1882 Chinese Exclusion Act which, until the 1940s, outlawed the immigration of Chinese citizens. Largely the result of anti-Chinese prejudices in the West, the act also indicated that support for post-Civil War segregation in the South reflected feelings that transcended regional boundaries.

The Exclusion Act, the only one in the United States ever to ban a specific ethnic group, also marked the beginning of a new era of immigration policy in which powers previously exercised by the states shifted to the federal government. This sea change had been ushered in by a 1875 Supreme Court decision. In *Henderson* v. *Mayor of New York*, the Court declared as unconstitutional the state laws controlling the reception of immigrants, such as state immigration commissions and port authorities, arguing that these usurped the powers of Congress to regulate foreign commerce. The Court's decision effectively ended the decentralised administration of immigration policy. Prior to the late nineteenth century, immigrants had arrived at a variety of ports, none of which had any formal immigration facilities. This changed in 1855, however, when the establishment of the landing depot at Castle Garden marked the emergence of New York as the dominant port of entry.

The fact that the Supreme Court decision coincided with the drive to restrict immigration was a crucial factor in providing the basis for effective and centrally imposed anti-immigration legislation during the ensuing decades. Anti-immigrant sentiments became more widespread as the 'new' immigrants, who formed an urban, low-skilled, non-Protestant working class, flocked to the United States. A key impetus for further restrictive legislation came from the findings of the Dillingham Commission set up by Congress in 1907 to investigate immigration. Chaired by Senator William Dillingham, the Immigration Commission maintained that many of the new immigrants could not be assimilated and were the cause of no small proportion of the country's economic ills. In turn, complex federal laws excluded people on a variety of grounds. In 1891 Congress excluded from admission people likely to become public charges, people with certain contagious diseases, 'convicts, lunatics, idiots' and polygamists. Prohibitions for anarchists and subversives were added in 1903, and laws passed in 1907 excluded people with 'mental defects' and those who had committed crimes of 'moral turpitude'. By 1892 New York's Ellis Island and, by 1910, the West Coast's Angel Island immigration station, had become the first – and sometimes only – stop for many immigrants. In 1917, when existing restrictionist legislation was codified, literacy tests designed to exclude immigrants from Southern and Eastern Europe were put in place. Likewise, an Asiatic Barred Zone, which included all of India, Afghanistan and the Arab countries as well as East Asia and the Pacific, and from which no immigrants could come, was written into the statutes.

Anti-immigrant sentiment, rekindled by the Red Scare, the hysteria of the First World War and the resumption of large-scale immigration from

Italy and Eastern Europe in the immediate aftermath of the war, culminated in the notorious quota laws of the 1920s. The Quota Act of 1921 and the National Origins Act of 1924 dramatically reduced the number of immigrants from Southern and Eastern Europe on the basis of racially and ethnically constructed quotas blatantly designed to favour immigrants from Northern and Western Europe. They also banned completely the immigration of people from East Asia by declaring them 'aliens ineligible for citizenship'. As indicated earlier, however, the primary result of the restrictive laws of the 1920s was not to cut the number of immigrants, but to change their ethnic composition, though not necessarily in the way nativists of Anglo-Saxon descent had anticipated.

In the aftermath of the Second World War, restrictionist laws were gradually loosened. The 1952 McCarren–Walters Act, though retaining limits based on national origins, for the first time set up quotas for previously excluded Asian nations. The landmark 1965 Immigration and Nationality Act finally replaced the quota system based on national origins with equal per-country visa allotments and hemispheric ceilings based on a preference system that privileged certain skills and family ties to US citizens and permanent residents. It also provided opportunities for those without needed skills or family links, and adjustment-of-status options for those who had entered the country as tourists, students or temporary workers. The law, however, imposed numerical limits on immigrants from the Western hemisphere, though provisions for admitting relatives and refugees meant that the quota was frequently exceeded. In effect, the 1965 legislation allowed increasing numbers of Asians, Latin Americans, Caribbeans and Africans to enter the country. Moreover, refugee legislation, such as the Cuban Adjustment Act of 1966 and the Refugee Act of 1980, not only put the status of those fleeing their homelands on a clearer legal footing but opened the way for hundreds of thousands of them to enter the United States.

Legislation passed between the 1970s and 1990s created a uniform system and gradually increased both regular and refugee admission quotas. Support for immigration from a diversity of countries prevailed over the legacy of restrictionism and the desire for cultural homogeneity. In 1986 the Immigration Reform and Control Act for the first time provided for an amnesty for illegal immigrants. By the mid-1990s around 3 million undocumented persons had been granted permanent residence. In the same vein, the Immigration Act of 1990 increased numerical limits and skills-based preferences, sought to diversify sources of immigration, clarified the complex security and health-related grounds for exclusion and deportation, and repealed the ban on communists.

By the early 1990s, however, restrictionist sentiment was on the rise again. The failure on the part of Congress to provide an effective system enforcing the law prohibiting the employment of undocumented workers, stories of people smugglers, porous borders and the high concentration of many immigrants in a small number of states engendered fears of ethnic and cultural besiegement among many Americans of European ancestry. In contrast to the early part of the century, however, few opponents of immigrations were openly racist. Instead, they took recourse to social policy as a symbolic vehicle for infusing their sentiments into the immigration debate. In 1994 a majority of voters in California passed Proposition 187, which barred illegal immigrants from receiving health care, welfare and educational benefits, and required service providers to report suspected illegal immigrants to the Immigration and Naturalization Service (INS). Although the new law was ruled unconstitutional, the effective grass-roots campaign and electoral success gave an indication of the new restrictionist mood. It is also no coincidence that half the savings attributed to the landmark 1996 federal welfare reform legislation were due to the restrictions it placed on immigrant access to welfare and social security benefits. The image of immigrants as welfare scroungers was thus a way of asserting racial stereotypes without having to resort openly to discredited racism.

In summation, the history of immigration policies shows that the liberal state, while laying claim to universalist principles of political equality, democratic participation and equal protection under the law, frequently inscribed particular ethno-cultural norms and racially based exclusions. It is a reminder of the American dilemma of the tensions between the republican promise and the effective denial of citizenship rights.

Immigration and American nationalism

The contrast between universalist democratic aspirations and exclusionary practices also challenges the myth that ethnic identities merge into the American creed that transcends ethnic loyalties. In the same way as exclusionary practices were at the core of a putatively democratic political order, American nationalism, while claiming to overcome ethnic particularities, was an amalgam of nativism, pluralist assimilationism and outright ethnopolitics. Ironically, demarcating ethnic and racial particularity was a core component in the construction of an American national identity.

Basic to the success of the United States as a nation has been its ability to construct a powerful nation-state by integrating people from a wide variety of ethnic, linguistic, cultural and religious backgrounds without provoking major religious warfare, ethnic schisms or systematic persecution. In the words of historian David Hollinger in *Postethnic America: Beyond Multiculturalism* (1995), the United States 'is endowed with a *non*-ethnic ideology of the nation', but 'possessed by a predominantly *ethnic* history'. In marked contrast with the European model of building advanced industrial nations within the framework of ethnic nationalism and homogeneity, the United States amalgamated diverse ethnic groups into a single cultural-linguistic space and a national identity based on civic culture, constitutionalism and commitment to democratic values. Public schools, the workplace, the armed forces, higher education, civic interaction and cross-cultural intermarriage are often identified as the main agents of assimilation. Sometimes called the 'melting pot', 'assimilative pluralism' or even the 'genius of American politics', this remarkable combination of ethno-cultural diversity with national unity and loyalty to the country's institutions has been mythologised by St John de Crèvecoeur in his *Letters from an American Farmer* (1782). 'He is an American, who leaving behind him all his ancient prejudices and manners, received new ones from the new mode of life he has embraced, the new government he obeys, and the new rank he holds', this acute European observer of life in America wrote. '[H]ere individuals of all nations are melted into a new race of men'.

In many ways, however, this non-ethnic ideology is the problem, rather than the solution. The emergence of an American identity and successful nation-state is only in part based on the ability of liberal democracies to cope with diversity by means of political participation and economic opportunities. The successful participation of immigrants in American life was more commonly predicated upon ethno-political self-assertion and ethnic institution building. Although the right to political participation itself was derived from republican principles of citizenship, the acquisition of effective political power was often through urban party machines built on ethnic foundations. Party machines in many urban centres, such as Boston and New York, for example, relied upon the Irish or Italian vote. Likewise, immigrant institutions, such as churches, self-help societies, fraternal lodges, schools, universities, hospitals, banks, credit unions, insurance organisations and newspapers were often the key to gaining access to economic resources, jobs and social status. Ethnic political organising and institution building made immigrants both stronger and more vulnerable. They provided opportunities for socio-economic advancement and political influence, even though they become at times the focus for nativist attacks and political marginalisation. What is crucial, however, is that most immigrant groups created different religious, economic, family and church structures, while at the same time claiming an American identity. The more recent resurgence of ethnic particularism in the aftermath of the civil rights movement can be understood as yet another manifestation of ethno-racial 'identity politics' that ultimately turned out to be a step towards, rather than away from, participation in American life.

This indicates that the American experience was as much about the persistence and creation of ethnic differences as about commitment to shared values and institutions and assimilation into a common culture. Well into the twentieth century the United States remained a nation of ethnic enclaves and neighbourhoods, many immigrants never feeling the need to learn English because they spent their lives among people from their own country or region. In *Boss: Richard Daley of Chicago* (1971) journalist Mike Royko noted about Chicago in the 1950s: 'The neighbourhood towns were part of larger ethnic states. To the north of the loop was Germany. To the northwest Poland. To the west were Italy and Israel. To the southwest were Bohemia and Lithuania. And to the south was Ireland'. To this day, the United States contains viable ethnic, religious and linguistic subcultures ranging all the way from those of the Native Americans to those of the Amish of Pennsylvania and Ohio.

Ironically, immigration to the United States was often deeply implicated in shaping national and ethnic identities in Europe itself, showing once again that although ethnic categories are contingent and socially constructed they have real social and political consequences. The language of nationality is largely an invention of the nineteenth century and became a reality largely in the context of the legal and bureaucratic classification of immigrants. Many immigrants who came from Southern and Central Europe prior to the creation of the Italian and German nation-states in the 1860s and 1870s saw themselves as Sicilian or Thuringian, rather than as Italian or German, until that identity was imposed upon them by the social experience of immigration. In the same vein, Czechs and Slovaks, divided by religion, socioeconomic development and status within the Austro-Hungarian Empire, would find the American experience one that made their Old World differences appear much less relevant and helped lay the foundation for the first Czechoslovak state after the First World War. Ethnic labels were similarly fluid and often depended on the locality in a country where immigrants settled. Upon moving to New Mexico or Texas, a resident of the state of New Jersey of French Canadian origin may well find that he or she will be considered an Anglo. Finally, in one of the most curious examples, the United States became a major source of armaments, money and supplies for the Irish fight for independence from Britain, while at the same time the English and the Irish in the United States were largely indistinguishable from another because both were classified as whites.

By the twentieth century, ethnic categorising had largely replaced traditional distinctions based on religion. Throughout a large part of the nineteenth century religion, rather than ethnic origin, defined the position of immigrants in the United States. Many Protestants from places such as Norway, Sweden and northern Germany found access to resources, careers and status much easier than Catholic, Orthodox, Greek, Catholic or Jewish immigrants from southern Germany, Poland, Ireland, Mexico, Russia or Greece. Likewise, the nativist impulse of the Know-Nothing Party and the ubiquity of 'No Irish need apply' signs in the 1850s was mainly directed against the perceived threat authoritarian and hierarchical Catholicism posed to republican institutions. Although religion remained important on a social level, the nation-state and its bureaucratic apparatus classified immigrants according to a set of ascribed ethnic and racial characteristics. Though increasingly laying claim to scientific objectivity, these categories were highly malleable. Irish immigrants, who in the nineteenth century were often considered to be barely above 'Negroes', were seen as 'white' in the latter part of the century.

In spite of a long history of discrimination, particularly after the Mexican-American war in 1848, it was never clear where Mexican Americans belonged on the racial scale. In the 1920 census they were counted as whites. By 1930 they had been assigned a separate Mexican category. By 1950 they were again white. Today they are collapsed into a broad category called Hispanics. After many transmogrifications, federal civil rights law in the United States today recognises six mutually exclusive racial and ethnic categories: American Indian, Asian, African American, Hispanic, Pacific Islander and White. Not until the 2000 census were Americans able to mark more than one category, reflecting the high intermarriage rates, cultural intermingling, multiple identities and growing level of comfort with racial hybridity. However, this has thrown decades of policy making into disarray by complicating civil rights enforcement, anti-discrimination monitoring, voting rights and reapportionment, and targeted social programmes.

In short, racial and ethnic categories written into state and federal law determined the debate about immigration and the process of assimilation to a much larger extent than the notion of America as a land of opportunity based on common ideals. American national identity, rather than dissolving distinct ethnic affiliations, categorised immigrants on the basis of shifting clusters of discreet bio-cultural groups into which traditional cultural, regional and religious identities were collapsed. Within this iden-tity, 'whiteness' became the normative core that allowed for the diminu-tion of differences between European immigrants.

Immigration and industrial capitalism

Finally, we need to consider the relationship between immigration and free enterprise, which held out the promise of economic opportunity without regard to race or creed. Being closely intertwined with the growth of industrial cap-italism under the auspices of the liberal state, the rags-to-riches myth has been an integral part of the American dream for many immigrants, holding out as it does the promise of economic opportunity. Noting in an interview with the *Wall Street Journal* that she still had her second-hand sewing machine, which she had bought in order to support herself, Ruth Westheimer, a German Jewish refugee and well-known therapist, added that 'part of my per-sonal American Dream is the hope that I'll never have to use it again'.

There is little doubt that immigration was ultimately economically ben-eficial both for the majority of immigrants and for the national economy of the United States. Though there is great controversy about this, numer-ous studies show that immigration has not depressed wage levels overall, though it often had this effect over short periods of time. Findings by econ-omic historians indicate that three-quarters of immigrants arriving in the United States between 1840 and 1850 had moved up the economic ladder. In general, the nation's expanding economy, urban growth, fluid social struc-tures and the continuing influx of people created a setting in which immi-grants thrived. Labour participation rates were high, and the growing market created by the newcomers helped absorb productivity gains. Moreover, immigration mainly attracted those of an ambitious and inventive turn of mind anxious to get ahead. Despite lower wages many were able to accu-mulate capital, meanwhile contributing to the nation's overall wealth by paying taxes. As most people emigrated in their prime, the expenses for their schooling having been paid abroad, it was an arrangement that profited both the United States and the immigrants themselves.

In light of these findings there is a tendency to associate pro-immigration sentiments with enlightened and tolerant multiculturalism, and to view restric-tionist campaigns solely as expressions of racism and bigotry. Nothing could be further from the truth. The call for restrictions has as often as not been indicative of the way economic élites have successfully pitted differ-ent ethnic groups against each other. By the same token, the advocates of open immigration have been less interested in high-minded ideas about cultural diversity than in ensuring a continuous supply of cheap labour. As the historian Matthew Frye Jacobson has put it, 'economically, the United States could never get quite enough "multiculturalism"'.

Immigrants working on railroads, in textile mills and in mines provided a ready pool of cheap and easily replaced labour to operate the industrial machine. Because immigrants could be hired at lower wages than native workers they significantly reduced the cost of production. Employers' reliance upon cheap labour also promoted the shift from skills-based production to use of machinery operated by unskilled and semi-skilled workers. This, in turn, created economies of scale and encouraged mass production. It also brought about economic inequalities and an ever growing gap between rich and poor. In the early nineteenth century the northern economy had been dominated by the independent yeoman farmers and artisans idealised by Thomas Jefferson. However, the subsequent growth of cities, industrial capitalism and factory production led to wealth being concentrated in the hands of small élites. In 1840 the nation's richest 1 per cent controlled about 20 per cent of all wealth, a significant proportion of it being tied up in slaves. By the end of the century, in spite of the abolition of slavery, the proportion had increased to around 30 per cent. A typical business unit in the nineteenth century was owned by individuals or small groups. By the turn of the century this had changed, with large consolidated corporations exerting disproportionate economic and political control over the nation's affairs, as exemplified by the fact that the five major railroads were owned by two banks.

Many restrictionists saw limits on immigration as a way of strengthening the bargaining power and organising capacities of labour unions. The conservative craft-based American Federation of Labor (AFL) made immigration restriction one of its main political goals. It fought the importation of cheap labour in the same way business used protectionist tariffs to fight the importation of cheaper foreign goods. The AFL and other unions clearly recognised that unskilled or semi-skilled immigrants, frequently single young males interested in seasonal labour, willing to work long hours and often difficult to unionise, provided a cheap and constantly replenished labour pool and created intense job competition that drove down wages. The availability of cheap labour also speeded up the process of industrial deskilling and mechanisation. Jobs traditionally requiring trained mechanics and artisans, who exercised a measure of autonomy and control over their workplace, were replaced by mechanised and repetitive tasks in large factory settings, where managers oversaw the routine work of unskilled labourers.

Restrictionist campaigns on the part of labour unions, however, came at a great cost. They effectively cemented the ethnic, skills-based and gender divisions that had formed the bedrock of the cheap labour economy. Poles and Italians, as well as women and African Americans, were commonly excluded from labour organisations dominated by 'old stock' Americans of Irish or English descent. Many labour unions forestalled the creation of effective cross-ethnic and cross-racial alliances by organising skilled labourers along craft lines, shunning both industrial unionism and the unskilled. As a result, the story of American immigration is riddled not only with strikes against factory owners but with inter-ethnic conflicts between Irish, Polish, African American, Mexican American and other groups of workers. The reason why so few African Americans migrated to the North before the First World War was not only the continuous influx of European immigrants, which cut off job opportunities, but also the virulent racism of many white workers.

The extent to which immigration and socio-economic conflict were intertwined was nowhere more apparent than in the American West. By the mid-nineteenth century the West, where Indians, Europeans, Asians, Africans and Latin Americans intermingled, had become the country's most ethnically and racially mixed region. Gold Rush California and the Great Plains, in particular, were noted for having exceptionally high percentages of foreign-born immigrants and for being segmented largely along racial lines. Far from resembling the melting pots celebrated by frontier theorists, they were societies in which the status of the individual depended largely on a mixture of skill and ethnicity, managerial and skilled occupations being mostly in the hands of white Europeans while the rest of the workforce was largely made up of unskilled Chinese, Mexicans and Filipinos. Divided into different social tiers and organised in different unions, each eyed the other with suspicion. Employers exploited these divisions, using the newly arrived foreign workers to undermine union organising and to break strikes. In the aftermath of the strike wave in the 1890s, western railroads, accurately recognising that the ethnic homogeneity of the workforce had contributed to the cohesion of the strike movement, actively set about recruiting Japanese, Eastern European, Mexican and African American workers in order to create job competition, drive down wages and break unions.

The 'wageworkers' frontier' in the often isolated mining and lumber camps and company towns of the West was thus characterised on the one hand by the constant attempt by business to replace skilled, expensive labour with cheaper unskilled immigrant labour, and on the other hand by the efforts of craft-based unions to retain workplace control and autonomy by means of racial exclusion. Attempts at forging cross-ethnic labour ties by creating industrially based unions – such as the Western Federation of Miners and the International Workers of the World – provoked a ferocious backlash from employers and their political henchmen. As in the South, where invoking the 'colour line' also sustained the stranglehold of economically powerful élites, western capitalists often resorted to playing the race card.

To sum it up, what is often forgotten in the fashionable celebration of 'cultural diversity' and the 'contributions' of various immigrant groups is that the growth of American industrial capitalism has depended in no small measure on deliberately exploiting ethnic differences in pursuit of corporate profit. Paradoxically, America's patterns of integration and exclusion have helped keep alive socio-economic tensions while at the same time contributing to the nation's economic success.

Conclusion

The United State is a 'nation of immigrants', not just because it became a destination for millions of people, but because immigration is at the core of the country's national identity and its capitalist economy. The success of the United States as an immigrant nation, however, is not simply the story of how people from a wide variety of countries and continents were integrated on the basis of republican principles, civic nationalism and free enterprise. Rather, the study of immigration provides insights into both the unity and the fissures of American society. Republicanism, while presenting itself as embodying universal norms and values, effectively racialised democracy by tying the preservation of republican institutions to racial hierarchies and exclusions. Civic nationalism, claiming to integrate and overcome ethnic particularities, frequently made economic power and political influence for immigrants dependent upon the assertion of 'identity politics' and ethnic institution building. And the system of free enterprise, while promising economic opportunity, helped foster racial and ethnic conflict to sustain the supply of cheap labour.

What makes the study of immigration and its relationship to American history especially intriguing is that these conflicting patterns are constituent elements of the functioning of the United States as a liberal capitalist nation-state. The shifting boundaries between political participation and exclusion, ethnic assimilation and segregation, and economic opportunities and exploitation helped conceal the contradictions between republican ideals, civic nationalism and industrial capitalism. The story of the American immigrant experience is thus about how newcomers positioned themselves within these shifting definitions, how they themselves effected shifts in the way ethnic boundaries were drawn, and how these changes, while sustaining new exclusions and discriminations, helped perpetuate the myth of the United States as the 'land of the free'.

Further Reading

Barkan, Elliott Robert, *And Still They Come: Immigrants and American Society, 1920 to the 1990s* (1996).

Borjas, George J., *Heaven's Door: Immigration Policy and the American Economy* (1999).

Gjerde, Jon, *Major Problems in American Immigration and Ethnic History: Documents and Essays* (1998).

Jacobsen, Matthew Frye, *Whiteness of a Different Color: European Immigrants and the Alchemy of Race* (1999).

Mink, Gwendolyn, *Old Labor and New Immigrants in American Political Development: Union, Party, and State, 1875–1920* (1986).

Neuman, Gerald L., *Strangers to the Constitution: Immigrants, Borders, and Fundamental Law* (1996).

Peck, Gunther, *Reinventing Free Labor: Padrones and Immigrant Workers in the North American West, 1880–1930* (2000).

Reimers, David M., *Unwelcome Strangers: American Identity and the Turn Against Immigration* (1998).

Suro, Roberto, *Remembering the American Dream: Hispanic Immigration and National Policy* (1994).

Takaki, Ronald T., *Strangers from a Different Shore: A History of Asian Americans* (1986).

Websites

Arizona State University Im/migration web page: www.asu.edu/clas/history/asu-imm

H-Net Humanities & Social Sciences Online – H-Ethnic (online discussion group with many links to resources): www.h-net.org/~ethnic

Immigration and Ethnic History Society (provides useful links): www.iehs.org

CHAPTER 8

Nineteenth-century American literature

Allan Lloyd Smith

E uropean, and particularly British, writers dominated the American literary landscape at the beginning of the nineteenth century. Not only were the Europeans able to draw on established traditions, they also spoke to a much larger audience, and in the absence of a copyright agreement their books could be published in the new United States as cheaply as any local productions and, much to the advantage of the publisher, without payment to the European author. The American readership was small and, apart from the few urban centres of Boston, New York and Philadelphia, both scattered and agricultural. Booksellers acted as publishers and frequently ran small lending libraries. A fair proportion of the population was illiterate, many were foreign born, and most were busily engaged in finding a livelihood. To make matters worse a widespread prejudice in religious and community leaders held that reading fiction and poetry tended, if not to deprave entirely, at least to encourage wrong principles and inhibit forceful action. Young people in particular were thought to be at risk of moral damage and of being led into a dangerous fantasy life by the suggestions of romances and the then popular form of the gothic. So at this point a life as a professional author was unfeasible and attempted by very few.

One who did make the venture into professional writing was Charles Brockden Brown, a young Philadelphian then resisting family pressure to become a lawyer. Brown produced four novels in less than two years (1798–9): *Wieland, Arthur Mervyn, Edgar Huntley* and *Ormond*. None of these books made literature financially viable as a career, but together they resulted in his subsequent canonising as the 'father' of the American novel. Nothing could be less fatherly than the riotous gothic fictions of murder, conspiracy, somnambulism and guilt his pen produced, but a filial anxiety is evident in these novels and it may well be that the recent overthrow of the British parent government, an effective regicide in symbolic terms, together with concerns about the chaotic forces unleashed by the even more recent French Revolution, had some effect in his imaginative productions. Certainly he sent a copy of his tale of a fatherless family, *Wieland*, to Thomas Jefferson, perhaps only in hope of an influential champion, but perhaps also having in mind the book's implication that an unguided freedom may be catastrophic. If the Wielands' little utopian democracy results in Theodore Wieland's religious lunacy and murder of his family then the suggestion could be that the larger utopian democracy of Jefferson's vision also risked tragedy.

Brown's lurid stories were based on a realism of sorts: Wieland's story came from a newspaper article and Brown frequently expressed his belief that science would lead to explanations of even the most irrational behaviour. In this he was a product of the Enlightenment culture of his late eighteenth and early nineteenth-century milieu. A scientific interest provided justification for exciting and morally questionable fictional themes, which he argued to be legitimate contributions to knowledge. He was also imitating the English novelist and social philosopher William Godwin, whose gothic novel *Caleb Williams* explored injustices of class and the British legal system by portraying the persecution of a servant who learns of his master's act of homicide. The gothic novel was at the peak of its popularity at this time, partly as a result of the Enlightenment openness to investigation of new areas of thought and society, including aberrant psychology and extreme actions. Brown, like Mary Shelley in *Frankenstein* or James Hogg in his *Confessions of a Justified Sinner*, used the fashionable gothic form to explore vexed social, scientific and psychological issues then coming into focus, rather than to investigate the legacies of feudal oppression and nostalgia for a vanishing past that characterised the work of Ann Radcliffe and the earlier gothicists. In this he anticipated Poe, Hawthorne and the later American writers in this form, setting the agenda that led Leslie Fiedler later to observe in *Love and Death in the American Novel* (1966) that American fiction has been 'bewilderingly and embarrassingly, a gothic fiction, non-realistic and negative, sadist and melodramatic – a literature of darkness and the grotesque in a land of light and affirmation'.

By the first decade of the 1800s the popularity of gothic fiction had declined, and it had become material for satirical treatment. Thomas Love Peacock's *Nightmare Abbey* (1818) and Jane Austen's *Northanger Abbey* (1803, 1818) both mocked the genre, and when Washington Irving touched on it in 'The Tale of the German Student' (1824) or 'Dolph Heyliger' (1822) it was with a comic turn. In the expansive and increasingly prosperous new United States his genial disdain for European traditions and dark visions of the past seemed more appropriate. Irving's great contribution to the new literature expected of the new nation was to invent an indigenous folk past in stories like 'Rip Van Winkle' (1819) or 'The Legend of Sleepy Hollow' (1820). To do so Irving focused on the old Dutch communities of New York State, revising stories from European folk tales to fit American circumstances. The tales were embraced as authentic American traditions and have remained popular instances of an American mythology despite – or because of – their self-admitted element of spoofery.

Across Europe at this time dedicated collectors of folk tales and ballads like Walter Scott were compiling anthologies of ancient culture, in an effort partly inspired by the growth of nationalism and a romantic search for the spirit of peoples and place that could legitimate and inspire the nationalist ideals. The new United States had fewer legends to draw upon, being constituted by people from a range of different national origins who were not inclined to celebrate its truly indigenous, that is Native American, traditions. Irving's old Dutch communities could therefore be seen as a suitably safe and unifying celebration of an American folksy antiqueness, a tongue-in-cheek version of the Europeans' search for their historic national identities. In fact if we look closely at Irving's stories they offer an ironic subtext that comments on ideological issues disguised within the search for supposed origins. In 'The Legend of Sleepy Hollow' the ungainly Ichabod Crane stalks the neighbourhood as a peripatetic Yankee schoolmaster, related to the 'Jonathan' caricature of New Englanders at the time. His greedy attention fastens upon Katrina von Tassel, plump daughter of a local farmer, with an eye to winning the fertile farmlands along with the daughter. Ichabod is seen off by Katrina's Dutch suitor, Brom Bones, who exploits Crane's Cotton Matherish superstitiousness and a local legend of a headless horseman to send him running. But Ichabod's subsequent career is successful, Irving hints; and in fact the economic and political invasion of the old Dutch fiefdom in New York State by the Yankees was historical fact by the time he wrote the tale.

Similarly, 'Rip Van Winkle' tells the timeless (originally German) tale of a man who sleeps for 20 years after drinking from a magic flagon. As Rip's 20 years' sleep includes the period of the Revolution, he wakes to a changed world of urgent politics outside the new hotel instead of the old village inn. Irving's story is of the recent rather than the timeless past, and it contains political satire in that the villagers have retained the picture of George III of England as the pub sign, simply relabelling it 'George Washington'. Irving was born and grew up New York City during the years of the Revolution when the city was forced to host the British, and he was named Washington in honour of the American leader. He would have been aware that the Dutch-speaking villages of New York State were largely Royalist, as the unchanged sign in the story subtly suggests, in opposition to the villagers' overt Republican protestations.

Irving's life as a professional writer illustrates something of the American literary situation at this time. For his first publications he used pseudonyms: Diedrich Knickerbocker for *A History of New York* (1808), or Geoffrey Crayon, Gent, for *The Sketch Book* (1819) in accordance with the view that writing should properly be only an amateur activity for a gentleman, whose real identity would be protected. His style conformed to the elegant usage of Addison or Steele, and for most of his career he responded to the appeal of Europe, describing English life and tales in *Bracebridge Hall* (1822) and *Tales of a Traveller* (1824). In the later 1820s Irving lived in Spain, producing historical accounts and biographies such as his *Life and Voyages of Christopher Columbus* (1828) and *The Alhambra* (1832). In 1829 he became secretary to the American Legation in London, returning to the United States in 1832, when he wrote several accounts of the American West, including *A Tour of the Prairies* (1835), perhaps in response to the view that he had become too much of a European. But in other respects his position differed from most contemporary writers, especially so in that his success in the European market was well rewarded by his publishers, who were able to assume a British copyright for works first published in Britain up until 1849, when a judge ruled this illegal.

Most Americans had neither his success in finding British publishers, nor the rewards that should have come from European publication. Hawthorne's books, for example, were freely pirated and sold in cheap editions in Britain, even on station bookstores, without recompense to the author. In the American market publishers could pirate the works of the best foreign authors such as Scott or Dickens for nothing, but to publish an American would be more expensive because of the need to pay royalties, making these books higher priced. Unless an American author had private means, therefore, a literary career involved work as editor of a magazine (for Brown the *Monthly Magazine and American Review*, for Poe the *Southern Literary Messenger*), or at least as a frequent contributor to the many newspapers and journals that thrived in the first half of the century.

James Fenimore Cooper was an exception to these constraints, inheriting a fortune at the age of 20. He became the first successful serious American novelist with his five Leatherstocking books: *The Pioneers* (1823), *The Last of the Mohicans* (1826), *The Prairie* (1827), *The Pathfinder* (1840) and *The Deerslayer* (1841). Despite time-consuming and obsessive lawsuits, which did his reputation much harm (as when he refused picnic-goers their traditional practice of using a point on his land at Otsego Lake), Cooper wrote many other novels and political commentaries. These included *The Spy* (1821), about Harvey Birch, an unacknowledged patriot secret agent in New York State during the American Revolution; *The Bravo* (1831), a historical thriller set in the Venice of the Doges; and *The American Democrat* (1838), setting out his own political reservations about the new Republic. Cooper's clumsy style, which was splendidly pilloried by Mark Twain in 'The Literary Offences of James Fenimore Cooper' for its ridiculous plots and leaden humour, requires a certain patience of the reader, but this need not obscure the power of his narrative drive or the significance of his insights into the American world.

The first of Cooper's Leatherstocking books is *The Pioneers,* in which Natty Bumppo (also known as Leatherstocking, the Pathfinder or Hawkeye) makes his first appearance, in this instance as an old man about to be driven west by the restrictions and laws of increased settlement, which see him locked up for shooting deer out of season. The novel centres around the need for laws, but also the inadequacy and intrinsic unfairness of the law, in a complex meditation brought out through illustration – as in the evident unreasonableness of penalising Natty for his modest and necessary shooting, while allowing the settlers their wasteful destruction of entire flights of pigeons by cannon, and the netting of excessive amounts of fish, beyond what they could conceivably eat or preserve – but also plot issues concerning rightful ownership.

Judge Marmaduke Temple, the owner of these lands, became rich through the trust placed in him by Oliver Edward's father, Colonel Edward Effingham, a British Loyalist in the Revolutionary War, which makes young Oliver Edwards a rightful – if not technically the legal – heir. Behind his claim, however, is the claim of Chingachgook, the Mohecan (or Mohican) chief, now an old drunk known as Indian John, who eloquently explains how the contested land was taken from the original inhabitants. Whether or not wampum was accepted for the lands, the validity of the Indian claim seems irrefutable, and Cooper was unable to address it, instead simply settling the rival Temple/Effingham claims by the timeworn device of a liaison between Elizabeth Temple and Oliver Effingham at the conclusion; a spurious resolution that was to appear again at the end of Hawthorne's novel *The House of the Seven Gables* in 1851.

The right to ownership of the land concerned Cooper through his own family history, but primarily he responded, like all the writers of this period, to the awesomeness of the land itself. This is no kindly landscape; it is rather a nature that is inimical to humans whatever puny efforts are made for its containment. It was his responsiveness to the power of the landscape that became Cooper's great novelistic strength and brought his initially quaint figure of the aged frontiersman Natty Bumppo to the imaginative centre of his books, instead of the comparatively stiff plots of romance and social interactions that were supposedly their subjects. The land compels respect, and in its darker modes produces a kind of natural gothicism of the dark forests and the terrors of a sublime landscape, peopled by hostile Indians and endlessly threatening a labyrinthine disorientation in those who, unlike Natty, are unversed in its mysteries. But in Cooper's larger tale, seen through the whole series of novels, he offers what might be called a sort of gigantic pastoralism: ultimately an optimistic vision offset by pathos and reservations about what is being lost in the great westward expansion that came to be legitimated as 'manifest destiny'.

That darker side of magnificent American nature persists throughout the literature of the nineteenth century, appearing in novels such as William Montgomery Bird's *Nick of The Woods* (1837), in which a demented Indian-killer leaves a bloody cross drawn on the breasts of his victims. The Indians believe this to be an evil spirit, called the Jibbenainosay, but he is in fact an outwardly pacifist Quaker, aptly named Nathan Slaughter, who has been driven insane by the treacherous murder and scalping of his wife and children by the Shawnee Chief Wenonga. The darkness of the landscape is visible again, if obliquely, in Poe's tales and poetry, especially in his strange novel *Arthur Gordon Pym* (1837), now displaced on to the South Pacific, as it is too in Herman Melville's *Moby-Dick* (1850) in the chapter on the whiteness of the whale, which deals with a horror at the centre of nature, expressed through the terror that whiteness can evoke in the soul. The beauty and the terror of American nature produced inevitably a dual response. There was, on the one hand, a celebration of its serene magnificence and supposed beneficence of the kind to be seen in the work of Emerson, Thoreau and Whitman. Alternatively, there was a stricken dismay at its violence and cruelty, including the fears of the settlers with, possibly, a sense of original sin and guilt derived from the Calvinist doctrines of the Puritan originators of the culture; and also, the repressed awareness of an underlying genocidal treatment of its indigenous people, together with the enormous guilt of the use of slavery in this utopian world.

Edgar Allan Poe, a southerner who was disappointed in his early aspirations to be a part of that doomed antebellum aristocracy, wrote tormented versions of the fall of feudal society in 'The Masque of the Red Death' and 'The Fall of the House of Usher', where nature, turned malign, enters the privileged realms as degeneracy, collapse and death. When Poe imagined aboriginal society it was, as in Pym's imaginary ultimate southland of Tsalal, with horror, as the home of treacherous black natives with black teeth, who abhor the colour white; 'the most wicked, hypocritical, vindictive, blood-thirsty, and altogether fiendish race of men upon the face of the globe'. This is a land seemingly inscribed with ancient messages in the shape of the fissures with which it is riven, spelling out the Ethiopian root 'to be shady', the Arabic 'to be white' or in Egyptian 'the region of the south', according to Poe's spoof editorial commentary, which he concludes by quoting 'I have graven it within the hills, and my vengeance upon the dust within the rock'. Like the Weir lands of his mysterious poetry, this place is haunted, already written (with echoes within Tsalal language of the writing on the wall at Belshazzar's feast, 'mene mene tekel upharsin': 'thou art weighed in the balance, and found wanting'), suggesting the curse on the sons of Ham (or black people), but beyond that, as in Poe's poetry, a tragic nature itself.

In his sense in this novel of a preordained tragic nature, Poe was perhaps in keeping with the Calvinist roots of the dominant American culture, but distinctly out of step with its present expansionist commercial and political optimism, and with his near contemporaries Ralph Waldo Emerson and Henry David Thoreau. They, along with Margaret Fuller, William Ellery Channing, Bronson Alcott and other reformers, constituted the transcendentalist group centred around Emerson's village, Concord, and their Boston publication, *The Dial*, in the 1830s and 1840s. This movement also saw nature as a kind of writing, a message from beyond, but saw it, following Emerson, as a tranquil apparition that shines benevolently around us, a reassurance from a pantheistic God, present through all things in an emblematic nature. Poe was scathing about the transcendentalists and their Boston 'frog puddle', mainly through personal and professional spite, but it could be reasonably argued that he himself also held to an inchoate belief in some pantheistic principle behind the surfaces of the universe – as his prose-poem cum astronomical thesis *Eureka* explains – and that he had simply failed to understand the fundamental rethinking of perception that underlay Romantic metaphysics.

Of reading Coleridge, Poe said: 'I tremble, like one who stands upon a volcano, conscious, from the very darkness bursting from the crater, of the fire and light that are weltering below'. The shift in gestalt that informs such poems as 'The Ancient Mariner' or 'Depression, an Ode', in which it is not the thing perceived but the involved perceiver, the act of perception itself that creates true meaning; this appears to have escaped him. In terms of M. H. Abram's clarifying account of Romantic epistemology in *The Mirror and the Lamp* we might say that Poe remained on the eighteenth-century Enlightenment part of the divide, staring into the mirror rather than becoming the illuminating lamp that creates and transfigures. Or, we might say, banging on the doors of the crypt; because Poe's formulation of the supernatural as quite another realm, the 'mystic', led him to a series of tales and poems that dramatise in effect the funeral moment of his period's extravagantly funereal culture. His protagonists approach the grave, believing, hoping – indeed dreading – that there is something beyond, but they constantly fall back, given the answer 'Nevermore' (by the Raven) or 'now – now – I am dead' (by the corpse of M. Valdemar). Berenice's communication from the grave is in the rattle of her ivory teeth falling from a box on her cousin's desk; Madeline Usher rises from the dead to fall back, taking her brother with her; an idly daubed sail magically spells out a word when it is hoisted in 'MS Found in a Bottle', spelling out as in an ironic mirror only the protagonist's own quest: 'DISCOVERY'.

Something of the Coleridgean idea of the imagination as transformative power informed Nathaniel Hawthorne's speculations as much as Poe's. But where Poe looked for an alternative realm in the 'mystic' – the supernatural regions verging on the occult or revelations sought if never found beyond the grave – Hawthorne looked for a more particular transfiguration of the everyday by the imaginary and, conversely, a recognition of the real within the fanciful. He set out this dialectic most cogently in the 'Custom-House' introduction to *The Scarlet Letter* (1850), in which he writes of the 'neutral territory, somewhere between the real world and fairy-land, where the Actual and the Imaginary may meet, and each imbue itself with the nature of the other'. The penchant for the 'mystic' acted it seems as a sort of defence against the disturbing material to which 'romance' might give expressive freedom. In *The Marble Faun* (1860), for example, Hawthorne's profound horror at his themes – the lake of blood that constitutes Roman history, the diabolism of his gothic Capuchin monk/model, incest and parricide embodied in his sculptress Miriam with its roots in the terrible real life of Beatrice Cenci, and the act and consequences of murder – is offset by the fanciful speculations about one of his characters' supposed faun's ears, and displaced into the safer realms of art appreciation. Even here, however, Hawthorne suggests there is no escape: Hilda restricts herself to copying masterpieces exactly but in doing so exposes herself to the dangers of voyeurism and consumption by the forces she tries to distance, while Miriam's inner self is exposed in the sculpture Kenyon makes of her as Cleopatra, and in the pictures she herself paints, of vengeful women committing atrocities, like the painting of Judith holding up the head of Holofernes, or Jael driving the nail through the head of Sisera.

In the tales making up his *Legends of the Province-House* Hawthorne explored how the past might be rediscovered imaginatively through the medium of romance. 'Lady Eleanore's Mantle' is a commentary on the fatal nature of pride and, at another level, her pox-ridden shawl is a representation of the infection of tyrannical and aristocratic Old World values. As Evan Carton puts it in *The Rhetoric of American Romance*, 'The mantle, "on which a dead woman embroidered a spell of dreadful potency", is passed from British to American hands; the taint it conceals is the price of the authority it manifests'. That the source of infection is ultimately the oppressed poor of England should also be noticed, and as this instance suggests, Hawthorne's work is at once allegorical and more complex than allegory is usually understood to be: he produces unfolding and ambiguous allegories that resist interpretative finality.

Such over-coded signifying objects are characteristic of Hawthorne's work: a shawl, a portrait that contains some secret, a black veil worn without explanation by a minister, a magic well fed by the spring that is the ultimate (and historical, material, political) reason for a family curse, and of course, the scarlet letter itself. When this structure works it produces a resonance that invites the reader to choose some particular interpretation while suggesting that to stop there would be to miss some further meaning: like those who read the celestial scarlet letter in a meteor, and think that it refers to the death of Governor Winthrop, or see the letter that Hester wears as signifying either adulteress or angel. Her little daughter Pearl's imitation of the letter in eel grass should be sufficient reminder that its meanings are not so simply pinned down. That letter is fresh and green, a renewal, but it is also implicitly satanic, in that the choice of *eel* grass hints at the presence of the serpent.

The cascading allegories become dazzling in 'Rappaccinni's Garden', which engineers an Escher-like reversal of field and ground: is it the garden and Beatrice that are poisonous, or Giovanni and the rest of the world? Is this garden a version of Eden – and if so, is Hawthorne promoting the infamous Gnostic heresy that Satan is the true redeemer, bringing knowledge to an oppressed Adam? All that rummaging Hawthorne did in the attic of the Old Manse he rented in Concord (where Emerson had recently written his famous essay 'Nature' in 1836) makes his knowledge of such heresies more than plausible.

Like Cooper, Hawthorne complained of the lack of a usable history for American writers. In his influential essay 'Nature', Emerson had deplored the opposite: 'Our age is retrospective. It builds the sepulchres of the fathers. It writes biographies, histories, and criticism. The foregoing generations beheld God and nature face to face; we, through their eyes. Why should not we also enjoy an original relation to the universe?' But Hawthorne, Cooper – and later Henry James – thought that the determined present tense of America, where 'actualities' were so 'terribly insisted upon' as Hawthorne put it in his preface to *The Marble Faun* (1860), was damaging to the writer's creativity. Harthorne continued:

> No author, without a trial, can conceive of the difficulty of writing a Romance about a country where there is no shadow, no antiquity, no mystery, no picturesque and gloomy wrong, nor anything but a common-place prosperity, in broad and simple daylight, as is happily the case with my dear native land. It will be very long, I trust, before romance-writers may find congenial themes either in the annals of our stalwart Republic, or in any characteristic and probable events of our individual lives.

This particular whistling in the wind was of course in the face not only of his already written American romances and tales, but precisely in the teeth of the historical tempest: the American Civil War began the very next year. And it must be added that many other writers as well as himself had in fact found congenial themes in the annals of the Republic, even in the accounts of Salem witchcraft that underlay his great *Scarlet Letter*, which provided the basis for John Neal's Rachel Dyer (1828), as well as more general annals of the Republic, mined by James Fenimore Cooper in several novels besides his Leatherstocking series: *The Spy* (1821), *The Wept of Wishton-Wish* (1829) and *Satanstoe* (1845), to mention a few, or by James Kirke Paulding in his *Westward Ho!* (1832).

In poetry, too, there were efforts to find suitable American resources for a national literature. Four poets in particular – Whittier, Longfellow, Holmes and Lowell – were regarded as the representative poets of their time, from the 1830s until as late as the 1880s. Theirs was a public poetry, in several senses. First, they were immensely popular, Henry Wadsworth Longfellow especially so after his 'Hiawatha' in 1855. Second, they engaged with public themes: the founding myths of the nation and its politics, as in John Greenleaf Whittier's 'Ichabod' (1850), an attack on the great orator Daniel Webster over his advocacy of the Fugitive Slave Law, part of the infamous 1850 compromise with the South:

> All else is gone; from those great eyes
>   The soul has fled:

> When faith is lost; when honor dies
>   The man is dead!

Whittier devoted much of his life to antislavery polemics, both as poet and as newspaper editor, as opposed to the more occasional abolitionism of James Russell Lowell in his vernacular *The Biglow Papers,* or Longfellow in 'The Slave's Dream'.

If in one aspect the Boston poets emulated a Tennysonian grandeur and sonorosity, in another they worked towards a very ungenteel American freshness and simplicity – what Whittier called his 'Yankee pastoral'. It was an element to be seen in later poetry by Robert Frost or William Carlos Williams, as well as Edward Arlington Robinson, and before them in Whitman and Thoreau. Besides such poems as Whittier's famous 'Snow-Bound' can be placed Oliver Wendell Holmes's satire of the logical religious system of Calvinism, 'The Wonderful "One-Hoss-Shay"' (1858), as a contraption that lasted perfectly for a hundred years but then

> Went to pieces all at once, –
> All at once, and nothing first, –
> Just as bubbles do when they burst.
>
> End of the wonderful one-hoss-shay.
> Logic is logic. That's all I say.

These poets were also public in another sense: this was poetry to be read aloud to the family around the fireside. There perhaps lies both the reason for their success and for the later rejection of their work as overly polite and unduly rhythmical and melodic. This is poetry that means what it says – and nothing more. The element of predictability and complacency, its irrefutable confidence, makes it difficult for readers now to accept, just as the insistent rhythms that gave this poetry coherent form when read aloud seem to jar when considered in silence. But a work like Longfellow's 'Cross of Snow', written in response to his beloved wife Fanny's tragic death through burning at the domestic hearth, demonstrates the considered and deeply felt power that might be achieved at the intersection of public statement and private trauma.

Against the patriarchal culture of these Boston Brahmins Emily Dickinson's poetry voices the response of the Other. Silenced, in that she never published her work, and intensely private, to the extent of reclusiveness, she adopted neither the public certainties of the genteel tradition nor its easy recuperations of meaning. Her idiosyncratic punctuation, extensive ellipsis and interest in fragmentation, together with a personalised vocabulary and personification of abstractions, make it doubtful that she would have received any significant audience even had she been an outgoing and astutely self-promoting poet. Holmes might mock at the old stark religion as a decrepit shay, but Dickinson felt it in the bone, and took questions of spiritual being to be no laughing matter. Oddly enough, her nearest contemporary in terms of style – and to some extent subject – was Edgar Allan Poe, whose poetry similarly forced rhythm to its limits and beyond, and aspired to move past the ordinary meanings of words towards some further realm of enigmatic abstraction. Dickinson's poems often seem to offer lyrical expression of Poe-esque situations:

> As if my life were shaven
> And fitted to a frame,
> And could not breathe without a key,
> And 'twas like midnight, some . . .

or:

> As all the heavens were a Bell,
> And Being, but an Ear,
> And I and Silence, some strange Race
> Wrecked, solitary, here.

Without Dickinson's exquisite rhetorical scalpel, Poe's poetry nevertheless seems to hail from the same realms, from 'an ultimate dim Thule – / From a wild weird clime that lieth, sublime, / Out of space – out of Time'. Like hers, Poe's insistent rhythms contradict while controlling the shapelessness of the experience attested, to the point when, as in 'The Raven', that insistence becomes almost a joke, the irony of a meaningless response to hysterical personal grief. Marginal in very different ways, both writers reach for gothic tropes when seeking to address ontological disaster.

The American transcendentalists could pursue the 'mystic' with an enthusiasm the equal of Poe's, and the invocation of divine afflatus hangs about the work of the lesser figures of this group like a miasma around some philosophical House of Usher. Bronson Alcott's 'Orphic Sayings' provide excellent examples (this reformer, Louisa May Alcott's eccentric father, would not grow root vegetables, allowing only those vegetables that aspired upwards). But Emerson and Thoreau understood the power of Romantic philosophy to spark across the gap between self and world defined by Lockean materialist views in which the mind receives and reflects upon sensations that must always be separate from either the self or the world. In that view the inner self must always be an exile, able only, as Coleridge says about the stars in his ode 'On Depression', to 'see, not feel, how beautiful they are'.

The Romantic position derived somewhat tenuously from Kant's argument that abilities to understand such categories as space and time must be already inherent in the mind; it was extended by speculators like Novalis towards a celebration of intuition as opposed to merely calculating knowledge. In the act of perception both self and world are created, and so the world is not simply some pre-existing other to be viewed in different lights but is actually brought into being for the subject by its apprehension. That insight opens up new reaches, not only for the possibility of an integrated life, but also for the possibility of art as a meaningful interaction between the self and the no longer endlessly alienated otherness of the world. Thus Whitman was able to claim: 'See, steamers steaming through my poetry'. His implication is that a full realisation of the act of perception in words can be equivalent to the thing perceived in 'real' life.

It followed that any one person's experience or intuition of life would be equivalent to any other's; that in fact truth could not be taught or handed on, but must be the product of immediate experience, felt on the pulse. That produced the paradox of an essayist and orator such as Emerson advising his audience not to listen to others, even himself, but to find truth in themselves and their own experiences. 'Trust thyself', he boomed in 'Self-Reliance': 'every heart vibrates to that iron string'. It also produced an interest in the concrete, living, phrase that would induce the appropriate experience in the audience, as is caught here, where the generality that every heart 'vibrates' is immediately anchored by the particularity and weight of 'to that iron string'. With the same sure sense of an exact correspondence between image and idea, he advocated that the healthy attitude would be 'the nonchalance of boys who are sure of a dinner', complaining instead that 'man is as it were clapped in jail by his consciousness', and 'society everywhere is in conspiracy against the manhood of every one of its members' but 'nothing is at last sacred but the integrity of your own mind'.

Emerson's confidence in the rightness of this individualist independence had him advocate that we 'affront and reprimand the smooth mediocrity and squalid contentment of the times', and made him sure that 'no man can violate his nature' as 'all the sallies of his will are rounded by the law of his being'. This rested upon his argument that 'the primary wisdom' is intuition, while 'all later teachings are tuitions' and, in that 'deep force, the last fact behind which analysis cannot go', all things have their origin. To these involuntary perceptions a perfect faith is due, because 'perception is not whimsical, but fatal'. And what lies behind intuition? That is where we find Emerson the child of the Puritans, the ex-Unitarian minister, secure in his belief that

> the Supreme Being, does not build up nature around us, but puts it forth through us, as the life of the tree puts forth new branches and leaves through the pores of the old. As a plant upon the earth, so a man rests upon the bosom of God; he is nourished by unfailing fountains and draws at his need inexhaustible power.

Emerson might play with the idea of deviation from accepted moral truth: 'if I am the devil's child, I will live then from the devil. No law can be sacred to me but that of my nature' he asserts in 'Self-Reliance'; but this freedom is founded on the belief that, as he says in 'Nature' (1836), 'the moral law lies at the center of nature and radiates to the circumference', and therefore it follows that a true faith in oneself will be moral.

Emerson's version of heroic individualism can be understood against the context of American frontier experience, the optimism of western expansion and industrial growth and the relative material security and prosperity of the New World. His thought is also rooted in some of the central tenets of Puritanism: the requirement of individual accountability before God, the need for self-scrutiny and honesty, the valuing of other qualities than the material, and the belief that the natural world is emblematic: 'The visible world and the relation of its parts, is the dial plate of the invisible'. To this he added the shift into subjectivity begun by Kant and developed by the Romantics, Berkeleyan idealism, and some of the elements of eastern philosophy. In the assumption that the world is as it must be, his philosophy was politically and socially quiescent: 'Discontent is the want of self-reliance: it is infirmity of will. Regret calamities if you can thereby help the sufferer' he instructs, 'if not, attend your own work and already the evil begins to be repaired'. More disturbingly, he argues that 'Power is, in nature, the essential measure of right', and even, anticipating Nietzsche: 'The doctrine of hatred must be preached, as the counteraction of the doctrine of love, when that pules and whines'. Emerson can celebrate the 'iron face' of grinding debt as a teacher 'needed most by those who suffer from it most', and he sees the inequality of property as being like snow: 'if it fall level today, it will be blown into drifts tomorrow', according to 'the surface action of internal machinery, like the index on the face of a clock'.

Equally, Emerson's philosophy has revolutionary import. Emerson might not himself be the devil's child of the antinomian heresy he suggests, but his doctrine of self-reliance empowers everyone to live according to their own perception, whether that be of the rightness of things or the view that the time is out of joint. Indeed, he increasingly thought it so himself, saying 'in Christendom where is the Christian?' and speaking of the need to move out from the shadow of the past, or, of the corruption of language, how we must 'pierce this rotten diction and fasten words again to sensible things'.

Henry David Thoreau took Emerson's inspirations seriously, building himself a cabin in the woods to test out his ability to live independently of the joint-stock corporation of society, and looking for the meanings of nature with a naturalist's close attention. Thoreau went to the woods to live deliberately, to reduce life to its essentials and see what it contained. That he should do so by building a cabin with his own hands out of cheap materials and growing or catching his own food aligns him with the frontier ideology that promised land and fortune to the enterprising; that he should build it on Emerson's land and make regular visits home for dinner suggests the largely symbolic nature of his venture. Two years at Walden Pond were condensed into one in *Walden* (1854), so that his book could follow the flow of the seasons. Better than any other production of the transcendentalist ethos, Thoreau's book shows how the vision of integration in and through nature could express a transfigured perception. He developed Emerson's intuition that the appearances of nature may be metaphorical, seeing his lake as an emblem of the human soul, frozen then 'alive again', reflecting the sky and yet of unknown depths. His naturalist's observation of the patterns in thawing sand and clay on the banks of the nearby railroad cut makes him think of lichens, coral, birds' feet or leopards' paws, brains, lungs or bowels – a 'grotesque vegetation'; and he concludes, seeing the similarities in these shapes, that 'The Maker of this earth but patented a leaf'.

Walden is a call to wake up, a reminder suitable to American perceptions of a new life in a new world, that life is now, and not some other time: 'Some are dinning in our ears that we Americans, and moderns generally, are intellectual dwarfs compared to the ancients, or even the Elizabethan men. But what is that to the purpose? A living dog is better than a dead lion'. At the same time, Thoreau disputes the frantic purposes of most American improvements and ambitions, noting that it takes more time to earn the money for a railroad ticket than it would to walk the distance, and observing that the 'sleepers' of the railroad are the bodies of those who died in its building. 'Why should we be in such desperate haste to succeed,' he asks, 'and in such desperate enterprises?'

Thoreau's early effort at a sort of performance art, making his life an experiment in living, a reformist colony of one, looks less distinctly odd in the speculative context of the 1840s. He was not the only experimenter engaged in a reassessment of the conditions of social and individual life; in fact the woods were full of them. In his study *The Communistic Societies of the United States,* Charles Nordhoff counted over 2,000 such experiments; some small, like Thoreau's, others becoming quite large, such as the George Rapp's colony at Harmony in Pennsylvania and its offshoot, New Harmony in Indiana. The small town of the Indiana colony was later bought by the English reformer, George Owen, only to go under due to the divided aims of its members; the original Rappite settlement, Harmony, remained peopled by a group of millenialist believers who were opposed to marriage and hence ever dwindling, until finally just six were left to inherit another sort of earthly paradise, when oil was discovered on the land and the Humble Oil Corporation (which was to become a founding part of Esso) was born.

Even the sceptical Nathaniel Hawthorne briefly succumbed to the attractions of alternative life, when looking for a home for himself and his bride-to-be Sophia, sister of the transcendentalist reformer Elizabeth Peabody. Along with George Ripley and Margaret Fuller, Elizabeth Peabody was a major proponent of Brook Farm, the utopian socialist project that Hawthorne joined in 1841. Their idea was that poetry and manual labour on the farm might go hand in hand in an elevated but natural lifestyle. Afternoons of shovelling farmyard manure soon taught Hawthorne the contrary, and the experience left him with both a protracted lawsuit to try to recover his investment and the material for a biting satire of the communitarian impulse, *The Blithedale Romance* (1852). Hawthorne was closely if uncomfortably connected with the transcendentalists. He and his new bride lived for a time in the same Old Manse at Concord where Emerson had earlier written his essays and lectures. He even bought Thoreau's rowing boat (although he changed its Indian name to 'The Pond Lily'). In the woods around Concord he would meet – and more often attempt to avoid – various adherents of the Emerson cult, including especially the charismatic feminist Margaret Fuller, whom he later satirised as the beautiful free-living Zenobia in *The Blithedale Romance*. Hawthorne portrays his idealistic Blithedalers as visionaries of more style than substance, engaged in elaborate pantomimes of the pastoral and likely to be found at convenient moments back in town dressed in their usual finery.

Thoreau's more serious refusal to accept the dictates of others, or even of the state itself, fetched him up in jail for refusing to pay his taxes, arguing that 'under a government which imprisons any unjustly, the true place for a just man is also a prison'. In his 'Resistance to Civil Government' (1849), an address reprinted as 'Civil Disobedience' and which has become enormously influential after his lifetime, Thoreau spelled out his political credo:

> When a sixth of the population of a nation which has undertaken to be the refuge of liberty are slaves, and a whole country [Mexico] is unjustly overrun and conquered by a foreign army, and subjected to military law, I think that it is not too soon for honest men to rebel and revolutionise. What makes this duty the more urgent, is the fact that the country so overrun is not our own, but ours is the invading army.

Such independence of thought and insistence on personal action is at once the strength of the transcendentalist reformist impulse and yet also its weakness. Thoreau considered that 'any man more right than his neighbors, constitutes a majority of one already' and elaborated his belief in the power of withdrawal from implication in acts of the state when he claimed:

> I know this well, that if one thousand, if one hundred, if ten men whom I could name, – if ten *honest* men only, – aye, if *one* HONEST man, in this State of Massachusetts, *ceasing to hold slaves,* were actually to withdraw from this copartnership, and be locked up in the county jail therefor, it would be the abolition of slavery in America. For it matters not how small the beginning may seem to be: what is once done well is done for ever.

Whatever weakness there is in this position, Thoreau's aphoristic arguments had powerful effects in the development of strategies for political opposition; the doctrine of peaceful non-resistance also inspired Ghandi in India, and subsequently civil rights and Vietnam protests at home. Thoreau's inspirational call for a life within rather than against nature has continued to inform movements for the protection of wildlife and landscape, and more recently the ecology movement.

But the ideas of the transcendentalists had more immediate literary consequences: Walt Whitman in particular acknowledged his debt to Emerson: 'I was simmering, simmering, Emerson brought me to the boil'; just as later American poets were in turn to see in Whitman a pioneering breaker of stale traditions: as Ezra Pound put it, 'I owe a debt to you, Walt Whitman'. Whitman's sense of the organic interconnection of all things, his democratic recognition of life as being like the leaves of grass, leading him to obliterate hierarchies by using parataxis, and even simply listing of sensory impressions, came at least in part from Emerson's revitalising openness of vision. A chain of insights links Thoreau's appreciation of the excremental organic quality of the patterns in thawing mud with Emerson's Idealist argument that

> A correspondent revolution in things will attend the influx of the spirit. So fast will disagreeable appearances, swine, spiders, snakes, pests, mad-houses, prisons, enemies, vanish; they are temporary and shall be no more seen. The sordor and filths of nature, the sun shall dry up and the wind exhale. (*Nature*, 1836)

In the same vein, Emerson's belief that 'there is no object so foul that intense light will not make beautiful' seems to be behind Whitman's willingness to extend the subjects of poetry, to include the 'unpoetic', not only the 'mystic amorous night' but also the 'sluff of bootsoles' and 'the blab of the pave'; how 'The suicide sprawls on the bloody floor of the bedroom' and 'The malformed limbs are tied to the anatomist's table / What is removed drops horribly in a pail'. Emerson's sense that 'it is not words only that are emblematic; it is things which are emblematic' and thus 'every natural fact is a symbol of some spiritual fact' informed Whitman's search for the true poetic images – the steamers steaming through the poetry – that anticipated and later in part inspired the modernist search for the 'adequate' natural image. But less intransigently optimistic contemporaries had their doubts.

Herman Melville could not avoid the influence of transcendentalist ideas, but he incorrigibly saw the other weight in the scales. Throughout his writing there is an awareness of suffering, inequity and even a malignity in man and nature. In *Moby-Dick*, although Ishmael subscribes to nature's 'linked analogies' to some extent, the true proponent of Emersonian doctrines of self-reliance and idealism is Captain Ahab. Ahab agrees that nature is merely a mask of appearances, behind which lies the deeper truth . For him, however, that deeper truth is evil:

> All visible objects, man, are but as pasteboard masks. But in each event – in the living act, the undoubted deed – there some unknown but still reasoning thing puts forth the mouldings of its features from behind the unreasoning mask. If man will strike, strike through the mask! How can the prisoner reach outside except by thrusting through the wall?

The result of Ahab's trusting of his intuitions, and striking out for man against the pantheist spectre, is catastrophe, although his destruction, a correctly prophesised fatality, ironically proves the madman right.

Melville's whaling ship is also a factory, an outpost of the industrial order, and one with hints of an American imperialist mission. With personal experience of the American presence in the south seas, and, of course, of whaling ships and naval life, Melville took a pessimistic view of the emerging national identity. He commented powerfully on the effects of the missionaries in the Pacific in *Typee,* urban poverty and despair in *Redburn* and *Israel Potter,* industrialisation and the oppression of women in 'A Tartarus of Maids', abuses in the navy in *White-Jacket* and *Billy Budd,* slavery and slave rebellion in 'Benito Cereno', and technology and slavery in his story 'The Bell-Tower'. Much of his political and social commentary was oblique, no doubt because he was well aware that his audience did not want to accept it, and perhaps also because he had a complex mind that did not settle easily into any one perspective. As Hawthorne said of him after a meeting in England, 'He can neither believe nor be comfortable in his unbelief; and he is too honest and courageous not to try to do one or the other'. 'Benito Cereno' is both a critique of slavery and an implication of complacent North Americans in its practices, and yet at the same time a racist account of some immitigable evil in the black leader of the insurrection, Babo. 'You are saved', says the northern Captain Amasa Delano to the slave-ship's captain Benito Cereno, at the end of the story. 'What has cast such a shadow upon you?' 'The negro', Cereno replies.

'Bartleby the Scrivener' can be read as an indictment of the commercial system of Wall Street that turns workers into robotic objects at the whim of their autocratic employer, or, equally, as an existential fable about the power of negativity in the individual. 'I prefer not to', insists Bartleby, and refuses to follow instructions, ultimately at the cost of his life but to the subversion of the lawyer's complacent world picture. 'The Tartarus of Maids' explores the appalling working conditions of mill girls working in a paper factory up in the New England mountains, slaves to giant machinery and dying from consumption brought on by their conditions of work. An insistent undertext establishes that the girls are emblematically also victims of *nature*'s machinery; the female reproductive mechanism is represented in the factory process, which takes exactly nine minutes to develop the paper pulp from its two giant vats full of 'white, wet, woolly-looking stuff', through a room of a 'strange blood-like abdominal heat' into the final sheets, all under the supervision of the manager (named Cupid). At the end of the sequence a giant machine impresses each sheet with a little heart, ironically signalling the commodification of sentiment that lets women be exploited. The mills, reached through the 'Mad Maid's Bellow's-pipe' and the 'grim Black Notch' beyond, are driven by Blood River, and to add to the black comedy Melville's narrator, the only other man involved in the story, is a seed merchant, seeking to buy paper for his seed packets. How Melville managed to get this story past the editor's of *Puttnam's* polite family magazine remains a mystery. Perhaps, as in Poe's story of 'The Purloined Letter', the startlingly offensive material was made so very prominent as to become invisible.

The reformist ethos of 1840s and 1850s New England, fuelled in part by the transcendentalists' insistence on the need for freedom from the tyranny of the past and the ability of the individual to stand firm and change the world, and stemming also from religious evangelism, resulted in some powerful and impatient statements of the utopian vision and American fallings short from that. Melville's 'Bell-Tower' stages such criticisms obliquely, in its covert referencing of the cracked Liberty Bell and its manacled – hence enslaved – robot figure who murders his inventor, but other writers were more open.

An important new literary form emerged during the American nineteenth century: the slave narrative. In the antislavery movement texts by survivors of the 'peculiar institution' were a powerful persuasive resource, among them the harrowing accounts of the *Narrative of the Life of Frederick Douglass, An American Slave, Written by Himself* (1845) and Harriet Jacobs's life story, written under the pseudonym Linda Brent in 1858, and published in 1861 as *Incidents in the Life of a Slave Girl*. As Douglass's title attests, the issue of authenticity in writing such life stories was a vexed question, not least because their very existence undermined many of the pro-slavery arguments about black inferiority. Jacob's book in particular came under question regarding the extent of the role of her editor, Lydia Maria Child, a matter only recently settled in favour of Jacob's authentic authorship. In addressing the central contradictions of a culture that attempted to unite its disparate elements under the ideology of individual equality, liberty and respect for women, these writers developed a rhetoric of simplicity and immediacy that, along with the influence of the frontier, may be seen as one of the determinants of a drive towards realism and unsophisticated, uninflected 'truth' in later American writing.

Harriet Beecher Stowe's *Uncle Tom's Cabin* (1852) makes evident the force of an essentially religious critique of slavery as morally damaging not only to its victims and the slaveholders but to the supposedly non-complicit northerners who found themselves party to the Fugitive Slave Law of 1850. Stowe aimed her hugely influential novel at middle-class Christians who would be susceptible to arguments based on the sanctity of the family and the need to translate biblical teachings into personal morality. She told the dramatic story of escape from slavery of a young couple, and the tragedy of Tom, whose non-violent Christian faith results in his Christ-like martyrdom. Stowe showed that arguments concerning 'good' masters meant nothing against the economic imperatives of slavery, and demonstrated the elements of sexual exploitation within the slave trade. The darkening course of her increasingly gothic novel follows a reverse trajectory from that of the popular slave narratives, which offered a pattern of escape from horror towards northern freedom and at least some hard won fulfillment.

Why should a white middle-class intellectual woman without personal experience of the institution have had such a famously profound effect on attitudes towards slavery? In part it was because she demonstrated that, to reverse a later feminist aphorism, the political is personal. Her Ohio characters, Senator and Mrs Bird, put their sympathetic feelings above the law when aiding Eliza after her spectacular escape over the ice floes in the river. As Jane Tomkins has argued, more than this, the thrust of Stowe's work was in tune with evangelism within the Christian American culture, articulating a deeply felt belief that the judgements of another world are more important than the travails of this one. From Stowe's point of view, and that of her chosen audience, Tom's miserable end is not a sadistic and mean conclusion to an insignificant life but, beyond all questions of reform or political exigency, it is a spiritual triumph. Another reason for Stowe's impact is her calculated appeal to a female readership: she focused on the traumas of broken families in an address to the fellow feelings of other women, especially mothers. The combination of showing, not telling, and dramatising in personal terms the emotional and spiritual costs of slavery, produced an argument that out-stepped political considerations. Her message in effect, to those like Hawthorne who felt that slavery was a great evil but one that should be progressively eliminated, was a simple one: whatever the niceties of dispute, this evil must not be. In a context of an unenfranchised female population, supposed to exercise political rights only through their influence on the more privileged males, and increasingly vocal in addressing this inequity, her emotive appeal had enormous force.

Rebecca Harding Davis, a well-educated middle-class woman who felt the personal frustration of being denied access to a career, wrote in 1860 of the horrifically deprived existence of the workers she had observed in her home town of Wheeling, Pennsylvania. *Life in the Iron Mills,* despite its original warm reception, was largely forgotten until recent feminist reappraisals of the American literary canon. Harding Davis powerfully evoked the squalour and degradation of workers' lives, contrasting their suffering with the complacency of the owner's friends visiting the iron mill. One of the furnace-men displays extraordinary self-taught artistic ability in creating a figure sculpted from the korl refuse: 'There was not one line of beauty in it: a nude woman's form, muscular, grown coarse with labor, the powerful limbs instinct with some poignant longing . . . like that of a starving wolf's'. When asked what he might do with such workers the owner replies: '*Ce n'est pas mon affaire*. I have no fancy for nursing infant geniuses. I suppose there are some stray gleams of mind and soul among these wretches.' Later he claims 'I do not think. I wash my hands of all social problems – slavery, caste, white and black. My duty to my operatives has a narrow limit, – the pay-hour on Saturday night'. In this story of cruel necessity Harding Davis anticipates the post-Civil War turn into realism and naturalism that marks the later decades of the century; what is extraordinary is to find it here so early, and not as a product of European naturalist influence from writers like Zola. It is fresh, spontaneous and harrowing; stemming at least in part from Rebecca Harding Davis's own sense of marginality as an educated and independent-minded woman in a time and place that valued neither attribute.

The kind of realism that Harding Davis developed in this novella provides a useful introduction to the distinction between realism and naturalism in later nineteenth-century American fictions. Her observation of the desperate conditions and thwarted aspirations of foundry workers is in its way still a form of romance: it is realism, but a heightened, intensified version, focusing on the reduction of life to its creeping essentials in the life of her loyal protagonist Deborah, and yet also insisting on the superb stifled artistic talent of Deborah's hero, Wolfe. Ideas of free will are reduced to the choice of suicide; the fatal theft is presented as inevitable, and not fully Wolfe's own chosen action, the foundries are represented as luridly as the pits of hell, and even the qualified happiness of Deborah's old age is due to an exceptional rescue. In all this, Harding Davis anticipates the work of the naturalists later in the century: Hamlin Garland, Frank Norris, Stephen Crane and, to an extent, Theodore Dreiser.

The Civil War was a coming of age that left the antebellum period seeming in retrospect a time of comparative innocence. This new industrialised warfare led all the Western nations to rethink their armaments and military strategy, with consequences reaching to the Crimea and even the First World War. In the United States it provoked a new realism – and even cynicism – about the American polis. As Melville expressed it in his poem 'The Conflict of Convictions' (1860–1):

> I know a wind in purpose strong –
>   It spins *against* the way it drives . . .
>
>   Power unanointed may come –
> Dominion (unsought by the free)
>   And the Iron Dome,

Stronger for stress and strain,
Fling her huge shadow athwart the main;
But the Founders' dream shall flee.

The gigantism of factories and railway lines, armament supply and iron-clads, and the mass distribution and disposal of men in the forces announced the coming of the modern. That this should have been an internal conflict of brother against brother gave it a peculiarly modern absurdist element, well caught by the stories of Ambrose ('Bitter') Bierce, a western humourist and survivor of the campaign. 'One of the Missing' details the plight of a human killing machine, sniper Jerome Searing who delights in his work of producing widows and orphans, but finds himself staring into the muzzle of his own rifle when a collapsed building traps him in such a way that the smallest movement will set off its hair trigger. At last Searing steels himself to take the risk of disturbing the wreckage – but dies of fright. Another of Bierce's heavily ironic Civil War fables tells of a young southerner who defies his Confederate father to join the Union army. During the war he has to shoot a mounted enemy scout who will otherwise report the position of the troops. But the impressive figure on the cliffs is his own father. Following his duty – and his father's own advice in their leave-taking – he shoots the horse from under its rider, and so, a thousand feet below, a Federal officer sees the astonishing sight of 'a man on horseback riding down into the valley through the air'. Another of his tales has a man ordered to bombard his own family home. Bierce's savage wit has an after-the-fall maturity as he explains these dilemmas with a subtle awareness of their oedipal dimension, of just how the political is now personal, of how the nation is torn apart in the struggle.

The unprecedented scale and atrocity of the war was captured in the new scientific technique of photography, one that was to have so much effect in the development of literary realism. It took some time for writing to catch up with the new medium in its ability to freeze the moment and include convincing amounts of credible detailing; when it did, arguably writing leapfrogged the photograph and invented the cinema before the event. Stephen Crane's novella of the Civil War, *The Red Badge of Courage,* in 1895 much post-dated its subject but shows how attention to kinetic impression and restricted point of view, near and far focus and emblematic detail, as well as a sense of speeded-up and slowed-down temporal sequence would soon emerge in cinematic narrative. Impressionism in art encouraged attention to immediate perception instead of mediated description, and Crane was closely associated with such development in painting through several

New York artist friends. Without personal experience of the war, he studied accounts and photographs to produce his story of a callow youth who runs from battle but is accidentally wounded. Being seen as a hero, he becomes one, and acts in later battles with a blind frenzy of heroism, feeling a rather spurious maturity: 'he had been to touch the great death and found that, after all, it was but the great death. He was a man'. Henry Fleming's world is one of monsters and machines. He is 'aware of the machinery of orders that started the charge', the 'whirring and thumping of gigantic machinery', and yet in another perspective the battle troops are 'like two serpents crawling from the cavern of the night'. Just as the earlier organicism of the Romantics and their American incarnation, the transcendentalists, can be seen as a reaction against the new world of science and industrialisation, the later nineteenth century interest in realism can be understood as a continuation of this process – an attempt to come to terms with the irresistible mechanical and electrical forces unleashed after the Civil War.

Additionally, America was more and more a country of immigrants, and the newer immigrants came not from Northern and Western Europe but from Eastern and Southern Europe or, in the case of California, from Asia, and, in the southern states, from Mexico. The immigrants clustered in the hugely expanding cities, where industrialism provided work, but where they were resented for accepting lower wages and for their perceived foreignness, in language and cultural practices. As the corporations grew and monopoly capitalists flourished, farm prices were driven down by railroad and grain storage cartels, and industrial wages were depressed by cheap labour, encouraging alternative visions of socialism, anarchism, populist agrarian resistance and, later, urban Progressive reform. The challenge for writers was to respond to and capture aspects of these several new Americas; to explore difference and come to terms with the new real. Some, regional realists, like Sarah Orne Jewett, Mary Wilkins Freeman, Kate Chopin, detailed the immediacy of life and its local legacies, catching dialect patterns and different regional mores. Mark Twain returned imaginatively to the pre-war South of Hannibal and the Mississippi River, where he reprised the problems of slavery from a post-Reconstruction distance. Hamlin Garland documented midwestern rural poverty and the financial exigencies of farmers under siege from distributors and banks.

The writers' economic understanding was deepened by increasing awareness of Marxist theory, but socialist arguments were undercut by the spread of Darwinist assumptions about human origins and development, especially when such concepts were applied to society in the form of Social

Darwinism. Herbert Spencer influentially held that social development would work most effectively if no attempts were made to ameliorate the costs of inevitable progress through unionism or charity, which would merely impede development towards the best possible society. Those who disagreed, like the novelists Edward Bellamy, Ignatius Donnelly or Jack London, foresaw a catastrophic and revolutionary future, albeit one that might be followed by a utopian reorganisation of the state. But Jack London's work in particular shows the tension between competing doctrines of Darwinist and sometimes Nietszchean ideas of individual supremacy and the imperatives of communal struggle. In *The Iron Heel,* for example, the oppressed proletariat has to be led in their revolutionary struggle by a superman figure.

The realists' position might be best seen as embodied in the extensive works of William Dean Howells, who documented the ordinary – largely middle class – centre ground of the new 'gilded age', in which genteel norms increasingly struggled against unwelcome perceptions of otherness. Howells responded to class differences, changes in fortune, industrial malpractices and political catastrophes, like the affair of the Haymarket bombing and subsequent trial of the supposed anarchist perpetrators. Unfairly criticised by the humourist critic H. L. Mencken for his middle ground position as the purveyor of a realism of teacups, in which little wooden men and women went illustratively about their business, his novels and stories nevertheless provide one of the best panoramas of the rapidly changing American society.

The gist of the naturalists' dispute with such explorations of the everyday was that truth about human behaviour would only emerge under more extreme conditions, when economic pressure, instinct and biological inheritance, or social conditioning could be clearly seen, and when the individual's comfortable assumption of free will would be exposed as mere self delusion. Frank Norris's essay of 1901, 'A Plea for Romantic Fiction', explores this difference with the realists:

> Realism stultifies itself. It notes only the surface of things . . . Realism is minute, it is the drama of a broken teacup, the tragedy of a walk down the block, the excitement of an afternoon call, the adventure of an invitation to dinner . . . But to Romance belongs the wide world for range, and the unplumbed depths of the human heart, and the mystery of sex, and the problems of life, and the black, unsearched penetralia of the soul of man. You, the indolent, must not always be amused.

However unfair this may be to the realists, who could indeed find drama in an afternoon visit, and even horror seated in the drawing room, its call to arms reflects the pressure of new understandings of that 'unsearched

penetralia' of the soul which were to lead on to representations of the unconscious and to new forms of fiction, in which the exploration of processes
of mind, its stream of consciousness, dreams and nightmares, would
become one of the forces behind modernism. And yet the enthusiastic crudity of Norris's manifesto suggests at the same time the price to be paid
for deterministic explanations of behaviour, whether in his novels like
McTeague, The Octopus, The Pit or *Vandover and the Brute,* or those of
Theodore Dreiser and Stephen Crane.

Henry James's subtle response to the issues concerning realism came in
one of his most cunning stories, 'The Real Thing' (1892) in which an illustrator struggles to use as models two aristocratic hangers-on who have fallen
on hard times. Major and Mrs Monarch are themselves unquestionably the
'real thing':

> It was in their faces, the blankness, the deep intellectual repose of the twenty
> years of country-house visiting that had given them pleasant intonations. I
> could see the sunny drawing rooms, sprinkled with periodicals she didn't read,
> in which Mrs Monarch had continuously sat; I could see the wet shrubberies
> in which she had walked, equipped to admiration for either exercise.

But as inspirations for exactly their own sort of people, they prove hope-
less, wooden, gigantic. His lower-class usual models, the blowsy Miss Churm
and an Italian vagabond called Oronte, do the job perfectly, so much so that
the Monarchs end up just making the tea. Still, James's joke is multilayered:
the illustrator's art is to create such confections as the Russian princess ('Golden
Eyes') in the *Cheapside* magazine, leading the reader to conclude that perhaps this is part of the problem; the real thing he seeks is itself a fake, kitsch.
At bottom, of course, the whole story is in itself an illustration of the 'real
thing', and James pulls it off without our even noticing his illustration of
the real conducted around – and as it were despite – the debate about it.
There is in short no point in arguing about it; the real artist simply does it.

James's realism was for the most part a realism of the everyday, albeit
often the everyday of rich and exceptional people. But he began by writing ghost stories in the manner of Hawthorne, and always retained a sense
of the gothic depths behind his polite society. Of this, the 'Turn of the Screw'
(1898) is his most celebrated example, finding in the situation of a governess looking after two beautiful children in a remote house horrors far in
excess of the familiar ghost story, precisely through the realism of his
approach. Everything is seen through the eyes and consciousness of the
embattled young governess, to the extent that the horrors she sees may be
only from her own imagination. But what has often been missed by critics

taking one side or another in the intended mystification of whether the governess hallucinates or actually sees the ghosts of Quint and Miss Jessel stalking the children, is that the horrors suggested are themselves real nightmares of the contemporary society: the horrors of what these two real or imaginary ghosts, but in any case real enough former servants, may have been doing with these delicious children. And for that matter, what the governess herself is now doing to them through her supposed protection. As a result of her efforts, Flora is driven into hysteria, and Miles to death. There is the final turn of the screw – unless, that is, yet another and even more final turn is to consider what James is doing to his audience: the sophisticated readers who will appreciate his little tale about children exposed to 'the very worst action small victims so conditioned might be conceived as subject to'. His tale is intended for the delectation, amusement and arguably even sexual frisson of those who, in James's own words in his preface, are 'not easily caught . . . the jaded, the disillusioned, the fastidious'.

The end of the nineteenth century, then, saw in some respects a return to the beginning, in an appreciation of the romance – which some critics like Harry Levin and Richard Chase have argued dominated nineteenth-century American writing – and the gothic – which, according to Leslie Fiedler, was from the beginning the hallmark of this fiction. James's work is protomodernist in its attention to formal issues such as point of view, consciousness, 'lucid reflectors' and so forth, but retains romance and gothic features in its attention to what Hawthorne earlier called the 'deeper psychology'.

The literary world was now immensely different, with new focus on immigrant and minority writers, with women like Edith Wharton, Kate Chopin and Charlotte Perkins Gilman prominent among serious novelists; new subjects; and, in the practices of realism, naturalism and, embryonically, modernism, new formal treatments. Yet the literature of the later nineteenth century recognisably maintained its earlier, distinctively New-World provenance.

Further reading

Bradbury, Malcolm, and Richard Ruland, *From Puritanism to Postmodernism: A History of American Literature* (1992).

Carton, Evan, *The Rhetoric of American Romance* (1985).

Chase, Richard, *The American Novel and its Tradition* (1957).

Fiedler, Leslie, *Love and Death in the American Novel* (1960).

Fussell, Edwin, *Frontier: American Literature and the American West* (1965).

Gray, Richard, *A History of American Literature* (2004).

Irwin, John T., *American Hieroglyphics: The Symbol of the Egyptian Hieroglyphics in the American Renaissance* (1980).

Lawrence, D. H., *Studies in Classic American Literature* (1923).

Levin, Harry, *The Power of Blackness* (1958).

Martin, Jay, *Harvests of Change: American Literature 1865–1914* (1967).

Marx, Leo, *The Machine in the Garden: Technology and the Pastoral Ideal in America* (1964).

Reynolds, David S., *Beneath the American Renaissance: The Subversive Imagination in the Age of Emerson and Whitman* (1989).

Slotkin, Richard, *Regeneration Through Violence: The Mythology of the American Frontier 1600–1860* (1973).

Smith, Henry Nash, *Virgin Land: The American West as Symbol and Myth* (1950).

Sundquist, Eric, *To Wake the Nations: Race in the Making of American Literature* (1993).

Tomkins, Jane, *Sensational Designs: The Cultural Work of American Fiction 1790–1860* (1985).

CHAPTER 9

Industry and technology

Christopher Clark

I f one claim of the United States for the world's attention has been rooted in its political systems and ideologies, its weight as a technological leader and industrial power has been equally prominent. Any account of the broad sweep of American history has to address the sheer power, scope, and wealth of the United States economy and the means by which the United States achieved its world-leading position. The United States had started out as an overwhelmingly rural and agrarian society, and some of its founders – notably Thomas Jefferson – probably hoped that it could stay that way. But within a century of gaining its political independence the new nation was becoming a leading industrial power. By 1894 United States manufactures almost matched in value those of Britain, Germany and France combined. Industry, and the technological developments that lay behind it, had become central both to American power and to the world's image of the United States as a dynamic, inventive culture. Throughout the twentieth century, too, industry and technology remained hallmarks of American accomplishment and influence, critical not only in substantive economic terms but in symbolising America's role as the archetypal 'modern' society.

Commentators have long emphasised the significance of inventiveness and technical prowess in the nation's history. America's first internationally renowned celebrity, Benjamin Franklin, epitomised to foreigners and to his own countryfolk the virtues of practical ingenuity and pursuit of 'useful knowledge'. During the mid-nineteenth century, while the historian George Bancroft was crafting his narrative of America's history as a triumph of democracy, other writers were celebrating its technological accomplishments. Compilers of a book entitled *100 Years' Progress of the United States* (published in 1871) focused on '[t]he means by which a few poor colonists have come to excel all nations in the arts of peace, and to astonish the people of Europe with their achievements through the development of their inventive genius'. Disregarding the recent Civil War they declared that 'the true subjects for a history of the United States' were not military or political heroes, but the inventive figures – 'Franklin, Whitney, Morse, and a host of others' – whose work was bringing the nation to the threshold of industrial pre-eminence. It seemed only fitting that the climax of the nation's centennial celebrations in 1876 should be an industrial exposition in Philadelphia whose own centrepiece was an impressive Machinery Hall. Since then, America's story has often been told in terms of its practical and material progress.

Much early work in technological history was written with a focus on machines themselves, and on the logic that made particular techniques successful. Writing of this kind continues to enjoy popular and scholarly attention. But the best histories of technology and industry have for long now been attentive to wider social, cultural and political contexts and to complex and powerful connections with an array of broader issues. What appears at first as a paradox – that such industrial and technological leadership should have emerged in what was initially an overwhelmingly rural society – in fact holds a key to understanding the early stages of America's industrial success. Connections between town and country, farm and factory, nature and machine, helped shape the processes that drove industrial expansion. This essay examines four main phases of American industrial and technological change, in at least three of which agriculture and rural societies played significant parts. Between the Revolution and the Civil War a new manufacturing economy grew up in close connection with patterns of rural economic life. After the Civil War, as American manufacturing achieved recognisably 'modern' dimensions of scale and scope, rural America was still expanding and helped shape industrial growth. Even in the twentieth century, as industrial and urban activities outstripped their rural origins, agricultural production itself became increasingly industrialised. Only in the recent, what I have called 'postmodern' phase, with its tendency to conceal the processes of production, have connections between agriculture and industry been obscured by other concerns. Meanwhile, the cultural processing of all these changes, the means by which they were interpreted and made intelligible to the generations who experienced or inherited them, drew significantly on themes developed in the rural, agrarian American self-image. National mythologies and self-perceptions as often incorporated industry and technology into a pastoral vision as they drew sharp distinctions between the worlds of farm and factory.

From colonies to Civil War

The roots of American industrial development had been laid during the colonial period. By the early 1770s about one-seventh of world iron production was being carried out in the iron works of Maryland, Pennsylvania and New Jersey. Household-based textile production, urban craft trades in the major port towns, and shipbuilding on the New England coast and Delaware River punctuated the strongly agrarian character of early American output. Some British officials became concerned that manufactures in parts of the American colonies would become competitors for Britain's own industries. Indeed economic historians now point to exports of raw materials and producers' goods from Britain to North America as evidence of the growth of colonial manufacturing. The rigours of the Revolution, deriving both from war and from the dislocation of leaving the British Empire, helped expand some of these activities and gave fresh political stimulus to a concern with 'domestic manufactures'. Franklin, Alexander Hamilton, Tench Coxe and other post-revolutionary champions of American manufacturing were by no means alone in seeing industrial development as a means to secure a hard-won political independence. Franklin's posthumous popularity derived in part from his image as a wise, self-fashioned craftsman.

Developments following the Revolution fell into two predominant categories: the transfer of technologies to America from abroad, and the development of new techniques within the existing household-based framework of American manufacture. The most dramatic innovations, often celebrated by historians as marking the start of an American industrial revolution, involved the establishment of machine-based factory processes, especially in the textile industry, at various locations in the Northeast. This involved the introduction of new textile technology from England, such as that installed in the early 1790s at a small spinning mill at Pawtucket Falls, Rhode Island, by an English emigrant, Samuel Slater, with the financial backing of Providence merchants. Over the following decades, many more mills, usually using water power to drive spinning and weaving machinery, sprang up in southern New England, in the Delaware Valley and Philadelphia region, and at other sites in the eastern states. In Philadelphia, they were established in connection with urban handloom weaving, mainly conducted by men. In southern New England, mills conducted on the 'family' or 'Rhode Island' system hired women and children to do much of the factory work, drawing on recruits from farm families, or leasing land to farmers and labourers whose family members would work in the mills. In eastern Massachusetts from 1814 onwards, a group of Boston merchants invested in large-scale textile production in mills employing hundreds of workers, first on the Charles River, and subsequently at sites on the Merrimack River, beginning in the 1820s with the town of Lowell, named after one of the founders of the enterprise. Lowell grew rapidly into an industrial city with thousands of workers and an array of large mills drawing water power from the company's dams and canals. Much of the mill labour consisted of young women recruited from farm families across New England, who were accommodated in supervised company boarding houses. One of the first American towns to be established purely for manufacturing, Lowell was viewed in its first two decades as a model settlement, attracting travellers and observers from Europe and around the United States.

But though they were important, such large-scale developments remained somewhat exceptional in pre-Civil War America. Most manufacturing remained in the hands of craft workers and farm families labouring in small shops closely connected with family households. Both in the countryside and in the established towns and cities of the northeast coastal regions, from Maryland to Maine, small-scale producers turned out an increasing array of goods, from shoes, tools and implements, to pumps, metalware, furniture and clocks. Though the adaptation of imported techniques was highly significant in early American industrial growth, this diffused but active craft production system was also an important seedbed for innovation. One British economic historian, Stephen Broadberry, who specialises in the history of industrial output, has calculated that American manufacturers had achieved higher productivity than their British counterparts by as early as 1820, at a point when factory production was still in its infancy.

Together with imported technology, the widespread diffusion of mechanical skills across rural and urban populations was a key influence on the character of early American manufacturing. It helped the emergence both of higher output and of the pursuit of further mechanical improvements. As well as adapting British techniques to early factory textile production, for example, American manufacturers in a variety of specialisms went further than those in Britain to install machinery where British manufacturers relied more on hand-powered equipment. American machinists were quicker to adopt standard jigs and templates to assist in the production of machine parts in batches. In some industries, including gunmaking and clockmaking, they went further than their British cousins by seeking to develop systems for producing interchangeable parts for standardised products. Where British machine-builders, for example, relied on skilled craft workers and fitters to assemble complex mechanisms that were still essentially hand-built, Americans aimed to reduce such reliance on skill by employing machines to assist in the manufacturing process. This helped foster new skills that would in the long term underpin the systematic development of American mechanisation.

Among the hallmarks of antebellum industry was the development of techniques not just for using machines to help make finished goods, but for helping produce the machines themselves, and for turning out the tools that helped fashion them. This development in depth of mechanical skills had a number of consequences. It fostered its own diffusion and replication. It helped ensure growing independence from reliance on inventions and innovations from other countries. It also helped bring about industrial diversification. One hallmark of many northern manufacturing centres as they expanded was the range of activities that grew up in them. Textile towns such as Lowell became centres not just of cloth production, but of machine building. And machine-builders in turn moved into new fields as development continued: Lowell and other early manufacturing towns became some of the first places to build steam locomotives as railroads began to expand in the 1830s and 1840s.

But why did American manufacturing take a different course from that in Britain? A pioneering explanation was provided by the Oxford-based historian H. J. Habakkuk in an influential book, *American and British Technology in the Nineteenth Century*, published in 1962. Habakkuk noted that early American machines were usually regarded as 'labour-saving' devices and that although the United States population was expanding rapidly in the nineteenth century, its land area was growing still faster. As a place with plentiful land and relatively scarce labour, wages were therefore high. Here, it seemed, was the incentive to manufacturers to introduce machinery to reduce the number of workers required and lower the unit costs of the wages required to pay them. American technological prowess, Habakkuk suggested, had its roots in the fundamental conditions of a land-abundant, labour-scarce national economy. Historians since then have found much to endorse, but also much to revise in this formulation. Migration to frontier land was not readily an option for many industrial workers, because of the costs of travel and setting up farms in new regions. Building machines took skill, and it was not self-evident that employers should use expensive skilled labour to save costs in the way Habakkuk had suggested. Early nineteenth-century America was as much characterised by capital-scarcity as scarcity of labour. Above all, the period of most rapid expansion of machine-based industries postdated the 1850s, and occurred when growing waves of immigrants from overseas were helping to end the nation's chronic, historic labour shortages.

More than labour scarcity, however, the rural, household-based character of much early manufacturing did help foster the adoption of mechanised techniques. Small-scale manufacturing often involved the co-ordination of work by several producers, many of whom were only part-time makers of items. Furniture makers, tool makers, and wagon builders early developed simple devices that would enable wooden chair seats or handles fashioned in one workshop to be fitted up to other components made elsewhere. Gunmakers, often under government contract, and clockmakers, operating under private incentives to cut costs to create markets for their goods, experimented with developing these techniques for the fashioning of parts for machines, with the greater accuracy and finer tolerances that this would demand. As American manufacturers exhibited a system for standardised manufacture of gun parts at the Great Exhibition in London in 1851, the British government was sending commissioners to the United States to examine and learn from these examples of what one of them called 'the American system of manufactures'.

Interest in inventiveness and experimentation with devices and techniques was broadly diffused among the population. Evidence from the patenting system set up by the federal government suggests that inventiveness became more 'democratised' between 1790 and the 1840s. Most patentees only made one application; they included women as well as men, and came from many different parts of the country, especially from rural areas. Most patents were concerned with refinements to tools and devices; for improvements to axes alone, for example, 81 patents were issued between 1830 and 1873. Popular mythology celebrated, even sentimentalised, the rural roots of industrial inventiveness. In his poem, 'Whittling – a Yankee Portrait', published in 1857, the New England clergyman John Pierpont evoked the myth of a Yankee farm boy making things with his hands:

> Thus, by his genius and his jack-knife driven,
> Ere long he'll solve you any problem given
> Make it, said I? Ay, when he undertakes it,
> He'll make the thing and the machine that makes it.

Pierpont not only evoked the pastoral image of the origins of industrial technology, but in that last line captured one of the essential facets of early American industrial advance – the capacity not just to use machines, but to build them and to use new techniques to do so.

The self-image of a nation of inventive men and women had powerful ideological ramifications. Inventiveness readily lent itself as a theme for nineteenth-century celebrants of exemplary individuals; the English *Lives of the Engineers*, by Samuel Smiles (1861–2), had had an American progenitor in Henry Howe's *Memoirs of the Most Eminent American Mechanics* (1840), whose inventions provided narrative devices for charting industrial progress. Technical change produced industrial growth, and so lay behind national greatness. Above all, the decentralised, relatively egalitarian character of early manufacturing underpinned what historians have referred to as a widespread 'producer ideology': the political conviction that makers of goods were particularly valuable to society, and that they should earn the fruits of their labour by receiving adequate rewards. Indeed the celebration of 'Yankee ingenuity' by writers like Pierpont was not just an assertion of national greatness. The term 'Yankee' referred to New Englanders (and soon northerners in general), and claims about practical ingenuity were part of the sectional struggle that would lead to the Civil War. Many of the most prosperous parts of the South concentrated on staple-crop production for exports, using slave labour, and after about 1810 had fallen behind the North in technical developments. By 1860 the South had only 15 per cent of US manufacturing establishments and accounted for only one-tenth of industrial output. Yankees, their champions argued, cultivated ingenuity because they worked for themselves, were rewarded with the fruits of their labour, and did not rely on chattel slaves to do their work for them. The North's emerging industrial prowess had moral, as well as economic, causes.

Technical developments, though they were partly linked by a certain practical logic, were far from being inevitable. They were in fact socially rooted, as the different antebellum experiences of the North and South demonstrated. From the 1840s onward, marked increases in levels of immigration from Europe, prompted in part by economic dislocations in Britain and Germany, and by the disaster of the Irish famine, fed growing numbers of workers into the American economy. While immigrants moved to most parts of the United States, they tended disproportionately to avoid the South, and to settle in areas where non-slave farming, manufacturing or construction activity could provide employment prospects. Although it was not the sole reason for the North's eventual military success in the Civil War, the region's economic diversity and technical dominance of manufacturing, supply and transport requirements essential for military operations were key factors in the defeat of the Confederacy and the consequent abolition of slavery.

Industrial concentration: from Civil War to the Great Crash

Groundwork for the subsequent expansion of American industry and technological change had been laid before the Civil War, often in the context of the interaction between agriculture and manufacturing. Much early manufacturing involved turning organic raw materials, including vegetable and animal fibres or skins, timber and other resources that were the produce of farm economies, into consumer goods, such as cloth, clothing, shoes, furniture and wagons. Yet the transportation demands of linking widely dispersed population centres had spurred the development and growth first of roads, then of canal systems, and latterly of railroads. Railroads, in turn, coupled with the demands of machine building for a whole range of processes, fostered the expansion of new iron-based and coal-powered technologies, which were to grow rapidly in the middle decades of the nineteenth century. Machine building and machine techniques also encouraged the production of new tools, and – with the introduction of mechanical reapers and other implements – the early stages of the mechanisation of agriculture too.

Accelerated by the transportation developments of the antebellum period, by the growing incentives of a nationally organised market, and by the impetus of civil war, American industry after the 1860s began to respond to different stimuli than those rooted in a household-based craft economy. Under the stimulus of war production, population growth and higher capital expenditure, the Civil War period marked a significant turning point in the development of industrial strength. By the 1880s employment in manufacturing and mining would for the first time exceed that in agriculture. Farming itself, except in the South, was becoming more mechanised, and processing activities such as meat-packing developed on an industrial scale. Iron, steel and coal became the central components of technologies that would prove to be the foundations of American industrial pre-eminence. The newest product, steel, was still in its infancy in the 1860s, with annual output no more than about 30,000 tons. New Bessemer-type furnaces and, later, open-hearth furnaces permitted a massive expansion of steel production, which in 1900 alone exceeded 11 million tons. Steel provided rails, bridges and trains for the rapidly growing railroad system, and for a host of other manufacturing and construction purposes. From the 1880s onwards steel-frame building techniques produced the first urban 'skyscraper' office buildings that would become the prime symbols of American modernity. Technical logic across a variety of fields impelled further innovation – in chemicals, telephony and electrical devices – while economic logic spurred industrial concentration.

Manufacturing firms grew. Whereas in 1869 the average American manufactory still employed fewer than five workers each, by 1906 the average size had reached 67 workers, and 83 per cent of industrial workers were in plants with more than 50 employees. Factory owners, keen to advertise their work, commissioned from artists handsome portrayals or 'birds' eye views' of their works buildings, stressing their size and solidity. Surveys of production technology in the 1890s concluded that considerable shifts towards mechanisation had occurred in the previous three decades, and that working conditions for many employees were now different from those of the antebellum period. Concentrated in factories on an increasing scale, the work employees did was also increasingly subdivided into specialisms that formed parts of larger systems. Though the antebellum period had witnessed the introduction of machine-building techniques based on interchangeable parts, historians have demonstrated that it was only later in the century that interchangeability became broadly feasible in the production of a range of products, from sewing machines and typewriters, to watches and bicycles. The subdivision of work enabled many tasks to be accomplished by relatively unskilled labour, but even the skilled craftspeople who were required to make the whole system function found themselves individually responsible for diminishing proportions of the total work involved in any product. As the scale of factories grew, work itself came to be part of a larger system, whose operations were dictated by considerations far from the workbench. The Centennial Exposition of 1876 furnished a striking instance of the ramifications of new industrial systems. The Machinery Hall at the exposition's heart housed one thousand exhibits, all powered by a single steam engine, the world's largest. Industrial technology, the exhibition demonstrated, had come to be more than a collection of machines and workers: it was now a system of interdependent parts, capable of more than its individual components could produce.

As firm sizes and capital investment grew, increasing influence was exercised by large corporate entities that could muster the resources to employ new technologies and organisational methods. But the concentration and co-ordination of activities was not driven by technology alone. As in the past, its social contexts shaped the process of technical change. Growing workforces had engendered the growing influence of labour unions, particularly among skilled male workers. The 1870s and 1880s witnessed unprecedented levels of strike action and other conflicts over wages and working conditions. To contemporary observers no facets of the new industrial society demanded more attention than the conflict between capital and labour, and the growing power of corporate enterprises. Pursuing both competitive advantage over rival firms and greater control over their own workforces, manufacturing companies sought to exercise increased influence over technical functions that had hitherto been the province of craft workers. Perceiving that usually 'the boss's brains were under the workman's hat', managers took steps towards co-ordinating the facets of production, standardising methods and instilling rigorous discipline on workers. The effort to extract optimum output from them led to the adoption of new techniques of shop-floor organisation and management. By the end of the nineteenth century time-and-motion studies, premium-rate methods, production planning and the rudiments of systems design were being introduced to factory work by an emerging generation of industrial managers and psychologists. Most famous was the engineer Frederick Winslow Taylor, whose experiments in 'scientific management' symbolised a generation of efforts to secure greater management control over work practices and production. As the historian Lewis Mumford would write in the 1930s, the clock became 'the key machine of the modern industrial age'.

Among the outcomes of such efforts were new techniques of closely managed production that emerged in the new automobile industry in the first two decades of the twentieth century. Determined both to extinguish rival companies and to develop a mass market for inexpensively produced vehicles, the Michigan manufacturer Henry Ford evolved what seemed to be the culmination of various nineteenth-century developments in the new production-line methods introduced at his company's Detroit factories. Adopting the principles of efficient plant layout and division of tasks from the scientific management movement, the principle of interchangeability from nineteenth-century machine production, and sequencing and belt systems from the gravity-driven slaughterhouses of the meat-packing industry, Ford evolved the moving assembly line, in which the speed of production was controlled by management and the line itself became the single most effective instrument of labour discipline. First called 'Fordism', assembly-line methods of bulk manufacture became referred to as 'mass production' after an encyclopedia article ghostwritten for Ford coined the term in 1925. By 1928 the Ford Motor Company had turned out over 15 million of its standard car, the Model T, the prime symbol of the inexpensive goods of this new machine age. Ford's vast River Rouge plant, built between 1917 and 1927 on a 2,000-acre site outside Detroit and, in the words of the historian David L. Lewis, 'easily the greatest industrial domain in the world', contrasted most dramatically with the household-based craft workshops of the previous century.

Institutional changes also fostered further technological developments towards the end of the nineteenth century. From abroad, in chemicals and some electrical applications, and from domestic developments in telephony, electricity, and ultimately automobile and aviation technology, emerged many of the elements of what, even today, we would recognise as 'modern' forms of energy supply, manufacturing and communication. Concentrated industry occupied distinctive geographical locations. The industrial districts of the antebellum period had expanded. The nation's chief manufacturing zones now stretched across a vast region bounded by Boston and Baltimore to the East and by Chicago and the Great Lakes in the West. This rapid growth had been fuelled not only by organisational and technical change, but by the rising numbers of immigrants drawn to the United States from much of Europe and from other parts of the world, exceeding one million a year by the early twentieth century. Typical industrial areas, moreover, were no longer rural, but urban. Landscapes by the precisionist painters Charles Demuth (1883–1935) and Charles Sheeler (1883–1965) convey a sense of the exclusion of nature from large industrial sites.

Most large cities and towns of the industrial belt became important manufacturing locations as well as commercial, cultural or political centres. Some developments were co-dependent, and formed elements of new technological systems. Steel frames permitted the construction of tall buildings. Electric power permitted these to be illuminated. The electrically controlled hydraulic safety elevator (lift) enabled buildings to be constructed to ever greater heights. Electricity powered the urban transport systems that carried people to work. New chemical and petroleum-based technologies began to produce new materials for clothing and for equipping buildings and houses. Other developments marked ambiguous or potentially subversive relationships with these emerging systems. Automobiles and, during the early twentieth century, the emergence of wireless transmission, signalled the possibilities of more dispersed social processes, less dependent on the construction of specific systems based on nodal concentrations of activity. Even as the American industrial and commercial city grew into its symbolic position at the apex of modern technological development, the seeds of the city's complex later history and partial decline were already being sown.

Stimulus for industrial investment had come from the existence of large, growing and prosperous domestic markets for a burgeoning array of consumption goods. By the turn of the twentieth century new technologies were being applied not just to the production of such goods, but to their design and function as well. American private households, especially those among the prosperous upper and middle classes, became important receptors for a growing pattern not just of consumer goods but of mechanised household appliances. The roots of this had been laid earlier, with the adaptation of simple hand-operated devices to a variety of domestic uses, but the spread of electric power supply to urban and suburban areas after 1890 began a gradual process of home mechanisation that was to be a prominent hallmark of twentieth-century middle-class culture. By 1920, one in three American homes had electricity; a decade later, the proportion was more than two in three. That decade in particular saw the rapid expansion of electric-powered domestic appliance consumption. Advocates promoted these new machines as labour-saving devices on the order of factory technologies, and they were presented as means of liberating women, who did most household work, from much of housework's drudgery. Lighten specific tasks they undoubtedly did, but it would take more than a change in technology to alter the overall character of most married women's lives, or to shift from them the overall burden of domestic labour.

The age of industrial concentration and complex systems seemed to justify a strongly rooted confidence in progress. Efficiency reformers from the late nineteenth century onwards, some identifying themselves with the Progressive movement, sought to apply the precepts of organisational rationality to a wide range of activities, from politics to the running of domestic households. They elevated the status and significance of experts – professional people (usually men) whose unique specialist abilities should give them particular influence over their chosen areas of knowledge. The expansion and diversification of engineering as a professional field epitomised this process. In 1880 the United States had about 7,000 professional engineers. New professional bodies and the development of college and university curricula in various subfields expanded engineering markedly within two generations. By 1900 there were 45,000 engineers, and by 1930 some 225,000. The same period witnessed a significant shift in the social character of invention itself. Though the heroic figure of the lone inventor remained dear in popular imagination, inventiveness was in fact being industrialised. Thomas Alva Edison, widely famed as America's most prominent and prolific inventor, was noteworthy not just for the array of important developments with which he was associated – especially in early applications of electricity – but also for pioneering new methods of industrial research and development based on capital investment and collaborative effort. Far from being a lone inventor, he was the head of a team of engineers and technicians who adopted factory methods for the very process of invention itself. The application of science to an increasing range of industrial and technological problems intensified the process. The General Electric Company opened an industrial laboratory in 1904; by 1917, there were some 375 such laboratories, and by 1931 about 1,600.

The cult of the expert reflected the concentrated organisation of industrial manufacturing by removing inventiveness from the domestic, individual environment and corporatising it. Ordinary (non-expert) people were now seen as the subjects, not the agents of industrial progress, a sentiment summed up in the slogan devised for the Century of Progress world fair held in Chicago in 1933 to mark that city's centenary: 'Science finds – industry applies – man conforms'. Meanwhile, during the 1920s and 1930s, Henry Ford was expending a portion of his personal fortune on collecting historic machines and other artefacts from around Europe and North America. Placing them before the public at what became the Henry Ford Museum in Dearborn, Michigan, Ford sought to celebrate the achievements of the inventor, a figure whom his own activities and that of his era had done so much to eclipse. While the older claims of a 'producer ideology' had in fact been subsumed in the new power and prerogatives of large companies, and in the counter-efforts of organised labour, the mythology of the individual inventor was sustained in the popular imagination.

The state and the industrial complex

In 1929 a journalist had welcomed the newly elected president, Herbert Hoover, as 'the great engineer who would solve all our problems', effusing confidence in a private-enterprise system founded on technocratic expertise. Most technical developments had emerged in the private sector, and the rapid growth of American industry was taken by economists and politicians as evidence of the wisdom of leaving such matters to private initiative. Hoover's predecessor, Calvin Coolidge, had complacently remarked that 'the business of the United States is business'. Industry and technology would, indeed, remain predominantly in private hands. But the period of the Great Depression and the Second World War would introduce a significant and growing role for government as a sponsor of industrial and technological development. Many of the major technical advances from the 1930s to the 1970s would owe much to government initiative or involvement.

In fact, this was not something new. From the late eighteenth century onwards military requirements had inspired developments in firearms technology that had laid important groundwork for the machine systems that underpinned modern industry. Various scholars regard the federal arsenals and the West Point military academy as significant progenitors of technical and organisational innovation. In the later nineteenth century the growth of railroads and interstate commerce led government increasingly to adopt a regulatory role. Faced with international competition and the growing complexity of machine technologies, the government founded the National Bureau of Standards in 1901 and charged it with seeking to establish consistency and interchangeability across systems and manufacturers' products. Though many of the Bureau's achievements may at first glance appear mundane, and though they were frequently not readily visible to the users of goods, such efforts at regulation were in fact fundamental to the operation of a set of technologies whose complexity grew annually at exponential rates. Having a standard set of screw threads, for example, or basic standards for electrical components and a whole host of other materials, turned out to have enormous significance when lack of co-ordination could have made the industrial system as a whole collapse in chaos. Standardisation, while never wholly achieved, nonetheless became a characteristic of early twentieth-century industry, of which Henry Ford's announcement that 'you can have any colour you like as long as it's black' was only the most famous emblem. Though attention to style and consumer demand would in time cause even Ford to abandon the insistence on uniformity, the cosmetic variety that was introduced to a whole array of products was often only a mask for the fundamental standardisation that enabled a machine-based industrial system to function.

Government's role would not remain limited to holding the ring for industry, however. The First World War to a limited degree, and the substantial collapse of the industrial economy after 1929 both spurred a closer involvement that the Second World War would only underscore. Between 1929 and 1933 economic depression drove down industrial production, especially in some of the more technically challenging sectors. Under Franklin Delano Roosevelt's New Deal, government agencies played an active part, particularly in stretching the sinews of industrial technology to places that private effort had failed to reach. Regional hydro-power schemes, such as those in the Tennessee Valley and on the Columbia River in Oregon and Washington, developed sources of electric generation to supplement older coal-based technologies. Publicly owned dams provided energy for a massive extension of the electricity distribution system. The Rural Electrification Administration brought to many rural areas the power connections that had been enjoyed already by town dwellers, and which by the 1940s linked the great majority of American houses to electric supplies. This of course enabled rural people to start to make use of the appliances and communications technologies that electricity permitted, and in due course to expand significantly the markets for such goods. New Deal agricultural programmes fostered fresh investment in tractors and other agricultural machinery, helped extend technical change to farming in the South, and assisted in the diffusion of fertilisers and new hybrid seed technology.

The Second World War brought government into industrial production even more directly. The conversion of depressed peacetime factories to the manufacture of tanks, guns, ships, aircraft and munitions, and the rapid extension of production capacity in these and a host of other areas quickly banished unemployment and initiated a massive economic boom. Between 1941 and 1943 manufacturing output for war needs grew from 15 per cent of gross national product to 40 per cent, reaching $40 billion a year. On the foundations of mass-production technology in steel, automobiles, electrical goods, chemicals, plastics and other fields, the wartime United States was able to outstrip both its enemies and its allies in the production and supply of war materiel. The massive secret Manhattan Project to create atomic weapons exemplified the linking of scientific research with industrial production. All these efforts underpinned not just military victory over Germany and Japan, but the projection of American power around the world during and after the war. Again, these developments fostered manufacturing in new regions. Partly to prepare for the Pacific war, partly to utilise available labour, significant sections of the aviation, electrical and shipbuilding industries were developed on the American West Coast. Similarly, many aspects of the new nuclear industries were located in the interior Southwest and Pacific Northwest.

In contrast to the aftermath of the First World War, however, the end of war in 1945 did not mark the withdrawal of government from its close connections with industry. Two parallel developments helped shape the continuation of a partnership for military strength and economic prosperity. Planning, tax policies and post-war government investment in programmes such as the GI Bill of Rights helped engender a successful reconversion of wartime industries into peacetime producers, leading to the substantial domestic economic prosperity of the 1950s. Public agencies responsible for road and bridge construction provided much of the infrastructure for a booming automobile industry, climaxing in the mid-1950s with the initiation of the still-active Interstate Highway building programme. Simultaneously, continuing government sponsorship of military production and development, now directed towards sustaining the Cold War against the Soviet Union, created a large and powerful symbiosis of military and business interests that President Dwight D. Eisenhower would eventually dub the 'military-industrial complex'. In aviation, electronics, atomic power and space technology, this symbiosis of government and industry produced many of the key developments with which the United States proclaimed its world leadership in the middle to late twentieth century. These developments, culminating in the unique effort to send people to the Moon in the late 1960s and early 1970s, further sustained the view of American history as one exemplifying extraordinary technological achievement.

A postmodern era

By the time astronaut Neil Armstrong was taking his vaunted 'giant leap for mankind' onto the lunar surface, however, shocks to the political and economic system were starting to call into question this long-standing faith in industrial progress. Having broadly celebrated technological achievements in his classic *Technics and Civilization* of 1934, Lewis Mumford was three decades later penning warnings about the dehumanising character of industrial society. Initially spurred by the revelations, in works such as Rachel Carson's *Silent Spring* (1962), that industrial activity was despoiling and polluting the landscape, the new environmental movement challenged the power of industrial technology to appropriate or transform nature for exploitative purposes. The political conflicts arising from the Vietnam War directed increasing critical attention at the activities of the military-industrial complex which, while it has certainly survived and continued to grow, has never since done so with the complacent acquiescence that it enjoyed at the height of the Cold War. While atomic power and the space programme at first seemed to mark the opening of new frontiers in the 1960s, scepticism as to their risks and benefits quickly followed the political disillusionment of the Vietnam era. Soon, the oil-price shocks of 1973 and 1978 initiated a severe economic recession and restructuring. Established patterns in US manufacturing activity were among the principal victims.

Large-scale industry found itself subjected to vigorous overseas competition for the first time. The most visible changes occurred in the automobile industry, as Japanese manufacturers using 'lean production' techniques outstripped the great Detroit carmakers whose more rigid mass production methods still derived from Ford's revolution of early in the century. Steel and other traditional heavy industries declined. The Northeast–Midwest industrial zone that had dominated American manufacturing for over a century suffered plant closures and job losses, and by the 1980s parts of the region were commonly being referred to as the 'Rust Belt'. Manufacturers moved part of their production to new plants in the South or West, especially where state 'right to work' laws enabled employers to evade or break the power of labour unions. This shift of industrial employment to the 'Sun Belt' encompassed some of the most important demographic and sociopolitical changes in late twentieth-century America, shifting the regional centres of power and underscoring the ideological decline of New Deal-era liberalism.

At the same time, new technological developments enabled the replacement of older industrial work with new employment patterns that reflected the massive growth of electronics, computing and other new technologies.

In part also, these important changes entailed new investments in education and technical skills, as older manufacturing practices and knowledge were superseded by 'higher value-added' intellectually based techniques, most noticeably in fields such as bioscience and biotechnology. These changes encompassed a shift in emphasis from manufacturing employment in the traditional sense towards work based on service functions and the handling and communication of information. Knowledge and data became the raw materials and output of these new 'industries' as much as the tangible products themselves. In a culture increasingly obsessed with 'lifestyles' and consumption, interest in and knowledge about techniques of production faded. Many facets of production, indeed, became concealed or were ignored. Mechanical processes had been visible and intrinsically comprehensible, but microtechnology worked in hidden ways, accessible only to specialist understanding. Even the inventors celebrated by earlier generations came to appear insignificant or just eccentric, while American business culture's new heroes were hailed more for their wealth or leadership skills than for their technical ingenuity.

One byproduct of all these changes was undermined confidence in historical accounts based on a linear narrative of technological progression. The future trajectory of industrial change seemed so much harder to predict than when the compilers of *100 Years' Progress* published their confident assertions of continued upward movement. Atomic technology in its military forms had spelled the potential for destroying the world. Atomic power and many aspects of the space programme came to be seen as dead ends. The histories of industry and technology no longer appeared so straightforward. New technologies no longer seemed simply beneficial. Household machinery, introduced during the twentieth century under the guise of 'saving' women's labour in the home, often did nothing to reduce the real burdens of housework. There was a new interest in industrial history's failures as well as its successes, and a realisation that (as with the survival of the QWERTY keyboard) habit and 'path-dependence' could be a more powerful determinant of success than intrinsic technical merit. The model of large industrial concentrations no longer seemed so central to historical explanations. Historians now accustomed to a society of backyard start-ups and 'just in time' production methods wondered if the narrative of industrial concentration adequately addressed past developments. As they looked, so they found: even during the heyday of corporate mass production, small firms as well as big ones had, it turned out, played a significant role in American industrial and technological development. Small businesses, rapid start-up and failure rates, production for market niches, and adaptive technologies were just as important in what the historian Philip Scranton has called the 'figured tapestry' of later nineteenth-century industrial development as large firms, corporate stability, standardisation and steady technological evolution. Fordism and its equivalents had never been as dominant a part of the picture as traditional accounts had suggested.

American industry in national and international contexts

These shifts towards 'postmodern' interpretations of American industry will also influence accounts of its place in wider world history. The narratives of producerism, heroic inventiveness and technological progress enabled accounts of US industry to be assimilated readily to wider themes in American history. Invention by individuals and the spread of homegrown technologies helped nourish the myths of popular democracy and social mobility that have underscored mainstream accounts of American development. When, as president, John F. Kennedy harnessed the image of the frontier to the commitment to space exploration, he tied modern technical advances explicitly to general understandings of the nation's past. Similarly, as the cultural historian of technology David E. Nye has demonstrated in several books, popular reception of new machines and technical systems over long periods traced patterns close to broader assertions about the character of Americans' encounters with their landscapes. From the seventeenth century to the twentieth, there were prominent and influential beliefs that settlers on the North American continent were furthering a 'second creation', rendering the land that God had shaped more sacred by improving on God's work. As the scale of human interventions in the landscape grew, so too did the transfer of emotion from the land itself to human creations. From Puritans and early continental explorers to the tourists who flocked to Niagara Falls in the first half of the nineteenth century, many Americans experienced the wonder, awe and terror that came from encounters with 'sublime' natural phenomena. Increasingly, though, from railroad trains to the wonders of electricity, hydropower dams and highway developments, modern Americans would derive these emotions instead from the 'technologically sublime' products of their society's own ingenuity.

Such views underpinned two characteristics of common beliefs about technology: that utilitarian approaches to nature were justified, and that the United States was uniquely an expression of presumed human mastery of the Earth. 'The surpassing beauty which our forests add to our natural scenery', a writer in *100 Years' Progress* noted in 1871, 'is not to be compared with the solid advantages which are derived from the immense variety, as well as the quantity of their lumber'. A vast landscape, granted by providence to an ingenious and inventive people, was an unsurpassed opportunity for human self-advancement. Exploiting and improving on the gifts of nature's God served personal material ends and national political ends simultaneously. But this American-exceptionalist interpretation of technological history had never squared well with the wider history of industry and technology, and the recent developments in the field reviewed in this essay underscore the interdependence of US developments on those taking place elsewhere.

Each of the four phases of industrial change discussed here contained important elements of US involvement in developments overseas. The first episode, embracing the pre-Civil War origins of American industry, entailed an intersection of domestic social structures and cultural patterns with technology transfer across the Atlantic, the growth of international commerce, and the arrival of substantial numbers of skilled and semi-skilled immigrants on America's shores. Similarly, the mid-twentieth century rise of state involvement and the creation of the military-industrial complex coincided with the final abandonment of America's political and diplomatic isolationism and its emergence as a global power. The challenge of the Second World War and the US policy of worldwide engagement following the war each provided international contexts for American technology and industrial methods. Meanwhile, as many recent studies have suggested, the other two episodes – of 'industrial concentration' from the 1860s to the 1920s, and what I have called the 'postmodern' phase from the 1970s onward – both owed much to successive iterations of what is now often called 'globalisation'.

Various scholars have posited a 'first globalisation' that coincided with mid-nineteenth century trade liberalisation in the British Empire and the unprecedented extension of new communications systems and connections. Not only did new inventions like the telegraph (dubbed 'the Victorian Internet' by the writer Tom Standage) speed the transmission of information, but steamships, railroads and postal systems furthered the extension both of state power and of commercial activities. Although stimulated in part by the logistical demands of the Civil War, the rapid subsequent growth and consolidation of American heavy industry was sustained during the later nineteenth century by large capital flows and by rising levels of transoceanic migration. The relative freedom of capital and labour markets during this phase enabled the United States to deploy its technical and organisational skills to great effect. The United States was only part of a much wider global system of trade, finance and consumption, but its size, prosperity and natural resources enabled it to become one of the foremost participants in this system. Its huge markets, its agricultural output and its mineral assets all assisted in projecting American industry to the world-leading position it attained by the 1890s. Early in the twentieth century more than half of the world's biggest companies were American, and the United States was the single largest 'importer' of immigrant labour.

The second, more recent era of globalisation, initiated by the collapse of the Cold War and the re-emergence of international economic liberalism, is also marked by massive intercontinental flows of goods, capital and working people, and is often associated with the projection of American-style economic activities abroad. But the United States' experience of this second globalisation phase has been altogether more ambiguous than that of the first. The partial relaxation since 1965 of immigration restrictions imposed in the 1920s induced large numbers of people once again to head for the United States from many parts of the world, but recently these migrants have been more likely to provide labour for the burgeoning service and information economy than for manufacturing. To an increasing (and, in some views, alarming) degree, American demand for manufactured goods has come to be satisfied by producers elsewhere, especially in the high-technology zones of Japan and Western Europe and in the 'cheap labour' economies of East and South Asia and parts of Latin America. Along with much manufacturing, substantial amounts of machine and machine-tool production, and even many research and development functions, have been moving offshore. To some commentators these developments are marks of an incipient decline in relative power and influence of the United States. Globalisation, though by its critics often treated as synonymous with 'Americanisation', turns out to have broader roots. Now only one-fifth or fewer of the world's largest companies are American-based. Although many facets of modern global capitalism incorporate 'American' methods, influences from elsewhere, especially from Asia, are coming to play increasingly significant roles. Though the United States projects unrivalled military power, its ability to continue to exercise economic influence and leadership could be compromised by the relative weakness of its industrial base. The debates over these and similar issues will continue to shape current affairs and historical interpretation well into the twenty-first century.

Further reading

Chandler, Alfred D., *Scale and Scope: The Dynamics of Industrial Capitalism* (1990).

Cowan, Ruth Schwartz, *More Work for Mother: The Ironies of Household Technology from the Open Hearth to the Microwave* (1983).

Cowan, Ruth Schwartz, *A Social History of American Technology* (1996).

Engerman, Stanley L. and Kenneth L. Sokoloff, 'Technology and industrialization, 1790–1914', in Stanley L. Engerman and Robert E. Gallman (eds), *The Cambridge Economic History of the United States,* Vol. II, *The Long Nineteenth Century* (2000), chap. 9.

Hounshell, David A., *From the American System to Mass Production: The Development of Manufacturing Technology in the United States, 1800–1932* (1984).

Hughes, Thomas P., *American Genesis: A Century of Invention and Technological Enthusiasm, 1870–1970* (1989).

Meyer, David R., *The Roots of American Industrialization* (2003).

Montgomery, David. *The Fall of the House of Labor: The Workplace, the State, and American Labor Activism, 1865–1925* (1987).

Nye, David E., *America as Second Creation: Technology and Narratives of New Beginnings* (2003).

Pursell, Carroll W., *The Machine in America: A Social History of Technology* (1995).

Riordan, Michael and Lillian Hoddeson, *Crystal Fire: The Birth of the Information Age* (1997).

Scranton, Philip, *Endless Novelty: Specialty Production and American Industrialization, 1865–1925* (1997).

Smith, Merritt Roe and Gregory Clancey (eds), *Major Problems in the History of American Technology: Documents and Essays* (1998).

Technology and Culture: the principal journal in the field (quarterly, 1959–present).

Websites

American Textile History Museum, Lowell, Massachusetts:
www.athm.org/home

Hagley Museum and Library, Wilmington, Delaware:
www.hagley.lib.de.us

The Henry Ford Museum, Dearborn, Michigan:
www.thehenryford.org/museum

National Museum of American History, Smithsonian Institution,
Washington DC: http://americanhistory.si.edu

The Society for the History of Technology (SHOT): (maintains weblinks
to resources in the field): www.shot.jhu.edu

CHAPTER 10

The twentieth-century American novel

John Whitley

A literary historian has no right to assume that a period of writing will organise itself into neat mathematical units, or even that its formal opening will automatically be auspicious. The year 1900 produced little significant American fiction, if compared with 1899 (Kate Chopin's *The Awakening*, Henry James's *The Awkward Age*, Frank Norris's *McTeague*) or 1901 (Henry James's *The Sacred Fount*, Norris's *The Octopus*). 1900 brought some interesting but minor writings by Charles Chestnutt (*The House Behind the Cedars*), Stephen Crane (*The Whilomville Stories*), Mark Twain (*The Man That Corrupted Hadleyburg and Other Stories*) and *The Touchstone*, an early novel by Edith Wharton. Fortunately for the writer of an essay on this topic, 1900 was also the year of the initial publication of Theodore Dreiser's first novel, *Sister Carrie*. This was, to be sure, an exceedingly modest début, since its acceptance by Frank Norris's publisher (Doubleday, Page & Co.), following Norris's enthusiasm, was largely negated by Doubleday himself, who had been away when his firm accepted the work. He found the book immoral and feared many adverse reactions. Dreiser refused to release the publishers from their contract and the book was published but in a very limited number of copies and with no promotion from the publishers. It sold poorly and was not published again until 1907, by a different firm. An inauspicious beginning to the great novels of the twentieth century!

Dreiser was a late and major practitioner of realism and naturalism. I use both terms because they are often used interchangeably and do have much in common. Of relevance to the discussion here is that realism emphasised the representative rather than the exotic or exceptional. There is, in this writing, often a commitment to aspects of the writer's time, to expressions of currents of popular feeling, and to the relations between the individual and the social world. Thus matters previously considered too unpleasant or controversial to figure in the pages of novels are now given an airing, such as divorce in William Dean Howells's *A Modern Instance* (1882) or a child's awareness of adult sexuality in James's *What Maisie Knew* (1887). Naturalism shares with realism some commitment to an objective account of external reality and a tendency toward impersonal techniques; a penchant for third person narrative rather than first person. This last tendency is often dramatically reversed with the onset of modernist fiction, mainly because the omniscient narrator is not a character in the story and hence is not tied to his/her own vision and necessary selectivity (as with the narrator of *The Great Gatsby* or the narrators of *The Sound and the Fury*).

What is perhaps the strongest difference between realism and naturalism lies not so much in the subject matter as in its intellectual background. Naturalism was much influenced by Social Darwinism and its concomitant sense of determinism. Humans do not do what they choose but what they are forced to do by environment and heredity. The novelist's study of humanity is thus akin to that of the social scientist, at a time when the social sciences are beginning to gain ground in the curricula of major American universities, and is removed from many of the moral conventions of the nineteenth-century social novel. These aspects could be applied to any of the strata of society but, because of the impact of industrialisation, urbanisation and immigration and the resulting problems of crime, prostitution and alcoholism, there is a tendency to concentrate on sordid subject matter: dire poverty in Hamlin Garland's *Main-Travelled Roads* (1891); prostitution in Crane's *Maggie: A Girl of the Streets* (1893); capitalist greed in Norris's *The Octopus* (1901) and Dreiser's *The Financier* (1912); alcoholism in Crane's *George's Mother* (1896); and syphilis in Norris's *Vandover and the Brute* (1914).

Dreiser's fiction conforms to much of the above. *Sister Carrie* takes an archetypal fictional American situation: the movement of a young person from the country to the city; the movement from innocence to experience. This movement can be seen in American novels as different as Twain's *Huckleberry Finn* (1885), Fitzgerald's *The Great Gatsby* (1925), Salinger's *The Catcher in the Rye* (1951), Herman Wouk's *Youngblood Hawke* (1962) and James Leo Herlihy's *Midnight Cowboy* (1965). The late nineteenth century saw huge and speedy expansions of major American cities and the fascination with urban society and its mores rapidly transferred to the novel. Crane's interest in prostitution and alcoholism arose from his time as a journalist in New York. Norris's *McTeague* is solidly grounded in an extensive knowledge of San Francisco, and Dreiser's work as a reporter in New York, Pittsburgh,

Toledo, St Louis and Chicago contributed significantly to his first novel. He had not seen a large American city till he was 13 and his capture of the kind of feelings that first look arouses occurs in the opening chapter of *Sister Carrie*:

> To the child, the genius with imagination, or the wholly untravelled, the approach to a great city for the first time is a wonderful thing . . . The street, the lamps, the lighted chamber set for dining, are for me. The theatre, the halls, the parties, the ways of rest and the paths of song – these are mine in the night. Though all humanity be still enclosed in the shops, the thrill runs abroad.

Dreiser treads carefully here. The city is only that seen for the first time. If it holds 'hope', it is mostly for the weary. But while two kinds of people, the innocent and the ignorant, are bowled over by the experience, so is a third party, 'the genius with imagination', presumably Dreiser himself. Thus the novelist can see beyond the superficial allure of the city to something more. The change from one sphere or condition to another is not simply day to night or natural light to artificial, but the capacity of the urban scene to invigorate the imagination, by allowing it to sense 'the wonder' – that great necessity of the American imagination – evoked by the positivist flood of detail released in the literature of naturalism. Another attempt to capture the essence of the new and huge metropolis can be found in John Dos Passos's 1925 novel, *Manhattan Transfer*. There the city is depicted in a new style requiring the fracturing of normal syntax so as to convey a sense of the continual flux of city life:

> Glowworm trains shuttle in the gloaming through the foggy looms of spiderweb bridges, elevators soar and drop in their shafts, harbor lights wink. Like sap at the first frost at five o'clock men and women begin to drain gradually out of the tall buildings downtown, gray faced throngs flood subways and tubes, vanish underground . . .

There seems to be a memory of the first chapter of *Sister Carrie* in *The Great Gatsby*, which was first published in the same year as *Manhattan Transfer*: 'The city seen from the Queensboro bridge is always the city seen for the first time, in its first wild promise of all the mystery and the beauty of the world'. The quotation does not give any hint of Fitzgerald's famed ability to hold opposites in tension; the beautiful view and the dead man in the hearse that pulls up alongside them; the bad city party against the glitter of West Egg; the dream and the nightmare. What Dreiser was hinting at, however, is made clearer by the literary context of Fitzgerald's novel. Naturalism, copied slavishly in

Fitzgerald's second novel, *The Beautiful and Damned* (1922), rarely allowed for the quality of seeing and extracting/formulating meaning from what is seen and evaluated. As we move further into the twentieth century the concerns of modernism are with the complexities of seeing and ordering experience. Certainly, the educative nature of experience is not accepted with the same alacrity as in the nineteenth-century *Bildungsroman*, so that what the narrator sees and senses remains complex and mysterious. This is emphasised by modernism's interest in both first-person narrative and the use of several narrators; in manipulations of time schemes and the general assumption that mysteries cannot be solved so easily by narrative structures; they can only be considered from various viewpoints. Who or what is Gatsby? What does he *mean*? Nick Carraway cannot tell us; he can only try to build a picture based not only on what *he* sees but also complicated by his personal predilections and aspirations and his capacity to see Gatsby as a model.

Melville, rediscovered in America during the inter-war years, points toward modernism in the chapter 'The Doubloon' in *Moby-Dick*, where the meaning of the Ecuadorian gold coin nailed to the mast cannot be discerned through a *mélange* of individual responses. In Willa Cather's 1918 novel, *My Ántonia* (and Cather has, in recent years, been shown to be a good deal more of a modernist than had been previously thought), the narrator, Jim Burden, whose responsibilities in the narrative are indicated by his surname, constructs an account, in his restricted and unhappy life, of the effect on that life of his relationship with Ántonia. To him, she stands for his past and pastoral moments of youth and innocence, as well as the land and the persistence of the settlers. He refers to the memoir he is writing as 'the thing about Ántonia' and at the end gives it the title *Ántonia*, and finally adds *My*. This does not indicate the total capturing of her essence, for the narrative makes it clear that no male narrator could begin to grasp fully the meanings of her story using male strategies, What is underlined is the personal nature of the viewpoint. This also indicates the modernist search for intuition; a vision or insight not released by the details of the narrative (description, character, irony) but lying somewhere behind all the obvious techniques. In a famous essay entitled 'The Novel Démeublé' (1922), Cather wrote about 'the inexplicable presence of the thing not named' in novels, and commented elsewhere that 'the highest processes of art are all processes of simplification'. The endless parade of social data in naturalist fiction is not for her; fictions must suggest more than they can describe. Though their works offer many strong contrasts, these critical comments of Cather's can lead us directly to Ernest Hemingway.

Three major novelists

Hemingway's career began in the 1920s and extended to the beginning of the 1960s. His greatest work, both as a novelist and as a short story writer, came in the inter-war years, including the novels *The Sun Also Rises* (also known as *Fiesta*, 1926), *A Farewell to Arms* (1929) and *For Whom The Bell Tolls* (1940) and the short story collections *In Our Time* (1925), *Men Without Women* (1927) and *Winner Take Nothing* (1933). Hemingway was a member of what Gertrude Stein called 'the lost generation': those writers and critics who turned their backs on the values of the pre-war world and, finding no artistic stimulus in the post-war American society, became expatriates. He was influenced by Stein's use of repetition, her emphasis on the present moment and her attempts to capture the particular essence of her subject without trying to give that subject a contextual backing. Much has been made of Hemingway's 'toughness' and his style has been linked to his training in journalism, but his style is inseparable from his world-view. His experiences as an ambulance driver in the war caused him to distrust abstractions, reliance on others and romantic views of life. Each person must find their separate peace through action, self-reliance and a code of restraint. In the story, 'Big Two-Hearted River: Part One', Nick Adams, having received a psychic wound in the war, goes camping in the Michigan woods:

> With the ax he slit off a bright slab of pine from one of the stumps and split it into pegs for the tent. He wanted them long and solid to hold in the ground . . . Nick tied the rope that served the tent for a ridge-pole to the trunk of one of the pine trees and pulled the tent up off the ground with the other end of the rope and tied it to the other pine. The tent hung on the rope like a canvas blanket on a clothesline. Nick poked a hole he had cut up under the back peak of the canvas and then made it a tent by pegging out the sides. He pegged the sides out taut and drove the pegs deep, hitting them into the ground with the flat of the ax until the rope loops were buried and the canvas was drum tight.

Taken in the context of the story, this style is highly mimetic of Nick's emotional state. The past has no lessons to offer and the future is, at best, very uncertain. Only consecutive actions in the present have any meaning and only through those can the protagonist exert any control over his life. Adjectives are avoided, as are literary reminiscences. Thus his style becomes his way of dealing with his wound. Much the same can be seen in *The Sun Also Rises*, where the novel's narrator, Jake Barnes, wounded like Nick, only now physically emasculated, has to adopt a particular style of restraint and adjustment to define the period, explain the expatriate nature of the 'lost generation' and to protect himself from despair, always lurking on the edges of Hemingway's world.

Hemingway and Fitzgerald were friends, often very uneasily so, and both have been taken to define major aspects of American literature of the 1920s and 1930s. Yet they are, fundamentally, very different and, again, style and content are inextricably linked. Unlike Hemingway, Fitzgerald borrows heavily from literary antecedents, The structure of *Gatsby*, in its use of the neophyte/adept pairing, looks back to both *Moby-Dick* and Conrad's *Heart of Darkness*, and everywhere one finds echoes of Fitzgerald's favourite poet, John Keats. Not only did the Romantic poet give Fitzgerald the title of his last completed novel, *Tender is the Night*, but *The Great Gatsby* is suffused with the Romantic fear of time and a herd-like society. The Keatsian technique of synaesthesia, whereby the impression gained is described in an unexpected mixing of senses, as in 'yellow cocktail music'; a sense of the artist constantly battling a philistine world; and the attempts to seek a numinous vision, the green light in the distance: all these aspects make Fitzgerald a Romantic writer where Hemingway was emphatically not. Fitzgerald was also a more committed *American* writer. *Gatsby* is generally regarded as one of the most brilliant and complex attempts to delineate the 'American dream' and *Tender is the Night*, although it deals with expatriate Americans in Europe, would show, if subjected to rigorous footnoting, how many references there are to American culture and how Dick Diver and his wife, Nicole, bring to the European area of action many of the problems of that culture. In his final, unfinished novel, *The Last Tycoon* (1941), Fitzgerald, now an unsuccessful screenwriter, turned to the Hollywood novel, thus joining John O'Hara (*Hope of Heaven*, 1938), Nathanael West (*The Day of the Locust*, 1939) and Budd Schulberg (*What Makes Sammy Run*, 1941) in finding the 'dream dump' an appropriate symbol of a nation that had lost its way.

The third great writer, William Faulkner, probably the greatest of the three in terms of the quality and consistency of his fictional output, was a southern writer. This implies a strong interest in cultural memory, for southern society is ruled by the twin fixations of the Civil War and slavery. Indeed, Faulkner's greatest achievement, *Absalom! Absalom!* (1936), is about one man's attempt to piece together, from memory, oral history, letters, memoirs and public records, the essence of the South in terms of his own family history. Like Willa Cather (Nebraska), James T. Farrell (Chicago), John Steinbeck (California), Eudora Welty (the Mississippi Delta) and Erskine Caldwell (Georgia), Faulkner soon settled down to writing about families in his 'own little postage stamp of native soil'. As with Jane Austen, narrowness of locale does not indicate narrowness of vision. Faulkner used an array of modernist techniques – complex time-schemes, multiple narrators, stream of consciousness – in order to bring his characters into byzantine relationships with the history, class structure, racial divides, economics and myths of his very own community, Yoknapatawpha County, and its county seat, Jefferson. What remains most impressive about Faulkner's work, however, is not that he is the finest writer of regional works in American literature, but his marvellous grasp of psychology and the relation of the human consciousness to timeless verities. It is not easy to illustrate from Faulkner's work because each of his novels is different in both large and subtle ways and his style moves in different directions to accommodate these shifts. Here is a passage from 'Barn Burning' (1938):

> The boy crouched on his nail keg at the back of the crowded room, knew he smelled cheese, and more: from where he sat he could see the ranked shelves close-packed with the solid, squat, dynamic shapes of tin cans whose labels his stomach read, not from the lettering which meant nothing to his mind but from the scarlet devils and the silver curve of the fish-this, the cheese which he knew he smelled and the hermetic meat which his intestines believed he smelled coming in intermittent gusts momentary and brief between the other constant one, the smell and sense just a little of fear because mostly of despair and grief, the old fierce pull of blood.

The sentences here are far removed from Hemingway's. The extraordinary length of Faulkner's sentences seems to stem from his attempts to see time as unwinding slowly from a spool and then rewinding. It is endless, not sectioned. Also this length is needed to try and capture the working of the human consciousness; intricate, perverse, erratic, doubling back on itself, and repetitive. Here, a small boy is sitting in a courtroom where his father is accused of arson. He is hungry and this is conveyed brilliantly by the use of 'dynamic', a word usually associated with movement and energy, applied to a tin can which assumes this force to the boy in his hunger. 'Hermetic' may, and indeed should, mean 'completely sealed in its wrapping' but could also mean 'magical', which enhances its powerful attraction for the boy and leads to the larger, more universal terms that are to follow. The hunger modulates into bigger, grimmer words as his consciousness of his surroundings expands and the courtroom becomes oppressive. The passage ends with 'blood', a much-used word in Faulkner's work, because it denotes violence linked to the blood of family and heredity. Faulkner is a historical novelist at a time, in the 1930s, when the historical novel was very popular, for reasons of both parallelism and escapism. Unlike his popular counterparts,

Hervey Allen (*Anthony Adverse*, 1933), Kenneth Roberts (*Northwest Passage*, 1937) and Margaret Mitchell (*Gone With The Wind*, 1936), Faulkner refused the easy assumption that the past is a foreign country where they do things differently, and, instead, contemplated the persistence of human evil and hope across a century or so.

Other writers

Five other writers should briefly be mentioned in the period before the Second World War. Sherwood Anderson seemed to embody much of the artistic spirit of his time. Embroidering the break-up of his marriage, he allegedly walked out on his commercial occupation as well as his wife, moved from the country to the city and took up creative writing. Much more importantly, he influenced, in various ways, both Hemingway and Faulkner and produced the first major work of American literature after the First World War. *Winesburg, Ohio* (1919) is one of the first works of American fiction to show the influence of Freud in various studies of sexual and cultural repression. Following E. W. Howe's *The Story of a Country Town* (1883), Anderson showed that the notion of the small midwestern town as the moral and spiritual heartland of America was a myth disguising the intellectual paucity, the narrow provincialism and the destructive legacy of Puritanism in such a place. In doing so, he paved the way for the biting criticisms of the midwestern 'booboisie' that made H. L. Mencken famous in the 1920s and 1930s. Anderson made two significant contributions to the development of American fiction. He virtually created the short-story composite, wherein a collection of short stories develops toward a novel form by being linked through character, themes and, particularly, place. Works that are indebted to him for this would be Faulkner's *The Unvanquished* (1938) and *Go Down, Moses* (1942), Hemingway's *In Our Time* (1925), William March's *Company K* (1933), John Steinbeck's *The Long Valley* (1938) and Eudora Welty's *The Golden Apples* (1949). Anderson also, though admittedly very tenuously, created a recording intelligence in the character of George Willard, a person to whom the other inhabitants of Winesburg tell their stories and whose career is influenced by what he so learns. George is the merest sketch for Nick Carraway and Chick Mallison (in Faulkner's *Intruder in the Dust*, 1948), but the line of descent is there. As well as being the year that *Winesburg, Ohio* was published, 1919 was also the date of first publication of Mencken's *The American Language*, subsequently much revised and expanded, which influenced American writers by its defence of American

English in terms of the richness and flexibility it derived from its 'melting pot' development.

Sinclair Lewis became, in 1930, the first American author to receive the Nobel Prize in literature. Another midwesterner, Lewis made his name with his satiric portraits of that part of the country in *Main Street* (1920), *Arrowsmith* (1925), *Elmer Gantry* (1927) and, pre-eminently, *Babbitt* (1922). *Babbitt*, as a satire of American consumerism, is frequently brilliant, and Lewis's use of the mock-heroic style, whereby grandiose attitudes are attached to the meretricious objects of a philistine, materialist society, is splendidly achieved. A much less serious *Gatsby*, perhaps. For America and the rest of the world, Lewis set down the American male of the day. The problem with the novel, as many have seen, is that George Babbitt works well as an example of what David Riesman was later to call the 'other-directed' American: someone whose individual traits have been lost in a conformity that makes the human and non-human almost interchangeable. This might reasonably lead to some sympathy for Babbitt as a victim of society, but Lewis tries to make him a 'round' rather than the 'flat' character this kind of novel requires, by giving him the impulse to rebellion, flashes of insight into lost artistic opportunities, and the recurring image of the 'fairy child' (Keats again!) who represents his imaginative longings. Fitzgerald could keep in balance Gatsby the dreamer and Gatsby the slave of the consumerist world, Lewis cannot. Babbitt is not given a sufficient personality to cope with this weight of meaning and so the novel is awkwardly skewed.

John Dos Passos made significant contributions to the modernist impulse in early twentieth-century American fiction with his great trilogy, *U.S.A: The 42nd Parallel* (1930), *1919* (1932) and *The Big Money* (1936), in which he sought to encompass the life of the American nation between 1900 and 1929. He achieved this by intermingling four distinct techniques: a fragmentary chronicle of the lives of a dozen fictional characters; potted biographies of leading figures of the time; stream-of-consciousness passages called 'Camera Eye'; and newsreel impressions of social occurrences, where he made use of cinema techniques.

Judging by the tastes of undergraduates, John Steinbeck's popularity has never waned and, though too much of his fiction is marred by sentimentality and melodramatic excess, he wrote one undoubted masterpiece, *The Grapes of Wrath* (1939). Here the plight of an 'Oakie' family in the Depression years, through careful use of biblical allusions and mythic structures, attains the status of a true, national and deeply felt quest, and is also, through an inventive and superbly detailed use of the intercalary chapters, linked to an analysis of Depression America in terms of its effects on the family unit. Steinbeck is, at his best, a wonderful writer and yarn-spinner. William Golding once remarked, in reference to the opening chapter of *Grapes* – where 'Every moving thing lifted the dust into the air; a walking man lifted a thin layer as high as his waist, and a wagon lifted the dust as high as the fence tops, and an automobile boiled a cloud behind it' – that readers knew, on perusing this opening, that they were hooked by a master storyteller.

Nathanael West's death in an automobile accident in 1940, while still in his mid-thirties, robbed American literature of a distinctive voice, and one that may have looked forward to post-war literature more decisively than any of his contemporaries. West had time to complete only four short novels; of these, *The Dream Life of Balso Snell* (1931) was surrealist babble and *A Cool Million* (1934) was a splendid and funny joke but one that, because it lacked variety, way outlasted its welcome. However, the other two, *Miss Lonelyhearts* (1933) and *The Day of the Locust* (1939), created astonishingly assured black comedies out of two symbols of the adulteration of values in America: the agony columnist and the motion picture industry. West's world is one of absurdity, grotesquerie and entropy – the notion that energy is leaking out of humanity and into the things of the world. It is a Dickensian vision without that novelist's positive sense of humanity. In these novels natural chronology is warped, particularly in movies, and offers no suggestion of progress. Language does not mean what it says and bears no particular relation to gesture, action or facial expression. Love is equated to pain and frustration; nature does not heal the spirit and the only realistic expectation is death.

New voices and social developments

The First World War seemed like a genuine watershed in the development of American fiction – almost as though two or three pages of its history had been accidentally turned over at the same time. It is difficult to have quite the same feeling about the Second World War. Although Fitzgerald and West are dead, on consecutive days, Faulkner and Hemingway are still writing powerful and significant novels. Changes are, however, certainly there. The war produced war novels, of course. So did the First World War, and the earlier efforts seem, in retrospect, more impressive and forward-looking than the later. Dos Passos in *Three Soldiers* (1921), e. e. cummings in *The Enormous Room* (1922), March's *Company K* and Hemingway's *A Farewell To Arms* seek to find stylistic and structural correlatives for the process of trying to make sense of a chaotic situation. Though that is true of some of the later writing, such as John Horne

Burns's *The Gallery* (1947) and John Hawkes's *The Cannibal* (1949), it is often easy to feel that the needs of the market for blockbusting bestsellers and Hollywood for war movies looms – for example in Irwin Shaw's *The Young Lions* (1948), Herman Wouk's *The Caine Mutiny* (1951), James Jones's *From Here To Eternity* (1951) and Leon Uris's *Battle Cry* (1953) – larger than the possibility of literary experiment. A sort of exception may be made of Norman Mailer's monumental *The Naked and the Dead* (1948), but only in part. Mailer draws on the naturalistic tradition, as do the others, but he, like Dos Passos, makes gestures towards a modernist technique in his interruptions of the narrative with potted biographies of his characters, playing these off against the approaches to experience embodied in these very different soldiers.

American fiction after the Second World War saw the rapid rise in importance of the Jewish novelist. There had been powerful novels about Jews by Jews before this – Abraham Cahan's *The Rise of Davis Levinsky* (1917), Mike Gold's *Jews Without Money* (1930) and, especially, Henry Roth's *Call It Sleep* (1934) – but they were few and far between. It needed the addition of more years and another generation before they came of age. The Jewish novelist was also the city novelist par excellence and came into prominence with a knowledge of the Holocaust and, therefore, great feelings of anger, guilt and fear. Nathanael West changed his surname from Weinstein, and Jewishness does not greatly impinge on his fiction. The same could be said of Norman Mailer, J. D. Salinger and Joseph Heller (*Catch-22*, 1961), and also, for the first 20 years of his career as a playwright, Arthur Miller, who did, however, publish a very powerful if rather schematic and hysterical novel about anti-Semitism in America, *Focus* (1945). This reticence is overshadowed by the very Jewish fiction of Bernard Malamud, Edward Lewis Wallant, Philip Roth and, especially, Saul Bellow. In their novels, particularly Malamud's *The Assistant* (1957), suffering becomes a key condition for understanding the meaning of existence and the necessity of becoming fully human. Traditional values often clash with the extreme materialism of post-war American society (in Roth's *Goodbye, Columbus*, 1959). These are primarily humanist novels, searching for ways to reach out to people, and to understand and love them. In Wallant's *The Pawnbroker* (1960) a German survivor of the prison camps, now living in America, learns to overcome his cynical fatalism through a friendship with a Puerto Rican boy who works in his shop. In Bellow's *The Victim* (1948) a supporting character, Schlossberg, a drama critic, encapsulates Leventhal's problems and points the way for him by his advice:

> Good acting is what is exactly human. And if you say I am a tough critic, you
> mean I have a high opinion of what is human. This is my whole idea. More
> than human, can you have any use for life? Less than human, you don't either.

Perhaps *The Victim* is Bellow's most Jewish novel. After that he broadens out into larger, more picaresque novels, though *Herzog* (1964) shows him to be the most naturally intellectual of modern Jewish novelists in the ease with which he makes one Jew's search for self-knowledge a paradigm of the urban problems of the time and a way, through ideas, to an acceptance of the human condition.

The 1950s in America was also the decade of 'youth culture', when teenagers separated themselves from the culture of their parents to assert their own identity and stress the importance of peer-group politics. That theirs was a subculture rather than a counterculture and their revolt rather irrelevant is well caught in the title of the most famous 'teenpic' of that decade, *Rebel Without a Cause*. If James Dean became the principal icon of teenage rebellion, its principal guru was J. D. Salinger. Before he fell into complete silence in the mid-1960s, Salinger wrote a number of excellent short stories and one very good novel, *The Catcher in the Rye* (1951). Few American novels have been discussed so frequently or banned in high school and college libraries so often. This novel has also been much misunderstood, since it is usually seen as either a severe critique of American consumerism and lack of ideals or as a sentimentalised view of a misunderstood young man. There are undoubtedly both these elements in the novel, but its chief claim to high standing is as a masterly portrait of teenagerdom. The world seems vacuous and 'phony' because of the solipsism of the young imagination, while the funny and embarrassing contradictions of Holden's character are easily explained by his loneliness, his non-directed and thus promiscuous reading and, very much, because of his lack of a peer group. The novel was much imitated in works like John Knowles's *A Separate Peace* (1958) but, lest we view the children of *Huckleberry Finn* – relatively innocent, uninitiated, carrying the precarious hopes of the adult world – as a persistent strain of American heroism, the darker side of youth was forcefully portrayed in Calder Willingham's *End As A Man* (1947), about a psychopath in a cadet school, and William March's *The Bad Seed* (1954), about a child murderess. March's novel was published in the same year as William Golding's British novel, *Lord of the Flies* which, as American society moved from the 1950s to the 1960s, replaced *The Catcher in the Rye* as required college hip-pocket reading.

With major steps in the development of civil rights occurring during this period, African American literature more than kept pace. Early progenitors of this were James Weldon Johnson's *Autobiography of an Ex-Colored Man* (1912); Jean Toomer's *Cane* (1923), a collection of sketches held together by the tension between the black experiences of the South and the North; Nella Larson's *Quicksand* (1928) and *Passing* (1929), which chronicle the problems of a part-white woman who is also a lesbian; and Zora Neale Hurston's *Their Eyes Were Watching God* (1937), the fictional work of a cultural anthropologist who celebrated black life with great attention to language, humour and the strength of community spirit. Like the Jewish novel, these examples of excellence appeared sporadically and without achieving any significant influence in their own time, despite the emergence of the 'Harlem Renaissance' in the 1920s. The same might be said of Richard Wright. He is best known for *Uncle Tom's Children* (1938), a collection of stories based on his experiences as a young man in Mississippi, and *Native Son* (1940), a major novel with a brutal black murderer as its central protagonist, whose growth in understanding of his racial identity is matched, in naturalistic terms, by growing anger, bitterness, resentment and defiance. Wright's influence can be seen, long after the publication of his book, in the first great play by a black American, Lorraine Hansbury's *A Raisin in the Sun* (1959), but, sooner than that, in the writings of James Baldwin and in Ralph Ellison's wonderful novel *Invisible Man* (1952). Baldwin response to the power of *Native Son*, in *Go Tell It on the Mountain* (1953) and, less impressively, in *Giovanni's Room* (1956) and *Another Country* (1962), is to oppose what he feels is Wright's 'rejection of life'. He tries to counter this by emphasising the role of religion and sex in black life, both of which intensify the narrator's feelings of guilt but also lead him to accept the burdens of love. *Invisible Man* is a joyous literary triumph; a picaresque black comedy that takes on board the history of black Americans from Booker T. Washington to the Harlem riots. Of particular importance to an understanding of this novel are the 'Prologue' and 'Epilogue' that frame the story. The 'Prologue' situates the hero's escape into a floodlit hole as indicative of despair at the black predicament, but the 'Epilogue' moves him to reject an absurdist view in favour of some form of social action:

> I suppose it's damn well time. Even hibernations can be overdone, come to think of it. Perhaps that's my greatest social crime. I've overstayed my hibernation, since there's a possibility that even an invisible man has a socially responsible role to play.

Other black writers of this time were Ann Petry (*The Street*, 1946), Ishmael Reed (*The Free Lance Pallbearers*, 1967), Chester Himes (*If He Hollers Let Him Go*, 1945, and *The Primitive*, 1955) and Paule Marshall (*Brown Girl, Brownstones*, 1959, and *Soul Clap Hands and Sing*, 1961).

It took the development of civil rights in the 1950s and 1960s to rediscover the work of writers like Toomer and Hurston in the latter decade. The same is true of earlier women writers such as Kate Chopin and Mary Austin

(*Earth Horizon*, 1932). As American fiction neared the wave of feminism in the late 1960s and early 1970s there were reappraisals of Carson McCullers and Flannery O'Connor: southern novelists without Faulkner's sense of place and time whose characters are deformed and grotesque, inhabiting a gothic southern world in a manner that Malcom Cowley once called 'Dixie Gongorism'. The inhabitants of this world find violence, corrupt sexuality and intense religiosity. Feminist *Bildungsromans* include Shirley Jackson's *Hangsaman* (1951) and Sylvia Plath's *The Bell Jar* (1963). Mary McCarthy's *The Group* (1963) expresses main concerns of the time through entirely feminine viewpoints that are shown to lack a developed vantage point or a language to express it. Alison Lurie's *The Nowhere City* (1965) provides amusing comment on West Coast sexual mores, and the early fiction of Joyce Carol Oates (*Expensive People*, 1968, and *Them*, 1969) shows how significant aspects of the American dream are male-oriented and very much not shared by American women.

Those fundamental indicators of the American mentality of the 1950s, the suburbs, find their commentators in John Cheever (*The Wapshot Chronicle*, 1957, and *The Wapshot Scandal*, 1964) and John Updike (*Rabbit, Run*, 1960, and *Couples*, 1968). The former creates a white Protestant community, ostensibly to combat the anomie of large cities, but increasingly to show similarities between the two, while Updike shows the paucity of flight and sex as substitutes for older moral codes that need to be revivified through art. These two are examples of reputations that have not worn well: Cheever because of ill-disguised misogyny and Updike because of rather too much massaging of the male ego.

The 1950s produced the 'Beat Generation' of which Jack Kerouac's *On The Road* (1957) is the iconic novel. Endlessly popular with young people, the novel has not had the critical attention it deserves. Its sense of rebellion ultimately seems vapid, but Kerouac can see the falsity of some of its flight from convention, and the novel's deep sense of American space, beauty and timelessness is a meaningful updating of transcendentalist visions.

New voices, new styles

In a collection of pieces entitled *The New Journalism* (1973), Tom Wolfe, the author of *The Kandy-Kolored Tangerine Flake Steamline Baby* (1965) and an excellent account of the antics of Ken Kesey and the Merry Pranksters, *The Kool-Aid Acid Test* (1968), argued that the novel as a chronicle of society had had its day and needed to be replaced by a new kind of journalism that would perform the task of showing the interplay between people and the forces around them: 'The crucial part that reporting plays in all story-telling, whether in novels, films, or non-fiction, is something that is not so much ignored as simply not comprehended'. It was soon clear what he meant. After demonstrating his powers as a novelist, Norman Mailer turned to report-ing with *The Armies of the Night* (1968), an account of the protest march on the Pentagon in 1967, arguing that American politics had become so absurd that the line between fact and fiction had become blurred. The sub-title of the work is *History as a Novel, the Novel as History*. Truman Capote, in *In Cold Blood* (1966), an account of a particularly brutal and senseless murder in rural Kansas, found that events seemed naturally to shape the crime into a nightmarish battle between the haves and the have-nots, so that the fictional arrangement of the facts made sense of the apparently senseless. At this time, indeed, novels began to mix history and fiction to great effect, even if the history is, itself, fantastic. E. L. Doctorow's *The Book of Daniel* (1971) and *Ragtime* (1975) do this; first in the matter of the Rosenberg case and then about race relations in the early 1900s, where a fictional char-acter, Coalhouse Walker, representing dispossessed blacks, meets real events and people, such as Emma Goldman and Booker T. Washington in a some-times anachronistic account of early twentieth-century history 'from the bottom up'. John Barth's *The Sot-Weed Factor* (1960) is based on colonial Maryland history and a little-known poem by Ebenezer Cooke. Thomas Pynchon's colossal *Gravity's Rainbow* (1973) takes the operations of the German V2 rocket in the Second World War as the starting point for an examination of the random, entropic nature of the modern world. It is a deliberately excessive novel, mixing something of a plot with anti-plot chaos amid a welter of ideas, figures and data.

What made Tom Wolfe feel that journalism needed to replace the novel? More than anything it was the development, in the late 1960s and early 1970s, of metafiction. The prefix 'meta-' is usually taken to mean 'going above and beyond', and its extensive use at this time coincides with post-modernism, in accounts of which it is possible to find such terms as 'metahistory', 'metanarrative' and 'metalanguage'. These terms are wholly in keeping with primary notions of postmodernism: the emphasis on the cultural manufacture of seemingly natural aspects of life and the balancing acts between self-reflexivity and history/politics. Metafiction is fiction that is often self-referential or parodic, as in Richard Brautigan's *A Confederate General from Big Sur* (1964) and *The Hawkline Monster* (1974); Donald Barthelme's *Snow White* (1967) and *Unspeakable Practices, Unnatural Acts* (1969);

and John Barth's *Chimera* (1972) and *Letters* (1979). It demonstrates a very wary attitude to reality, always assuming that that exists. Many of these authors, as if to underline the constructed nature of reality, delight both in the endless play of language (Vladimir Nabokov, *Lolita*, 1955/8; Robert Coover, *Pricksongs and Descants*, 1969; John Hawkes, *The Lime Twig*, 1961) and in drawing attention to their fictions as artefacts (Nabokov, *Pale Fire*, 1962; Coover, *The Universal Baseball Association, Inc*, 1968; William H. Gass, *Willie Master's Lonesome Wife*, 1968), but with the further design of drawing attention to the fictionality of the outside world. More than one author in the second half of the century – Philip Roth comes to mind – has stressed the difficulty of concocting plots to match the extraordinary reality of the United States. Metafiction moved to the farthest extreme from the nineteenth-century belief in the progress of the central character, the validity of the essential self and the solidity of the external world in which its characters strive to make their place.

By the 1980s realism was making something of a comeback, even if the routes were rather tortuous. The critic, Jerome Klinkowitz, coined two phrases to show different directions for admittedly loose definitions of 'realism'. One was 'experimental realism', referring to such works as Paul Auster's *New York Trilogy* (1985/6), Leonard Michaels's *Going Places* (1969) and *The Men's Club* (1981) and Walter Abish's *How German Is It* (1881). Here many of the features of metafiction are in evidence: the parody of detective stories that allows for serious possibilities of 'detecting' meaning; the generous use of literary sources; self-reflexivity; but also a greater attempt to reconstitute the validity of memory and design. Writers such as Abish and Stephen Dixon (*No Relief*, 1976) seek to avoid transparent signifiers and concentrate on 'the self-apparent word', whereby the texts do not offer a window on to the 'real' world, but draw attention to the acts of composition and their relationship to the richness of the human imagination. Klinkowitz has also written a book on the new American 'novel of manners' where, discussing such writers as Thomas McGuane (*Nobody's Angel*, 1982, and *Something to be Desired*, 1984); Dan Wakefield (*Selling Out*, 1985), and Richard Yates (*Young Hearts Crying*, 1984), he found that the term no longer suggested the decorum and order of a society that might be tempered by the wit and humanity of newcomers, but rather the focus on the compositional aspects of manners in the novel and the relationships of characters to the new signifying systems in the world around them. *Young Hearts Crying*, in particular, owes something to Scott Fitzgerald and follows a deceptively simple but very subtly written story of a couple too tied to their conventional, if high, expectations of life to read the signs around them coherently and make the right choices.

'Dirty realism' is a term used to describe novels and stories, mostly from the 1980s, that eschew fantasy, playful use of language, parody or self-reflexivity. Instead, they concentrate on working or lower-middle-class lives in mundane surroundings, and banal dialogue and small surprises. They can, to be sure, feel like watching paint dry or bread bake, but, in some of these writers, notably Richard Ford (*A Piece of My Heart*, 1976, and *The Sportswriter*, 1986); Raymond Carver (*What We Talk About When We Talk About Love*, 1981, and *Cathedral*, 1983); Bobbie Ann Mason (*In Country*, 1985) and, especially, Jayne Anne Phillips (*Machine Dreams*, 1984, and *Fast Lanes*, 1987), while the characters are limited in vision and edged to the peripheries of the material world, there is a satisfying solidity to the world described and a vivid sense, often through the vernacular, of half-forgotten neighbourhoods and real problems in getting through the day:

> There are a few high-priced shops behind mullioned windows-men's stores and franchised woman's undergarments salons are in ascendance. Book stores are down. Aggressive, sometimes bad-tempered divorcees (some of the seminarians ex-wives) own most of the shops and they have given the square a fussy, homespun air that reminds you of life pictured in catalogs (a view I rather like). It is not a town that seems very busy. (*The Sportswriter*)

The term 'magic realism', first attributed to Borges and describing fantastic places and happenings while retaining a realistic view of politics and society, is more obviously linked to non-American writers, such as Salman Rushdie and Gabriel García Márquez, but could be applied to the fiction of John Irving (*The World According to Garp*, 1978, and *Hotel New Hampshire*, 1981) and Toni Morrison.

Morrison herself points to strong developments in black fiction, particularly in her novels *Sula* (1971) and *Beloved* (1987) and those of Alice Walker (*Meridian*, 1976, and *The Color Purple*, 1983), to such an extent that Morrison could arguably now be the most celebrated living American novelist. Walker creates what she calls a 'womanist ' view and emphasises the plight of the black woman, torn between the sense of blackness foisted on her by a white society and her sense of black womanhood defined in reaction to the macho posturing of black men. Toni Morrison, a greater writer, draws, like Alex Haley, on African-inspired oral history and traces, in an epic sweep, the relations between black history, community and wider, eternal aspects of life. In her best-known novel, *Beloved*, acute use of symbolism, psychology and historical awareness is harnessed to one of the truly great ghost stories.

The melting pot

No account, however brief and superficial, of the twentieth-century American novel, can end before it remarks on the intense growth of cultural and racial multiplicity that has been manifested over the past quarter of a century. Among Native American novelists, N. Scott Momaday (*House Made of Dawn*, 1968, and *The Ancient Child*, 1989) is distinguished by his use of Kiowa tales and sensitive descriptions of the Rainy Mountain lands of Oklahoma. He makes interesting use of a mix of viewpoints and styles. Leslie Marmon Silko (*Ceremony*, 1977) is a Laguna Indian from New Mexico who writes powerfully of the links between mankind and nature and the terrible wounds made in that nature by such advances as uranium mining. Louise Erdrich (*Love Medicine*, 1984, and *Tracks*, 1988), a Chippewa, is noted for being a marvellous stylist with a strong sense of the comic and a gift for intertwining myth and realism.

Maxine Hong Kingston (*The Woman Warrior*, 1976, and *Tripmaster Monkey: His Fake Book*, 1989) is a Chinese American who, like the distinguished playwright, David Henry Hwang, mingles Chinese philosophy and legend with a strong critique of the difficulties assimilating to the American way of life, especially as a woman. She is noted for subtle and inventive stylistic devices and derives strength from her autobiographical material.

Chicano/a writers such as Helena María Vimontes (*The Mother*, 1985), Sandra Cisneros (*The House on Mango Street*, 1984, and *Woman Hollering Creek*, 1991) and Rolando Himojosa-Smith (*Sketches of the Valley*, 1973, and *Rites and Witnesses*, 1982) write perceptively of the problems of living in a disjointed borderland between two cultures.

Ralph Ellison once said that the search for identity 'is *the* American theme. The nature of our society is such that we are prevented from knowing who we are. It is still a young society, and that is an integral part of its development'. The above listings suggest that the 'melting pot' of American society is now producing a truly multicultural range of fictions; an experimental and epic variety of writing that seeks to find new voices and capture the immense potential and frustration of holding together such a vast, complex and contradictory culture.

Popular formulae

There has been no room in an essay of this length to deal with the contributions of American writers to popular culture. There has always been, however, a willingness, on the part of American writers, to consider all forms of writing as equally creative. In the history of American literature, what is one to call *Letters from an American Farmer*? *Walden*? *The Education of Henry Adams* (a work of the greatest importance to the development of modernist literature in the first half of the twentieth century)? *The Ugly American*? *Zen and the Art of Motorcycle Maintenance*? Certainly, American novelists have never been afraid to use popular literary formulae for serious purposes. Science fiction has been used profoundly by Kurt Vonnegut (*The Sirens of Titan*, 1959, *Slaughterhouse Five*, 1969, and *Breakfast of Champions*, 1973), by Thomas Pynchon (*V*, 1963, and *Gravity's Rainbow*, 1973) and Ursula LeGuin (*A Wizard of Earthsea*, 1968, and *The Left Hand of Darkness*, 1969). Detective fiction, especially of the 'hard-boiled' and conspiratorial kind, has been inflected with considerable cultural significance in the novels of Paul Auster (*City of Glass*, 1985, *Ghosts*, 1986, and *The Locked Room*, 1986), Ishmael Reed (*Mumbo Jumbo*, 1972) and Truman Capote's *In Cold Blood* (1966). Influences from science fiction and the detective story are brilliantly modulated in the work of perhaps the most significant American novelist of the past 20 years, Don DeLillo.

DeLillo has said, in a rare interview, that 'my work has always been informed by mystery' and 'I think fiction rescues history from its own confusions'. For DeLillo, American society since the 1960s has become increasingly dominated by conspiracies, technology, banks and policy agencies. His characters find themselves enmeshed in a tremendous cultural obscurity that needs a plot to sort it all out. He describes sights with meticulous care, particularly those of the city, its various kinds of buildings and artefacts. Names, language and movement seem to disguise more than they reveal. So the detective has to be an artist ready, not merely to interpret chaos but, finally, to impose an arbitrary order upon it, even if that hints at further chaos down the line. Nicholas Branch, in *Libra*, is trying to piece together the gigantic puzzle of the Kennedy assassination, but finds himself overwhelmed by detail. In other words, he lacks what DeLillo suggests so often and richly that the artist must have: 'a sense of something extraordinary hovering just beyond our touch and just beyond our vision'. DeLillo manages to convey both the misery and the endless fascination of American lives.

Not an ending

Earlier, I quoted from an interview with Ralph Ellison that was first published in the *Paris Review* in 1955 and later reprinted in his 1964 collection of essays, *Shadow and Act*. Its concluding paragraph will serve as a conclusion to this essay:

I feel that with my decision to devote myself to the novel I took on one of the responsibilities inherited by those who practice the craft in the Unites States: that of describing for all that fragment of the huge diverse American experience which I know best, and which offers me the possibility of contributing not only to the growth of the literature but to the shaping of the culture as I should like it to be. The American novel is in this sense a conquest of the frontier; as it describes our experience, it creates it.

Surveying the richness and variety of fiction in the United States over the past century, it is clear that so many talented artists have described their fragments so masterfully that they have made lasting contributions to American culture and set out, with courage and great skill, on the perpetual attempt to conquer the frontier.

Further reading

Bell, B.W., *The Afro-American Novel and its Tradition* (1987).

Bradbury, M., *The Modern American Novel* (1992).

Fetterley, J., *The Resisting Reader* (1978).

Hassan, I., *Radical Innocence* (1961).

Hilfer, T., *American Fiction since 1940* (1992).

Lee, B., *American Fiction 1865–1940* (1987).

O'Donnell, P., *Passionate Doubts: Designs of Interpretation in Contemporary American Literature* (1986).

Pizer, D., *Realism and Naturalism in Nineteenth Century American Literature* (1966).

Rideout, W.B., *The Radical Novel in the United States 1900–1954* (1956).

Scholes, R., *Fabulation and Metafiction* (1979).

Stevick, P., *Alternative Pleasures: Postrealist Fiction and the Tradition* (1981).

Tanner, T., *City of Words* (1971).

Young, T. D. (ed.), *Modern American Fiction: Form and Function* (1989).

CHAPTER 11

Twentieth-century American poetry

Daniel Kane

A merican poets in the twentieth century not merely registered the impact of modernism but were its exemplary figures. People looked to the United States for new voices and forms of experimentation, and for a democratic verse that would expand on the work of Walt Whitman and Emily Dickinson. Inherited tone, content, form, poetics and even the lines dividing poetry from other genres were all questioned radically by American poets at the turn of the century. 'Make it new' was Ezra Pound's iconic imperative to his contemporaries and heirs. It is this urge towards newness and innovation that characterises the best of twentieth-century American poetry.

What was Pound reacting against in his desire to 'make it new'? To help us answer this question, we must look back to the nineteenth century, particularly to the period, dominant in Britain, known as Victorian poetry (so defined because it was written during the reign of Queen Victoria, 1837–1901). Most of the popular American poetry in the United States during the Victorian period depended on a fairly stable, British-centered notion of composition that adhered to traditional poetic forms (the sonnet, for example) and stable metres. The most widely used metre in English-language poetry at the time was iambic pentameter, a metrical pattern consisting of five iambic feet per line. An iamb, or iambic foot, consists of one unstressed syllable followed by a stressed syllable. Examples of iambic pentameter include British poet Alfred Lord Tennyson's 'Come Down O Maid' ('Come down, O maid, from yonder mountain height') and American poet John Greenleaf Whittier's 'The Fair Quakeress' ('She was a fair young girl, yet on her brow').

As Christopher MacGowan asserts, much nineteenth-century American poetry did not distinguish itself rhythmically or thematically from British poetry.

> Rhymed lyric poetry was to the fore, and such poetry was directly addressed to the reader, usually expressed the feelings of the poet – feelings that were heightened in some way – and, even if the emotions conveyed were not entirely those of pleasure, the lyric quality of the poem, its rhyme, and its summary conclusion, were intended to make reading it a pleasurable, uplifting experience.

With the advent of American poets Walt Whitman and Emily Dickinson, however, readers were able to see that American poets could break resolutely from their Victorian inheritance in order to create a recognisably new poetics. In the preface to the 1855 edition of *Leaves of Grass*, Whitman wrote, 'A great poem is no finish to a man or woman but rather a beginning'. This was (and is) a truly radical proposition to make. Whitman not only rejected inherited British forms of poetry that most of his American contemporaries slavishly imitated, he also proposed a model for the poem that was defined by its very openness, embodied in the idea that a poem is always a 'beginning'.

Formally speaking, Whitman gave us free verse as we know it today. He rejected the use of the then-standard iambic line, replacing it with a rhythm based partly on the Psalms and Gospels and predicated more on the human breath. He also celebrated people, including homosexuals, prostitutes and slaves, with a candour that had not been seen before, exulting in the body and sexuality with an often explicit and always loving diction. ('How beautiful is candor! All faults may be forgiven of him who has perfect candor'). Such a project set the stage for an innovative American poetry, and the poets who followed Whitman – including Ezra Pound – were determined to extend his experiments in form and content.

Emily Dickinson's wry humour and telegraphic style and her use of the hymn measure to transmit a dark, philosophical and often erotic vision likewise proved extremely influential to succeeding American poets. In her wonderful book *My Emily Dickinson*, Susan Howe provides us with a potential reason for Dickinson's ongoing influence on American poets:

> [B]y 1860 it was as impossible for Emily Dickinson simply to translate English poetic tradition as it was for Walt Whitman. In prose and in poetry she explored the implications of breaking the law just short of breaking off communication with a reader. Starting from scratch, she exploded habits of standard human intercourse in her letters, as she cut across the customary chronological linearity of poetry.

As the nineteenth century progressed into the twentieth century, Dickinson's and Whitman's work stood as a kind of model for other ways of writing in distinction to inherited British forms. We should note that Whitman and Dickinson were not just radicals in terms of their form, but also in terms of their content. They allowed for all kinds of sensuousness, political radicalism and gender trouble to make their way into verse.

Though Ezra Pound spent most of his life away from the United States, he had what could generously be described as mixed feelings about British poetry. Milton was compared unfavourably to Dante: 'Consider the definiteness of Dante's presentation as compared with Milton's'. Wordsworth was damned with faint praise: 'Read as much of Wordsworth as does not seem to be unutterably dull' ('A Few Don'ts for Imagists'). Referring to British poet Walter Savage Landor, Pound asserted, 'The decline of England began on the day when Landor packed his trunks and departed to Tuscany' (*How to Read*). Ezra Pound's subsequent focus on innovation, informed partly by Whitman's example, guaranteed that the history of twentieth-century American poetry would be riven with conflict between poets who believed in the continuing relevance of inherited, predominantly British poetic practices, and poets who took Pound's imperative to heart by committing themselves to experimentalism. For the purposes of this essay, then, I would like to refer to *a* history of twentieth-century American poetry: one that is tilted in favour of an innovative poetics.

Modernism, American-style

Modernist poets in the first three decades of the twentieth century extended Whitman's experiments in form and content. Poets including Ezra Pound (1885–1972), T. S. Eliot (1888–1965), Gertrude Stein (1874–1946), Wallace Stevens (1879–1955), William Carlos Williams (1883–1963), HD (1886–1961), Marianne Moore (1887–1972), e. e. cummings (1894–1962) and Hart Crane (1899–1932) called for new ways of imagining what constitutes a poem. Answering Whitman's appeal for a specifically American voice in poetry, many of these writers incorporated distinctly regional and dialect speech into their verse.

Highlighting Whitman's perhaps inadvertent focus on the material nature of language freed from conventional reference, Gertrude Stein wrote in 'Poetry And Grammar':

> And then Walt Whitman came. He wanted really wanted to express the thing and not call it by its name. He worked very hard at that, and he called it

Leaves of Grass because he wanted it to be as little a well known name to be called upon passionately as possible. I do not at all know whether Whitman knew that he wanted to do this but there is no doubt at all but that is what he did want to do.

As if to inscribe Whitman's importance to twentieth-century American poetry, Ezra Pound in his delightfully cranky early poem 'A Pact' wrote: 'I make a pact with you, Walt Whitman –/ I have detested you long enough', acceding at the close of the poem,

It was you that broke the new wood,
Now is a time for carving.
We have one sap and one root –
Let there be commerce between us.

Once again, the idea of newness is presented here as prima facie good ('It was you that broke the new wood'). Interestingly in terms of Pound, who spent most of his life in Europe, we find that poetry is conceived as emanating organically out of America; 'We have one sap and one root' is a metaphor for Pound's and Whitman's 'roots' in the United States.

Despite the cosmopolitanism of nearly all the modernist poets mentioned above, all identified their country of birth as containing the necessary ingredients crucial for a new poetry and poetics. As T. S. Eliot, who lived in London for most of his life, said in an interview with Donald Hall: 'In its sources, in its emotional springs, [my poetry] comes from America'.

Imagism and vorticism

Putting his commitment to newness into practice, Pound invented 'imagism' and, later, 'vorticism'. These were roughly defined movements lasting from about 1912 to 1917 that were attempts by Pound and his contemporaries to mark themselves as innovators breaking away from the turgid practices of their British nineteenth-century ancestors.

In 'A Retrospect', Pound defined some basic approaches to writing that he thought would refresh contemporary poetry:

1. Direct treatment of the 'thing', whether subjective or objective.
2. To use absolutely no word that did not contribute to the presentation.
3. As regarding rhythm: to compose in sequence of the musical phrase, not in sequence of a metronome.

Pound's ideas were greatly informed by his reading of Asian literature. He was especially taken with Japanese *haiku*, poems of 17 syllables that usually present only two juxtaposed images. *Haiku* do not bother with figurative devices like analogy, allegory or even metaphor. Pound was impressed by this economy in writing, and was inspired to write his celebrated imagist poem 'In a Station of the Metro' which, like *haiku*, juxtaposes two images:

> The apparition of these faces in the crowd;
> Petals on a wet, black bough.

Similar imagist moments occur in the work of other modernists. William Carlos Williams's famous poem 'The Red Wheelbarrow' contains only a red wheelbarrow 'glazed with rain / water / beside the white / chickens'. HD's poem 'Oread' yokes together conventionally unrelated items including 'sea' and 'pines', resulting in a visually startling and emotionally violent poem that ends with the lines 'Hurl your green over us. / Cover us with your pools of fir'.

As imagism developed and was taken up by writers with whom Pound was not so willing to be associated, Pound invented vorticism. Vorticist principles applied not just to poetry but to sculpture, painting, music and more. Pound wanted to make the poetic image more intense and dynamic. He wanted to make the image *move*, as he explained in his essay 'Vorticism':

> Vorticism is an intensive art. I mean by this, that one is concerned with the relative intensity, or relative significance, of different sorts of expression. One desires the most intense, for certain forms of expression *are* 'more intense' than others. They are more dynamic. I do not mean that they are more emphatic or yelled louder.

Despite Pound's insistence that adherence to vorticism did not mean poets 'yelled louder', the publication of his and Wyndham Lewis's literary journal *BLAST*, announcing the invention of vorticism, certainly sounded like ranting, albeit erudite ranting. The journal was replete with scurrilous statements and outrageous manifestos. For example, a regular column in the magazine aimed to 'blast' and 'bless' various aspects of literary and social culture. English humour, do-gooders, sportsmen and aesthetics were blasted; trade unionists, music halls, hairdressers and aviators were blessed. Even the cover of *BLAST* was designed to shock. With the single word *BLAST* superimposed in black blockish letters over a garishly pink background, the cover influenced generations of artistic outlaws. (The Sex Pistols modelled the cover of their album *Never Mind the Bollocks* after *BLAST*.)

Imagist and vorticist poets rejected standard rhythm and rhyme and practically stopped using iambic pentameter, the metre of choice for almost all the major British and American writers since Chaucer. The new poetry introduced shifting rhythmic and thematic patterns – Eliot's *The Waste Land* is one of the best examples of this. The poem jumps from song to talk to blank verse to prose, mixing the 'low' speech of barmaids with the 'high' rhetoric of classical literary allusions. Imagism and vorticism in part encouraged poets to let all sorts of new sounds, shapes and images into their poetry, and allowed traditionally competing or dissimilar discourses to co-exist on the same playing field.

Competing modernisms

Imagism and vorticism aligned its adherents and readers to a specifically European modernism by invoking language associated more with continental movements like cubism, German expressionism, and Italian futurism than with American free-verse traditions. This marked one of the first instances of tensions within modernism between a specifically American strain and its more cosmopolitan manifestation. Such tensions were revealed in the feud between William Carlos Williams and T. S. Eliot, as well as in the American poet Robert Frost's highly publicised disdain towards free-verse forms and in Wallace Stevens's heightened aestheticism.

The publication of Eliot's *The Waste Land* (1922) initiated a debate between what it meant to be an American writer liberated from European literary inheritance and what it meant to be a Western writer working within a canonical lineage. Williams in particular believed that Eliot was too attached to European culture and traditions. The enormous popularity of Eliot's *The Waste Land*, a work that contained multiple endnotes referencing Greek myth, Ulysses and Arthurian legend, was anathema to Williams. Williams's project aimed to inscribe colloquial American speech and quotidian action – be it eating plums, going to the doctor, waiting for a bus – into poetry. He therefore saw *The Waste Land* as a huge step back for American poetry. As he wrote in his *Autobiography*:

> Then out of the blue *The Dial* brought out *The Waste Land* and all our hilarity ended. It wiped out our world as if an atom bomb had been dropped upon it and our brave sallies into the unknown were turned to dust . . . I felt at once that it had set me back twenty years, and I'm sure it did. Critically Eliot returned us to the classroom just at the moment when I felt that we were on

the point of an escape to matters much closer to the essence of a new art form itself – rooted in the locality which should give it fruit.

Robert Frost, perhaps the world's most widely known twentieth-century American poet, staked a kind of middle ground between Williams's radical demotic practice and T. S. Eliot's apparent élitism. Though he was affiliated initially with Ezra Pound (who wrote a favourable review of Frost's poems for *Poetry* magazine), Frost was mostly to reject the free-verse techniques of his peers in favour of a more traditional blank verse. (Frost once said he would as soon play tennis without a net as write free verse!) That said, the language that Frost used was surprisingly informal and recognisably American, as we find in these lines from 'The Mending Wall':

My apple trees will never get across
And eat the cones under his pines, I tell him.
He only says, 'Good fences make good neighbors.'
Spring is the mischief in me, and I wonder
If I could put a notion in his head:
'Why do they make good neighbors? Isn't it
Where there are cows? But here there are no cows . . .'

While some critics are tempted to minimise Frost's work by referring to it as 'regional' or 'minor', there are some modern moves in these lines: an ability to synthesise a formal metre (in this case iambic pentameter) with language as it is actually spoken, as well as ironic commentary and ambiguity.

Wallace Stevens, now regarded as one of the most significant poets of the twentieth century, largely avoided coterie affiliation, though like many of the modernist poets he was influenced by Pound's theories. He worked in quiet isolation as an insurance executive in Hartford, Connecticut, yet created a body of work that is startling in its commitment to emphasising how the imagination determines 'reality'. Unlike the poetry affiliated with the Pound/Eliot tradition, Stevens's poetry was not used to re-establish a link with a privileged literary past. Unlike Frost, Stevens did not employ regular metres in the service of a typically American vernacular. Unlike Williams's work, Stevens's poetry was not identifiably regional in its sources, nor was it hostile to non-American discourses. The influence of French symbolists and English Romantics on Stevens's work is evident throughout his oeuvre, though Stevens transcends these influences to create a startlingly original voice. His diction is as deceptively light and surface-oriented as it is committed to articulating a philosophy of aesthetics. The final lines from his poem 'Metaphors of a Magnifico' attest to Steven's ability to mix complexity with a deeply pleasurable whimsy:

> The boots of the men clump
> On the boards of the bridge.
> The first white wall of the village
> Rises through fruit-trees
> Of what was it I was thinking?
> So the meaning escapes.
> The first white wall of the village . . .
> The fruit-trees . . .

These lines suggest that the world in Stevens's poetry is almost entirely conceptual. Action ('The boots of the men clump') is contingent on imagination ('Of what was it I was thinking'). 'Reality' as we know it is an act of the mind, highly subjective and open to multiple interpretations ('So the meaning escapes'). What is especially remarkable about Stevens's poetry is his anticipation of postmodern gestures – for example, this poem evinces a playful resistance to closure, evident in the fact that it ends with non-conclusive ellipses. Stevens, with his almost dandyish evocation of a dreamy European-Americanism and his practically lighthearted use of fragmentary techniques, was a true original, and was a model for major experimental poets in the post-war years, particularly John Ashbery (discussed below).

The visual and the verbal

Since we have been discussing the role of the image in poetry, as well as the influence of European and American aesthetics on the genre, it is important to point out that visual artists informed and were informed by their literary counterparts. Modernist poets were affiliated with artists and sculptors including Wyndham Lewis, Pablo Picasso, Henri Gaudier-Brzeska and Georges Braque. Not content to use art merely to imitate nature, these artists presented a new reality that depicted radically fragmented objects. To effect such changes, material as disparate as newspaper, wallpaper and cloth was collaged into the canvases, and no single element was centred on the visual field. Poets treated language in a similar fashion. In 'This is Just to Say' Williams recycled a note he left for his wife on the refrigerator into a poem ('I have eaten / the plums / that were in / the icebox'); in *The Waste Land* T. S. Eliot collaged the spoken words of a barmaid ('HURRY UP PLEASE IT'S TIME') into the text, and so on. Writers including Williams, Pound, Eliot and Stein decentred the way we tend to look at things by linking unlikes – petals, faces, chickens, wheelbarrows, pine, sea all appear in no privileged order.

Much of the fragmentation in modernist poetry was employed to evoke the writers' belief that a cohesive, unified Western culture was fragmented, perhaps beyond repair. The senselessness and slaughter of the First World War in particular belied any positive assertion of a 'progressive', 'enlightened' West. Pound, Eliot and affiliated writers tended to present their fragmented views of human subjectivity and history as something tragic, and worked to make art that would at least attempt to provide some coherence and meaning in an otherwise fractured world. T. S. Eliot's line 'These fragments I have shored against my ruins' in his poem *The Waste Land*, and Pound's 'And I am not a demigod, / I cannot make it cohere' from 'Canto 116' are good examples of poets trying or failing to use art to regenerate culture.

We should also consider that modernist poetry coincided with a period in American history in which commercial and artistic photographic images and films were widely distributed. Thanks to improvements in black-and-white photography, amateurs who did not have much time, money or technical savvy could still learn how to take pictures. By 1907 colour photographs were produced with the three-exposure camera. This prompted a move away from representation and realism and towards abstraction. These facts might help us understand how we end up with poems that are as stark, lovely and fundamentally abstract as Williams's 'The Red Wheelbarrow' or Stevens's 'Thirteen Ways of Looking at a Blackbird', or why Pound was so committed to creating images independent of overly descriptive language.

In terms of the influence of film on developing poetics, we find that HD served as contributing editor for the film journal *Close Up*, wrote film-influenced poems including *Projector*, and appeared in the films *Wing Beat* and *Borderline*. Recognising the similarities between Gertrude Stein's work and experimental film, director Kenneth MacPherson wrote to Stein:

> I really want to ask now if perhaps sometime you would send a poem or article for *Close Up* in which this development of experimental art is concerned . . . The most modern tendency seems so linked up in this way and the kind of thing you write is so exactly the kind of thing that could be translated to the screen that anything you might send would be deeply appreciated.

Stein responded by sending two prose pieces, 'Mrs Emerson' and 'Three Sitting Here'. Of Stein's 'Mrs Emerson', Anne Friedberg, an editor of the book *Close Up 1927–1933: Cinema and Modernism*, writes:

> To interpret [Stein's 'Mrs Emerson'] literally as about cinema would be forcing meanings on Stein's intentionally slippery polysemic play. Yet the 'new

houses' without windows could easily be cinema theatres; the 'kindly amazing lights', the films; the 'recent disturbances fit the first change in silent rugs', the transition to sound.

The objectivists

In the 1930s a second generation of modernist poets – all of whom expressed aesthetic allegiance to Pound and Williams particularly – came into prominence. The publication of the February 1931 issue of the magazine *Poetry* announced the arrival of the so-called objectivist poets. Louis Zukofsky (1904–78), Charles Reznikoff (1894–1976), George Oppen (1908–84), Carl Rakosi (1903–2004) and, later, Lorine Niedecker (1903–70) were all affiliated with this group. Zukofsky, Reznikoff and Oppen went on to form the Objectivist Press, publishing their own books as well as work by William Carlos Williams. Although the objectivists were basically ignored by critics and the reading public, the 1960s and 1970s found renewed interest in their work via the cheerleading of younger popular poets including Allen Ginsberg and writers affiliated with the 'language' and second generation New York School groups described below. Currently, the objectivists are recognised as highly influential and are admired by writers throughout the contemporary American literary scene.

While objectivist poets were connected to first generation modernists, they distinguished themselves from their predecessors in a number of ways. Apart from Lorine Neidecker (who was from rural Wisconsin), objectivists were committed to pluralism, evoking the ethnic and religious ghettos where New York's Jews, African Americans, Puerto Ricans and others demarcated their own communities. Reznikoff especially was a poet par excellence of the City. As George Oppen's wife Mary Oppen recalls, 'Charles walked every day to and from his work, across the bridge to Manhattan, to the Bronx above George Washington Bridge along the Hudson River; stopping to write a word, or pausing quietly, as other walkers passed him by, to think'. Harvey Shapiro writes, 'The span of his writing begins with Jews on the lower east side [*sic*] and ends with the Puerto Ricans there. His subject . . . was the City. He wanted us to see it clearly'.

Oppen's work can be read as a critique of modernism. For instance, the poem numbered '1', from Oppen's first book *Discrete Series*, works as a plain-speak parody of Pound's 'Canto 1', partly by mimicking the nautical imagery of Pound's line 'And then went down to the ship':

The three wide
Funnels raked aft, and the masts slanted

> the
> Deck-hand slung in a bosun's chair
> Works on this 20th century chic and
>   efficiency
> Not evident at 'The Sailor's Rest.'

The use of 'this' to refer to the twentieth century impels us into presence, into a distinct moment in history independent of a privileged lyric tradition. Contrary to much of Pound's and Eliot's work, such a poem emphasises what is known and can be seen now, as opposed to rather mournfully serving as a conduit to and elegy of an idealised past.

It is also important to recognise, as Stephen Fredman notes, that the objectivists 'make a strong claim for our attention based on their inventive negotiations between literary modernism and a Jewish heritage'. This focus on 'Jewish heritage' served as a welcome counterbalance to Pound's and Eliot's at-times virulent anti-Semitism and élitist cultural and social politics. In his poetry, Pound railed against what he believed to be a Jewish banking conspiracy, and volunteered to give anti-Semitic radio speeches for Mussolini during the Second World War. Eliot's anti-Semitism was also visible in his poetry – in 'Gerontion', for example, Eliot writes 'And the jew squats in the window sill, the owner, / Spawned in some estaminet of Antwerp, / Blistered in Brussels, patched and peeled in London'. Objectivists implicitly critiqued such noxious positions throughout their poetry.

Objectivist poets continued to distinguish themselves from their immediate predecessors by committing themselves to progressive and socialist politics. Early sections of Zukofsky's life-long epic poem *A* were concerned with the political and economic situation of the United States in the late 1920s, and evoked the struggle between capitalists and the working classes. In Reznikoff's multi-volume work *Testimony*, composed from selections of witnesses' testimony as recorded in law reports, we learn of blacks railroaded by racist criminal-justice systems, sexually abused women and girls, exploited orphans, immigrants mired in poverty forced to work in unsafe conditions, and so on. The dry, legal tone of Reznikoff's writing works as an ironic counterpoint to what is ultimately a moving and disturbing condemnation of American capitalism in the twentieth century.

Oppen felt so strongly about politics that he decided to stop writing poetry for 25 years in order to devote himself to progressive politics. Regarding Oppen's 25-year silence between the publication of *Discrete Series* in 1934 and *The Materials* in 1962, Michael Davidson, in his introduction to George Oppen's *Collected Poems*, suggests that Oppen felt 'he could neither write poems in service to social causes nor sequester those causes in hermetic formalism', while Eliot Weinberger agrees that Oppen's work during that time was 'agitation and organization, in which poetry could have no place without compromising itself'.

The Harlem Renaissance

Pound and Eliot tended to mourn what they thought was the death of a coherent Western culture, and the objectivists worked to point out that such coherence is compromised in the first place by the presence of marginalised social, religious and ethnic figures and competing ideologies. These writers were some of the dominant figures in an evolving modernism, yet we should be careful not to assume that they had the last word in terms of what could be done in American poetry.

A linked movement of poets, novelists, choreographers, dramatists and artists based in New York City's Harlem neighbourhood, a predominantly African American community, thrived in the 1920s. The 'Harlem Renaissance' lasted to the onset of the Great Depression, and used art in a variety of socially and politically charged ways – for race building and image building, for creating hybrid genres like jazz poetry or revitalising conservative forms like the sonnet, for progressive or socialist politics, for racial integration or separation, and to give voice to the musical and sexual freedom of Harlem nightlife. Poets associated with the Harlem Renaissance included Langston Hughes (1902–67), Esther Popel (1896–1958), Sterling Brown (1901–89), James Weldon Johnson (1871–1938), Countee Cullen (1903–46), Claude McKay (1891–1948) and Jean Toomer (1894–1967). As a result of the ending of slavery, the wish of former slaves to start a new life and the economic plight of the rural South after the Civil War, American blacks were becoming an urban people. The Harlem Renaissance, therefore, should be seen as a cosmopolitan phenomenon and thus linked to modernism as a whole.

Harlem became predominantly black during the First World War, when enormous numbers of African Americans came north to work in the war industry. What made Harlem so different from other black urban communities was its role as a centre for black culture, protest and thought. The National Association for the Advancement of Colored People (NAACP) was formed there, and militant thinkers including W. E. B. DuBois and black nationalist organiser Marcus Garvey based their headquarters in Harlem. As a result of all this activity, young black intellectuals were drawn to Harlem, and the more who came, the more followed. Harlem was also a centre for fun. The Prohibition Act (1920), which outlawed the sale of alcohol, encouraged entrepreneurs to open up dozens of illegal drinking clubs (known as speakeasies). Big-band music by artists including Fletcher Henderson, Jimmie Lunceford, King Oliver and Fess Williams became a kind of sound-track for the neighbourhood and source material for its poets and artists.

In Stephen Watson's book *The Harlem Renaissance*, we learn how the poetry of the period both informed and was informed by the social scene of Harlem. Alelia Walker turned her town house into a parlour-nightclub-salon, nam-ing it 'The Dark Tower' after a newspaper column by poet Countee Cullen. Langston Hughes's poem 'The Weary Blues' was lettered on the building's wall. Jazz musicians often played in speakeasies well into the early hours of the morning:

> [M]oonlighting performers dropped into the clubs that had paid off the police
> for 'special charters.' 'Jazzlips' Richardson or the dancing Bon Ton Buddies,
> fresh from playing *Hot Chocolates* at Connie's, for example, might do a turn in
> exchange for food and drink . . . The activity at institutions like the Sugar
> Cane continued in high key until piercing seven o'clock whistles warned that
> a new work day was about to begin.

Variety magazine less graciously described Harlem nightlife as 'A seething caul-dron of Nubian mirth and hilarity'.

We should consider the Harlem Renaissance scene within the overall con-text of modernism, especially as the racial politics of black and white artists affiliated with modernism remain complex. Early in the century, Europeans and Americans had 'discovered' the sophistication of African culture. In 'Melanctha' (a chapter in her book *Three Lives*), Gertrude Stein imitated the cadences of black American English. Post-impressionist painters including Picasso were influenced by African sculpture and painting; this was espe-cially true of cubism, which, like African art, tended to analyse form rather than reproduce it. Images including Picasso's 'Les Demoiselles d'Avignon' and the American photographer Man Ray's picture 'Noire et Blanche' are all examples of modernist art as it is informed by African imagery.

White writers including Carl Van Vechten served as intermediaries between the white 'downtown' world and black 'uptown' world. Vechten became friends with Cullen and Hughes; he gathered manuscripts by black writers for Yale University; he wrote as passionately about the blues as he did about Stravinsky; and he arranged to have Langston Hughes's first book *The Weary Blues* published. Writers outside New York, like William Faulkner, made it a point to have Vechten serve as tour-guide to Harlem. Such cultural exchange went both ways, as Vechten invited black artists to his salons downtown.

We can understand the poetry of the Harlem Renaissance, then, as actively engaged in at-times hostile and at-times friendly conversation with white modernism. In his book *The Souls of Black Folks*, W. E. B Dubois argued that the black person sees 'himself through the revelation of the other world. It is a peculiar sensation, this double-consciousness . . . One ever feels his two-ness – an American, a Negro; two souls, two thoughts, two unreconciled striv-ings; two warring ideals in one dark body'. The term 'double-consciousness', as it is been used and adapted by contemporary literary critics including Henry Louis Gates, refers to the conflicting experience of feeling as if one is a mem-ber of a privileged, non-racial artistic milieu called 'modernism', only to then recognise oneself as a 'Negro' with all the political and social ramifications that the term entails. Many African American intellectuals in the 1920s were torn between representing the historical and contemporary oppression of coloured people and participating in a relatively apolitical modernist discourse.

Langston Hughes's 'double-consciousness' found expression in his adaptation of modernist poetics. Like Pound and Eliot before him, Hughes moved away from forms associated with British and European tradition, but this time for the purposes of creating a specifically *African* American voice. Jazz, blues and the idea of Africa as political refuge and artistic symbol, influ-enced his early poetry.

Hughes's famous poem 'The Negro Speaks of Rivers' was written on an envelope on a train as Hughes was crossing the Mississippi River at sunset. Fitting in with the overall strategy of 'making it new', Hughes creates rhythms that evoke the force of the Negro spiritual, thus raising a formerly marginalised form to the status of poetry and adding African source mate-rial to the American canon. The fact that the poem suggests the source of human experience ('the Euphrates when dawns were young') is specifically African in origin, a radical gesture in the light of Pound and Eliot's ten-dency either to ignore or lambaste African American contemporary repre-sentations and cultural history. In their various, often conflicting ways, the work that was produced by Hughes and other poets affiliated with the Harlem Renaissance added strategic and necessary representations of black identity and cultural diversity to modernism.

Post-war American poetry and the New Criticism

As the United States struggled through the Great Depression and then, after the Japanese attack on Pearl Harbor, entered the Second World War, a new generation of poets and critics arrived on the scene. A number of them wrote directly out of their military experience or their status as conscientious objectors, including Randall Jarrell (1914–65), Anthony Hecht (1923–), Karl Shapiro (1913–2000), Richard Eberhart (1904–), William Stafford (1914–93), John Ciardi (1916–86), James Dickey (1923–97), Richard Hugo (1923–82), William Everson/Brother Antoninus (1912–94) and Howard Nemerov (1920–91).

Post-war American poetry was to prove rich and controversial. Competing interests between writers affiliated with a mode of criticism called 'New Criticism' and those writers determined to inject a new romanticism and formal radicalism into American poetry set the tenor for much of the debate related to poetry to this day.

The broadly based group of critics and writers affiliated with the New Criticism included John Crowe Ransom (1888–1974), Allen Tate (1899–1979) and Robert Penn Warren (1905–98). New Critics were against interpreting literary texts in the context of the author's life and contemporary historical conditions. W. K Wimsatt and Monroe Beardsley, two well-known New Critics, came up with the term 'intentional fallacy' to argue strongly against any interpretation that aimed to discover what the author's intended meaning was. The word 'autotelic' was coined to refer to a text that is theoretically complete within itself, independent of any relation to the author's life or intent. Influenced in part by T. S. Eliot's essay 'Tradition and the Individual Talent' (published in Eliot's book *The Sacred Wood*), New Critics argued that good literature was produced as part of an evolving Western tradition or 'canon'. They located the beginning of this tradition in Ancient Greece and traced it up to their own time, setting themselves up as tastemakers who would protect the production and interpretation of poetry from what they considered to be vulgar reading practices and a steadily declining popular culture. Primary to the New Critical approach was the belief that formal and technical approaches to analysing literature should be privileged as modes of interpretation.

Poets affiliated with New Criticism included Howard Nemerov, John Hollander, Robert Lowell, Anthony Hecht, Karl Shapiro and Richard Wilbur. Most of these writers wrote formal verse, employing steady iambic measures in service of content that was generally apolitical. Such form and content worked in tandem with New Critical reading practices that emphasised elucidation of formal characteristics of a given work over the consideration of a poem in its social, historical, and/or biographical context. The first stanza of Howard Nemerov's poem 'The Goose Fish' is telling in terms of its relationship to the New Criticism:

On the long shore, lit by the moon
To show them properly alone,
Two lovers suddenly embraced

So that their shadows were as one.
The ordinary night was graced
For them by the swift tide of blood
That silently they took at flood,
And for a little time they prized
    Themselves emparadised

These lines, clearly rhymed and scored in an easily identifiable iambic hexameter, almost sound as though they could have been written at any point in the last 200 years in either Britain or America. There is no indication here of a 'native' American voice *à la* William Carlos Williams; the poem does not purport to interpret 1950s American culture and politics; there is no hint of the radical experiments in prosody initiated by poets, including Stein and Pound, decades earlier. The stanza presents its own entirely self-enclosed dramatic scenario, thus adding to the overall effect of the poem as a system that is 'closed' to such effects as digression, stream of consciousness, contingency and so on. Situating itself firmly within the Western canonical tradition, the stanza alludes to Milton's *Paradise Lost* in the line 'Themselves emparadised'. The stanza is an example of what New Critic Cleanth Brooks might have described as a 'well-wrought urn': a poem that, while able to create internal paradoxes and ambiguities, is always able to be resolved (using New Critical strategies) in order to produce a 'correct' reading independent of author, culture and time.

Confessional poetry

Interestingly, many of the poets that found favour with the New Critics of the late 1940s and 1950s would by the late 1950s reject New Critical approaches to writing and interpretation. Led initially by Lowell's example (and despite the fact that Lowell was formerly a formalist writer endeared by Ransom and other New Critics), mainstream American poetry took a turn in 1959 with the publication of Lowell's book *Life Studies*. In his review of the book, the literary critic M. L. Rosenthal was prompted to call the poems 'confessional' and thus the 'confessional' movement in poetry was born.

Confessional poetry coincided with the ever-growing threat of the Cold War and an increasingly paranoid, atomised, geographically dispersed American culture. In her book *Pursuing Privacy in Cold War America*, Deborah Nelson links confessional poetry to tensions that were manifesting themselves across the social, cultural and political spectrum during the 1950s, including the advent of television, the middle-class shift from the cities to suburbia, Senator Joseph McCarthy's hunt for communists throughout American institutional life, and the increasing use of psychoanalysis. (The impulse towards a more personal, anguished lyric typical of much of *Life Studies* and affiliated work is, historically speaking, parallel to the increasing popularity of Freudian analysis. Poets associated with the confessional grouping, including Sylvia Plath, Anne Sexton and John Berryman, all took workshops with Lowell in Boston, and all were at some point in their lives committed to psychotherapeutic analysis.)

Robert Lowell's book *Life Studies* was seen as a major shift in mainstream American poetry because much of it was written in a relatively loose free verse and was packed with all sorts of personal details of his and his family's scandalous life and history. Readers could not help but interpret the book as a wilfully biographical gesture. For example, the poem 'Skunk Hour' features a speaker who is a practically transparent representation of Lowell. The speaker, apparently as mentally unstable in the poem as Lowell was in real life, admits his 'mind's not right' and lets us know he 'watched for love-cars'. He continues in this vein:

> . . . I hear
> my ill-spirit sob in each blood cell,
> as if my hand were at its throat . . .
> I myself am hell,
> nobody's here –

Here we find Lowell confessing to being a peeping tom (he is watching people make out in their 'love cars') and to being mentally unbalanced. As if to remind us that this is 'literature' as opposed to a therapy session, Lowell quotes from Milton's Satan in the lines 'I myself am hell / nobody's here'. The speaker is at once Lowell confessing his wretched state as he is, according to the critic James Breslin, 'projecting as demonic self'.

Over and over again we see writers affiliated with the confessional group foregrounding their mental illness, their vulnerability and their overall angst in the world, then projecting that 'demonic self' through a mythical persona containing distinctly psychological overtones. Sylvia Plath's poem 'Daddy' is a good example of such a move. The speaker compares her father to a Nazi – 'I thought every German was you' – and herself to a concentration camp victim: 'An engine, an engine / Chuffing me off like a Jew / A Jew to Dachau, Auschwitz, Belsen'. According to Plath:

> The poem is spoken by a girl with an Electra complex. Her father died while she thought he was God. Her case is complicated by the fact that her father

was also a Nazi and her mother very possibly part Jewish. In the daughter the two strains marry and paralyze each other – she has to act out the awful little allegory once before she is free of it. (Quoted in Rosenthal, 81–2)

Nazism, Freudian terminology and mythos all weave together as Plath projects herself through a Jewish persona.

The 'academic' and the 'avant-garde'

Both the poets amenable to New Critical practice as well as some of the writers beginning their confessional journey were anthologised in 1957 and 1962 in the books *New Poets of England and America* and *New Poets of England and America: a Second Selection*, edited by Donald Hall, Louis Simpson and Robert Pack. The publication of these books initiated what is the still hotly debated 'cold war' between so-called mainstream verse associated with *New Poets of England and America* and a burgeoning counter-cultural verse, represented most clearly in 1960 with the publication of the anthology *The New American Poetry*.

The New American Poetry, edited by Donald Allen, showed the American reading public that there was a rebellious, adamantly American experimental verse tradition well under way in American letters. Poets included in this book were to prove profoundly influential on succeeding generations. Among them were so-called 'Beat' poets Allen Ginsberg, Gregory Corso, Jack Kerouac and Peter Orlovsky; New York poets Barbara Guest, John Ashbery, Frank O'Hara, James Schuyler and Kenneth Koch (also known as New York School poets due to their affiliation with the New York School of painting); Black Mountain poets Charles Olson, Robert Creeley, Paul Blackburn, Joel Oppenheimer and Edward Dorn; San Francisco Renaissance poets Helen Adam, Robert Duncan, Michael McClure and Jack Spicer; and unaffiliated poets including future black arts revolutionary Amiri Baraka (then known as LeRoi Jones), gay lyric poet John Wieners, and others. Representing the polar opposite of the values and reading strategies championed by the New Critics, the new poetry was often experimental in form and politically, sexually and socially insurrectionary in content.

Many of the poets in Allen's anthology felt that writing in *New Poets of England and America* represented an unacceptably 'academic' trend in American poetry, and identified *The New American Poetry* as opposed to the dominant formal verse represented by Hall, Pack and Simpson's books. This is not to say that poets in *New Poets of England and America* were *not* using free-verse techniques as well as traditional forms and measures. The conflict,

rather, was due to the fact that for Hall, Pack and Simpson, 'new' generally meant young poets writing new poems that were literally *about* relatively traditional themes written in restrained metres. What made them
'academic' was the way they valued mythological allusions, a kind of rational take on experience, and a relatively élitist, non-populist use of language.
Many poets and readers who favoured *The New American Poetry* believed
that 'academic' poets were writing from a distinctly middle-class, privileged
perspective.

'Anti-academic' poets were reclaiming and extending the exuberant
spirit and free-verse techniques of Whitman, the experimental method and
tone of Dickinson, and the radicalism of the poetics Ezra Pound of Gertrude
Stein, Wallace Stevens and William Carlos Williams. As Allen put it in his
introduction to the book:

> These new younger poets have written a large body of work [that] has reached
> its growing audience through poetry readings . . . it has shown one common
> characteristic: a total rejection of all those qualities typical of academic verse.
> Following the practice and precepts of Ezra Pound and William Carlos
> Williams, it has built on their achievements and gone on to evolve new
> conceptions of the poem . . . They are our avant-garde, the true continuers of
> the modern movement in American poetry.

Poems within *The New American Poetry* addressed and even celebrated drug
use, homosexuality and other 'dissident' behaviours in distinction to the
genteel and cautious approach evident in the 'academic' *New Poets of England
and America*. More important, however, was the fact that most poets in *The
New American Poetry* were committed to *formal* experimentation, often in combination with surprising content. We can look to Allen Ginsberg's legendary
poem 'Howl', where Whitmanic long-breath lines are employed to depict
raunchy sex: 'who howled on their knees in the subway and were dragged
off the roof waving genitals and manuscripts, / who let themselves be fucked
in the ass by saintly motorcyclists, and screamed with joy, / who blew and
were blown by those human seraphim, the sailors, caresses of Atlantic and
Caribbean love'; John Ashbery's neo-surrealist techniques in 'How Much Longer
Will I be Able to Inhabit the Divine Suepulcher . . .': 'Stars / Painted the garage
roof crimson and black. / He is not a man / Who can read these signs . . .
his bones were stays . . .'; Frank O'Hara's quotidian notation of a lunchtime
walk in 'The Day Lady Died': 'it is 1959 and I go get a shoeshine / because
I will get off the 4:19 in Easthampton / at 7:15 and then go straight to dinner / and I don't know the people who will feed me'; Gregory Corso's dada
antics in 'Marriage': 'I deny honeymoon! I deny honeymoon! / running

rampant into those almost climactic suites / yelling Radio belly! Cat shovel!';
Helen Adam's haunting ballad 'I Love My Love': 'She combed her hair with
a golden comb and shackled him to a tree. / She shackled him close to the
Tree of Life. "My love I'll never set free. / No, No. / My love I'll never set
free"'; Kenneth Koch's proclamation in his poem 'Fresh Air': 'GOODBYE, cas-
trati of poetry! farewell stale pale skunky pentameters' and so on. Clearly,
such poems were eclectic in terms of content, typography, tone and rhythm.

Many of the poets in *The New American Poetry* rejected the social, political and literary establishment, focusing on the New Critics as enemies in
the war between 'academic' and 'avant-garde' poetry. As Jonah Raskin put
it in his cultural history of Allen Ginsberg's poem 'Howl':

> Ginsberg wanted a revolution in the classroom, a radical change in the way
> that poetry was taught. He was prepared to chase the New Critics from the
> halls of academia. Interpreting a poem without placing it in a social and
> historical context, and without discussing the life of the poet – which many of
> the New Critics insisted on – made no sense at all to him . . . In order to
> understand *Howl* . . . it was important to understand the Cold War and the
> warring impulses in his own character and personality.

This 'revolution' that Raskin refers to was manifested in the hundreds of
public poetry readings that Ginsberg and most of the poets in *The New
American Poetry* foreground as a necessary site for the dissemination and reception of new poems. In conscious opposition to the model of a poetry reading as a formal affair wherein the esteemed poet stands on a podium
declaiming his or her verse to a quiet and respectful audience, alternative
poetry readings took place in cafés, bars and art galleries where at times
raucous audience participation was part of the poetry experience.

Especially famous readings included the Six Gallery reading in 1955 that
took place in San Francisco – readers and audience members included a virtual who's who of the developing poetic counterculture on both the East
and West Coasts, including Ginsberg, Philip Lamantia, Michael McClure,
Gary Snyder, Philip Whalen, Kerouac (who mythologised the reading in his
book *Dharma Bums*) and others. The Six Gallery was seen as a direct blast
against complacent 1950s consensus culture. Raskin insists the event

> helped create the conditions for both the San Francisco protests against the
> House Un-American Activities Committee in 1960 and the Free Speech
> Movement at Berkeley in 1964. The Six Gallery reading was living proof that
> the First Amendment [guaranteeing freedom of speech] hadn't been destroyed
> by McCarthyism and the committees that investigated artists, playwrights,
> Hollywood directors, and TV screenwriters.

Public poetry readings helped create poetic communities throughout the United States as they encouraged participants to disseminate and publish poetry as quickly as possible. Accompanying the growth of poetry readings in the 1950s and especially during the 1960s was a parallel revolution in the growth of literary journals. Cheap, easily reproducible mimeograph and small-circulation magazines, including John Ashbery's *Locus Solus*, Cid Corman's *Origin*, Charles Olson's *The Black Mountain Review*, Amiri Baraka and Diane Di Prima's *Floating Bear*, Ed Sanders's *Fuck You/ a magazine of the arts*, Ted Berrigan's *C* and countless others, appeared and proved highly influential throughout the mid-1950s and 1960s.

The alignment of experimental aesthetics with leftist politics and community was part and parcel of *The New American Poetry*. Amiri Baraka connected aesthetics with the contemporary political condition of the mid-1960s:

> I was always interested in Surrealism and Expressionism, and I think the reason was to really try to get below the surface of things . . . The Civil Rights Movement, it's the same thing essentially, trying to get below the surface of things, trying to get below the norm, the everyday, the status quo, which was finally unacceptable, just unacceptable. (Quoted in Kane, 13)

In his manifesto *Projective Verse* (republished in *The New American Poetry*), Olson linked the development of new poetry to the poet's individual breath and body:

> The line comes (I swear it) from the breath, from the breathing of the man who writes, at the moment that he writes, and thus is, it is here that, the daily work, the WORK, gets in, for only he, the man who writes, can declare, at every moment, the line its metric and its ending.

On a far more irreverent note, New York School poet Frank O'Hara wrote in his anti-manifesto *Personism* that 'Personism' was

> founded by me after lunch with LeRoi Jones [Amiri Baraka] on August 27, 1959, a day in which I was in love with someone (not Roi, by the way, a blond). I went back to work and wrote a poem for this person. While I was writing it I was realizing that if I wanted to I could use the telephone instead of writing the poem, and so Personism was born . . . It puts the poem squarely between the poet and the person . . . The poem is at last between two persons instead of two pages.

Poets affiliated with *The New American Poetry* were challenging the conception of the poem as a static text on the page, independent of author, history, culture and overall social context.

John Ashbery

While many would argue that a number of poets in *The New American Poetry* transcended their regional affiliations to become writers appreciated by all factions in the American poetry scene, perhaps no poet has succeeded as well as John Ashbery. Influenced by writers as diverse as Wallace Stevens, Ronald Firbank, Raymond Roussel and Gertrude Stein, Ashbery reminds us that, despite the preponderance of poetic 'schools' and 'movements', the most important poetry tends to be written by writers who resist classification.

From a very early age, Ashbery was shy, bookish, and intellectual. In his early poem and self-portrait 'The Picture of Little J.A. in a Prospect of Flowers', Ashbery describes his appearance:

> My small self in that bank of flowers:
> My head among the blazing phlox
> Seemed a pale and gigantic fungus.
> I had a hard stare, accepting
> Everything, taking nothing

Ashbery seems to present himself here as a kind of distrustful outcast (suggested by 'a hard stare'), though the lines also suggest a complicated mix of the gentle, the geeky and the learned. Such a 'picture' in many ways represents him to this day. Ashbery continues to be suspicious of collective movements – we know this because of his lifelong promotion of unaffiliated 'outcast' writers who never quite fit into any movement (like John Clare, Raymond Roussel and Laura Riding Jackson), and through his well-publicised resistance to being labelled as a New York School poet.

In 1955 Ashbery received a Fulbright grant to study French literature in Paris. He fell in love with France and was to live there for the next ten years (with occasional trips back to New York City). His stay influenced his developing poetics, which work to reject any simple binary separating 'American' poetry from the rest of the world. While living in France, Ashbery produced his third book, *The Tennis Court Oath*, which has been denigrated by 'establishment' critics, including long-time Ashbery supporter Harold Bloom, even as it has been lionised by experimental or avant-garde critics and poets affiliated with the so-called language school. This latter group sees in *The Tennis Court Oath*'s fractured narratives, collaged texts, plagiarised source materials and overall experimental tenor a major postmodern statement and model for future innovative poetry.

1976 was a banner year for Ashbery when he received the literary equivalent of a triple crown, winning the National Book Critics Circle Award, the Pulitzer Prize and the National Book Award for his book *Self-Portrait in a Convex Mirror*. This event marked Ashbery's shift from his position as 'poet's poet' to international poetry stardom (as it were). Ashbery has written over 20 books of poetry, works of literary criticism, a number of plays, the novel *A Nest of Ninnies* (written in collaboration with fellow poet James Schuyler), the hybrid prose-poetry text *Vermont Notebook* (with drawings by artist Joe Brainard), translations of French literature, and more. Overall, he has produced writing that variously induces trances, mixes playful and high-rhetorical dictions, combines mundane musings with transcendent gestures, and resists closure while extending real philosophical inquiries into the nature of writing, identity and the poet's place in the world. His influence on contemporary poetry can be said, without fear of histrionics, to be profound.

Poetry, the 1960s and New York

The New American Poetry in many ways set the standard for progressive verse in the 1960s and 1970s. Ashbery and the New York School poets generally were to prove especially influential, generating dozens of imitators and even a group of poets that is now being referred to as the second generation New York School. Poets affiliated with the second generation include Anne Waldman, Ron Padgett, Ted Berrigan, Bernadette Mayer, Alice Notley, Michael Brownstein, Lorenzo Thomas, Clark Coolidge, Joe Ceravolo and Lewis Warsh. The younger members of this loosely knit group made its base at the Poetry Project, a reading series that began in 1966 and is still housed at St Mark's Church in New York's East Village neighbourhood. The Poetry Project was rife with illegal and fun activity, including a pirate radio station transmitting poetry from the belltower of the church and days-long poetry readings/parties where people would enjoy illicit substances and even make love in the pews as poets performed their work.

The social world fed directly into the poetry produced by this vibrant group. Collaborative poems, anonymous poems, serial poems and performance poems were all part of the new forms being developed in New York and beyond. Parallel to the growth of communes and the leftist critique of capitalism and ownership, Bernadette Mayer's writing workshops at the Poetry Project emphasised collaboratively produced works where no single author would get credit. Poetry readings themselves became far more varied in nature, often stretching the boundaries between what constituted a poetry reading and what constituted a 'happening' or performance. For example, Bernadette Mayer and Clark Coolidge advertised a reading at the Poetry Project where they did not bother showing up, instead arranging for a screening of a film of them being chased around a home as they read from the Yale volume of Gertrude Stein's work; poet Jackson Mac Low organised what he called 'simultaneities', where audience members along with the author would intone sections of Mac Low's texts; John Giorno installed strobe lights and fog machines in a given performance space, distributing drugs including LSD and marijuana as tapes of himself reading his highly repetitive, hypnotic poems played in the foreground. This was the 1960s, after all. Poets in New York and elsewhere, influenced as much by the counterculture and the Vietnam War protest movement as they were by the 'make it new' ethos of Pound, radicalised the poetry scene immeasurably.

Interestingly, traditional forms, including the sonnet and the sestina, were taken up and 'made new' by second generation writers. Ted Berrigan's book *The Sonnets* became a kind of cult favourite and remains highly influential for many American poets. *The Sonnets*, first published by Berrigan's C Press in 1964, perhaps best captures the essence of much that was valuable in American poetry of the 1960s and 1970s, and is worth consideration here as a model for the kind of ambitious writing that characterised the poetry scene of this era.

The most 'traditional' aspect of *The Sonnets* is that it can be read both as a cohesive book and as a collection of discrete poems. Thus the book is firmly within the context of historical sonnet sequences stretching back to Shakespeare's and Petrarch's sonnet cycles. As in Shakespeare's work, Berrigan addresses his poems to various characters. However, in her introduction to *The Sonnets*, Alice Notley points out '[B]ut where Shakespeare's plot is patterned chronologically [Berrigan's] is patterned simultaneously, and where Shakespeare's story is overt [Berrigan's] is buried beneath a series of names, repetitions, and fragmented experience that in this age seem more like life than a bald story does'. Phrases including 'I like to beat people up' and 'feminine, marvelous, and tough' are repeated throughout, lending a sense of consistency to the otherwise highly fragmented work.

Typical of much of the best poetry of the 1960s and 1970s, *The Sonnets* also works to threaten conventional definitions of authorship and originality. Lines from other authors are collaged into *The Sonnets* without attribution – one half of 'A Final Sonnet' is a word-for-word selection from Prospero's final speech in Shakespeare's *The Tempest*! *The Sonnets* is particularly noted for its references to New York School poets, and thus the reader can understand it as a work in conversation with select predecessor poets. However, unlike Pound's and Eliot's use of collage and fragmentation in the service of elegy, Berrigan employed the practice for celebratory purposes, illustrating his intention through abundant use of exclamation marks, whimsy and humour.

Poems in *The Sonnets* are significant for their lyrical beauty and their assault on sonnet conventions. No single poem conforms to the rules of established sonnet structure. Elevated language typical of traditional sonnets, including 'O let me burst, and I be lost at sea!', appears throughout *The Sonnets*, yet Berrigan combines it with a wholly contemporary rhetoric: 'fucked til 7 now she's late to work'. Altogether, *The Sonnets* radically extends the possibilities of the sonnet form, as it continues to evoke 1960s ideals including community building and democratic redistribution of wealth – particularly the wealth of predecessor poetry.

Slam poetry, the New Formalists, *L=A=N=G=U=A=G=E* and multiculturalism

Many of the themes and practices associated with the poetry scene of the 1960s and 1970s were analysed, adapted, adopted or rejected by succeeding poets of the 1980s and 1990s. The performative elements of the era were to find their most outrageous manifestation in the 1980s with the development of the 'poetry slam', an event where poets declaim their verse to a rowdy audience, who in turn judge the poets using scorecards. Centres for 'slam' or spoken-word poetry include Marc Smith's Green Mill Tavern in Chicago and the Nuyorican Poets Café in New York's Lower East Side, whose slams were initially organised by poets Bob Holman and Miguel Algarín. Slam poetry is especially notable for its populism – the work and performances draw from sources including hip-hop rhythms and rhymes, 1970s punk, comedy stand-up routines, and performance art.

Unlike most of the poetry discussed so far, slam poetry is particularly multicultural and reflects the racial, ethnic and religious diversity of the United States. The audience at the Nuyorican Poets Café is often composed, as Christopher Beach recognised, of 'middle-class whites from Queens and Bensonhurst, Latinos from the Lower East Side, blacks from uptown, and visitors who have come to this mecca of slam poetry from Chicago, Los Angeles, Boston, or Dublin'. As a glance through the slam anthology *Aloud: Voices from the Nuyorican Poets Café* shows, a large number of poets of colour make up the scene. Writers who began their careers at the Nuyorican who have gone on to achieve some measure of recognition include the African American poet and novelist Paul Beatty (whose book of poems *Big Bank Take Little Bank* was praised by Allen Ginsberg) and Edwin Torres (whose work combines Puerto Rican-inflected language with futurist experimentation).

As slam poetry thrived throughout the 1980s and 1990s, reaching a huge audience that generally would not be drawn to poetry while mostly failing to produce an enduring published body of work, other rumblings were felt in the poetry community. Similar tensions evident in the 'cold war' between *New Poets of England and America* and *The New American Poetry* re-appeared. Two roughly defined groups of writers emerged during this time – the 'New Formalists' and the 'language poets'. The New Formalists group rejected the experimental tenor of American poetry from the 1960s and the modernist insistence on innovation in favour of verse that rejuvenated standard metrics and structures. 'Language' poets (named after the magazine *L=A=N=G=U=A=G=E*, first published in 1978) critiqued the privilege that many 1960s poets placed on speech – indeed, the poet Robert Grenier became notorious for writing the slogan 'I HATE SPEECH'. At the same time, language poets extended the innovative impulses typical of the era, particularly those that challenged the primacy of the individual author and the stability of the relationship between signifier and signified.

The New Formalists – at times evoking Robert Frost's adherence to form and wide popularity – believed in re-establishing a populist role for poetry that its critics insist never really existed in the first place. The group's main spokesperson, Dana Gioia, famously wrote in his manifesto 'Can Poetry Matter', 'No longer part of the mainstream of artistic and intellectual life, [poetry] has become the specialised occupation of a relatively small and isolated group'. Gioia blames a variety of institutions and movements for the supposed decline of poetry in public life. The explosion of university-based creative writing programmes, the grants culture, and wilfully hermetic and difficult poets committed to experimentalism are all sources of horror for Gioia. He adds, 'The New Formalists put free verse poets in the ironic and unprepared position of being the *status quo*. Free verse, the creation of an older literary revolution, is now the long-established, ruling orthodoxy, formal poetry the unexpected challenge'. According to Gioia, the fact that some new poets are writing in relatively strict forms and metres is a revolutionary slap in the face to the free-verse establishment.

The anthology *Rebel Angels: 25 Poets of the New Formalism* evokes tradition (Milton's rebel angels in *Paradise Lost*) as it positions itself more literally as rebelling against free-verse orthodoxy. The editors of the book 'chose only poems in which the use of form was rigorous and commanding' and asserted that poems 'that were sound exercises in prosody, but did not move or convince us in human terms, were excluded'. The first lines of Emily Grosholz's poem 'Back Trouble' illustrate the editors' convictions:

And so to bed. My heart is full of poems,
my pillow full of feathers, unexpressed.
Old traveler, what ails you? Misery,

I've traced so many cities on the ceiling,
I couldn't lift my feet today,
much less my faithful suitcase: Amsterdam,
Florence, and Paris waver on the scrim
superimposed by bad, old-fashioned pain

Adhering to the editors' requirements for a traditional form, the poem is written in blank verse. Additionally, in light of the New Formalist's commitment to a mostly Western notion of literary tradition, it is significant that the poet chooses to transmit a sense of sophistication via her references to 'Amsterdam, / Florence, and Paris'. These are after all Old World cities notable for their roles as major centres of the Renaissance. Perhaps most importantly, language is used here transparently. In contrast to Stein's interest in 'express[ing] the thing' while 'not call[ing] it by its name', every word in Grosholz's poem depends on entirely conventional acts of naming – all the language is in a sense confined to its role of telling a clear-cut story with a paraphraseable narrative and easily understood metaphors.

This transparent use of language distinguishes the New Formalists most clearly from the language poets of the 1980s and 1990s. Language poets are known for applying the lessons learned from French poststructuralism (i.e. the work of Michel Foucault, Julia Kristeva, Jacques Derrida and Roland Barthes) to the development of their art. Poets affiliated with the group also share an abiding passion for and theoretical commitment to modernist predecessors Louis Zukofsky and Gertrude Stein, particularly Zukofsky's procedural techniques and Stein's use of language independent of conventional meaning.

Charles Bernstein and Bruce Andrews were the original editors of _L=A=N=G=U=A=G=E_ magazine, which ran for 13 issues between 1978 and 1980. Featuring important articles on poetics, politics and literary lineage, the magazine provided a groundwork of poetics and theory that many of the writers affiliated with the group engaged with throughout the 1980s and 1990s. While language writers tended to congregate in New York and San Francisco, the group as a whole was nationally represented in other areas, including Washington, DC. Language writers include a high percentage of women poets, such as Rae Armantrout, Fanny Howe, Susan Howe, Lyn Hejinian, Tina Darragh, Hannah Weiner and Carla Harryman, along with Ron Silliman, Barrett Watten and Bob Perelman. Representative anthologies include Silliman's _In the American Tree_ and Douglas Messerli's _Language Poetries_.

Language poets were committed to questioning the 'natural' approach towards referential language that writers like Grosholz take for granted. In his book _Content's Dream_, Charles Bernstein wrote, '"Natural": the very word should be struck from the language'. Bernstein and his colleagues were determined to threaten any conception of the poem as a 'natural' way into an author's privileged personality, insisting that literary persona and the appearance of a recognisable 'voice' were language games as opposed to essential expressions of self. As Bernstein added, 'Personal subject matter & a flowing syntax, whatever those descriptions mean to a particular writer, are the key to the natural look'.

Language writers produced book-length poems determined by procedural techniques as well as a multitude of collaborative texts. Ron Silliman's *Tjanting*, for example, begins with

Not this.

What then?

I started over & over. Not this.

Last week I wrote 'the muscles in my palm so sore from halving the rump roast I could barely grip the pen.' What then? This morning my lip is blisterd.

Of about to within which. Again & again I began. The gray light of day fills the yellow room in a way wch is somber. Not this. Hot grease has spilld on the stove top.

Tjanting continues in this manner for almost 200 pages. The way the book is structured is quite surprising – it follows the progression of the Fibonacci number system, with the result that the number of sentences in each paragraph equals the number of sentences in the previous two paragraphs. Thus, *Tjanting* ends up as a 19-paragraph work with the following number of sentences in each paragraph: 1, 1, 2, 3, 5, 8, 13, 21, 34, 55, 89, 144, 233, 377, 610, 987, 1597, 2584, 4181. The implications of such procedural work are both aesthetically compelling and politically progressive. Such a work tends to undermine the associations we might have regarding authorship – that the author is a privileged, special person who writes according to magical moments of inspiration, that the author's poem is a projection of his or her 'soul', that the structure of a poem is unique to the sentiment of the author, and so on. What Silliman does here is point out that poetry is *writing* and, subsequently, that perhaps *anyone* can democratically choose a structure, start writing, and see what happens. Poetry is language and language (following the precepts of Ludwig Wittgenstein, a philosopher much adored by language writers) is a game.

The poet Bruce Andrews is especially concerned with foregrounding language as inherently ideological. He writes a poetry of extreme disjunction in order to, as he put it in his essay 'Writing Social Work and Political Practice', promote a poetics 'of *subversion*: an anti-systemic detonation of settled relations, an anarchic liberation of energy flows . . . So: a spectrum stretching from "stylistic display" work to a more disruptive political work – within the mostly self-contained linguistic system, of the sign'. Towards that revolutionary end, Andrews writes texts, including this selection from his poem 'Mistaken Identity':

> Profit margin american cream dream cultures of vultures
> A social predicament, the losers are self-preoccupied
> Jellyfish FBI – are you a vending machine?
> Who fights the free? – at least the exploited ones have a future
> Dayglo ethics, corporate global chucksteak
> Lose the flag, nightstick imitation value goosing me
> Estados Unidos, suck o loaded pistol

Here, disjunction is used to undermine the pleasant associations we conventionally attach to words like 'free' and phrases like 'American dream'. The multiple interruptions, the abundance of neologisms, the juxtaposition of dissimilar words like 'flag' and 'nightstick' all work to create an ominous, politically charged landscape critical of the United States and its capitalist ideology. Such gestures are hallmarks of language poetry's political approach to prosody.

The 1970s, 1980s and 1990s also saw the emergence of identity-based poetry that reflected the multicultural conditions of the United States. Poetry anthologies organised around the theme of multiculturalism began to appear, often directly addressing the ways in which 'minority' literatures were frozen out of representative, canon-making poetry anthologies, including the *Norton Anthology of Literature*. Representative works include *Quiet Fire: A Historical Anthology of Asian American Poetry, 1892–1970*, featuring poets including Joy Kogawa, Jessica Hagedorn and Lawson Inada; *Paper Dance: 55 Latino Poets*, showcasing Hispanic American poets Jimmy Santiago Baca, Julia Alvarez and Pedro Pietri, among others; the evocatively titled *Unsettling America: An Anthology of Contemporary Multicultural Poetry*, which includes work by Amiri Baraka, Alberto Rios, Louise Erdrich and Ntozake Shange; and many others.

Unsettling America is generally illustrative of multicultural poetry. The editors aim to include a wide range of writers – Native Americans, Asian Americans, Latinos, African Americans, Italian Americans, Jewish Americans and other so-called 'minority' groups are represented here. Much of the work in the book serves to question what it means to be an American. The notion of America as a 'melting pot' is radically interrogated – the writers' variance from a white, male-dominated mainstream is emphasised so that difference can resurface, assimilation can be critiqued, the ways in which race is constructed can be analysed, and so on.

The editors of *Unsettling America* assert:

> The nostalgic vision of a simple, harmonious past, emphasizing the strenuous but rewarding settlement of this country by heroic pioneers, obscures the long history of oppression within the United States: the decimation of native peoples, the enslavement of African Americans, the exclusion of Chinese Americans, the lynching of Italian Americans, the internment of Japanese Americans during World War II, the increase in anti-Semitism and neo-Nazi violence, and the economic exploitation of migrant workers.

In an effort to complicate this 'nostalgic vision', much of the work in *Unsettling America* aims to affirm those voices and themes that were frozen out by the dominant power structures that institutionalised racism.

In her introduction to *Unsettling America*, Jennifer Gillan discusses Native American poet Louise Erdrich's poem 'Dear John Wayne', a work that describes a group of Native American teenagers watching a John Wayne film at a drive-in. Gillan quotes the following section of the poem:

> How can we help but keep hearing his voice
> the flip side of the sound-track, still playing:
> *Come on, boys, we've got them*
> *where we want them, drunk, running.*
> *They will give us what we want, what we need:*
> *The heart is a strange wood inside of everything*
> *we see, burning, doubling, splitting out of its skin.*

Gillan frames this poem in the context of American racism generally and the oppression of Native Americans specifically:

> Erdrich expresses her double consciousness as both American and Other . . . While the western heroic narrative encourages her to identify with the hero, she also recognizes herself as the villain. Unfortunately, she cannot choose to ignore the myth, since it operates in the way others view her and the way she views herself. As Erdrich discovers, cinema is a powerful tool for disseminating the codes of Americanness and establishing the unAmerican.

The tacit message in such an interpretation is that poetry, particularly a poetry that affirms and projects a race-based consciousness, can do much in terms of countering the dominant, racist narrative of the United States. In the same spirit, Gillan quotes the following lines from Puerto Rican/American (or 'Nuyorican') poet Miguel Algarín:

> I learn off the radio waves
> of 98.7 Kiss F.M. salsa/disco jams,
> that come from a Sony,
> bought even though I need a coat,
> even though I'm behind on my payments
> for the Trinitron Remote Control Color T.V.
> that I picked up at Crazy Eddie's last month.

Gillan believes that such a poem, via its implicitly critical take on consumer culture, shows how the author's identity 'has been reduced and watered down to easily accessible transmissions from the electronic frontier'. Like the Erdrich poem quoted above, Algarín criticises the ways in which American popular culture serves ominous ideological agendas. Such a critique is a first step in reclaiming the voice of the 'Other'. As Gillan adds, poems such as these 'proclaim the complexity of the American identity and articulate alternative histories of American cultural relations . . . Through the power of their writing, [the poets] refuse to accept the designated boundaries that say that the issue of who or what is American is settled once and for all'.

American poetry into the twenty-first century

American poetry in the 1990s and into the twenty-first century continues to be marked by controversy and dissension. Currently there is talk of 'post-avant' (Ron Silliman's term) or 'post-language' poetry. Young writers associated with the 'post-avant' include Lisa Jarnot, Jennifer Moxley, Ange Mlinko, and Anselm and Eddie Berrigan (Ted Berrigan's sons). There are also many poets affiliated with academic creative writing programmes who are now publishing books – prize-winners among this group include Cate Marvin, Rick Barot, Matthea Harvey, James Kimbrell and Brenda Shaughnessy.

Again, what is especially important to consider is that there is no single history of American poetry in the twentieth century. Instead, there are multiple histories of the genre, each one bearing its own ideological, racial, social and historical stamp. *This* particular history, for example, is flavoured by the author's personal, literary and aesthetic predisposition towards the progressive and experimental in American poetry. Another author might take an entirely different tack, spending more time discussing, say, Edna Vincent Millay than Gertrude Stein. Another author might foreground the work of 'minority' poets while dismissing language poetry as hopelessly academic and distanced from any serious public. For critics averse to thinking about poets in groups, yet another history of twentieth-century American poetry might fruitfully be presented as a series of individual achievements independent of coterie affiliation – thus, instead of referring to 'imagists' it would focus on Pound; instead of 'objectivists' it could focus on Oppen; instead of 'modernism' it would focus on Wallace Stevens, and so on. Hundreds of well-known 'avant-garde' and 'academic' writers, including Jerome Rothenberg, Jack Spicer, Robert Bly, Sharon Olds, Gwendolyn Brooks, Cornelius Eady and Galway Kinnell, could have featured prominently here, but did not. *This* particular history is one among many. By whatever criteria, however, one thing all critics can agree on is that the twentieth century was a remarkable time for American poetry specifically and for world poetry generally.

Further reading

Algarín, Miguel and Bob Holman (eds), *Aloud: Voices from the Nuyorican Poets Café* (1994).

Allen, Donald, *The New American Poetry* (1960, reissued 1999).

Andrews, Bruce and Charles Bernstein (eds), *The L=A=N=G=U=A=G=E Book* (1984).

Breslin, James, *From Modern to Contemporary: American Poetry 1945–1965* (1983).

Chang, Juliana (ed.), *Quiet Fire: A Historical Anthology of Asian American Poetry, 1892–1970* (1996).

Cruz, Victor Hernández, Leroy V. Quintana and Virgil Suarez (eds), *Paper Dance: 55 Latino Poets* (1995).

Fredman, Stephen, *A Menorah for Athena: Charles Reznikoff and the Jewish Dilemmas of Objectivist Poetry* (2001).

Gillan, Maria Mazziotti and Jennifer Gillan (eds), *Unsettling America: An Anthology of Contemporary Multicultural Poetry* (1994).

Gioa, Dana, *Can Poetry Matter: Essays on Poetry and American Culture* (1992).

Kane, Daniel, *All Poets Welcome: The Lower East Side Poetry Scene in the 1960s* (2003).

MacGowan, Christopher, *Twentieth Century American Poetry* (2004).

Pound, Ezra, *'How to Read' (1929), Literary Essays of Ezra Pound* (1954).

Nelson, Deborah, *Pursuing Privacy in Cold War America* (2002).

Raskin, Jonah, *American Scream: Allen Ginsberg's 'Howl' and the Making of the Beat Generation* (2004).

Rifkin, Libbie, *Career Moves: Creeley, Zukosfsky, Berrigan, and the American Avant-Garde* (2000).

Rosenthal, M. L., *The New Poets* (1967).

Watson, Steven, *The Harlem Renaissance: Hub of African-American Culture, 1920–30* (1995).

Whitman, Walt, *Poetry and Prose* (1982).

CHAPTER 12

Twentieth-century American drama

Christopher Bigsby

I t is one of the curiosities of American Studies courses in universities that they place so little emphasis on drama and theatre, perhaps because in most American universities they exist in separate, and sometimes mutually hostile, departments, one dealing in texts and the other in performance. Poetry and the novel are seen as central, along with literary theory. There is a concern with gender studies and ethnic studies, those component elements of a contested American identity. Yet little attention is given to the most public of the arts (privately created but publicly consumed), a present-tense art with a history of registering shifts in the psychological, social, political subsoil.

In Ancient Greece the citizenry assembled together in an open-air theatre to see their myths enacted, their heroes celebrated, their values staged. So important was this experience that the rich were required to subsidise the poor, not a practice embraced with much enthusiasm in America. Today, of course, film and television seem to perform that public function. But film and television are not present tense. They are unresponsive, requiring the viewer only to submit, become passive absorbers, obedient consumers in the cultural marketplace.

Theatre, by contrast, is collaborative. It bears the impress of those who come together to create an experience that differs from performance to performance, and is necessarily responsive to audiences that can never be safely assumed to be homogenised. It is also a constant reminder of the performed nature of experience, of the extent to which not only the self but also social forms, political realities and individual personas are constructions. At key moments in American history the theatre has been called upon to engage directly with political developments. It has been one of the places where America has debated with itself, whether in Revolutionary times or when actors spilled out on to the streets in the 1960s, liberated from theatre buildings as they insisted citizens should liberate themselves from the suspect imperatives of political casuists. Plays were performed on picket lines and in public parks (sometimes in the face of injunctions to the contrary). Communities consolidated their sense of cultural, religious, ethnic and gender identity by staging dramas specific to themselves.

Today, few American cities are without a theatre. Few of those theatres fail to produce plays by American writers. It was not always so. American theatre was often derivative, while those outside New York had to await the blessing of a road company travelling through with the good news of yesterday's accomplishments. It is so no more. Theatre is always embattled, struggling for resources and attention, the more so at a time when technology has provided a wonderland of distractions, but it is there, often at the heart of the community, its very embattled status frequently generating a reactive energy. Not-for-profit theatres, often a painfully precise designation, have become generators of new drama rather than recipients of recycled hits.

The American playwright, no less than the novelist or poet, has created an art deeply implicated in the values and assumptions of a Protean culture. Arthur Miller has said that a basic theme of American writers is an argument with the American dream. True or not, it is clear that it is in part through its drama that America has sought to understand itself, and often to contest values propounded and embraced as casual assumptions, simple pieties, rather than self-evident truths.

For all its Puritan origins, America has always shown a hunger for theatre, if also an equal and opposite distrust of its seductions. There was something sensuous, lubricious about a public art that placed the body at the centre of attention. Historically, the actor had always been the subject of distrust, and the theatre has been suspect, both because of its deceits (in Rome, actors, too skilled at simulating, could not run for public office) and its association with immorality (prostitutes were drawn to theatres as places of assignation, while in the last decade of the nineteenth century an actor in New York was refused burial in holy ground). The theatre was, however, where Americans looked not merely for entertainment but to see their private and public anxieties acted out. As pioneers opened new territory, so theatre followed swiftly behind, on wagons and show boats, arriving courtesy of the railroad, which spread like nerve fibres through the body of the young country. In the Revolutionary War, theatre had been both banned and enthusiastically embraced. George Washington was an avid theatre-goer as, 80 years later, albeit briefly, was Abraham Lincoln.

What was lacking, and would continue to be lacking, were American writers who could create drama commensurate with the new land. The dominant playwright was William Shakespeare, performed, initially, by British actors, as anxious to make their fortunes in America as their descendents would be as they took the plane to Hollywood. It is this fact that lies behind the humour of the two confidence tricksters in Twain's *Huckleberry Finn*, whose parody of Shakespeare depends on the reader's knowledge of his works. The most popular domestic play was an adaptation of the century's most successful novel, *Uncle Tom's Cabin*, whose melodrama stood justified by a social reality that presented itself in melodramatic fashion. There were American playwrights who sought to rise to the challenge, playwrights who registered a changing America in which the city had become the defining experience, but few of these can compel attention today. The most popular of mid-nineteenth century playwrights was the Dublin-born Dion Boucicault, a specialist in melodrama and comedy, like Bronson Howard who followed him. Augustus Daley celebrated the frontier, while James A. Hearne wrote what passed for realist plays set in the city, as did David Belasco and, later, Clyde Fitch. Ibsen might be too heavy for turn-of-the-century American audiences but Belasco could be relied on to deflect tragedy into comedy.

Among the best known of nineteenth-century actors was a man who it was once thought might prove the greatest Shakespearian actor of his generation. That this did not turn out to be so was because he was seduced by money and fame, not an unknown temptation for actors, or anybody else. He was so successful in a particular part that he bought the play and appeared in it 6,000 times, earning $35–40,000 a year. The play was *The Count of Monte Cristo*. The actor was James O'Neill, and those seeking a portrait of him have only to turn to one of the greatest works of twentieth-century American theatre, *Long Day's Journey Into Night*, by James O'Neill's son, Eugene.

From the Provincetown Players to the Federal Theatre

The story of Eugene's O'Neill's emergence as a dominant presence in American drama began with two people who had fled the Midwest. Susan Glaspell and Jig Cook had run off together from Davenport, Iowa, and found themselves in Provincetown, situated on the incurving end of Massachusetts Bay. There they founded a small theatre group, the Provincetown Players.

It was an amateur group, which performed in a waterfront wharf. They wrote and staged their own plays, part of a group of young intellectuals excited by the ideas of a century still young and undefined. Glaspell, in particular, though she had never previously written a play, proved a genuinely original talent. *Trifles* (1916), a deceptively simple play about the perspicacity of a group of women, remains popular to this day, while *The Verge* (1921) is as demanding as anything written by the writer who would emerge as the best known of the Provincetown writers, Eugene O'Neill.

O'Neill was a young man who on one level had little to recommend him. He had married and abandoned a young woman, attempted suicide and was a dedicated drinker. On the other hand, he had a startling talent. Repelled by his father's theatre, which he regarded as declamatory, detached from the lives of ordinary people, he began his career writing plays about the sea and those pressed to the margin of social attention.

O'Neill was eclectic, if we mean by that that he stole from everyone and that he sought to renovate apparently outmoded forms. He was an admirer of the Irish Players but also of the German expressionists. He would write plays six hours long *(Strange Interlude*, 1926–7), plays in which a character was played by two actors, in which the soliloquy reappeared. At a time of casual racism, he placed an African American at centre stage (*The Emperor Jones*, 1920) and wrote a play that featured an interracial marriage (*All God's Chillun Got Wings*, 1923). In *The Hairy Ape* (1921) he created a play that seemed to offer a Marxist model of society, yet he was no ideologue. His was a restless talent, which galvanised the American theatre. In 1936 he was awarded the Nobel Prize for literature, which had the effect that that prize sometimes has in that no new play by O'Neill reached New York for 13 years between 1933 and 1946.

O'Neill's vision was a tragic one. Effectively he wrote only a single comedy, *Ah, Wilderness!*, a nostalgic piece written in 1933 but set in 1906. Even then, the following year he began to sketch out a sequel in which he consigned the characters to a series of bleak fates. His own life was no less problematic. One brother died from measles, another from drink. His mother was an addict. One of his sons committed suicide; another was an alcoholic and addict, while he disowned his daughter, Oona, when, at the age of 18, she married a man of 54 – Charlie Chaplin. Out of this experience, however, came some of the greatest plays in the American canon: *The Iceman Cometh* (1946) and *Long Day's Journey into Night* (1956), both set in 1912, the year of his attempted suicide but also the year he had begun to write.

Both are plays that stage the lives of characters trapped in part by their own suspect natures but equally by the limits set on desires and needs by circumstance. They are hermetic works in which increasingly desperate figures are victims of an irony that goes beyond their own natures. In a brief play, *Hughie*, O'Neill would press this in the direction of the absurd, as a man effectively pitches nothing more than language against the bleak fact of an ineluctable death. In the other two plays, though, he acknowledges a tension between his tragic instincts and a desire to offer himself, and those to whom he had been linked by blood or friendship, a retrospective grace. There is, perhaps, a kind of sentimentality waiting in the wings, a wish to absolve if not justify. These are character born on a dark star and are the source of one another's pain, but they are equally the only source of consolation available.

There is something more than a sustaining tolerance at play here. Contempt, blame and suspicion are still capable of dissolving in the instant as O'Neill's characters recognise in themselves what they seek to condemn in others. Yet contact is no sooner made than broken. These are painful plays to watch but there is an honesty to them that cuts through the posturing of characters, whose desperate strategies O'Neill exposes even as he acknowledges their necessity.

A number of American critics (including Mary McCarthy and Eric Bentley) were disposed to dismiss what they saw as the crudity of O'Neill's language and his suspect celebration of the victim. It is hard to agree. O'Neill launches an assault on the sensibility. He creates a poetry in the theatre that depends not simply on a structured language but on rhythms generated out of character and the alternating pulses of hope and despair. There is a relentlessness to his greatest plays, but it is the relentlessness of honesty. His characters strike poses, hide behind affectation or a borrowed language, but once stripped of this by pain they are deeply affecting and eloquent in their despair and love alike.

The Provincetown Players flourished not only in Massachusetts but also in Greenwich Village, which in the early years of the century was a maelstrom of radical ideas. This was the age of the 'new Negro', the 'new woman', of socialism, anarchism and syndicalism. Freud became fashionable enough for Cook and Glaspell to mock it in a play (*Suppressed Desires*, 1915). In one sense the birth of twentieth-century American theatre was merely part of a renaissance in the arts, the arrival of modernism, a new sense of internationalism that opened the door to influence from abroad, hence O'Neill's eclecticism. American playwrights were alert to European theatre, and the impact of Chekhov, Ibsen and Strindberg is clear from O'Neill through to Arthur Miller, Tennessee Williams and Edward Albee. In much the same way, Beckett, Ionesco and Pinter would leave their marks on playwrights of the 1960s, 1970s and 1980s. By the same token, however, American drama would increasingly be seen by Europeans as breaking new ground, in particular in its open sexuality and its democratic instincts, drawing, as it did, on all parts of society for its characters.

Following the Provincetown Players, and another group called the Washington Square Players, a new company was formed. The Theatre Guild staged its first production in 1919 and it was this group that would produce O'Neill's plays and many other works that would define the inter-war years. Elmer Rice, one of their authors, like O'Neill, was responsive to foreign influence. *The Adding Machine* (1923) was an expressionistic satire on the reductivism of modern industrial life, while *Street Scene* (1929) was a seemingly realist work that also staged the lives of those trapped by a world they cannot believe themselves to have created. Rice himself saw it as experimental in its pointillist deployment of incidents and characters.

The Theatre Guild, though, had no particular political or social agenda. It also staged the comedies of Philip Barry, William Saroyan's sentimental and lyrical *The Time of Your Life* (1939) and *My Heart's in the Highlands* (1939), and Robert Sherwood's *Reunion in Vienna* (1931), though the same playwright's melodramatic *The Petrified Forest* (1935) had pretensions beyond that, even if he admitted that somehow his big ideas seemed to devolve into mere entertainment. Maxwell Anderson did bring a critical moralism to bear in *Both Your Houses* (1933), but was drawn to historical verse drama in part, perhaps, precisely because it represented a coherence that he failed to find in the present. With *Winterset* (1935), however, he attempted to set a verse drama in that present. The play was inspired by the Sacco and Vanzetti case in which two Italian immigrants, with anarchist connections, were executed for a murder it was widely believed they did not commit.

There were those in the Theatre Guild, however, who were discontented, less for political reasons than because the Guild was a Broadway company, with Broadway values. They wished, at least initially, to explore the nature of acting. Cheryl Crawford and Harold Clurman thus broke away and formed the Group Theatre whose reputation would quickly become linked to the work of a single playwright – Clifford Odets. In 1935 two of his plays – *Waiting for Lefty* and *Awake and Sing* – did much to define the era. The former centred on a strike of New York taxi drivers and ended with actors and audience alike shouting, 'Strike! Strike! Strike'. The latter concerned a family, the Bergers, that had allowed itself to be defined by seemingly implacable economic circumstances and by its own resignation. This time it is less the necessity for social action that stirs Odets than the need for spiritual renewal. The cry is now not to strike but to 'awake and sing'.

The Berger family live in a tenement, but this is not a naturalistic work in which the characters are defined by their circumstances, as they would have been in a Dreiser novel. The urban pressures exerted upon them limit their possibilities, but they have conspired in their own irrelevance. For a young Arthur Miller, still in college, Odets represented something new, something to be emulated, not least in the language he created, which transformed ordinary speech into a kind of urban poetry.

Meanwhile, in the cast of *Waiting for Lefty* was a young actor who would later turn director and direct Miller's first great successes. His name was Elia Kazan. He was on the left, and the Group Theatre, in common with many others, responded to the fact of the Depression with plays that spoke of the need to transform the country. He was, indeed, for a time, a member of a communist cell in the Group Theatre, a fact that would be invoked against him in 1952 when he was called before the House UnAmerican Activities Committee where his decision to name names would create a gulf between him and Miller that would never really be closed.

The theatre was no less responsive than the other arts in the 1930s to the crisis in American society. A plethora of left-wing theatre groups was established that sought to rally the proletariat: the Workers Laboratory Theatre, which became the Theatre of Action; the Theatre Collective (a branch of the Workers' Laboratory Theatre); and Theatre Union, which produced George Sklar and Albert Malz's *Peace on Earth*, a pro-union anti-war play, and *Stevedore* (1934), which dealt with race relations. A League of Workers' Theatres was founded in 1932. Three years later it became the New Theatre League, responsible in 1936 for a production of Irwin Shaw's anti-war play *Bury the Dead*. To be sure, just as the proletarian novel was in truth read by few members of the proletariat, indeed by few people at all, so these groups reached only a very small proportion of the theatre-going audience, except when unions organised their own theatre visits for consciousness-raising purposes.

Perhaps the longest-lasting play of the 1930s, however, had little to do with radicalism, though everything to do with anxieties generated out of economic and social collapse. Thornton Wilder's Pulitzer Prize-winning *Our Town* (1938) was a celebration of an American community, a small New Hampshire town called Grovers Corners. It was an equivalent of those Norman Rockwell *Saturday Evening Post* covers that managed to be simultaneously reassuring and disturbing, in that their nostalgia suggested an irremediable loss never entirely dispersed by the invocation of familiar imagery.

In the depths of the Depression, when American values were being questioned, *Our Town* placed individual lives in the context not only of national pieties but eternal verities. Its theatrical experimentalism is a borrowed garb essentially concealing a wistfulness disguised as dispassionate realism. It is not hard to understand its continued popularity. It is emotionally compelling, sentimental and lyrical. With *The Skin of our Teeth* (1942), however, Wilder attempted something altogether more radical, influenced, as it was, by his reading of James Joyce's *Finnegans Wake* if also by a more domestic model, the zany *Hellzapoppin* (1941). It was *Our Town*, however, that established him as a standby for amateur and professional theatre for the rest of the century and beyond, offering back to America an idealised version of itself, wistful but resolutely virtuous and sustaining.

O'Neill had called *Ah, Wilderness!* a folk play and there is something of that about *Our Town*; something, too, of the nostalgia to which O'Neill had confessed. And this was a good time for nostalgia. Booth Tarkington's 1918 novel of family life, *The Magnificent Ambersons*, was filmed by Orson Welles in 1942, while *Meet Me in St Louis* was released in 1944. Both looked back to a seemingly innocent period to be contrasted to a suspect present, dominated now not by Depression but by war. What Wilder was not concerned to do, however, was contrast that past with a compromised present. His was not a left-wing perspective.

Lillian Hellman's, however, was. She was another of those who would be called before the House UnAmerican Activities Committee, but her most successful play of the 1930s, *The Children's Hour* (1934), was not so much a complaint about an inhuman capitalism – though *The Little Foxes* (1939) would indict a new South, deeply corrupt, acquisitive and devoid of human values – as it was about the coercive power of majority opinion. *The Children's Hour* is a study of two women accused of lesbianism but its real concern is with the suppression of truths, a failure of nerve and values alike. Two years later came her strike play, *Days to Come*, an unconvincing work, more than touched with the melodrama that would equally infect *The Little Foxes* and her wartime play, *Watch on the Rhine* (1941)

By far the most significant development in 1930s theatre, however, was the creation of the Federal Theatre, part of Roosevelt's Works Progress Administration (WPA) and designed, in the words of Harry Hopkins, WPA administrator, to be free, adult and uncensored. This was to put writers, directors, actors, designers and stage technicians back to work. It was not a building but an organisation with units spread across the country. Headed by Hallie Flanagan, from Vassar College, it flourished from 1935 to 1939, when Congress closed it for supposed communist subversion. During those years, however, it became the largest state-financed theatre outside the Soviet Union, which fact only serves to underline how exceptional these times were.

Flanagan had visited the Soviet Union (an offence that later resulted in her, too, being called before the House UnAmerican Activities Committee) and brought back ideas, being struck in particular by its immediately post-revolutionary theatre, energetic and inventive, before the hand of Soviet reactionary bureaucracy descended. One aspect of that theatre had particularly appealed to her and this led to what came to be known as the Living Newspaper – plays on immediate social and political issues constructed from material gathered by a team of researchers. These were large-scale productions, designed to employ as many actors as possible. They centred on issues of current concern. *Triple A Plowed Under* (1935) dealt with the agricultural situation. *One Third of a Nation* (1938) addressed the nature of slum life in America. The idea was to bring theatre closer to the people, which it did both by addressing issues of immediate concern and by making entry so cheap that money would be no bar. In the brief period of its existence, the Federal Theatre was attended by the equivalent of a quarter of the population of the United States. Theatre had historically been an interest of the few. Here was an organisation that changed that. It was also a theatre that played a role in opening up the arts to African Americans. The 'Negro Unit', directed by the not too noticeably black Orson Welles and John Houseman, employed black actors and technicians. One of its most famous productions was *The Voodoo McBeth* (1936), which located Shakespeare's play in Haiti.

Among those who briefly worked for the Federal Theatre and had a college play produced by it, albeit for a single night, was Arthur Miller, who returned to his Brooklyn home from the University Michigan in 1938. His early college plays had been committed works. Two were concerned with strikes, and one presented prison as an expression of the repressive nature of capitalist society. At the same time another young playwright, Tennessee Williams, was working for a radical theatre group in St Louis. He also wrote a prison play, first staged 60 years later by Britain's Royal National Theatre. Both men, in other words, were formed in the decade before the plays for which they are best known, even if their radicalism subsequently took the form of a questioning of national myths to do with material advance or conformity rather than a Marxist transformation of America.

Broadway, of course, had much more to offer than such serious fare, from Philip Barry's comedies to the musicals which for many around the world became synonymous with the American theatre. The so-called Great White Way never forsook the principles of capitalism even if well-meaning radicals did. Broadway was and would remain concerned above all with the bottom line.

Tennessee Williams and Arthur Miller

Following the Second World War, few of those who had dominated the inter-war years survived. O'Neill was now too ill to write, though the plays he had written in the late 1930s and early 1940s would finally reach Broadway in the 1950s, some staged posthumously. As the war finished, however, a new writer emerged – Tennessee Williams. His apprentice work in St Louis was unknown. Like Miller, he began his public career disastrously. *Battle of Angels* (1940), proved a depressing flop. *The Glass Menagerie* (1945), how-ever, ran for 516 performances.

Williams came from the South, a part of the country that had had to live with defeat, opting to substitute myth for history. He was homosex-ual, at a time when this was not merely illegal but attracted draconian pun-ishments. That he created a series of characters who found themselves on the margin of the social world, desperately inventing not only themselves but also their environment, was perhaps logical enough. He certainly chose to celebrate the poet in a prosaic world: the restless spirit seeking protec-tion in movement or transitory moments of love. One of his central images was of a bird without legs, which lived on the wind but was doomed to die if it should ever alight. Relationships were the source of salvation and doom in the same instant.

Something has broken Williams's characters and they struggle to sur-vive in the knowledge of that fact. This has a shadow of his early radical-ism but transposed now into a psychological battle with wider social implications. There is, after all, a radicalism of the soul, observed Arthur Miller when speaking of Williams, and there is certainly a critique of a soul-less materialism in his work, a distaste for the modern that he shared with another southern writer, William Faulkner. But even as Williams understood the need of his characters to take refuge in fantasy, in art, in transitory rela-tionships with no implications beyond the moment, he recognised, too, the danger of such strategies, lifting the individual out of contact with others and denying the only redemption on offer.

What his characters principally fear, however, like Williams himself, is death. Blanche DuBois, in *A Streetcar Named Desire* (1947), is terrified of age-ing. To step into fiction is to secure a temporary if factitious respite, to claim an immunity that can never be real. In like manner, Laura (in *The Glass Menagerie*), with a club foot and intensely shy, steps into the world of her glass menagerie, in recoil from a life that carries the stain of mortality, secure, as she thinks, like a Beckett character seeking to defeat the absurd by suc-cumbing to it. It is an irony clear to the audience but not to characters, who tell themselves that they can re-invent the world and then inhabit it, as Blanche is led off to a mental hospital on the arms of a doctor who she greets as if he were a redeemer.

Part of the shock of Williams's work was the extent to which sexuality was a language and a symbol. It is the source of a resistant spirit, pitched against the impotence and sterility of a world in which a soulless materialism has a grasp on power (*Cat on a Hot Tin Roof*, 1955, *Orpheus Descending*, 1957). It has the ability to re-animate those who have been tempted to surrender. The problem is that if sexuality implies continuity and commitment it breeds vulnerability, and those Williams's protagonists who are tempted to pause in their flight (an original title for *Orpheus Descending* had been *The Fugitive Kind*), suffer the consequences, being emasculated, burned with blow torches, driven to the edge of insanity. Williams's is a gothic sensibility, something he shared with other southern writers. It was seen at its most extreme in *Suddenly Last Summer* (1958), in which cannibalism and threatened lobotomies hint at his own fear of being consumed – by his own talent and by those who seemed intent to appropriate him, as by his guilt with respect to his sister, Rose, who had in fact suffered a lobotomy, which he had done nothing to stop.

Williams's own explanation for the violence of his work (another distinguishing characteristic) was that he was registering a threat apparent in the world at large – and here, perhaps, his own sexuality was especially relevant, along with the caustic racism of the South. He might not choose to include black characters in his plays – except on the margin – but in both *Orpheus Descending* (1957) and *Sweet Bird of Youth* (1959), he showed himself alert to the cruelties of a tradition that chose to lie about the basis of its wealth and power. In *Night of the Iguana* (1961) fascists penetrate the last retreat of a man on the run from himself as from society; a man who is trussed up like an iguana, which, we are told, can only escape by maiming itself. He, however, is offered the tenuous hope of a Williams character, as a spinster who shares his desperation declares the necessity for 'broken gates between people so they can reach each other, even if it's for one night only'.

Williams's career began to falter in the 1960s, which, with good reason, he called his 'stoned decade', being high on drink and drugs. A new generation of writers had appeared and the theatre was going through a period of experimentation. Williams himself had attempted radical experimentation in *Camino Real* (1953), allowing the action to spill over into the auditorium, and sought inspiration in a new European drama (*Gnadiges Fraulein*, 1966, represented a flirtation with the absurd), but his best work reached for a poetic realism that found its correlative in the stage designs of Jo Mielziner, who was also a key figure in the work of the other major figure who appeared in the immediate aftermath of the Second World War.

Like Williams, Arthur Miller began his career with a disaster. *The Man Who Had all the Luck* (1944), a fable that explored the seemingly arbitrary nature of fate, and left one man a success and another a failure, closed after four performances, leaving the question raised by the play embarrassingly relevant. For the moment Miller abandoned the theatre, in 1945 writing *Focus*, a novel that centred on American anti-Semitism, on the face of it a curious subject for the final year of the war. But it soon became apparent that Miller was a writer who wrote against the American grain. Beginning while America was still at war, he wrote *All My Sons* (1947), which placed at its heart a war profiteer and his son, a man who sees himself as an idealist and who feels guilty both for the death of his men in battle and for his involvement in a company that owes its success to the war, whether criminal or not.

Miller followed it with a play that appeared to question the American dream at the very moment Americans were desperate to pursue that dream at the beginning of a sustained economic boom. Nonetheless, both this play, *Death of a Salesman* (1949) and *All My Sons* proved immediate and considerable successes.

Believing that his first play had failed in part because of its stylistic experimentation, Miller rooted *All My Sons* in an Ibsenesque aesthetic. Indeed it is remarkably close in spirit and detail to a particular Ibsen play, *The Wild Duck*. Having succeeded in that, however, Miller determined that his next play would find its own form. *Death of a Salesman* takes place, in part, inside the mind of its central character, a man who looks back on his life in an attempt to discover the moment it had gone wrong, since he judges himself a failure by the world's standards. Miller offered a number of images for what he was trying to do. He treated time, he explained, as though he were cutting down through geological strata, as if he had devised an equivalent of the CAT scan in which it is possible to see different dimensions simultaneously. It is not, he insisted, a play built around flashbacks. It all takes place in Willy Loman's present, since memories are present tense even as they carry the shadow of the past. The play, he insisted at the time, was to be a tragedy of the common man – a man who wished above all to evaluate himself justly, to close the gap between what he would be and what he feared he might be.

Thanks to the skills of Jo Mielziner, it proved possible for every scene to blend into the next, with no pauses and no blackouts, so that it moved with the speed of the mind. The play was seen at the time, and seems in retrospect, a key moment in the history of the American theatre. Here was a play that sought to go to the heart of the American experience as a man sees his individual worth as a product of his social utility. Desperate to leave his mark on the world, to feel that he has lived the dream, he bequeaths it to his sons, unaware of the poison he hands them. One son learns nothing, determined to embrace the same illusions as his father. The other, with the soul of a poet (and Willy Loman, like America itself, is part materialist, part spiritual questor) recognises that his father had had all the wrong dreams.

Both plays were successful with the public but both provoked hostile responses from other groups. Miller was already under surveillance by the FBI and a report on the screenplay for *All My Sons*, held in his file, presents it as an attack on American capitalism and the family. It was banned from production on American military bases in Europe. The touring version of *Death of a Salesman* was picketed by the American Legion. It was the first sign, to Miller, of a shift in the culture.

Approached by two actors who had been blacklisted for their supposed association with the Communist Party, he agreed to write an adaptation of Ibsen's *An Enemy of the People* (1950). He followed this with as provocative a play as could be imagined in the context of the House UnAmerican Activities Committee investigation of writers, directors and actors; an investigation that had seen Clifford Odets, Miller's role model from the 1930s, Elia Kazan, director of *Death of a Salesman*, and Lee J. Cobb, who had played Willy Loman, all summoned by the Committee and required to turn informer. Miller travelled to Salem, Massachusetts, scene of the 1692 witchcraft trials, and returned with a play seen at the time as offering a direct parallel to contemporary witch-hunts: *The Crucible* (1953).

This was a work that would eventually become Miller's most frequently produced play. At the time, however, it had a modest run and when, the following year, Miller was invited to travel to Belgium for the French-language premiere of the play, he was refused renewal of his passport. He himself had become an enemy of the people. At the heart of *The Crucible* is the figure of John Proctor, who grudgingly challenges the court when it seeks to indict his wife. At first he is disabled by guilt, having conducted a brief adulterous affair with his wife's accuser. In the end he stands up against authority, his own integrity being implicated in the need to take a stand. Hemingway's definition of tragedy turned on the fact that, to him, a man could be destroyed but not defeated. It is in that sense that *The Crucible* was a tragedy.

When Miller followed this with *A View from the Bridge*, which featured an informer, there were those who thought he was responding to Elia Kazan's film of Budd Schulberg's *On the Waterfront* (Schulberg also having been a friendly witness before the House UnAmerican Activities Committee), which seemed to justify informing. The irony was that Miller offered his protagonist, Eddie Carbone, as a tragic hero. Written first as a one-act verse drama, it was rewritten for its British production (directed by Peter Brook). The American production was only a moderate success and no new play by Miller would appear on Broadway for a further nine years, during which time he married Marilyn Monroe and dedicated much of his energy to sustaining her in her battles with film studios and directors. The one product of those years was a film, *The Misfits* (1956), originally published as a short story, which Miller offered to his wife as a gift following a miscarriage. The film survives, the marriage did not, though a play based on his experiences while filming it, *Finishing the Picture*, was finally staged in 2004.

Miller returned to the theatre with a play that was an attempt to come to terms not only with his own experiences but also with those of a generation. *After the Fall* (1964), which marked the establishment of the Lincoln Center Repertory Company, and was directed by Kazan (perhaps bizarrely, also a character in the play), engages the fact of the Holocaust and the House UnAmerican Activities Committee, as it does the private betrayals of its central characters. Seen at the time as a response to Miller's failed marriage to Monroe, in fact it was an exploration of private and public betrayals. He followed it a year later with *Incident at Vichy* (1965), set in Vichy France and exploring the possibility of self-sacrifice in a context in which all human values seemed in abeyance.

Though set in the past this was, Miller insisted, a play for the day, a play of equal relevance to the situation in Vietnam, against which he had now begun actively to campaign. This connection between past and present is fundamental to Miller's work, which is, he once explained, about the birds coming home to roost. In a country liable to show a disdain for history, Miller was insisting on the connection between act and consequence, on moral responsibility for one's own actions and those of the culture. His next play, *The Price* (1968), about two brothers who meet to dispose of their dead father's furniture, makes precisely that connection. Only when the past has been acknowledged is it possible to confront the present.

The Price was highly successful, perhaps surprisingly so given the fact that the American theatre was undergoing a transformation at the time and that this play seemed sturdily realistic when realism was under pressure and the playwright seen as the source of a suspect authority. It was, though, the last success Miller would score in his own country for the next 30 years. What followed was a series of plays, well-received elsewhere in the world, but casually dismissed in America. They included *The Archbishop's Ceiling* (1977), set in a central European country (in fact Czechoslovakia); *The American Clock* (1980), which looked back to the 1930s from the perspective of a deeply materialistic decade; and *The Ride Down Mount Morgan* (1991), which featured a bigamously married man who believed he could have everything and that his integrity lay precisely in abandoning a sense of guilt. Miller's 1994 play, *Broken Glass*, can stand as a paradigm of his contrasting reputations. In the United States it had only a modest run. In Britain it won the country's premiere award: the Laurence Olivier Award for Best Play.

It was not Miller's last work of the twentieth century. In 1998 came *Mr Peters' Connections*, in which a man looks back through his life in an attempt to understand what its meaning might have been. He does so in a culture that, beneath its rhetoric of progress and the pursuit of happiness, seems equally adrift. It was an apt play for the millennium and, incidentally, no more a realistic work than many of Miller's plays, in spite of his reputation for realism. Indeed, from virtually the beginning of his public career Miller had been interested in the nature of reality – how it is defined and what its connection is with power

In two one-act double bills – *Two Way Mirror* (1982) and *Danger, Memory* (1987) – Miller pressed such concerns further, as he was to do in 2004 in *Finishing the Picture*, a study of power in its various guises, including the power that lies at the heart of art. Not the least of Miller's concerns was the question of how a moral world can be sustained in a context of competing notions of the real and the desirable. In a fiercely satirical play, *Resurrection Blues* (2002), set in Latin America but directly applicable to America, he painted a portrait of a deeply materialistic society with no interest in transcendence, in which the flickering images of advertising, like those in Plato's cave, proposed an alternative reality remote from human needs.

Miller's argument with America had been lifelong but it was the argument of a believer, albeit not a believer in the slogans of self-evident virtue and material progress. His was an existential world in which the individual is responsible for his or her own actions and thereby for the state of the culture. A primary metaphor – to be found in *The Golden Years* (written while he was working for the Federal Theatre) and *Broken Glass*, but also implicit in virtually everything he wrote – is of paralysis. His characters work their way towards acknowledging responsibility for their actions and hence for the integrity of the identities in which they need so desperately to believe.

Miller lived a public life and engaged many of the issues of his day. As a Jew, as someone raised in the Depression, as part of a generation that lived under the shadow of the atom bomb (and he spent some time drafting a play on the subject), he was acutely aware of the fragility of the social world, indeed of life itself. His theatre not only addressed that sense of contingency, it in itself constituted that sense of communality – the connection between people and between them and their society, whose lack was often the inspiration for his plays.

From Edward Albee to Amiri Baraka

Nor was Miller the only writer for whom that lack of connection has proved a stimulus and a theme. Not merely was *The Connection* the title of a 1959 play, written by Jack Gelber, in which a group of addicts sit around waiting for meaning to be offered to them, but another then-young writer, in that same year, produced a play in which alienation and estrangement were to be ended by an act of selflessness, of love, which seemingly had quasi-religious overtones. At a time when the American theatre seemed in a state of crisis, with Tennessee Williams on the cusp of his stoned decade and Miller four years into a nearly decade-long silence, Edward Albee's *The Zoo Story* (1959) seemed to mark the arrival of a vital new talent.

The American theatre itself was changing. O'Neill, Williams and Miller had all opened their career on Broadway. This was no longer a credible proposition. Production costs had risen. A commercial art required some guarantee of success and new playwrights were unlikely to provide that. The focus, therefore, moved to smaller theatres, where actors commanded lower wages and union agreements enabled costs to be lowered. The emergence of Off Broadway (not a geographical description but a designation that permitted lower than Equity rates to be paid to actors) made possible the emergence of new talents.

Edward Albee had been writing for several years, but *The Zoo Story*, a parable of the need for human contact, was the first he had offered for production. It made its way to New York by way of Berlin. When he followed it in 1962 with *Who's Afraid of Virginia Woolf?*, which did open on Broadway, it was clear that a new generation had arrived, though like Williams and Miller before him Albee was in his thirties at the time of his first success. This play, too, beyond its excoriating language, was a plea for simple human contact. George and Martha, unable to have children, have invented a fantasy child designed to bring them together. In fact it proves the source of contention. In the place of genuine human contact the couple offer a flood of language, a brilliant performance that simultaneously shocks and thrills a young couple with whom they spend the evening. The logic of the fantasy child, however, due to reach his twenty-first birthday that night, is such that he must now be surrendered. George and Martha thus end the night stripped of illusion, their language simplified. The play, Albee insisted, was as much a rejection of the 'pipe dreams' embraced by Eugene O'Neill's characters in *The Iceman Cometh* as it was of the fantasies embraced by so many of Tennessee Williams's characters, and there are lines in the play that parody the work of both writers.

Who's Afraid of Virginia Woolf?, though, was something more than a brilliantly articulate study of a disintegrating marriage, not least because that very articulateness was itself the source of self-deception. It was also offered as a comment on a society that seemed no less in thrall to illusion, no less dedicated to fantasy. Viewed in retrospect, however, there is a curious confidence to both *The Zoo Story* and *Who's Afraid of Virginia Woolf?* and even a sentimentality, albeit neutralised by a visceral power to the language and action. On the edge of a decade in which love would be offered as an antidote to scientism and violence, they seemed to propose an end to the vapid materialism of the 1950s and to the alienation that was a product of a dream of personal and national endeavour, by offering nothing more than an acknowledgement of the need for human contact.

It was not a confidence that lasted long. In 1963 the president of the United States was assassinated and Albee has confessed to feeling that possibilities were suddenly obviated. Perhaps as a consequence his subsequent plays tend to be marked by irony (*A Delicate Balance*, 1966), to focus on the closing down of options (*The Lady from Dubuque*, 1980) on impending death (*All Over*, 1971) and even apocalypse (*Box* and *Quotations from Chairman Mao Tse-Tung*, 1968), though he was still capable of offering a fable of human possibility, albeit hedged around with doubt, in the form of *Seascape* (1975).

Albee was a product of Off Broadway in his dedication to experiment. Few of his plays are best described in terms of realism and each one tends to break new ground. He drew his inspiration in part from T. S. Eliot's verse drama and, indeed, an early unpublished work was written in verse. Eliot's influence, however, beyond a fascination with the precision and rhythms of language, lies largely in a fascination with locating social and metaphysical issues in the context of contemporary realities.

Despite several Pulitzer Prizes, Albee was no more immune to American critical disregard than O'Neill, Williams and Miller had been. For nearly

30 years, with occasional exceptions, his plays failed in New York. They opened and closed on a Broadway that now seemed to have little time for his oblique metaphysics. He turned, increasingly, to working in Europe (in Austria and the Netherlands, in particular), in small American theatres and in universities. However, for those who, like F. Scott Fitzgerald, thought that American lives do not have second acts, he proved the contrary with *Three Tall Women* (1991), which had at its heart the device of a character played, at three different stages of her life, by different actresses. Brilliantly conceived and structured, it opened Off Broadway but swiftly moved to the Great White Way. When, a few years later, Albee followed it with *The Goat* (2002), a play that centred on a love affair between a man and a goat, it was something more than a *succès de scandale*. In one way it echoed the concern of Albee's first plays in that it interrogated the meaning and force of love, no matter its focus.

In a varied career, there are certain constancies in Albee's career. At the centre is a respect for language, its valences, its rhythms, and its power to deflect and access meaning. Thematically, Albee has insisted on the need to live an examined life, to distinguish the factitious from the vital. He once described himself as a demonic social critic, and that wider dimension of his art remains significant. At its heart, though, are more fundamental issues to do with a life made more urgent by the fact of death.

Albee's first play appeared at a critical moment in the American theatre and in American society. The Eisenhower years were making way for the Kennedy years. Power was shifting to a younger generation who would find themselves in revolt over the racial situation and Vietnam. In an age in which the performing self became a familiar trope and in which authority was distrusted, along with the language it deployed to justify war and sell America back to its citizens, the theatre became a central focus. This was not, though, the theatre of Broadway, with its high-price tickets. It was a theatre in which the division between audience and performer was to be eroded both because the audience was part of that performance and because artistic legerdemain seemed of a piece with political deceit. The existential drive of the period found a correlative in the stress on improvisation. It was a rare public demonstration or protest that was not accompanied by theatre groups – the Living Theatre, the Bread and Puppet Theatre – staging America's moral and political dilemmas on the street where the people were.

Julian Beck and Judith Malina's Living Theatre had been founded long before the 1960s but came into its own with that decade, along with Richard Schechner's Performance Theatre. As the decade progressed, so Off Broadway gave way to Off Off Broadway – performances staged in lofts, cellars, church halls and cafés. Young playwrights, who often doubled as busboys, cleaning tables, could write a play one day and see it performed a few days later. There was an immediacy to a theatre whose audience was changing. The middle-aged gave way to the young; black playwrights began to stage the drama of a swiftly changing situation.

James Baldwin turned to the theatre with *Blues for Mr Charlie* (1964), inspired in part by the murder of Emmet Till, a young black boy, as by an incident that he and James Meredith had learned about on a visit to the South. LeRoi Jones, poet and editor, with his Jewish white wife, of a literary periodical, scored a success with *Dutchman* and *The Slave* in 1964, and then changed his name to Amiri Baraka and began to write agit-prop plays designed to raise consciousness in the black community. Having opened his plays at the Cherry Lane Theatre, with support from Edward Albee, Baraka moved north into Harlem, staged plays on the street, divorced his white wife and married a black woman, later acknowledging his ideological reasons for doing so. He established a Black Arts Repertory Theatre, which proved a template for other such across America. Later he would move on to Marxist–Leninism, having discovered that the black control of America's inner cities would simply leave them in charge of a desert unless there were a radical change in American politics – a change that he managed, in the face of the evidence to the contrary, to convince himself might come about. Meanwhile, a young black man in Pittsburgh was inspired by Baraka but would not begin writing until some years later, when he became the most successful black playwright in American theatrical history. His name was August Wilson.

Sam Shepard and David Mamet

Among those drawn to New York at this time was a man who arrived from California, escaping from an oppressive family situation and in search of the source of musical and theatrical energy. Sam Shepard found employment at Theatre Genesis, at St Mark's in the Bowery, working as a busboy, and wrote a series of somewhat surreal sketches beginning with *Cowboys* and *The Rock Garden* in 1964. Theatre Genesis was his base until 1971, along with Café La MaMa. It was, he later confessed of the 1960s, a time of some confusion. That confusion could be generative but also disturbing. America was changing in front of his eyes, so much so that he briefly went to London, then presenting itself as the home of rock music. While there he wrote *Geography of a Horse Dreamer* (1974) which he directed at the Royal Court Theatre, very much a writers' theatre.

Thematically, Shepard grew increasingly interested in exploring the family, the relationship between men and women, between men and men, and locating these against a background of American myths and values. His has tended to be a theatre of loss, which stages the lives of individuals repelled by the very relationships they seek in a society in which people have only the weakest grasp on private or public meaning. Love, in Shepard's work, contains the seeds of violence. In *Paris, Texas*, a film that he wrote for Wim Wenders, the central character leaves his wife to protect her from his own brutality. Drawn back by love, he finally opts to leave again for the same reason, aware of his power to destroy what he needs beyond anything. In *Fool for Love* (1979) a man and a woman seek one another out in the knowledge that they must separate. In *A Lie of the Mind* (1985) a man beats a woman so severely that she loses the power of coherent speech. Every action seems to have an equal and opposite reaction, as if this were the natural law of a culture that celebrates the individual and turns the family into a national piety, but which sees violence as a vital component of the national psyche and witnesses the collapse of family life and national coherence. His family members tend to meet as strangers (*Buried Child*, 1978).

Shepard's characters seem to be passing through. His father worked for the military and the family was moved from place to place, finally settling in an undistinguished town on an undistinguished California highway (his Los Angeles, in *Angel City*, 1976, is more than touched with disaster). Perhaps that is why his characters, like Tennessee Williams's, tend to be on the move, with little in the way of roots (and his first play, he has confessed, was a poor copy of a Williams's play) and afraid of the vulnerability that comes with stasis. The plays take place in motels, cafés and anonymous cabins. Shepard even claims to have written *Simpatico* (1995) as he drove across the country, one hand on the steering wheel, the other holding a pen, and this in a country in which 17 per cent of the population moves every year – as if movement were progress instead of flight.

Shepard's characters' grasp of identity is so insecure that they are liable to exchange places, share characteristics, blend into one another. Even the genders, apparently so separate, so antithetical, can echo one another as if the confusion were contained within the self and was not simply a product of differing perspectives. In that sense the characters are shown as being at war with themselves, in a culture in which violence is definitional and communication an invitation to vulnerability.

Shepard's characters live intensely. They are liable to sudden bursts of unfocused energy. In *Fool for Love* the sound is amplified as if the characters live on the extreme, as if that were the only way of living. The external world does penetrate – the possibility of nuclear war in *Chicago*, 1965, the Gulf War in *States of Shock*, 1991, Bosnia in *When the World Was Green*, 1996 – but Shepard is more concerned to take the inward path. He tends to pitch a bleak modernity against the organicism of Native Americans, even if they have now been reduced to a corrupted remnant. Though he himself celebrates the natural world, even being drawn to the rodeo, itself a kind of quotation from a past no longer quite available, there is no suggestion that this was the moment that marked the beginning of decline and alienation. That seems to have occurred much further back in time, perhaps even at the very beginning with expulsion from Eden. That, after all, was the origin of violence and death, the moment women was born out of the rib of man and their ambiguous relationship was laid down.

That aside, Shepard's America is in a state of disintegration with old roles no longer sustainable, old principles no longer applicable. His characters tend to stare out into blackness, mere space, as if their location were not of any final significance. His real focus, though, is less on a national fate than on individual lives stripped of all but some inner compulsion. America is invoked but it is the baffled intensities of private existence that fascinate. His characters have suffered some wound. For the most part his plays are about living with the consequence. His is a theatre of trauma, of incomplete people baffled by the needs that direct their lives, aware of secrets to which they lack true access, secrets to do with their own natures and those they encounter. When the protagonist of *Paris, Texas* heads out into the desert, he is trying to escape the irony of his own contradictory nature. He abandons sociality, language and feelings, his distinguishing characteristics as a human being. This is the world of Samuel Beckett, except that Shepard can never quite settle for the final irony of figures who give birth astride the grave. His characters, trapped in their own nature and in a culture drifting on the wind, nonetheless seem committed to something more than mere survival.

If Shepard has a model it is Garcia Lorca, whose work was read to him by his father, the father who recurs as a point of reference in his work, as if he were trapped in an argument with a man to whom he was drawn even as he was repelled. For Lorca, too, passion and pain occupy the same space. Love is a destiny and a fate. Lorca wrote with the kind of intensity that is to be found in Shepard's work.

Sam Shepard is not only a playwright, screenwriter and director. He is also an actor, often playing the kind of laconic character implied in his invocation of Western values. David Mamet, whose *Sexual Perversity in Chicago* was voted Best Chicago Play in 1974 and which went on to win an Obie

Award in New York, was also once an actor, appearing as a child on radio and television in a series of plays commissioned by the Chicago Board of Rabbis. Though Mamet was to make a passing appearance in a film later in life, he has confessed that it was less than a triumph, though like Shepard he would go on to write for and direct movies. There is also, perhaps, another point of contact. If Shepard's portraits of a strained family life had in part been a product of his upbringing and the violence of his father, Mamet, too, as a child of divorced parents whose step-father had been liable to sudden and irrational outbursts of violence, would create a drama in which the family seemed hardly to function and the relationship between men and women was no less fraught than it was in Shepard's plays (in *The Cryptogram*, 1994, indeed, Mamet offered what seemed in part an oblique portrait of himself and the betrayals he witnessed).

Mamet had started his career as a playwright at Goddard College in Vermont, though he was raised in Chicago, a city that was home to some of the more exciting theatre of the 1970s and 1980s. *Sexual Perversity* concerned two couples, one male, one female, manifestly failing to make contact with one another. Brilliantly funny and occasionally obscene, it operated in a series of brief scenes, in part, perhaps, inspired by the playwright's time watching Chicago's improvisational Second City, at which, like Shepard at Theatre Genesis, he had cleaned tables. The play's depressing portrait of sexual relations would be reflected in later plays, as would the image of a society held together by nothing but baffled instincts. In *The Woods* (1977) Mamet created a fable that dramatised the differing needs and satisfactions of men and women, leaving them isolated and confused. In a number of plays, indeed, women were excluded altogether, as if they had no place in a society seemingly stalled, with no sense of purpose or direction, a society whose myths had been resolutely male.

One such was *American Buffalo* (1975), set, significantly, in a junk store full of detritus from Chicago's 1933 Exposition, whose motto had been 'A century of progress'. The irony is equally apparent from a group of men who plan, but do not carry out, a robbery, filling their time with pointless ventures, mouthing partially recalled American pieties about freedom, which they regard as sanctioning greed and rapacity. As they pass the time so police cars patrol the area. They meet only within the games they play, like O'Neill's derelicts in *The Iceman Cometh* – apparently mutually supportive but only up to a point. Eventually, however, there is a spasm of violence, itself no more than a cover for self-evident failure. In a sense this seems like a downtown Chicago version of Beckett, except that here, as in

Mamet's later plays, there is a brief moment of consonance, a sense of loyalty, albeit easily betrayed, which links two characters together even in this place of rusting dreams and corroding fantasies.

For Mamet, the men form a kind of family and in so far as they do he creates a harrowing portrait of a deeply uncommunal world. Just how uncommunal would become apparent in a later play, *Edmond* (1982), in which the anti-hero goes on a journey into the urban underworld, drained of anything resembling transcendence. For the most part the brutal reductivism of Mamet's characters is balanced by the play's humour. In *Edmond*, though, there is little more than a final ambiguous gesture to weigh against the reductiveness of the world he encounters.

Mamet has been astonishingly prolific. It has been said that if he went to the men's room he was likely to come out with a play. Thus at one moment he writes a play, set at the time of the Chicago Exposition, which takes as its ostensible subject the urban myth of a man who invents an engine that will run on water, *The Water Engine* (1977), and at another a two-hander in which two actors play out scenes and discuss the theatre while subtly revealing aspects of their own characters, their fears and ambitions, *A Life in the Theatre* (1977).

Despite his growing reputation, however, it was not until *Glengarry, Glen Ross* (1984) that he finally consolidated his position as one of America's leading playwrights. It opened at London's National Theatre and won a Pulitzer Prize in America. It is a play that offers a model of American society. Set in a real estate office, it features a group of salesmen set in competition with one another. The winner will receive a Cadillac, the runner-up a set of steak knives. The loser will be fired. Desperate to succeed, one stages a robbery to secure the leads – the addresses of likely clients. The police are called. Only one of the salesmen shows any loyalty. Otherwise what is on show is a paradigm of capitalist society: a dream that has devolved into nothing more than a battle for survival in which human needs are seized upon for advantage and language is a snare for the unwary.

However, one dimension of the play would prove paradigmatic. The salesmen may in effect be fraudsters, selling worthless land, but they are, for the most part, superlative actors. In so far as they are successful they are so because they offer people what they can be persuaded they want. They take advantage of those who wish to believe them because they exploit others' belief they live in a world in which trust has meaning. They are storytellers who understand the human need for story and for the most part they are masters of their craft. The irony is that in betraying others they betray themselves. The play ends much as it began as the salesmen continue their suspect struggle to succeed, enacting a degraded myth of possibilities.

Much the same was true of another play, *The Shawl* (1985), in which a confidence trickster masquerades as a medium. There is a mutuality between trickster and victim. The fraudster needs the woman to whom he spins his fictions, while the victim needs to be told the stories that appear to make sense of her life, and to address her anxieties and needs. The trickster and victim can both only play the roles they do because faith and belief survive, even if they are manipulated and betrayed. This is the balancing act that gives Mamet's plays something of their particular force. While offering a caustic view of human nature, he recognises that that nature extends to a human vulnerability that is potentially redemptive, just as it does to inventive skills and a sensitivity to need that implies a residual humanity.

A similar fascination with the trickster figure was apparent in a number of the films that he went on to direct, from *House of Games* and *The Spanish Prisoner* to *Heist*. The pleasure of these lies in the skills of those who spin fictions that clearly respond to the needs and desires of those who find themselves victims of these deceits.

In 1995, with *Oleanna*, Mamet staged a play that created immediate controversy, not least because it seemed related to an incident in which Anita Hill had accused a Supreme Court nominee, Judge Clarence Thomas, of harassment. In Mamet's play, a professor is accused of sexual harassment by a female student, an accusation that turns on an ambiguous gesture observed by the audience and which the audience, too, is therefore required to decode. In essence a study of power, *Oleanna* explores the extent to which language is a mechanism as well as an expression of that power – the degree to which reality is a construction susceptible to interpretation and manipulation. There is, it seems, no secure reality, since this is a product of language, a language that appears to be gendered.

Audiences were divided. For some, here was proof that Mamet was, indeed, misogynistic, the views of some of his characters being confused with his own. At least it seemed further evidence of the gulf that he apparently believed existed between the sexes. In the end, though, Mamet insisted that he regarded both characters as absolutely right and absolutely wrong. Each, in effect, was requiring the other to exist within a language and a fiction offered by the other.

For those who thought Mamet might be incapable of allowing women centre stage, in 1999 he staged *Boston Marriage*, a witty pastiche of nineteenth-century comedy reminiscent of Wilde and Shaw.

Gender, sexual preference, ethnicity and national origin

Women had not been absent from twentieth-century American drama (or, indeed, British drama) but it is true to say they had not been a major force, despite the work of Susan Glaspell, Rachel Crothers and Lillian Hellman. Things began to change in the 1970s, though Lorraine Hansberry's *A Raisin in the Sun* had staked a claim both for women and for black writers in 1959. Off Broadway and Off Off Broadway made space for those who saw theatre as a site for social and political aims. The 1960s saw the emergence of Adrienne Kennedy, Irene Fornes, Rochelle Owens and Megan Terry. In the 1970s a number of women's theatre groups were formed, in many cases with a clear polemical intent, though a report found that between 1969 and 1975 only 7 per cent of playwrights in funded not-for-profit theatres in America were women. The feminist movement set about recuperating women writers from the past, reconstituting a tradition that would provide a pre-history to present endeavours. As ever, the theatre was registering shifts in the culture. It was the 1980s, however, before the achievement of women writers was acknowledged with the award of three Pulitzer Prizes (women playwrights having won only three in the previous 60 years, just as they had won only four New York Drama Critics Circle awards between 1935 and 1983). The best of these, perhaps, was Marsha Norman.

In 1977, in *Getting Out*, Norman had staged the life of a woman released from prison to debate with herself (the part was played at different stages of her life by different actresses) her possible future. It was a powerful and original work. The Pulitzer Prize came for *'night, Mother* (1983), a disturbing play, disturbing for feminists as well as for audiences, in which a daughter explains to her mother that she is about to commit suicide. The play takes place in real time. The problem for feminists lay in the fact that the daughter apparently felt that the only way she could address her problems was to end her life. For her part, Norman argued that her character was taking control of her life in the decision to end it.

Wendy Wasserstein, another Pulitzer winner, offered a comic account of the life of a woman over several decades. *The Heide Chronicles* (1988) is, in effect, an ironic take on the women's movement as, later, *The Sisters Rosensweig* (1992) offers an account of three sisters who come to believe that they have betrayed aspects of themselves. Outside their windows, major events are taking place. Inside, they are struggling to accept who they are and what they have allowed themselves to become. With *An American Daughter* (1997), Wasserstein moved more directly into the public realm. Shocked by the attacks on Hillary Clinton and a woman nominee for the post of attorney general, she created a woman character who is similarly attacked and who has to struggle to come to terms with her possibilities in a world which will not resolve itself into moral simplicities. Concerned as she was to write plays that reflect 'how a group of people live at a certain time', her 2002 play *Old Money* exposed what seemed to her to be a new gilded age.

If there had been a paucity of women playwrights before, this was now manifestly no longer true. Tina Howe began writing in the 1960s, her first Off Broadway play, *The Nest*, dating from 1969. Stylistically inspired by the theatre of the absurd, she created a series of plays that show a fascination with slapstick – *Museum* (1976), *The Art of Dining* (1979) – while exploring serious themes to do with the nature of creativity – a concern, too, of the award-winning *Painting Churches* (1983), of *Coastal Disturbances* (1986) and *Approaching Zanzibar* (1989). Howe has also been concerned throughout her career, however, with the experience of women, in different stages of their lives, with *Pride's Crossing*, in 1997, taking the story to the moment of death.

Emily Mann created a series of affecting semi-documentary plays. *Annula Allen: Autobiography of a Survivor*, based on interviews she had conducted with a woman in London, had its first performance in 1977. Despite its roots in fact, however, part of the interest of the play lay in the degree to which it spun a series of complexities having to do with history, identity and the problematic nature of theatre itself. Certainly, Mann saw theatre as engaging the public world, as, in effect, a kind of court before which she could summon recent history.

Subsequent works included *Still Life* (1980), a play that she described as being about violence in America, inspired by the memories of a Vietnam veteran, and *Execution of Justice* (1981), provoked by the murder of San Francisco's mayor and its gay city supervisor by a homophobic ex-policeman. With *Greensboro* (1996), Mann returned to the question of American violence, inspired by the killing, in 1979, of members of the American Communist Party by the Ku Klux Klan.

For Paula Vogel, who describes herself as a playwright who is gay, rather than a gay playwright, sexuality is the subject and site of her drama. She acknowledges hers to be a dangerous theatre, challenging taboos, and political in that it sets out to confront audiences with a different way of seeing the world. *The Oldest Profession* (1988) features five prostitutes; *Hot 'n' Throbbin'* (1993) includes a woman who works on women's erotica; *The Baltimore Waltz* (1990) addresses the question of AIDS; *How I Learned to Drive* (1998) takes as its central character a paedophile. Vogel's achievement, though, lies not in the challenges she seems to throw out, but rather in her deft theatricality and her ability to seduce audiences as much by her technical skills as by the subject of her plays.

In contrast to Paula Vogel's self-designation, Tony Kushner was ready to describe himself as a gay playwright. A number of America's major playwrights had been gay, while not making that the centre of their work. Both Tennessee Williams and Edward Albee had begun writing at a time when to declare one's sexuality was to invite persecution and neither made their own sexuality overtly part of their drama. In the 1960s and thereafter, though, gay theatre began to establish itself. The founder of Off Off Broadway's Caffe Cino, Joe Cino, was gay and the work of a number of gay playwrights was first staged there, including Lanford Wilson's *The Madness of Lady Bright* (1964). Charles Ludlam founded the so-called Ridiculous Theatre Company and Ronald Tavel the Playhouse of the Ridiculous, while in 1967 all but one of the characters in Mark Crowley's *The Boys in the Band* (1968) were homosexual. The Gay Theatre Alliance was founded in 1978. Four years later Harvey Fierstein's *Torch Song Trilogy* opened on Broadway.

However, by the time Tony Kushner came to write *Angels in America* (its two parts, *Millennium Approaches* and *Perestroika* opened in 1990 and 1992 respectively), the fact of AIDS had become a dominant reality for gay Americans, more especially since politicians seemed reluctant to confront its implications. Gay liberation was no longer to be primarily a matter of securing social and political rights. It had become concerned with survival. It was the death of a friend from AIDS, indeed, that prompted Kushner to write a play whose subtitle was *A Gay Fantasy on National Themes*. It was a work, in other words, no longer designed, as a number of earlier gay plays had been, to focus primarily on the private world. This was to be an expansive work, almost Whitmanesque in spirit, that would link the personal to an unfolding history. Once, such a play might have flourished and died Off Broadway, seeking out an audience already predisposed to its theme and style. *Angles in America* made its way to Broadway, in itself a sign of a changing America. A first collection of lesbian plays, *Places, Please* had appeared in 1985.

At the same time, the last few decades of the twentieth century also saw a Balkanisation of the American theatre. Just as broadcasting in America gave way to 'narrow casting', with audiences seeking out specialist programmes that appealed to their special interests, and niche-marketing in magazines generated a plethora of new titles not designed for a mass market, so theatre began to fragment along lines of race, religion, ethnicity, national origin and sexual preference. Chinese Americans, Japanese Americans, Chicanos and Puerto Ricans turned to theatre as a place to display, interrogate and explore their identity. Collections of these plays began to appear: *Contemporary Chicano Theatre*, 1976; *Nuevos Pasos: Chicano and Puerto Rican Drama*, 1979; *Necessary Theater: Six Plays About the Chicano Experience*, 1989; *Between World: Contemporary Asian-American Plays*, 1990; *Cuban American Theatre*, 1991; *The Politics of Life: Four Plays by Asian American Women*, 1993; *But Still, Like Air, I'll Rise: New Asian American Plays*, 1997; *Seventh Generation: An Anthology of Native American Plays*, 1999. Few of these plays were bidding for mainstream attention. They spoke to other necessities. At a time when a quarter of the population was either black or Hispanic, and when other previously suppressed or marginalised groups were finding not only their voice but a new space to express themselves, a certain insecurity about national identity became evident.

The black theatre had long since established itself and in the person of August Wilson now had a playwright who, while writing what was in effect an alternative history of the twentieth century from the point of view of black Americans, had established himself as one of the country's leading playwrights, winning two Pulitzer Prizes and seeing his plays move from regional theatre to Broadway. *Jitney* (1982, subsequently revised), *Ma Rainey's Black Bottom* (1984), *Fences* (1987), *Joe Turner's Come and Gone* (1986), *The Piano Lesson* (1988), *Two Trains Running* (1990), *Seven Guitars* (1995) and *King Hedley II* (2001) explored the lives of those who lived on the margin of American society but at the centre of their own lives and communities. The arrival of these plays on Broadway, however, should not be seen as a sign that in Wilson's mind this took primacy over other theatres and other audiences. The story he told was the story of black men and women in America, the private rather than the public life of black men and women, and this was a story that had not been told.

American drama had entered the twentieth century as a marginal art – derivative, unadventurous, an entertainment that rarely engaged the realities of a country emerging into world dominance. A century on and that drama has moved to the centre of attention. Among the talents it has produced are John Guare, Lanford Wilson, David Rabe, Richard Nelson, Terrence McNally and many more. What had once seemed the poor relation in the arts is now for many the most vibrant and compelling drama in the world; a drama that reflects the contending elements of a society always in the making. There may no longer be a single audience. Broadway may not have the power and influence it once had. The theatre may have to compete for time and attention with the electronic media, with multi-channel global programming. It may ask more of its audience than the price of a book. But it has reached out to new communities, to those who once thought their concerns irrelevant to a culture announcing its indivisibility, and in doing so has staged the essential drama of America, which is, and it has always been, the invention of a culture and of the values to which it wishes to believe it commits itself.

Further reading

Bank, Rosemary K., *Theatre Culture in America 1825–1868* (1997).

Bigsby, C. W. E., *A Critical Introduction to 20th Century American Drama*, 3 vols (1982, 1983, 1985).

Boardman, Gerald, *American Musical Theatre* (1978).

Kolin, Philip C. and Colby H. Kullman, *Speaking on State: Interviews with Contemporary American Playwrights* (1966).

Meserve, Walter J., *An Emerging Entertainment: The Drama of the American People to 1828* (1977).

Miller, Jordan Y. and Winifred L. Frazer, *Drama between the Wars* (1991).

Roudané, Matthew *American Drama since 1960* (1996).

Smith, Susan Harris, *American Drama: The Bastard Art* (1997).

Witham, Barry B., *The Federal Theatre Project: A Case Study* (2003).

Wilmeth, Don B. and Christopher Bigsby, *The Cambridge History of American Theatre*, 3 vols (1998–2000).

CHAPTER 13

America and war

Brian Holden Reid

At the beginning of May 2004 President George W. Bush responded to the reports of widespread ill-treatment of Iraqi prisoners at the Abu Ghraib prison by American service personnel with the plea that Iraq 'must understand that what took place does not represent the America I know'. Mrs Laura Bush rallied to her husband's assistance with the claim 'that's not the picture of America'. Indeed she claimed that reports of abuse of prisoners were quite untypical of American military conduct. 'That's not the story of most of the troops who are in Afghanistan and Iraq. And it's certainly not the story of our country.' It is not the aim of this essay to suggest that the widely publicised (mainly because it was so copiously photographed) humiliation of Iraqi prisoners is somehow the 'real America'. The incident serves to illustrate a divergence between the view that a country might take of its conduct, and the way that its policies, especially in wartime, might be interpreted by the less-than-sympathetic citizens of other countries. At the Republican national convention in September of that year, Governor Arnold Schwarzenegger made the case for the 'greatness of America'. He stressed that 'we are the America that fights not for imperialism, but for human rights and democracy'. Schwarzenegger put the best possible gloss on American behaviour in war; the terrorists' 'hate', he proclaimed, 'is no match for America's decency'.

In this regard the United States is no different from other great powers. The great historian of the rise of the British Empire, J. R. Seeley commented in his seminal work, *The Expansion of England* (1883), on the 'indifference which we show towards this mighty phenomenon . . . and the expansion of our state'. He went on, in a state of some perplexity, to coin a famous phrase: 'We seem, as it were, to have conquered and peopled half the world in a fit of absence of mind'. That is to say, the acquisition of the British Empire was not consciously motivated, and thus Great Britain could not be deliberately expansionist, let alone predatory or conniving. Certainly others, least of all those ruled by the British (including, it must be said, before 1783 Americans, too), did not and have not interpreted the growth of the British Empire in these casual terms.

The British example is a pertinent one because the United States has inherited a significant portion of Britain's military tradition. Since the seventeenth century, the British nursed hostility to a large, standing army, disliked high defence spending (preferring voluntary enlistment to conscription), and thus relied on a small regular army. A reliance on naval power was deemed more suitable for the defence of personal liberty. British expansion, accompanied by protestations of altruism and moral standards ignored by other powers, led to accusations of hypocrisy and perfidy.

But suggestions that other great states have been subject to similar complaints of insincerity have not granted Americans much solace. Their view of America's place in the world, and therefore its conduct during wartime, has largely been shaped by notions of American exceptionalism. Numerous American leaders share an ardent belief that the United States has been uniquely blessed by divine favour. It is exceptionally abundant, exceptionally rich and exceptionally good. Its relations with other nations have been shaped invariably by a moral code *even* when self-interested. George W. Bush, like Ronald Reagan before him, is the authentic spokesman of such values. It is perhaps not surprising that neither president benefited from great popularity or even respect in Europe. George Bush has certainly been the target of the same kind of contemptuous denigration by Europeans as Reagan. There seems to be a view in Europe that if the United States has one exceptional quality it is the capacity to elect singularly incapable leaders.

Europeans tend to be sceptical, if not downright scornful of American exceptionalism, often denouncing it as pretentious, hypocritical, self-interested, or just plain conceited. Such a dismissal should be considered in the context of a relative decline in Europe's place in the world during a half century that saw the continuing rise in the power of the United States. Even though Europe's comparative decline has been halted (and indeed since the collapse of the Soviet Union Europe has witnessed something of a small revival), the anti-Americanism provoked by American claims to exceptionalism tends to illustrate the differences between Europeans and Americans rather than draw out their many similarities. Nonetheless, the ties remain close, as was evinced by the great wave of Western sympathy following the terrorist attacks on 11 September 2001 on the World Trade Center in New York and the Pentagon in Washington DC.

The influence of geography and culture

The American experience of war is a subject that has provoked extreme opinions and reactions. Virtually all American conflicts have sparked dissent, protest and unrest. Perhaps the easiest way to begin to approach it is to establish the nature of those forces that determined the 'story' of America in military terms. The influence of geography has been powerful. During its rise to world power the United States was separated by great oceans from those powers greater than itself. The young Abraham Lincoln, in his address before the Young Men's Lyceum in Springfield, Illinois, in January 1838, declared that 'All the armies of Europe, Asia and Africa combined' could not successfully invade the United States even if they were commanded by a Napoleon because of the great obstacle provided by the Atlantic Ocean. Even if an invader managed to cross the Atlantic safely, the sheer size of the American heartland presented an insuperable problem. By the Treaty of Guadalupe Hidalgo that terminated the Mexican War (1846–8), the United States gained half a million square miles of extra territory, not including Texas. By the end of the first decade of the twentieth century the United States formed an integral, continental republic of 48 states embracing some 3 million square miles. Its historical experience has thus been one that has enjoyed the comfort of 'space'. It also enjoyed during this period the advantage of being able to pick and choose the nature of its military interventions. (The one exception, the Civil War, 1861–5, represented the climax of a struggle over which social system – slavery or free labour – would prevail in the settling of these great spaces.) By 1900 the United States benefited from tremendous strategic advantages: it formed a compact, unitary state of great comparative wealth, surrounded by weak neighbours, and exploited an imbalance of power in its favour. The ability to enforce its interests in the comparative security of the Western hemisphere has contributed to the unilateral character of so much American foreign and military policy. The shelter and respite offered by its fortuitous geographical location has permitted a puny but pugnacious state – a veritable David that might easily have become a client of either Great Britain or France – to emerge as a Goliath that has supplanted both.

Second, the geographic and strategic advantages enjoyed by the United States fit its social form. The United States is a republican democracy. The source of its sovereignty lies with the people; they are able to concern themselves with what Thomas Jefferson termed 'the pursuit of happiness' – an opportunity that has been rare (especially outside the Western world) during the twentieth century. Thus 'foreign' wars can be a major distraction from the pursuit of happiness, and frequently Americans have attempted to distance themselves psychologically from such conflicts – and before 1941 could physically feel distant from them. Moreover, when the United States has participated in wars before 1975 it enjoyed the benefit of a long run of military success; before the Vietnam War the United States had never experienced the humiliation and trauma of defeat (although after 1865 the southern states had). This unbroken series of military victories was not only a source of great nationalistic pride but lent strength to the American belief that the United States fought wars honourably and cleanly. As the great French social scientist Raymond Aron wrote in his *Imperial Republic* (1974) of the Treaty of Guadalupe Hidalgo, in which, despite an overwhelming military victory, the United States paid Mexico $15 million for the territories seized, 'As was its custom, the United States paid for its territorial acquisitions in order to legitimise their conquest'.

Third, the United States, like other democracies, often experiences periods of self-doubt. It is a curious feature of American history that these have become more marked as the reach of American power has grown. Increasingly since the 1880s the American public has been persuaded into thinking that it could be attacked after all. In 1915 Eric Fisher Wood, in an article in *The Century Magazine*, argued that the 'very immensity' of the United States rendered it vulnerable; a number of strategic points on the East Coast contiguous to the Potomac, Susquehanna and Hudson Rivers to Lake Champlain – what Wood called 'this heart of America' – could be seized and the United States would be powerless to respond. 'Once occupied', Wood warned, descending into extraordinary fantasy, this area 'could easily be held by 400,000 German, British, or French troops against any army in the world'. Wood feared that the American economy would collapse and its population be reduced to penury – conditions that would resemble the days of the frontier. This kind of analysis has been applied to the 'threat' posed to the United States by Cuba or Nicaragua in the 1980s. The main strategic result of these debates has been an exaggeration of American vulnerability. During periods of crisis a widespread feeling grows that the United States is the underdog – the victim of the ambitions of others.

The two terms of the Reagan presidency (1981–9) have often been described as a period of revival – especially in self-confidence after the setbacks, humiliation and defeat encountered during the 1970s, the Watergate scandal, the resignation of Richard Nixon and the abandonment of Vietnam, as well as the resultant economic problems combining high inflation and industrial stagnation. Reagan himself had a sunny disposition, but the revival in self-confidence was sometimes more apparent than real. The incredible level of discussion of the extent of American 'decline' triggered off by a work of the British historian resident at Yale University, Paul Kennedy's *The Rise and Fall of the Great Powers* (1988), seemed to indicate that many Americans were convinced that the 'decline' of their military power *vis-à-vis* the Soviet Union would be permanent. Actually Kennedy's comments are contained in a 21-page section at the end of the book (the total length of which is 540 pages). A lot of the discussion was tinged with dire warnings that the United States might follow Portugal, Spain, the Netherlands, France and Britain and succumb to 'imperial over-stretch'. Kennedy's own argument appears to have greater subtlety: the United States could take action to reverse its *relative* decline. Of course, even this qualified argument has proved questionable. For in 1991 it was the Soviet Union not the United States that collapsed, adding its name to the list of fallen empires. Still, a lot of angst resulted from much misdirected discussion. The United States often expresses, despite the air of outward confidence, doubts about the wars it fights – including the Cold War, a war that involved no fighting at all between the major rivals.

A vital fourth consideration is the persistence of isolationist sentiment in America. Isolationism is an attitude of mind towards Europe rather than the world in general. It is not an American monopoly – the British are subject to bouts of 'splendid isolation', too – but is central to the American military experience because it binds together in cultural form so many of the geographic, social and political factors that have shaped the American approach to conflict. It was a commonplace of the immediate post-1945 years that isolationism had been vanquished by the Japanese attack on Pearl Harbor on 7 December 1941. This has never been true. American politics and defence policy were subject to isolationist resurgence in the 1970s and 1980s, and again at the beginning of the twenty-first century. The idea that the 'Europeans' enjoyed a 'free ride' on the back of burdensome, massive US defence expenditure led to calls for the withdrawal of American troops from bases in Western Europe. At the very least, strident demands were made to redeploy military resources in areas equally important to American interests, such as South Asia or the Pacific Rim lands.

A case can certainly be made that isolationism serves as a means of domestic healing. It permits Americans to seek solace by indulging a contemplation of their virtues and vices free of foreign (predominantly European) irritations; certainly domestic concerns seem to take precedence in isolationist periods. But far from being inimical to the process of 'globalisation' – the spread of the capitalist economy across the world – that has occurred over recent decades, it can be argued that isolationism will be able to draw renewed vitality from it in order to repair internal injuries. And indeed, as the American presidency gains power from its direction of foreign relations and military policy, no president is voluntarily going to give up these prerogatives to concentrate solely on domestic affairs. So it is possible to postulate that after a temporary period of disengagement, an American president would wish to engage again with the other great conglomerations of power.

Isolationism should not be confused with pacifism or a desire to withdraw from the world. On the contrary, such periods often exhibit bouts of belligerence – an open American willingness to use force in pursuit of national interests – especially when dealing with states far weaker than themselves. A good example can be found in US dealings with the states of the Caribbean basin during the early 1920s. The United States intervened in Nicaragua in 1920; it also took charge of Santo Domingo and Haiti, and its relations with Mexico were on the verge of breakdown. By 1924, through 'dollar diplomacy', the United States was running the financial (and thus foreign) policy of ten countries; in that year the US marines were landed in Honduras.

The United States has not succumbed, despite periodic resurgences of sentiment, to a sustained isolationist mood since the outbreak of the Second World War. After its triumph with the end of the Cold War, the United States has become 'isolated' in a rather different sense from that conveyed by the term 60 years ago. It is isolated in being the *only* superpower on the globe. Its international responsibilities across the spectrum, as they are undisputed, are far weightier than those of any previous power. The disparity of strength between the United States and other competing powers – contrary to the claims made by Professor Kennedy – is increasing in terms of economic resources, technological edge (often the two are related), political and cultural influence, and military power. American defence expenditure accounts for 28 per cent of the entire world's total. The scope for self-doubt under this tremendous burden of world leadership is therefore enormous. It might also promote a propensity for a display of pride and over-confidence. Senator J. William Fulbright at the beginning of his famous book *The Arrogance of Power* (1966) warns of the danger of conflating power and virtue, for a very great power 'is peculiarly susceptible to the idea that its power is a sign of God's favour, conferring upon it a special responsibility for other nations – to make them richer and happier and wiser, to remake them, that is, in its own shining image'. Self-righteousness, in short, can be just as much a product of isolation as of engagement with other powers.

The American conduct of war

Some historians claim that special characteristics might exist that define an 'American way of war'. In 1973 Russell F. Weigley wrote a large study of US strategy and military policy with that very title. It is perhaps instructive to consider the generally accepted American view of wars before proceeding to assess the characteristics of some form of US 'strategic culture' that prevails in US armed forces. It is also important to recall that the United States, like Great Britain before it, is first and foremost a naval power. It is now the greatest naval power of all time. The 'mission statement' of the US Navy declares baldly that 'The mission of the Navy is to maintain, train and equip combat-ready Naval forces capable of winning wars, deterring aggression and maintaining freedom of the seas'. The United States, in other words, is *not* a maritime power. It has developed during the twentieth century a massive 'military' navy entrusted with strategic tasks with little or no relationship to national maritime needs. It has an awesome capability with 372,624 personnel (54,076 officers, 4,308 midshipmen, 314,240 enlisted men), 289 ships, including 13 carriers, nuclear submarines, assault forces (and the US Marines are part of the US Navy) and 4,000 aircraft. At the end of 2004 more than half its ships were 'underway', that is, at sea away from American home waters, and 93 ships (34 per cent of the total force) were on deployment. Large navies, it is generally held by liberal democracies, are less threatening than great standing armies. For despite the size, power and sophistication of US armed forces over more than half a century, the characteristics that Americans tend to alight upon as differentiating their attitudes to war, say from Europeans, underplay the enormous offensive potential and ability of the United States to impose its will on other states. A survey of these attitudes would include the following – and to some extent they overlap or are related to one another.

Americans never seek to wage war

Wars tend to be foreign in their source. Such an argument reflects the assumption of space and choice with which Americans tend to approach war. It is assumed that the United States can conduct itself like a spectator and choose the time and place of its military intervention according to its interests and its judgement on the issues involved. The United States thus always acts defensively, never aggressively. 'If there is one principle more deeply rooted in the mind of every American', Thomas Jefferson once observed, 'it is that we should have nothing to do with conquest'. The corollary, therefore, to this assumption is that Americans only act in self-defence. The idea that the United States always acts defensively and is never the aggressor has been fortified by its military experience in the twentieth century: in 1917 it was forced to enter the First World War (despite Woodrow Wilson's declaration that it was 'too proud to fight') by unrestricted German submarine warfare against American shipping in the Atlantic Ocean; in 1941 it was the victim of a shameful Japanese 'sneak' attack on Pearl Harbor; and in 1947–8 (whatever the intricacies of scholarly debate) President Harry S. Truman presented the outbreak of the Cold War as resulting from the imposition of communist puppet régimes on the reluctant peoples of Eastern Europe. In May 1947 the famous Truman Doctrine enunciated a policy of 'containment' and declared the American intention to 'support free peoples who are resisting subjugation by armed minorities or outside pressures'.

The consequent nuclear stalemate that dominated the Cold War, and the emergence of deterrence theory to underwrite it, added a new dimension to the matter. Whereas for much of American history the armed forces had been ridiculed as wasteful parasites, and the claims of the US Army, in particular, to professional expertise were scoffed at (in such books as John A. Logan, *The Volunteer Soldier of America*, 1887), after 1945 (with the creation of the Department of Defense that replaced the old War Department) the armed forces found new civilian champions who hailed them as 'crusaders for peace'. Ronald Reagan, a consistent champion of high defence spending, put this with his customary lucidity: 'There are those who believe that men in uniform are somehow associated with starting wars', he wrote in September 1981. 'That's like saying policemen cause crime'. Military men were 'the peacemakers'.

In May 1983 Reagan returned to this theme. 'The paradox of military training is that young men are taught a trade which we hope and pray they will never use.' But the United States will respond with vigour to aggression. After the attacks of 11 September 2001 Governor Schwarzenegger justified the war in Iraq by playing on the most famous words he ever uttered as a motion picture actor, 'America is back – back from the attack on our homeland, back from the attack on our economy, and back from the attack on our way of life'.

Of course, the historical behaviour of the United States has tended to contradict this comforting assumption. The United States has been an expansionist power for much its history. In the 1840s it coveted Mexican territory. In July 1845 the independent republic of Texas accepted an American offer of annexation. American strategy sought to advance divergent columns into the Mexican heartland before its defence could be organised.

As a first step President James K. Polk ordered Zachary Taylor to advance to the Rio Grande River, a provocative act, since this had never been the agreed Texan border. During the following manoeuvres a force of American dragoons found themselves surrounded by a larger Mexican force and eventually surrendered. This skirmish permitted Polk to ask Congress for a declaration of war on the point of a technicality. Mexico, he claimed 'has invaded our territory and shed American blood on American soil!' A state of war existed, he announced, 'and notwithstanding all our efforts to avoid it, exists by the act of Mexico itself'. Polk's message embodied a conscious effort to conceal the degree of naked American provocation and lust for expansion shown in the months preceding the war. He also hid the determination of the United States to fulfil its 'manifest destiny' to dominate the North American heartland.

Perhaps it is primarily for this reason that in the mythology of the movement ever westwards of the American frontier, Indian tribes are not 'conquered', they 'vanish'. Indian tribes were doomed to virtual extinction because of the existence of white culture. This idea was given point in Edward S. Curtis's monumental work, *The North American Indian* (20 volumes, 1907–30) when he concluded that Indians 'are passing into the darkness of an unknown future'. In any case, despite Philip H. Sheridan's forthright remark that 'the only good Indian is a dead Indian', the whole thrust of American Indian policy was their *removal* from their territory, not their annihilation, let alone extermination. Sheridan, in his account in his *Personal Memoirs* (two volumes, 1888) of his dealings with the Cheyenne, Kiowas and Araphehoes, claimed that 'I showed by resorting to persuasive methods my willingness to temporise a good deal'. The later campaigns against the tribes of the Southwest, culminating in the pursuit and surrender of Geronimo to Nelson A. Miles in 1886, were designed to round up 'hostiles' with the minimum of casualties, and escort these representatives of an already militarily doomed people to the reservations. Thus the historical record, to some degree, supported the notion that the West was won without conquest – as Jefferson understood the term. Later in the twentieth century such an interpretation was subject to scathing attack by some American critics as a self-deluding conceit – mainly by those of the 'new left', radicalised by the protest against the Vietnam War.

Belligerent acts can be found in American history, in short, but attempts have often been made to explain them away by some kind of plot or conspiracy in which the United States is 'manoeuvred' by some cunning and unprincipled warmonger, despite itself, into fighting unnecessary wars. Such an 'evil genius' might be found in the White House. Hence the popularity in the late 1930s, especially among southerners, of the notion that President Abraham Lincoln had managed to 'manoeuvre' the Confederacy into firing the 'first shot' when it bombarded Fort Sumter in Charleston harbour on 12–13 April 1861, thus opening the Civil War. An alternative version of this approach, cherished by isolationists (but recycled in 1991 during its fiftieth anniversary by gullible journalists), was the even more bizarre idea that President Franklin D. Roosevelt deliberately 'manoeuvred' the Japanese into attacking Pearl Harbor on 7 December 1941 (thus enabling them almost to destroy one of the key forces – the battleships of the Pacific Fleet – with which he could have waged the war). Finally, on 4 August 1964, the US destroyers *Maddox* and *Turner Joy* claimed they had been attacked in the Gulf of Tonkin by North Vietnamese torpedo boats. Three days later Congress passed the Gulf of Tonkin Resolution authorising President Lyndon B. Johnson to take 'all necessary measures' to protect US forces from North Vietnamese 'aggression'. The ships did believe they had been attacked, but careful research reveals that no military action occurred – it was an error. As the ships had been in action two days before against three North Vietnamese torpedo boats, their crews were on a state of nervous, high alert. In short, Johnson's use of the incident did not result from artful invention, as later anti-war critics alleged, designed to clothe American aggression in a self-righteous raiment.

These sorts of suspicion – products of a penchant for conspiracy theories fortified by the emerging television age – have spawned a major cottage industry in recent years. The waging of the Iraq War after 2003 has undoubtedly stimulated it, giving rise to the widespread belief that both the British and American governments persuaded their electorates to support an aggressive war under a false prospectus.

American wars are short

American optimism – a 'can-do' sense of self-assurance – has contributed to a profound desire for rapid success in war. As Marcus Cunliffe observes, 'wars have rarely been welcomed by the entire American population, and never when their decisiveness is in doubt or their duration prolonged. The expectation . . . has been of swift success followed by an equally swift return to normal peacetime conditions'. Certainly great armies waged to fight specific wars have melted away with rapidity. For instance, in the case of the US Army, by March 1946 only 400,000 men of the great force of 3.5 million raised to fight the Axis Powers remained in uniform. But, in other ways, the historical record has tended to contradict the expectation of a quick victory followed by a return to 'normalcy'. Only two wars really fit – the

Mexican War that lasted 15 months, and the Spanish–American War of 1898, 'a splendid little war' lasting only four months. American participation in the First World War was also short – 18 months, but most observers were surprised by the speed of the Allied victory in 1918 and had predicted that it would continue into 1919, even 1920.

But what *is* a short war? Robert Cowley's anthology, *The Experience of War* (1992), drawn from articles published in the popular history periodical, *MHQ: The Quarterly Journal of Military History*, includes a contribution from Williamson Murray entitled, 'What Took the North So Long?' The reference is to the Civil War and the inordinate length of time that it took the North to mobilise its resources and defeat the South. As Murray rightly points out during that conflict, 'The mere creation of armies and their requisite support structure created problems that were neither readily apparent not easily solved'. To a European eye, accustomed to a Hundred Years War, or an Eighty Years War and their like, such a question, put in relation to a war that lasted almost exactly four years, seems misconceived. Of course, the frustrating ordeal of the Civil War is underlined not just by the passage of time but by the sheer number of battles (149 important engagements, 2,200 lesser actions) and the enormous casualty toll – as Murray claims, 'around 625,000 dead on both sides, equalling the total losses of all our other conflicts up to the Vietnam War'. The ferocity of the conflict – rather like the First World War – made it seem as if the war lasted longer than it actually did. But four years does seem a long time in the American timescale – a complete presidential term.

It therefore follows that American wars are characterised by directness: by a desire to strike at the critical point with a massive concentration of troops and firepower at the earliest moment. Such an attitude had determined Union strategy in the Civil War, even at the beginning. In the summer of 1861 the New York *Tribune* had rallied to the cry of 'On to Richmond', with calls for an immediate concentrated thrust against the new Confederate capital at Richmond, Virginia (the original rebel capital had been located at the more inaccessible Montgomery, Alabama). Most enthusiasts for such an advance were buoyed up by an optimistic expectation that the war could be won in one great battle, after which the city would fall. This optimism had an unfortunate outcome on 21 July when the Union forces recoiled from defeat at the First Battle of Bull Run. Nonetheless, Union strategy in 1864–5 was characterised by Ulysses S. Grant's efforts to concentrate Union resources in simultaneous onslaughts on the Confederate heartland. Grant bequeathed to his twentieth-century successors a certainty in the merits of powerful, rapid concentrations.

Such a strategy was seen to best effect during the Second World War. It underwrote the American debates with the British over the direction of the war in Europe from 1942 onwards. Dwight D. Eisenhower, later the Supreme Allied Commander, was adamantly opposed to 'giving our stuff [men and equipment] in driblets all over the world'. He advocated a massive build-up of American military resources in Britain 'and, when we are strong enough, go after Germany's vitals, and we've got to do it while Russia is still in the war, in fact only by doing it soon can we keep Russia in'. This objective could only be achieved by a massive cross-Channel amphibious operation at the earliest opportunity, followed up by an offensive across northern France to the Ruhr. In Eisenhower's opinion, the British response, calling for a greater effort to be made in mounting more indirect, smaller-scale operations in the Mediterranean theatre, was 'wearisome' – it eroded not only Eisenhower's patience with Britain but, he feared, would exhaust American interest in the war in Europe and lead to greater enthusiasm for operations against the Japanese in the Pacific. In the end, such arguments for a concentration in northwest Europe succeeded, but mainly because the United States came to dominate the Grand Alliance with Great Britain.

Hostility to alliances

Much of American military history, reflecting an isolationist attitude, has evinced a strong measure of hostility to alliances, especially with other great powers. Thomas Jefferson expressed this best in his First Inaugural Address: 'peace, commerce and honest friendship with all nations – entangling alliances with none'. American wars of the nineteenth century were fought without allies, although it was frequently forgotten that an earlier French intervention in the American Revolution (1775–83) was decisive in securing independence by breaking the British naval stranglehold on the North Atlantic, turning the North American war into a global conflict, and stretching British resources to breaking point. The dispersal forced on the British enabled the joint American–French forces to gain local superiority in the 13 colonies. Likewise the inability of the Confederacy to secure European military intervention in 1861–5 (not helped by its incompetent, ham-fisted diplomats) played a major role in the ultimate southern defeat.

With the rise of the United States to world power after the Civil War, and its easy victories over Spain in 1898, the combined dimension of warfare was forgotten. In 1917–18 the United States held its allies at a distance by becoming an 'associated power'. Clearly, this aspect of military policy reflects a unilateral tradition in foreign policy. The disillusionment in the

1920s with the policies and ideals of Woodrow Wilson helped inculcate within the US Army, in particular, a deep suspicion of working with allies. Planners during the inter-war years consequently did not consider the needs of fighting a future global war aided by allies. They thought only in terms of types of war that might be palatable to Congress and public opinion. They developed a series of 'colour plans' that had scant connection with the realities of international politics and military potential, except perhaps the 'Orange' series relating to Japan. Curiously, no colour plan was drawn up to counter any renewed threat from the main enemy of 1917–18, Germany. All plans, however, were determined by the main defensive strategic concept, namely, that the United States would defend its interests against foreign threat *alone*. American planning in the inter-war years thus reverted to a pre-1914 style of thinking based on the need to defend the continental republic. Implicit in the colour plans was an assumption of limited war – limited that is to say in terms of its participants and the scale of the forces involved. The type of conflict envisaged was thus very different from the one to which the United States had to adapt after 1941. It is a measure of Eisenhower's achievement in his role as Supreme Commander that he could transcend the limitations of this environment and (indeed his own prejudices) and work so effectively with allies, and not just the British, whom he found on first acquaintance in 1942 'stiff-necked'. He went on: 'They're difficult to talk to, apparently afraid someone is trying to tell them what to do and how to do it. Their practice of war is dilatory'. The criticism here should be compared with the scorn and sarcasm frequently openly displayed by George S. Patton Jr – a much more representative figure of the pre-1941 US Army. Even as late as August 1944 in the closing stages of the Battle of Normandy, as he advanced northwards to Argentan after encircling the Germans, he asked, 'Shall we continue and drive the British into the sea for another Dunkirk?' Eisenhower was not so foolish as to make a tactless parade of such sentiment.

The consistent American hostility to alliances carried over into the last half of the twentieth century and beyond. Robert E. Osgood's *NATO: The Entangling Alliance* (1962) indicates the limitations of America's affection for the first formal treaty of alliance it had signed (in 1949) with other significant military powers to ensure the defence of Western Europe against Soviet aggression. (In the event, the South East Asia Treaty Organization, SEATO, and the Middle East Treaty Organization, METO, proved to be pale and ineffective imitations of the original model.) The military arm of the North Atlantic Treaty Organization (NATO) adopted the wartime model of the Supreme Headquarters Allied Expeditionary Force (SHAEF) to produce its later refinement, the Supreme Headquarters Allied Powers in Europe (SHAPE) with an American supreme commander, and a British (later also a German) deputy. Many of the strains within the NATO alliance have been attributed to American high-handedness. In 1966 France left the military structure partly for that reason. These and other difficulties can be explained not just by America's irritation that its European partners (except Britain) in the 1980s failed to achieve an annual increase in defence expenditure of 3.5 per cent to meet the Soviet build-up. It also reflected a lack of US willingness to consult with its allies over important strategic issues.

As isolationist sentiments strengthened after the millennium, the administration of George W. Bush demonstrated a marked reluctance, while planning military action against Saddam Hussein's Iraq, to make the full use of the resources of international organisations such as the United Nations (UN) and alliances such as NATO. A more accommodating approach would undoubtedly have helped confer a measure of legitimacy on American military moves. 'Rather than gain leverage by means of international legitimacy', wrote General Wesley K. Clark in October 2003, 'the United States, even through the long summer of 2003, refused to cede political authority to the UN or grant meaningful authority to any other international organization'. In 2004 General Clark himself failed to gain the Democratic presidential nomination, so his is not a neutral political voice, but he is surely correct to suggest that additional legitimacy would have reduced the scale of the American task, even though the effort would have run against the grain of American military instincts.

Americans are reluctant to accept heavy casualties

The development of the notion that Americans are unduly fearful of sustaining heavy casualties in war has dominated views of the US conduct of war for at least 20 years. The phenomenon has a complex history and draws upon a variety of diverse sources.

Obviously, casualties are as far as possible to be avoided – something that democratic governments in particular are eager to demonstrate in time of war. Making the safety of one's own troops a first priority, however, may have unintended consequences. Thus, from the late 1960s onwards, mainly as a by-product of the protest movement against the Vietnam War, many Americans came to be highly critical of the conduct of their armed forces. Such critics held that the shameful, self-defeating, indiscriminate unleashing of overwhelming firepower in the Vietnam War reflected deeply ingrained, previously hidden and extremely unpleasant aspects of American history and national character. A wide variety of writers thought – reflecting a reverse exceptionalism – that the American armed forces were *the* villain of the piece: they were more brutal and savage, more destructive and more short-sighted than those of other countries. In *Sherman's March and Vietnam* (1984), James Reston Jr drew close parallels between the Civil War and Vietnam. Reston claimed that Sherman, and American generals who thought like him, bred into the American military psyche a hunger 'for victory by any means'. It was at this time also, mainly through the pessimistic and rather sentimental histories of Dee Brown (for instance, *Bury My Heart at Wounded Knee*, 1970), that the misconception gained wide currency that Indian Wars that 'won the West' took the form of genocide.

In 1975 the end of the Vietnam War coincided with striking changes in nuclear strategy and the balance of the Cold War. Throughout the 1960s and 1970s the nuclear confrontation with the Soviet Union was justified by an assumption of 'mutually assured destruction' (MAD) and the 'balance of terror'. As both sides were deterred from launching nuclear attacks, if the balance of terror was sustained, then it would ensure that nuclear weapons would never have to be used; nonetheless, even a limited nuclear exchange would still result in 'mega-death' – the loss of many millions of lives. Perhaps these figures were so huge that they were impossible to comprehend. At any rate, it was as a response to a marked deterioration of superpower relations and an increasing alarm at the possibility of impending nuclear war, that in March 1983 President Reagan delivered his famous 'Star Wars' speech announcing his intention to launch the Strategic Defense Initiative (SDI). This would employ advanced laser technology to shoot down ballistic missiles as they were launched and create an impenetrable shield as a defence against nuclear attack. Many (especially European) military critics of the programme warned that if this programme were successful it would negate nuclear deterrence and make great conventional wars, along the lines of the two world wars of the twentieth century, possible again. Thus conventional strategy seemed to be restored to pre-1945 levels of utility just at a time when the United States was psychologically quite unfit to exploit it.

The major concern within the Pentagon during the 1980s was to rescue the US Army from the brink of disintegration and restore its morale. In the light of the Vietnam conflict, the Nixon administration believed that the United States could no longer, unaided, 'undertake all the defence of the free world'. It was assumed as a given that after the first outright defeat in American history (that of 1865 was inflicted on 'insurgents', as Abraham Lincoln always called them) that the American people had lost their interest in and stomach for a fight, and could not be counted on to support military intervention abroad.

Reagan did not repudiate this policy after his victory in the 1980 presidential election, despite his confrontational rhetoric in describing the Soviet Union. Indeed the Weinberger Doctrine, named after his Secretary of Defense, Caspar Weinberger, emphasised the need for caution with regard to foreign adventures. The United States would only fight wars it thought it could win and only wage them if it suited American interests. If these counts were not met then American forces would be withdrawn, as they hurriedly were after the suicide attacks in 1983 on the American contribution to the international peacekeeping force in Lebanon. Spokesmen for the Reagan administration seemed to quiver with fear at the possibility of the arrival of 'body bags' and the outrage they would provoke. This seemed a very rapid switch from the casual acceptance of the deaths of many millions to a fear of the public's reaction to one serviceman losing his (or, as became increasingly possible, her) life. But such was the case as the Cold War gradually came to an end. Voices were heard boasting that it was an American triumph, due mainly to Soviet economic and financial exhaustion resulting from attempts to match Reagan's SDI programme.

This last claim is overstated, but it is certainly the case that a great victory had been won with the end of the Cold War without the loss of significant numbers of American casualties, and was thus a milestone in American military history. In a sense, a success of this order only strengthened what came to be termed the 'Vietnam syndrome' (the phrase was first used in 1976). Despite the great resurgence in self-confidence during the Reagan years (most evident in the Los Angeles Olympics of 1984), references to the Vietnam syndrome gained common currency during the 1980s to describe the long-running consequences of the Vietnam defeat and the fear of the reaction of the American public to any military expeditions that might incur sizeable casualties. Within the US armed forces senior officers were keen to express the view that this recent emphasis had roots deep in the American military experience, namely, that the United States had *always* been averse to accepting casualties; indeed this had been a central feature of all American wars, not least in the twentieth century.

There were grounds for challenging these assumptions on both historical and policy-related grounds. Few American generals before 1975 gave much thought to casualty-avoidance as an important objective in their plans. The Union general, George B. McClellan, is sometimes seen as having been too fond of his soldiers to sacrifice them in battle; if so, his half-hearted, piecemeal, frontal assaults at the Battle of Antietam, 17 September 1862, did more than any other factor to prolong the savagery of the single most bloody day in American history, with 12,000 casualties inflicted on each side. During the Second World War American commanders showed impatience with and sometimes open contempt for British worries over losses in battle. In the Italian Campaign Mark Clark treated any campaign that failed with low casualties as evidence of poor leadership. British troops, he sneered, lacked determination.

Clark and George S. Patton, too, were representatives of a generation of American generals that had missed the 1916 holocaust of Verdun or the Somme. Their successors in the two decades after 1980 – best represented by General Colin Powell, later Secretary of State (2001–5) – gained experience of battle in another 'futile' war: Vietnam, the American equivalent of the Western Front in the First World War. Powell imparted to American military policy a caution and defensiveness abandoned in the Iraq War of 2003–5. Powell, and those who shared his beliefs, respected the power of the Vietnam syndrome. But its received wisdom, too, can be disputed. The Triangle Institute for Strategic Studies (TISS) discerned a yawning gap between the views of ordinary Americans and those attributed to them by their leaders; the former, in general, thought that America should strike back with overwhelming force to attacks on US interests.

For the last two decades of the twentieth century American decision makers, both civil and military, had invented for themselves an excuse for inaction. Indeed the US armed forces, far from scorning the Vietnam syndrome before 2003, had embraced it; in some ways they became even more sensitive about accepting casualties than their civilian leaders. Ronald Reagan revealed in November 1983 that 'in the closely guarded sessions where our military chiefs were planning the Grenada missions (and they only had hours to do so) their top priority was to minimize casualties. And this they were doing with no prompting from us'.

In 2004 American fatalities in Iraq passed the 1,000 mark (a very small number compared with losses in earlier wars). The figure had little influence on either domestic support for the war or on the re-election of George W. Bush. It is thus possible to speculate that after the passage of a quarter of a century the ghost of the Vietnam syndrome has been exorcised.

Americans are slow to anger but furious when aroused

The wish to fight any war to a finish, to achieve complete or 'unconditional surrender', as first demanded in February 1862 by Ulysses S. Grant at Fort Donelson, is frequently considered a central feature of American warmaking. Alexis de Tocqueville in his *Democracy in America* (1835, 1840) had warned of this tendency. General Douglas MacArthur went so far as to claim, in his dispute with the Truman administration over the strategy to be pursued in the Korean War (1950–3), that 'in war there can be no substitute for victory'. The passionate desire to gain victory irrespective of the cost or political circumstances has sometimes led to much soul-searching among American intellectuals; it has also involved a tacit criticism of the capacity of democracy itself to conduct war sensibly or to find a suitable strategy to gain its desired objectives. This disquiet contributed to the rise of the 'realist' school of writers, who deprecate the excessively idealistic, unattainable, sentimental aims that Americans are prone to set themselves.

The distinguished American diplomatist and historian, George F. Kennan (b. 1904) is the spiritual foster father of the realist school. In his seminal work, *American Diplomacy 1900–1950* (1952), a book as much concerned with the conduct of war as foreign affairs, Kennan characterised pithily the process that culminates in a rising tide of American anger when confronted with the harsh reality that the United States is being forced to abandon its customary state of peacefulness. 'When it [the United States] has once been provoked to the point where it must grasp the sword', he observes, 'it does not easily forgive its adversary for having produced this situation'. Provocation 'then becomes the issue. Democracy fights in anger – it fights for the very reason that it was forced to go to war'. Consequently, the United States is determined to prevent an aggressor disturbing the peace again. The subsequent type of war (as in the Second World War or Iraq in 2003–4, which implies an important war aim is the transformation of the enemy's political system) 'must be carried to the bitter end'.

Kennan reflected in these comments the bitter disappointment felt in the early 1950s with the strategic fruits of the Allied victories in the Second World War. Kennan and other critics located the source of perceived American weakness *vis-à-vis* the Soviet Union in the nature of American society itself. He lambasted the 'deliberateness of the opinion forming process in a democracy', especially its broad ignorance of history. Americans lacked 'objective understanding of the wider issues involved', and thus have a 'difficulty . . . in employing force for rational and restricted purposes' in a way that permits a sensible correlation of foreign policy and strategy. Kennan then went on to make three significant criticisms of the American way in war, criticisms that have subsequently been recycled in various guises over the last half-century. First, Kennan argued that the United States paid insufficient attention to 'the power realities involved in given situations'. Second, its leaders often failed 'to appreciate the limitations of war in general – any war – as a vehicle for the objectives of the democratic state'. Their greatest weakness when formulating policies lay 'in something that I might call the legalistic–moralistic approach to international problems'. Third, Kennan contended that the enormous economic and social dislocation, the sheer chaos and destruction that had resulted from the two world wars, called into question the very utility of 'total' war. Indeed he questioned 'whether . . . there could ever be any such thing as total *military* victory'.

These notions have much more bearing on the history of the first half of the twentieth century than on other periods of American history. Marcus Cunliffe has pointed out that this kind of argument, namely that Americans have shown more crusading zeal than Europeans, have fought wars with greater ideological character, more selflessly and with more energy and commitment – though not without merit when dealing with specific issues – is really a reflection of American exceptionalism. Dwight D. Eisenhower called his war memoirs, *Crusade in Europe* (1948). Yet British writers, such as Major General J. F. C. Fuller and Captain Sir Basil Liddell Hart, have made similar criticisms and attacked the lack of restraint in Churchillian strategy during the Second World War.

The presumed determination of fighting to the finish contradicts previous assumptions about the way Americans fight wars: that they be short, dynamic and won with minimum cost. The shorter wars of the nineteenth century (the War of 1812, the Mexican War and the Spanish–American War) had little significant ideological content; most observers expected the Civil War to be short and fought for limited objectives. None of these wars compare in length and ferocity with the French Revolutionary and Napoleonic Wars (1792–1815), which sought to 'export' the ideals of the Revolution. The idealistic visions that inspired both Woodrow Wilson, and to a lesser extent Franklin D. Roosevelt, were made possible by the great change in the relative power of the United States since 1865.

The sense of failure that haunted writers such as Kennan when they considered the outcome of the Second World War has vanished, and had started to do so even before the collapse of the Soviet Union. The conjunction of American dominance, the rise of what John Kenneth Galbraith termed the 'affluent society', the banishment of fratricidal wars among the Western powers, transformed the way Americans viewed their past. The Second World War was recast as 'the best war ever': the ideal blend of successful strategy and idealistic expectation that permitted so much of the world to be made over in the American image. A reaction against the hypocrisy, incompetence and destructive fumbling in Vietnam only served to underwrite this transformation of the Second World War as a 'model' American conflict.

American strategic culture: its strengths and weaknesses

How do American servicemen solve the strategic and operational problems they encounter? How are the operational means – the troops, ships and aircraft deployed – utilised to meet the strategic end? The experience of the 1941–5 conflict has done more than any other factor to shape these questions, probably because it brought the United States into the environment created by international alliances that shaped the post-war world. It is often claimed that since the middle of the nineteenth century American commanders have enjoyed abundant resources. Even before Pearl Harbor and full military mobilisation, the United States had at its disposal a productive capacity greater than Germany and Japan combined. But successful operations are not conjured out of stockpiles of equipment alone; the resources must be utilised effectively. One of the strengths of American military operations since 1861 has been the skill of its logistical planning. Logistics is the art of supplying and moving armies. American staffs, however crude, have shown an aptitude for relating logistics to operational needs. Not for nothing did Major General Joseph Hooker in the spring of 1863 describe the Army of the Potomac as 'the finest army on the planet' before he went down to defeat at Chancellorsville. The United States (like Britain) came rather late to the 'general staff revolution' of the nineteenth century, not setting up a distinct general staff to run the Army until 1903. The impetus for these changes came from the uncharacteristic logistical blunders committed in 1898 in Cuba, as most American casualties resulted from tropical disease (of the 5,462 deaths, only 379 were lost in battle).

From 1917 onwards the US general staff developed a system based on production targets, equipment schedules and the concentration of this equipment and fighting troops at the decisive point. The accusation has frequently been made that as the conception is based on mass, American strategy is unimaginative and inflexible. Southern writers dedicated to the 'lost cause' were convinced that Grant beat Lee in 1865 only because of his superior numbers and logistic resources. British critics of American strategy after 1943, such as the Chief of the Imperial General Staff General Sir Alan Brooke, chaffed at their failure (again due to inferior resources) to inject greater opportunism into Allied planning. According to these critics, the combination of great quantities of men and material and the straitjacket conferred by the doctrine of Unconditional Surrender, announced by Roosevelt in January 1943 at the Casablanca Conference, seemed well matched. More than

60 divisions (the largest field army in American history) slowly lumbered forward, more concerned with grinding the Germans into dust than with gaining a specific objective, such as the capture of Berlin, which would have rewarded this gargantuan effort with a decisive and beneficial victory.

There is an element of caricature in such depictions. Their authors perhaps protest too much. The British have always been prone to congratulate themselves on their superior wisdom in military matters. Two other accusations have also been made that have a greater relevance to the Cold War. First, that American commanders have been indifferent to history, and second, that their plans have been blind to cultural differences and the symbols that other societies cherish. The supposed indifference to history seems overstated. Although the US armed forces have periodically evinced enthusiasm for engineering, 'systems' or computer-based methods, in some ways American commanders have shown themselves *too* conscious of the past. One thinks of an exhausted and harassed General William C. Westmoreland in Vietnam, wearily insisting on taking to read in bed imposing volumes on the French defeat at the Battle of Dien Bien Phu (1954), over which he invariably fell asleep, in a vain effort to prepare himself for his ultimate challenge – a battle he never had to fight.

It is wrong also to suggest that the US armed forces always have huge resources at their disposal. They have frequently been starved of resources, and not just in the nineteenth century. After 1945 the Truman administration attempted to cope with inflation by reducing defence expenditure. The opening rounds of the Cold War revealed that commitments had far outstripped capability. Indeed military expenditure fell from its high point in 1944 of 37.4 per cent of gross national product to a mere 4.4 per cent in 1948 (that is, 1 per cent lower than the 1941 level).

In terms of sheer numbers, American forces were outnumbered in the Korean War, the confrontation with the Soviet Union in Central Europe, and in its two wars against Iraq. The military analyst, Edward N. Luttwak, perceived in the 1980s that it was anomalous for a power that itself relied on attritional methods to attempt to face down the Soviet Union that had greater initial resources available: the inevitable result would be rapid defeat. Luttwak and others called for a fundamental rethink of American strategy. The result was a revival of thinking about operational art – the ability to bring military resources to bear to win campaigns that contribute to the ultimate victory. Military analysts inserted the 'operational level' between strategy and tactics. These efforts were timely because they assisted in rebuilding the US Army after the Vietnam defeat. First, the operational level allowed planners to conceive of military operations as a coherent whole geared to winning a decisive military victory (unlike in Vietnam); second, the reformers developed a concept of 'manoeuvre warfare' that combined all elements of manoeuvre (movement and firepower) to smash the enemy's cohesion and psychological equilibrium rather than rely on incremental attrition.

The bid to reduce casualties by placing an emphasis on manoeuvre rather than battle also dovetailed with an enthusiasm for exploiting new technologies. The US military has frequently been criticised for introducing new technologies (for instance, in the 1950s, tactical nuclear weapons) without giving a lot of thought as to how they might be used; the weapons themselves would provide the solution. The so-called 'revolution in military affairs' arising from digitisation seemed another moot point. However, the lightning victories of 1991 and 2003 over Iraq seemed to indicate that planners had got the balance between technology and doctrine right. In both conflicts, the US armed forces seemed irresistible in 'warfighting' mode.

The very success of the initial phase of the 2003 Iraq War revived the same sort of doubts that had been expressed over the American victory in 1945. American forces seemed too preoccupied with operations and sought to evade the political issues inherent in the termination of conflict. In particular, the eruption of guerrilla activity from autumn 2003 onwards seemed to catch the American military just as unprepared as it had been in Vietnam. The US Army paid the price for its reluctance to consider operations other than war, and especially peacekeeping (even though much of its historical experience – in its various Indian wars and in the Philippines, Lebanon, and Somalia – had been rooted in operations of this kind).

Post-1945 criticisms of the limitations of American strategy were not well founded. It is true that the Soviet occupation of Berlin, Prague and Vienna (given up in the demilitarisation of Austria in July 1955) pushed the European balance of power decisively in the Soviet favour, and required the stationing of American troops indefinitely to safeguard the security of Western Europe. Marshall and Eisenhower were blamed for this outcome by neglecting Berlin as an objective in 1945 and playing into Soviet hands by failing to occupy all of Germany. But far from neglecting the political-strategic dimension, the whole course of the American advance into Germany had been determined by it. Marshall intended that the US Army would be seen as the main victor over Germany (unlike in 1917–18). Thereafter he hoped that the United States would have untrammelled influence over the direction of the future peacemaking. Events took a very different course, but this was not due to political naïvety. The Roosevelt administration simply underestimated Stalin's ruthless determination to impose communist rule on the states of Eastern Europe and the barrier his paranoid nature placed in the way of forming harmonious relations with the Soviet Union.

It is still too early to judge whether the Iraq example has been the victim of equal polemical misrepresentation. In 2003 it was clear that the whole drift of the US Army doctrine envisaged the need for 'decisive operations' designed to secure the defeat of the enemy with minimum cost; a coherent campaign plan emerged based on manoeuvre and massive firepower, underpinned by the 'warrior ethos' nurtured among the Army's rank and file. Such an approach tends to ignore the harsh reality that the 'new world order' after 1991 demands intervention in the affairs of other states, and thus a more subtle and graduated use of force beyond the immediate battlefield. The United States had avoided altering its fundamental assumptions by falling back on air power as a panacea – such as the aerial bombardment of Serbia in early 1999 during the Kosovo crisis – campaigns that only required a limited despatch of ground forces. Pentagon analysts have consistently refused to acknowledge the importance of peacekeeping on the spurious grounds that it would detract from the importance of the primary mission – war-fighting. It is indeed ironical that, despite the enormous importance that the US Army especially (but the other services, too) attach to the Vietnam conflict, its prime lessons – in terms of nation building and counter-insurgency – have been ignored. George W. Bush consistently championed the view 'that our troops should be used to fight wars'. Consequently, after its rapid victory the United States revealed a dearth of planning that addressed the central problem of how it would run a prostrate Iraq, with little thought given to how it would respond to increasingly audacious terrorist action.

In sum, the American military experience has played a central role in the way Americans view themselves and their place in the world. Attitudes to war are intimately related to American views on foreign affairs, and these have been subjected to identical impulses. To understand American attitudes to war is to grasp American attitudes to peace, and together their resolution offers a way of discerning relative domestic values, especially conservatism. Over the course of more than two centuries the United States has been transformed from a David into a Goliath, although most Americans prefer to view themselves as somehow still the underdog rather than the swaggering bully. There are strong grounds to question *in detail* the existence of exceptional American attitudes to war. Yet these views remain historically important because the overwhelming majority of Americans believe in their historical efficacy.

Finally, is the awesome military power at the disposal of the United States evidence that it constitutes some form of empire? The United States is a republican democracy; it might not be an empire but it is an imperial power with diverse commitments consonant with its interests. The United States differs from many previous imperial powers because of the importance it attaches in the policy debate to public opinion. Ferocious debate and the expression of dissent have been frequent in American wars, sometimes to the point of causing convulsion (as in 1776, 1812, 1846, 1863–4, 1914, 1964–73 and 2003–5). Such currents of opinion are intermeshed in the contradictory views that Americans take of their place in the world and their willingness to use armed force. Hence the novelist Gore Vidal's conclusion, that the United States 'is possibly the last empire on this earth'.

Further reading

Two central books are Russell F. Weigley, *History of the United States Army* (2nd edn, 1984) and *The American Way of War: A History of United States Military Strategy and Policy* (1973). The best one-volume study is Allan R. Millett and Peter Maslowski, *For the Common Defense: A Military History of the United States of America* (rev. edn, 1994). The most important study of American military attitudes is Marcus Cunliffe, *Soldiers and Civilians: The Martial Spirit in America, 1775–1865* (1969). Also germane are three of Cunliffe's essays, 'The American military tradition' in H. C. Allen and C. P. Hill (eds), *British Essays in American History* (1957), pp. 207–24, 'Formative events from Columbus to World War I' (Part IA), in Michael P. Hamilton (ed.), *American Character and Foreign Policy* (1986), pp. 3–13, and 'America's imaginary wars', in his posthumous volume of essays, *In Search of America* (1991), pp. 373–85. Some of the essays in Cunliffe's *Festschrift* reflect on military history, see John White and Brian Holden Reid (eds), *Americana: Essays in Memory of Marcus Cunliffe* (2nd edn, 1998). A stimulating if not always persuasive account of the 'militarisation' of American society is Michael S. Sherry, *In the Shadow of War: The United States since the 1930s* (1995).

CHAPTER 14

American women

Elizabeth J. Clapp

The majority finds its past

A merica has long seen itself and been seen as a male under-taking. The archetypal American, whether a Puritan settler, a revolutionary Patriot, a Robber Baron, cowboy or twentieth-century cor-porate wheeler-dealer, has almost always been portrayed as male. American history has similarly been seen through male eyes. The American literary canon has also frequently been defined as masculine, sometimes aggressively anti-feminine, with women, if they are featured at all, being marginalised. The same may be said for other cultural forms. In the last few decades, how-ever, prompted in large part by the women's movement of the late 1960s, scholars have dramatically revised their understanding of both American history and culture. Alongside a new inclusiveness that has encompassed race, class and ethnicity in the study of both history and cultural forms, gender has become an important lens through which to examine America. As a consequence, far from simply writing women back into the historical and literary culture of America, scholars have begun to consider what dif-ference it makes to put gender at the centre of their studies.

Gender is a social construction and as such is dynamic, that is to say it can change over the course of time, or in different social settings. Sex on the other hand, is biologically determined. Thus while Americans may have changed their perceptions of what women's (and men's) roles should be over the course of time and according to their race and class, throughout American history women – whatever their social status – have shared the experience or potential of being mothers. As a consequence, the investiga-tion of American women in the past presents the student with a rather dif-ferent set of questions than those that might be asked in the examination of 'mainstream' American history. The traditional periodisation of history, based as it is on the makers of laws, wars, governments and the actions of élite men, does not necessarily have much meaning in studying women's lives. Often historical events had neither the same impact nor significance for women that they did for men, nor was the female experience always homogeneous.

If the female experience has been largely absent from the historical record, women have been similarly excluded from the study of American culture. Female contributions were rejected as worthless or sentimental, often because they did not conform to a male sense of what was of value. Influenced by Nathaniel Hawthorne's dismissive remark about a 'damned mob of scribbling women', a great deal of women's literature was ignored by critics because it was considered to be beneath their notice. It was not until the latter half of the twentieth century, when it was 'rediscovered', that scholars began to re-evaluate the influence of women and their literary output on the shaping of American culture.

In studying American women many scholars have used the concept of the 'separation of spheres' as an explanatory tool. The idea is based on a comment made by the French aristocrat, Alexis de Tocqueville, in his observations of the new United States in *Democracy in America* (1840):

> In America, more than anywhere else in the world, care has been taken constantly to trace clearly distinct spheres of action for the two sexes . . . You will never find American women in charge of the external relations of the family, managing a business, or interfering in politics . . . If the American woman is never allowed to leave the quiet sphere of domestic duties, she is also never forced to do so.

Women's role was thus to be found in the domestic sphere, uninvolved in the economy or politics, concerned only with her own household, husband and children. While Tocqueville's remark may not have reflected the reality of the situation, the idea of the separation of spheres remains a powerful analytical concept in helping us to understand American women from the colonial period to the late twentieth century.

The colonial experience

There were no white women among the English colonists who established the first permanent English colony in North America at Jamestown in 1607. The Virginia colony was initially intended to be only a trading and military outpost, and although a handful of women arrived in the colony in 1608 and with later arrivals from England, it was not until a decade or so later that English women were actively encouraged to settle in Virginia. By 1619, the colony's leaders had realised that Virginia's future depended on agriculture, specifically on the cultivation of tobacco as a cash crop, and this required a more settled population than had previously been the case. Sir Edwin Sandys, the treasurer of the Virginia Company which funded the Jamestown colony, observed that it was the 'want of wives' that had proved to be among 'the greatest hindrances' to the new plantation. He hoped that shipping out to Virginia 'an extraordinarily choice lot of . . . maides' would help 'make the men more settled & lesse moveable'. Sandys' was the first of a series of schemes to encourage young white women to emigrate to Virginia to marry male colonists and thus provide greater stability in the colony. Throughout the seventeenth century, however, white women remained scarce in the Chesapeake colonies, which meant that once they had worked out their indentures for the cost of their passage, they enjoyed an enviable status on the marriage market.

In many respects the lives these white female emigrants lived differed from those of their counterparts who remained in England. Not only did they have a much greater choice of partners and could therefore marry further up the social scale than their own social origins might have allowed, but the uncertainty of life in these colonies meant that if they were able to survive the 'seasoning period' and the dangers of childbirth, they were frequently widowed and married again, sometimes more than once, accumulating wealth and social status. Their daughters, not needing to work out their indentures, married in their teens, and like their mothers had their choice of marriage partners. But life was precarious and it was not until the 1690s that the region's white population began to grow through natural increase.

In other respects too, life was different for these women. In an area where labour was scarce, English notions of the proper sexual division of labour could not apply – women, like men, especially when they were servants, were expected to work in the fields. Even the wives of planters could not afford to confine their work to their house and its yards, but at peak seasons they were expected to work alongside their husbands and servants in the fields. Until the end of the seventeenth century even the most elevated planters' wives would be expected to support tobacco cultivation by providing support services, releasing the men to work in the fields.

As the Chesapeake colonies gradually became more settled, the work of white women began to change and to resemble that of their social counterparts in England. From the middle of the seventeenth century enslaved African men, and sometimes women, were increasingly being employed in tobacco cultivation, allowing white women to confine themselves to duties that had traditionally been defined by English society as female. Planters' wives began to concentrate their labour on their households and children, rather than working in the fields. Slowly the status of black slaves became defined by law as perpetual servitude, and by the 1660s as chattel slavery. With this change, black women as well as men became attractive slaves, as masters quickly realised the profits that could be made from slave women's reproductive potential, for the status of slave passed from the mother to her children. Thus, slave women would be valued both for their work in the fields and for their ability to produce more slaves – and profits – for their masters. As white women's work was removed from the field to the household and their role became increasingly unlike that of white men, white slaveholders drew little distinction between the work of their slave men and women. It was not until the mid-eighteenth century, as plantation economies became more complex, that some slave women were employed in the house.

While the lives of women in the early southern colonies differed markedly from those of their European sisters, the migrants who established the New England colonies in the seventeenth century had other purposes in mind. The aim of most of those who settled the northern colonies of Plymouth and Massachusetts Bay was primarily religious rather than economic. They wished to establish independent, pious communities organised to enable them to lead a godly life and work for the collective good, while setting an example for the rest of the world. These Puritan settlers relied on two strong institutions for the success of their mission – the Puritan church and the stable patriarchal family. Thus the overwhelming majority of those who migrated did so as part of a family, with the aim of establishing a permanent settlement. The relatively healthy conditions of New England resulted in marriages that lasted longer than they did in the southern colonies, and the availability of land meant that couples married earlier than they did in England, causing marital life to be remarkably stable and allowing husbands to dominate their wives and families. The even sex ratio also meant that, except in the earliest days of settlement, English ideas about the sexual division of labour could be adapted easily to this part of the New World. The daily work of a New England 'goodwife' and her daughters was centred around the house, garden and dairy, preparing food and looking after the children. Her tasks varied with the season, and as the colonies became more settled women began to trade their surplus domestic manufactures with other women, creating a female network of trade and gossip.

Puritan religion placed great emphasis on a hierarchical system of social relations, with the wife submitting to the authority of her husband, although the Puritan minister Samuel Willard placed the relationship between husband and wife 'nearest to equality' among 'all the Orders which are unequals'. The wife's submission to her husband in marriage reflected a more general belief in female inferiority, both in terms of her physical abilities and in her moral and intellectual capacities. One consequence was that although the Puritans believed that a knowledge of the Bible was important to everyone and therefore required that all children should attain a basic literacy, this was restricted to learning to read for girls, and only exceptionally did girls learn to write as well. Nonetheless, levels of literacy among women in New England were considerably higher than they were among women in the southern colonies, where formal education among slaves was virtually non-existent.

Puritan leaders had very clear ideas about women's place in both the household and in the church – a question that was frequently the subject of sermons and tracts. While the woman was to be submissive to her husband's authority at home, she was to be his 'helpmeet' and spiritual equal rather than his servant. This did not, however, mean that women should publicly articulate their religious beliefs or question the authority of their ministers, for to test the boundaries of female piety might lead to banishment from the colony, as Anne Hutchinson and several other women found to their cost. Some women did protest their place in New England society, but they did so quietly in the privacy of their own writings.

Tensions between the Puritan notion of the 'godly woman' and some women's desire for a measure of autonomy, were apparent in the prosecutions of women accused of witchcraft, which occurred sporadically throughout the seventeenth century and culminated in the extensive witchhunts in Salem, Massachusetts in 1692. Historians now suggest that most of the women accused of witchcraft seemed in some way to threaten the established order. Women or adolescent girls were frequently the accusers of other women, making them central to witchcraft allegations and giving them a position of power that superseded normal hierarchies of gender, age and social position. The Salem outbreak was also symptomatic of wider tensions centred around women's role.

The eighteenth century created new opportunities for some women in the American colonies, while narrowing them for others. The growth of the economy in the southern colonies brought with it an ever-increasing demand for black slaves, most of whom continued to be imported. As the plantation economy became more complex, some slave women learned specialist skills as they were assigned to work in the 'big house', but the labour of black women continued to be defined by their race as the majority worked in the fields alongside black men. Planters, who made their fortunes from the labour of their black slaves, began to build palatial houses with specialised uses of space, marking the increasing segregation of male and female spheres of activity among élite whites. These houses were filled with consumer goods imported from Europe – the visible signs of gentility – and white women's duties began to change to encompass a more genteel and leisured lifestyle, based on notions of refinement also imported from Europe. The idea of the 'lady' and, in the north, the 'pretty gentlewoman' was learned from English books and periodicals, and sometimes from an English education. Rather than attempting to forge a new ideal of womanhood as it gained power and wealth, the colonial élite sought to reproduce older aristocratic ideals of English womanhood.

Most women's lives in the years immediately preceding the Revolution were shaped by their roles as mothers and housewives. English notions of proper feminine behaviour dominated and the English Common Law dictated women's legal position. The circumstances of the early colonies gave women some rights over property that they did not have in England, but the increasingly commercial society of the mid-eighteenth century meant these rights did not have a great deal of significance. While literacy rates among women had increased by the mid-eighteenth century, few women had the skills or time to write other than to record their daily and spiritual lives in their private journals. Like their husbands and fathers, it is likely that colonial women saw themselves as English. The notion of a distinct American womanhood had yet to be formed.

The American Revolution

The American Revolution with its debates about liberty and independence, its battles and its political divisions, on one level seems to have had little to do with women. It was assumed that eighteenth-century women were unconcerned with politics, and men alone fought in armies. But the imperial struggle between Britain and her North American colonies involved many women as participants, and in its aftermath the position of women in the new Republic was widely debated. Women were members of the crowds that protested the Stamp Acts and they were essential to the success of the consumer boycotts during the 1770s – a fact that did not escape the notice of some of the Patriot leaders. Newspaper editors encouraged women to refuse to buy imported British goods, and to find alternatives to such items as tea.

Many women were well aware of the issues involved in the boycotts and hardly needed prompting. Such actions politicised their daily activities and gave new meaning to them. Women began to wear homespun rather than British manufactured cloth, and gathered together in highly public spinning bees in order to manufacture it, calling themselves the Daughters of Liberty. Some women wrote poems and essays urging patriotism and political principle, suggesting that women could show men how to be patriotic. While the boycott of British goods could be understood in terms of women's domestic role, the actions of some women became more overtly political. They signed public pledges not to drink tea; occasionally they took this even further. In October 1774, 51 women in Edenton, North Carolina, met to endorse the Nonimportation Association resolves: 'As we cannot be indifferent on any occasion that appears nearly to affect the peace and happiness of our country'. They declared it was their 'duty' to work for the common good, thus claiming a public voice and role. The ridicule with which this document was met on both sides of the Atlantic suggests its novelty. A British cartoonist lampooned the 'Edenton Ladies' Tea Party' as a grotesque and unnatural gathering, and even in the colonists' camp some men were alarmed. The colonists' leaders wanted female co-operation, but they wanted to set the limits of female activism, and they certainly did not want to encourage female autonomy.

The greater political awareness of many women during the revolutionary struggle did, however, cause some of them to raise the question of women's rights. In a private exchange of letters between John Adams and his wife in spring 1776, when John was a delegate to the Continental Congress, Abigail not only demonstrated her knowledge of political affairs, but asked John to ensure that the new nation's legal code should protect the rights of women: 'I desire you will Remember the Ladies, and be more generous and favourable to them than your ancestors. Do not put such unlimited power into the hands of the Husbands. Remember all Men would be tyrants if they could.' John refused to take his wife's concerns seriously. His response was like that of many other men at the time – an unwillingness to acknowledge that women's role had been altered by the conflict with Britain. But whereas many men might have seen women's input as merely supporting male resistance to the reassertion of imperial power, it is clear that increasingly many women conceived their activism in a more public and political way. Thus in 1780 Esther deBerdt Reed wrote a pamphlet entitled 'The Sentiments of an American Woman', couched in defensive and traditional terms, but which claimed the mantle of patriotism for American women in terms similar to those of many male Patriots: 'Born for liberty, disdaining to bear the irons of a tyrannic Government . . .'

The war had other effects and forced new roles on many women. Some followed their husbands and fathers and were active in the military, either as camp followers providing essential support services for the troops, such as cooking and laundry, or, very occasionally, disguising themselves as men and fighting in the army. Generally though women were left at home, often for long periods of time, to run the farm, business or other affairs while their husbands served in the army, or in the case of Loyalists sought refuge with the British. For many women this was a new experience, as they assumed tasks that had traditionally been defined as male. Some did so reluctantly, but many Patriot women particularly took a great pride in their growing expertise and developed a new self-respect as they began to act autonomously, making business decisions without referring to their husbands. War also brought many hardships, as property was destroyed, provisions were seized, friends and relatives were killed or died as the result of disease, and women were brutally attacked by enemy soldiers.

Despite female participation in the Revolutionary struggle, women were not central to Revolutionary thought. Jefferson's declaration that 'All men are created equal' reflected the Founding Fathers' limited vision of who constituted a 'citizen', for it referred only to white 'men'. The establishment of a republican government altered the relationship between the citizen and the state. During the 1780s and 1790s political leaders, social reformers and women themselves debated the question of white women's role in the new nation, for the activities and ideas of the Revolutionary period challenged assumptions that women should be defined as domestic, private and dependent. There was some support for greater female political participation, although only in one state, New Jersey, were women given the vote for a brief time between 1776 and 1807. The printing of Mary Wollstonecraft's *A Vindication of the Rights of Woman* in an American edition in 1792 raised further questions about women's status. The later revelation that Wollstonecraft had borne a child out of wedlock discredited many of her ideas, however, and reinforced a growing belief that womanhood should be defined within the bonds of marriage and motherhood. The solution that emerged from the debates surrounding the appropriate role for women in the new Republic was republican motherhood.

The republican mother

Republican motherhood resolved the difficulty of female citizenship by endowing women's traditional roles of motherhood and domesticity with political meaning. It became the republican woman's patriotic duty to instil in her children, particularly her sons, the virtues and values believed to be critical to the survival of the new Republic. As wives, too, women were to have a responsibility to the state, to ensure that their husbands remained true to these same virtues. Women now had a civic duty, an identity distinct from men, and a role that was essential to the welfare of the state. The political consciousness aroused by the Revolutionary struggle was directed back into the home, but by giving motherhood a greater value than it had had before.

The idea of republican motherhood stimulated a debate about women's education. During the colonial period most people believed that education was a means of promoting personal well-being and as a consequence most parents paid to educate their sons, not their daughters. Girls were considered to be unsuited for education beyond the basics, for it would make them unfit for their duties as wives and mothers, as the Connecticut poet, John Trumbell observed:

> And why should girls be learned or wise,
> Books only serve to spoil their eyes.
> The studious eye but faintly twinkles
> And reading paves the way to wrinkles.

Republican motherhood, however, required that women should teach their sons the precepts of good citizenship – patriotism, self-sacrifice for the public good, and virtue. In order that they could fulfil this important role, women needed to have high moral standards, and increasingly to achieve this they needed to be educated. As an 1822 article in *Masonic Miscellany* suggested: 'Female education is all important to the public welfare. The sons of Columbia who are to command her armies and direct her counsels, receive most of their impressions for the first twelve years of their lives, from the example and instruction of their mothers!' Thus those who advocated the education of women in the late eighteenth and early nineteenth centuries did so to prepare women to be better wives and mothers – few proposed that women should be educated for their own sake. The occasional writer even began to suggest that women were the intellectual equals of men, disabled only by their lack of education. Although the quality of schooling varied from region to region, and depended on class and race, women's education was transformed in the decades after the Revolution. By the middle of the nineteenth century the literacy gap between men and women in New England had closed, and though it was slower to do so in the South, there were significant improvements in white women's literacy there too.

Some women began to establish careers for themselves as writers. The Revolutionary era growth in print culture continued into the early Republic and provided women with the prospect of publication. Increasing numbers of newspapers began to seek a female audience and by the end of the eighteenth century periodicals aimed specifically at women were being published. These naturally attracted female writers. The development of a market for books of all kinds aimed at the new audience of literate women also created opportunities for female authors. Thus by the end of the eighteenth century American women were beginning to appear in a variety of forms of print media, and America's first bestselling book was by a female author, Susanna Rowson's novel *Charlotte Temple*. By early the following century, there were growing numbers of published female authors.

Bestselling novels by female authors such as Maria Cummins, Susan Warner, E. D. E. N. Southworth and Lydia Sigourney dominated the mid-nineteenth century literary marketplace. They were read by men and women alike, and although many of them sought to promote an ideal of femininity that emphasised women's role as mother and housewife, others were more subversive. Nor did women just produce novels; they wrote in many different genres, both fiction and non-fiction, for a variety of audiences and a diversity of purposes. While many critics considered these works to have little 'serious' cultural value, recent scholars have begun to recognise that this literature not only played an important part in shaping gender roles, but was often used by female authors to promote a religious and reformist agenda, sometimes offering a powerful critique of male society.

It was not just on the written page that women became more visible in the nineteenth century. The series of religious revivals in the early decades of the century, known as the Second Great Awakening, were an evangelical response to fears about the growing secularisation of American society, and the tensions caused by early industrialisation and urbanisation. The kind of emotional religion promoted by the revivals appealed particularly to women, and it was they who often brought other family members into the churches. Protestant clergymen, who in Puritan times had regarded women as temptresses and inciters to evil, now began to value them on account of their bringing men back to God. Through their sermons, tracts and popular literature, these clergymen joined women writers in constructing a discourse in which woman's role was defined as central to the moral well-being of the family and in which domesticity was women's glory. According to one writer, Catherine Beecher, it was women's role in a democratic society to be responsible for the moral and spiritual quality of the home, and as moral mothers they were the acknowledged superiors of men – giving women a role that extended beyond the private home into the public sphere.

Encouraged by their ministers, many women became involved in church-related activities. Female missionary societies, Sunday School societies and benevolent associations sprang up all over the United States, but especially in New England, providing support for male missionary and evangelical endeavours and raising funds for charitable causes. Alongside these, women established maternal associations to provide the support and infor-mation they needed in order to fulfil their roles as moral mothers. These female societies were guided by traditional gendered precepts and were con-servative in nature and as such were generally socially acceptable, but at the same time they encouraged women to become involved in activities beyond their own households. They also taught women organisational skills and involved them in a network of female organisations, which by the mid-1820s had spread across the country.

Many women were content to limit their benevolent activities to their local church organisations, but others, prompted by their sense of religious mission and armed with their new organisational skills, took their moral zeal further. They also directed their activism into more secular channels, and areas of social reform that were politically charged. Their establishment of female temperance societies and moral reform societies was often highly controversial, in part because the work these societies brought women more obviously into the public sphere, but also because they offered an auth-oritative critique of male society. Particularly contentious was women's involvement in the antislavery movement.

The perceived morality of their cause and their concern for family life among slaves attracted white women to the abolitionist crusade. Black women were also prominently involved in the movement as speakers on abolitionist plat-forms and in practical ways, as by helping slaves to escape. Not surprisingly, women abolitionists provoked the hostility of those outside the movement, who condemned these women for their involvement in a highly controver-sial cause, but also from male abolitionists, who did not approve of female abolitionists speaking in public, collecting signatures for petitions and tak-ing a prominent public, even political, role. Despite the radicalism of the cause, however, many of the women interested in it used conservative rhetoric to justify their part in opposing slavery. Thus Harriet Beecher Stowe in her great antislavery novel, *Uncle Tom's Cabin* (1852), by emphasising the virtues of motherhood and domesticity irrespective of race, presented a powerful chal-lenge. Former slaves added their own voices to the literary critique, highlighting – through their own experiences – the horrors of the institution. Harriet Jacobs'

Incidents in the Life of a Slave Girl (1861), in particular, emphasised the sexual exploitation that slave women suffered and questioned the way they were judged by the standards of white womanhood:

> But, O, ye happy women, whose purity has been sheltered from childhood, who have been free to choose the objects of your affection, whose homes are protected by law, do not judge the poor desolate slave girl too severely! If slavery had been abolished, I, also, could have married the man of my choice; I could have had a home shielded by the laws . . .

The hostility from men that women encountered in their antislavery work, prompted some of them to question the limitations put on women by American society and to link the two issues of slavery and the position of women. The Grimké sisters had been among the first women publicly to compare the restrictions on the lives of slaves and women during the 1830s, but it was not until 1848 that the first women's rights convention brought the growing dissatisfaction of some American women to public attention. The Seneca Falls Convention was organised by Elizabeth Cady Stanton and Lucretia Mott and met in upstate New York in July 1848. It was attended by a group of men and women, many of them Quakers and activists in other reform movements.

Stanton's use of the Declaration of Independence to convey women's demand for rights picked up from some of the earlier debates about women's place. Drawing on the tradition of American liberty for men, as epitomised by Jefferson's document, Stanton framed her demand for the equality of the sexes in the same language. Women's grievances against men replaced those of the colonists' against George III, and she concluded with a demand that women should be accorded their full rights as Americans: '. . . we insist that they have immediate admission to all the rights and privileges which belong to them as citizens of the United States'. The resolutions resulting from the convention called for equality before the law, improved educational opportunities, the breaking down of barriers to female employment and an end to the oppression of women by men. The resolution demanding woman's suffrage was the only one which did not pass unanimously.

The Civil War

The Civil War had a major impact on women's lives, as they were expected to take on new roles. White women in the South ran plantations and tried to manage the slave workforce while their husbands were away fighting.

Non-slaveholding women too, managed farms and businesses in the absence of their men, much like their counterparts in the North. The war also brought opportunities for women to overcome barriers to some professions that had for long been erected against them. Women on both sides of the conflict quickly organised themselves to create soldiers' relief societies in order to sew, assemble medical supplies, and provide other items for the soldiers. In the North these societies were co-ordinated by a central agency, the US Sanitary Commission, while in the South they remained independent local organisations. Women working for the Sanitary Commission, drawing on their pre-war experience in voluntary societies, raised money for the Union cause by holding fairs, door-to-door collections and other fund-raising drives. In the South, where there was no such tradition of voluntary activism, women's efforts were on a smaller scale.

By contributing in this way to their respective armies, women identified themselves with the cause and asserted their patriotism. Many women of the slaveholding class in the South no longer saw themselves as American. As the Louisianan Sarah Morgan proclaimed to her 1863 diary: 'I confess my self a rebel, body and soul. *Confess?* I glory in it! Am proud of being one, would not forego the title for any earthly one! . . . Yes! I am glad we are two distinct tribes! I am proud of my country'. These women supported a cause that sought to maintain the dependence not just of black men and women, but also of white women. Encouraged by the southern press, women pushed their men to join the Confederate army, and demonstrated their loyalty to the cause by sacrificing their men to it, to the extent that one northern newspaper editor put it: 'But for the courage and energy of the women of the South, we believe that the Rebellion would not have survived to this time'. However, when the war turned decisively against the Confederacy, and women found their homes destroyed, their authority challenged by their slaves and shortages of food, they began to demand an end to the war and the return of their men from the battlefield – circumstances that some historians argue led to the failure of morale and defeat of the Confederacy. Nonetheless, even after the war, women – especially those of the planter class – were important in maintaining the patriotic sentiments, gender codes and racial attitudes that preserved southern distinctiveness until well into the twentieth century.

For southern slave women, the Civil War had a quite different meaning. It was clear to the slaves from the outbreak of war that their freedom was at stake, and women as much as men sought to ensure that their agenda was not forgotten. Many slave men escaped to the Union military lines and offered their services to the army, and they were often followed by their wives and children seeking both protection and the chance to help the Union war effort. Others remained loyal servants throughout the war, but those slave women who stayed on the plantations sometimes suffered the revenge of cruel owners. Recent scholarship has suggested that African American women, whether slave or free, did more than white women to step beyond the proprieties of womanhood to secure the success of their cause, and were perhaps the most politicised of the war's participants.

In the North women expressed their loyalty to the Union through specifically female methods, since social codes prevented them from showing it by joining the military conflict. Rather than acknowledging the political nature of women's war work and patriotism, popular culture insisted that female loyalty was natural, and that women participated in the war effort as a consequence of their moral instincts not for political reasons. For many women in the North, however, there was some expectation of expanded rights as a result of their wartime economic and personal sacrifices. The antebellum discussion of women's rights, together with the reformist activities of many women, meant that there was a body of opinion that believed that the voluntary work women did for the state during the hostilities should be translated into full citizenship as a result of the war. Although the movement for women's rights was put on hold during the conflict itself, as a demonstration of loyalty and to advance the war, there was an anticipation that women would gain political advancement as a reward for their sacrifices.

Towards the 'new woman'

The end of the Civil War in April 1865 brought few of the gains that white women in the North might have hoped for, and only some of those that African American women sought. The Civil War ended slavery, but the slaves were freed with no property or income and with families scattered. In the aftermath of the war, many ex-slave couples legalised their marriages before judges and ministers, and spent a great deal of effort in tracking down family members. African American families sought to emulate white ideals of women's role, by withdrawing wives and daughters from field labour and allowing them to concentrate on domesticity – an action many whites in the South regarded as 'putting on airs'. Some ex-masters refused to accept this new situation. As one ex-slave from a plantation on Louisiana's Red River recalled, white men 'drive colored women out in the fields to work . . . and would tell colored men that their wives and children could not live on their places unless they work in the fields'. It was economic necessity, however, that most often drove black women back into performing tasks they had been forced to work at as slaves, but the meaning of this work had changed. Now women were working for the economic support of their families, rather than for a white master, although in most families it was the husband who strove to be the main breadwinner.

The question of the freed slaves' citizenship rights produced considerable controversy in both Congress and the southern states. It also caused a split in the abolitionist alliance, as women who had put aside their demand for women's rights to campaign for the abolition of slavery during the Civil War expected their fellow abolitionists to support their demand for the vote. As one activist of the period, Ernestine Rose, argued, voting was a basic right shared by all Americans: 'Human beings are men and women, possessed of human faculties, and understanding, which we call mind; and mind recognizes no sex, therefore the term "male", as applied to human beings – to citizens – ought to be expunged from the Constitution and laws as a last remnant of barbarism'. The Fourteenth Amendment to the Constitution, however, granted the franchise to all male citizens, using the word 'male' for the first time, and consequently denying women the right to vote on the grounds of their sex.

The decision that this should be the 'Negro's hour' created a division in the abolitionist alliance and a women's rights movement that focused increasingly on woman's suffrage as the means to ensure women full citizenship. It also led to the founding of two independent woman's suffrage organisations, established within a few months of each other in 1869 – the National Woman Suffrage Association (NWSA) and the American Woman Suffrage Association (AWSA). Throughout the latter half of the nineteenth century these two organisations remained, often bitterly, divided, pursuing the same goal but utilising different methods and appealing to slightly different constituencies. Between them they kept the issue alive, and even gained some victories in western states, until they set aside their differences and finally came together to form one organisation, the National American Woman Suffrage Association (NAWSA) in 1890.

While women's suffrage advocates made little progress in the late nineteenth century, changes in the American economy and in society altered many women's lives, creating new constructions of femininity. Industrialisation had a major impact on the work women performed and where they did it. Starting before the Civil War in the textile mills of New England, women entered the paid labour force, becoming some of the first industrial workers in America. The shift from home to factory-based manufacturing meant that the paid female workforce before the Civil War was almost always young and single.

These women worked in factories because the wages were better than in other female employments, such as domestic service, but women were only paid a half to two-thirds of what men earned for the same work. Middle-class observers frequently deplored the presence of women in factories, regarding it as unfeminine, as Orestes Brownson commented in 1840: 'She has worked in a factory, is sufficient to damn to infamy the most worthy and virtuous girl'. Such attitudes persisted, especially while the number of women in the paid labour force remained low.

Between 1870 and 1920 the number of women entering the labour force expanded rapidly, as did the variety of jobs they undertook. Many factors stayed constant – most women worked in sex-segregated workplaces, and were present in the workforce for short periods of time. Their wages remained low and working conditions were usually poor. Trade unions were generally uninterested in organising women workers, in large part because of the supposedly temporary nature of women's employment, but also because they believed that women depressed men's wages. Women continued to enter the workforce in ever-larger numbers, however, especially unmarried immigrant women, and African American women, both single and married. By 1920 the proportion of native-born white women in employment had risen, and most working-class women expected to spend a period in the labour force before they got married, although married white women tended not to work outside the home.

By the early twentieth century increasing numbers of middle-class women were going out to work, although this tended to be to professional employment rather than industrial work. The move began before the Civil War, as educated women became teachers, encouraged by Catherine Beecher's assertion that because women possessed superior moral and nurturing qualities, they were uniquely qualified for the profession. Beecher's quest to make teaching 'a profession for woman, a profession as honorable and as lucrative for her as the legal, medical and theological professions are for men', was remarkably successful, particularly as it coincided with an increased demand for schoolteachers. Nursing emerged during the Civil War as a respectable profession for educated women, a move that was consolidated with the establishment after the war of training schools. Like teaching, nursing drew upon women's traditional qualities of nurture and subservience to a male doctor, but when women tried to enter the medical profession as doctors, they were met with hostility from the male medical establishment.

The desire to enter the professions was encouraged by the expansion of higher education for women in the late nineteenth century. In the decades after the Civil War a number of well-funded private women's colleges were founded, including Vassar (1865) and Radcliffe (1894), with rigorous academic standards and curricula that matched many men's colleges. Many of the land grant universities in the West, established as a result of the Morrill Land Grant Act of 1862, were co-educational, although some were slow to admit women. Educational opportunities also expanded for African American women, with the aim of creating a black professional and leadership class. Advances in higher education for women were not always well received. Some critics believed that co-education would lead to immorality, while others believed too much education would ruin a girl's chances of a good marriage, and too much studying would put a strain on girls' nervous and reproductive systems, rendering them unable to give birth to healthy children. Such attacks were testimony to the strength of feeling against developments that seemed to undermine traditional notions of femininity.

Higher education had a profound impact on the first and second generations of female graduates, but many of these women found it difficult to find a place in society after they had graduated. Only slowly did professions such as law, medicine and academia open their doors to women, and many female graduates were unwilling simply to return to domesticity. Instead many of these women created new professions and institutions through which they could fulfil their commitment to public service. Much of the work these women did was for other women and children, bringing the values of middle-class domesticity and motherhood to deal with the problems caused by poverty, unrestricted urbanisation and industrialisation. Initially they tried to improve conditions by philanthropic and voluntary means, but it quickly became clear to many reformers that only legislation could produce a lasting solution to such problems as juvenile delinquency, factory conditions and child labour. Thus female activists spearheaded many of the Progressive era reforms that formed the basis of the early welfare state, entering the public sphere in order to lobby the legislature while using the rhetoric of the private sphere to justify the measures. They argued that women needed special consideration and protection by the state because of their actual and potential motherhood – an argument that was endorsed by the Supreme Court in the *Muller* v. *Oregon* case in 1908.

Women activists did not achieve the reforms they sought without a struggle, however, and their lack of political representation was increasingly a matter of concern. As Jane Addams, a leading female reformer who had not previously publicly advocated woman's suffrage, explained in an article entitled 'Why Women Should Vote' in the *Ladies' Home Journal* (1910):

> If woman would fulfill her traditional responsibility to her own children; if she would educate and protect from danger factory children who must find their

recreation on the street; if she would bring the cultural forces to bear upon our materialistic civilization; and if she would do it all with the dignity and directness fitting one who carries on her immemorial duties, then she must bring herself to the use of the ballot – that latest implement for self-government. May we not fairly say that American women need this implement in order to preserve the home?

By 1910 such arguments for the vote were not particularly new. The Women's Christian Temperance Union (WCTU) had endorsed the 'Home Protection Ballot' in 1876, as a means to accomplish temperance laws. By the late nineteenth century, the suffrage organisations themselves began to move away from 'natural rights' arguments to those based on woman's difference from men and the 'special qualities' she could bring to the political process. This shift in argument arose partially out of expediency, but also because by the end of the century many of the legal disabilities suffered by women had been removed. As more and more women became involved in public activity in the early twentieth century, the vote no longer seemed to be such a radical measure.

The changes in argument and new support for the suffrage gave a fresh momentum to the campaigns led by the NAWSA, although progress continued to be slow. Further energy was brought to the campaign with the formation of the Congressional Union (later the National Woman's Party) in 1913, which borrowed many of its tactics from the British suffragette movement. It was not, however, until America entered the First World War that the suffragists won the support of President Wilson and, in August 1920, the right to vote.

The 'New Woman'

The securing of the Nineteenth Amendment to the Constitution exposed many of the contradictions and tensions within the women's rights movement. The vote represented only a very narrow definition of citizenship for American women, focused on the relationship between the individual and the state, rather than the kind of collective action that women had been involved in prior to gaining the vote. While many women activists, and male politicians, assumed that women would use their vote collectively to push for social welfare reforms and other 'women's' issues, it quickly became clear during the 1920s that women voted in the same way as men, as individuals, and that the 'women's vote' would not materialise. Nor did the Nineteenth Amendment enfranchise all women – African American women in the southern states, like their men, were excluded from the polls by segregationist laws. The narrow concentration on gaining the vote also meant that once it was accomplished the women's suffrage movement no longer had a reform agenda, with the result that the movement fragmented quickly after achieving its goal.

Amid the coalition of women who had fought for the suffrage there were a number of activists who wished to push the demand for women's rights further. This was not, however, a group that was united by any one set of ideas or demands. It included those who had been demonised as 'sex radicals' before the First World War, such as Margaret Sanger and Emma Goldman, who demanded women's right to birth control information; those like Charlotte Perkins Gilman and Crystal Eastman, who began to call themselves feminists and challenged the emphasis on female difference while advocating female economic independence; members of the National Woman's Party who wanted to see an end to all remaining forms of discrimination against women; and the 'social feminists' who wanted to build upon their pre-war programme of protective legislation and social welfare reforms for women and children. Though each of these groups had some sympathy for the others' aims and there was some overlap between them, their co-operation foundered over the attempt by members of the National Woman's Party to introduce an Equal Rights Amendment (ERA) into Congress in 1923. The problem was that although the ERA might have increased the civil rights of professional women, it would have swept aside all the protective legislation for working-class women for which the social feminists were working. The ERA was defeated, but the conservative atmosphere of the 1920s meant that little further social welfare legislation was secured, and the feminist movement split.

If the vote did not secure equality for women, it did mark a recognition of a new construction of American womanhood. In the early 1920s popular culture began to reflect new ideals, identifying and glamorising a public role for women. In magazines and fiction, working girls were accorded a new respectability and given advice on how to succeed; but their ultimate goal was still to get married, as the social commentator Floyd Dell in *Love in the Machine Age* (1930) observed: 'The idea of work as a *goal* would be repudiated by working women; to them it is a *means to an end*, and the end is love, marriage, children, and homemaking'. The 'flapper', too, who shocked the older generation by shortening her skirts, cutting her hair and indulging in 'petting parties' and new sensual dances, ultimately conformed and married, often at a younger age than her mother. New cultural forms, such as films and advertisements, reinforced this message, showing young women not only how to secure a husband, but how to keep him by purchasing the right goods.

The Crash of 1929, and the Great Depression that followed, halted many of the trends of the more prosperous 1920s. As unemployment levels rose, many men lost their jobs, but because the job losses were initially in male-dominated industries, women workers were slower to lose theirs. This was not true of all women, for African American women were often displaced from their traditional jobs in domestic service, to make room for white women. Deeply ingrained beliefs about appropriate work for men and women meant that women were often able to find work where men were not, and women's work was frequently crucial to the family's economic survival. There was, however, a widespread and profound hostility to women working, especially married women. As one man reportedly asserted in 1931: 'If less women were employed it would make room for the employment of many of the idle men in our country . . . in the last analysis woman's true place is her home where she can see to the proper raising of her children while the man earns the living'. Both federal and state governments responded to such resentment by trying to limit government employment of married women, but as several scholars have suggested, the number of women workers still increased during the 1930s.

The Depression created other ambiguities. Many women experienced a return to a more traditional role as mother and housewife, reviving old skills in home manufactures in order to stretch resources, and sacrificing themselves to nurture their families and keep the home together. They did so, however, in a context where men were often unable to fulfil their role as main breadwinner, and where families had to move in with others in order to spread costs. Family life was also one of compromises, for birth rates dropped dramatically, as couples delayed marriage and married couples used contraception. Economic distress created a greater demand for birth control information and in 1936 its dissemination became legal. Franklin Roosevelt's New Deal ignored such contradictions, however, and based many of its policies on fixed assumptions about the male role as breadwinner and women's role as dependents requiring supervision and protection.

The irony of the New Deal was that while it entrenched traditional ideas about women's domesticity and motherhood in its welfare measures, women reformers initiated many of these programmes and drew on the experience of women in administering them. While few of these women achieved electoral office during the 1930s, more women were appointed to, and secured influence in, the federal government than ever before. The most important of these was Eleanor Roosevelt, the First Lady, who brought many of her network of friends from the settlement houses and reform organisations into government to staff new agencies. They were, however, unable to secure reforms that dealt with women as autonomous beings, seeing them only in the family context. Thus relief programmes aimed to provide male workers with jobs so that they could support their families, and, where there was no male breadwinner available, assumed that the state would provide means-tested benefits in the form of Aid to Dependent Children. Even those work projects that provided work for women assumed that women were only temporarily in the workforce, helping out their families during the emergency.

Such assumptions also underlay women's involvement in the workforce during the Second World War. As men were mobilised into the armed services, the United States suddenly found itself with a labour shortage. Many women, who had previously been employed in low-paid jobs, quickly filled better-paid jobs in the war-related industries, and others filled the places left by men in the non-defence industries. When married women began to take jobs for the first time in large numbers, commentators began to be alarmed that this would undermine their femininity, while some women were themselves fearful of the reception they might receive in the male domain of the workplace. To allay these fears and to mobilise women for war work, the government organised a propaganda campaign to persuade women that it was their patriotic duty to fill the jobs vacated by men, for the duration of the war. The Office of War Information, in alliance with commercial advertisers and the media, produced images such as 'Rosie the Riveter' – a woman who at one and the same time ably filled a man's job and retained her femininity. Films reinforced the idea, reassuring women that industrial processes and machinery were much like household appliances and housework, and movie stars made such work appear glamorous and exciting.

Women responded to the call with enthusiasm, although clearly many did so less from a sense of patriotic duty than because they were attracted by the opportunity to earn more than they had been able to in peacetime. The older, married women who now entered the workforce were also keen that their new status should not be temporary, despite the added burdens that such employment often created. From the beginning unions and employers worried that women would not be happy to return home at the end of the war, although government and the media consistently reassured Americans that women were only helping 'for the duration' and they would return to their traditional roles once the emergency was over. The ambivalence of many about women in the workforce was reflected in debates about what was seen as gender experimentation.

Women were also being constantly reminded that their presence in the workforce was on a different basis from that of the men they replaced. In many industries pay differentials were maintained throughout the war, even though women were doing the same work as men. Female workers frequently had to put up with the sexual harassment or ostracism of their male co-workers, and often found themselves relegated to the least skilled work because employers did not want to spend time and money training temporary personnel.

The Feminine Mystique and its challengers

Qualified as their experience was, women enjoyed their work and entered areas of employment that had previously been closed to them. Many understood also that they had helped make the victory possible and gained a new sense of themselves as American citizens. But the impetus encouraging women to enter the workforce had come from the government, as a response to an emergency, not from any change in social attitudes, and with the end of the war the propaganda machinery was employed to hasten the return to domesticity. Women had to relinquish their wartime jobs to the returning men, and they were urged to concentrate on their homes and families and to embrace domestic life. Public opinion was no longer in favour of women working outside the home, and because there had been little discussion of the political meaning of women's work during the war, there were few attempts by women's organisations to challenge such sentiments. The reality was that many women carried on working after the war and the number of married women in the workforce continued to rise following a trend that had begun before the war, a development obscured by the dominant ideology of domesticity.

The onset of the Cold War brought a new set of concerns, together with a yearning for stability in family and gender roles, as Betty Friedan was later to observe: 'We were all vulnerable, homesick, lonely, frightened. A pent-up hunger for marriage, home and children was felt simultaneously by several different generations; a hunger which, in the prosperity of postwar America, everyone could suddenly satisfy'. The period of the 1940s and 1950s saw young marriages as the norm, a low divorce rate, and a steep increase in the birth rate as the country produced the 'baby boom' – a phenomenon that cut across class and ethnic divisions. Popular magazines, movies and fiction all urged a family ethic on women, and a sense of 'togetherness', accompanied by an emotionally intense form of child-rearing. Social and political commentators attacked progressive women's organisations as suspect in this Cold War atmosphere, and women who were frustrated by their domestic role were condemned as deviant and the source of social problems. Popular culture promoted a vision of family life and domesticity in which the father was the breadwinner and the mother was a full-time housewife – a cosy ideal to protect Americans from the chill of the Cold War.

The mass media offered women contradictory messages, however. For, while on the one hand, they were told that their fulfilment lay in the home, on the other they were presented with images that offered alternatives to the mother and housewife role. Popular psychologists suggested equally conflicting roles for women, some of which emphasised domesticity, others that undermined it. Increasing numbers of married women worked outside the home in the post-war period, and were frequently criticised for doing so by conservative commentators, but that did not stop others from following them. For the most part, however, these were not jobs that offered women a sense of autonomy, or which were motivated by 'feminism', but a means to obtain a second income to buy the consumer goods necessary to aspire to middle-class domesticity.

Despite the emphasis on domesticity during the 1950s, there were individual women in both main parties, but especially in the Democratic Party, who remained politically active. In response to their work for his campaign during the close election of 1960, these Democratic women in 1961 persuaded President Kennedy to establish a Presidential Commission on the Status of Women. The commission, with its membership drawn from the trades unions, women's organisations and government agencies, was chaired by Eleanor Roosevelt. It examined women's place in the family, the economy and the legal system. Its report, published in 1963, emphasised the importance of childcare services, paid maternity leave and, most importantly, the persistent inequities women faced in the workplace, thus paving the way for the Equal Pay Act of 1963. It stopped short of demanding an Equal Rights Amendment, largely because the commission itself was split on the issue, but suggested instead that existing provisions in the Constitution should be used for promoting women's legal rights. Of perhaps greatest significance was the fact that the Commission existed at all, for it symbolised the national importance of women's issues, as well as creating a network of people with a common interest in women's status, which later became the National Organization for Women (NOW), the civil rights wing of a reinvigorated feminist movement.

The impact of the report was greater because of the publication by Betty Friedan of *The Feminine Mystique* in 1963. She eloquently expressed the frustration of many middle-class, college-educated suburban housewives, by describing the 'problem that has no name':

> If I am right, the problem that has no name stirring in the minds of so many American women today is not a matter of loss of femininity or too much education, or the demands of domesticity. It is far more important than anyone recognizes . . . It may well be the key to our future as a nation and a culture. We can no longer ignore the voice within women that says: 'I want something more than my husband and my children and my home.'

The book provoked an immediate response, as thousands of women wrote to Friedan thanking her and telling their own stories. It also provided the context for the debate over the Civil Rights Bill in 1964. In an attempt to derail the bill, a Southern Democrat added sex to its provisions as well as race, assuming that this would render the bill so ridiculous as to defeat it. The move backfired, as Congress passed the Civil Rights Act, creating in the Equal Employment Opportunities Commission a body that was quickly inundated with women's grievances.

By the mid-1960s the middle-class, professional women who had pushed for civil rights legislation for women and who formed NOW, were only one part of a burgeoning women's rights movement. Younger women who had been involved in the civil rights movement in the South began to question their treatment by male leaders of the movement; so too did young women in the student movement. These women formed a second branch of the women's movement – women's liberation. This had a quite different constituency, style and politics from NOW, through the creation of autonomous, women-only consciousness raising groups. Through these discussion groups, women began to connect their personal experiences to widespread sexual discrimination, and to develop an understanding that the 'personal is political'. From these beginnings the women's liberation movement launched a widespread attack on traditional attitudes and assumptions about women's role in American society. It was not a movement with a clear programme or distinct leadership, but rather one that used varied methods and in one way or another sought to encompass all facets of women's lives: sexuality, domestic violence, equality in the workplace. It staged protests outside the Miss World Competition, sought to abolish sexist language, and created women's studies. The issues were so diverse and they were raised by so many different groups that they affected virtually every aspect of American life.

The women's rights movement of the late 1960s and early 1970s sought a final end to the 'separation of spheres' that had dominated women's lives since the English settlement of North America in the early seventeenth century. It achieved some of its aims, but also provoked a conservative back-lash, which tried to maintain the traditional ideal of the male breadwinner, protecting and supporting an American home presided over by a full-time mother and housewife. American women have always been more complex than this conservative image might suggest. Race, ethnicity and class have affected women's ability to achieve this traditional ideal, but even white middle-class American women who were frequently instrumental in con-structing it have not always conformed to the ideals they have created. At all points in American history women have been present in the public sphere of work and politics, helping to shape the United States as a nation and influ-encing its culture. Despite the apparent masculinity of the American under-taking, it has always been a joint enterprise.

Further reading

Bauer, Dale M., and Philip Gould (eds), *The Cambridge Companion to Nineteenth-Century American Women's Writing* (2001).

Chafe, William H., *The Paradox of Change: American Women in the 20th Century* (1991).

Cott, Nancy F. (ed.), *No Small Courage: A History of Women in the United States* (2000).

Evans, Sara M., *Born for Liberty: A History of Women in America* (2nd edn, 1997).

Flexner, Eleanor, *Century of Struggle: The Woman's Rights Movement in the United States* (1959).

Friedan, Betty, *The Feminine Mystique* (1963).

Giddings, Paula, *When and Where I Enter: The Impact of Black Women on Race and Sex in America* (1984).

Kerber, Linda, 'Separate spheres, female worlds, woman's place: the rhetoric of women's history', *Journal of American History*, 75 (June 1988), pp. 9–39.

Kleinberg, S. J., *Women in American Society, 1830–1945* (1999).

Laurel, Thatcher Ulrich, *The Age of Homespun: Objects and Stories in the Creation of an American Myth* (2001).

Welter, Barbara, 'The cult of true womanhood, 1820–1860', *American Quarterly*, 18 (1966), pp. 151–74.

Website

Women and Social Movements in the United States (subscription
    website): http://womhist.binghamton.edu/index.html

CHAPTER 15

Popular culture

Nick Heffernan

Accordng to the US Census Bureau, American residents over the age of 12 each spent an average of 3,667 hours in 2003 on commercial amusements, over 40 per cent of the total hours available. The same average American spends over $760 per year on entertainment media, not including live events or the hardware – TVs, PCs, DVD players, games consoles and hi-fis – now so fundamental to the American appetite for home entertainment. That twenty-first-century Americans devote as much time to entertainment as to working or sleeping indicates the pervasive influence of popular culture on American social behaviour and national character. A torrent of mass-produced images, stories, spectacles and sounds now pours forth into every nook of daily life and cranny of private consciousness, making the United States not only the world's dominant military and economic power, but an empire of signs whose global supremacy is asserted as much through the pervasiveness of its popular culture as through its military reach or its command of international trade. Indeed, as its products form an ever-greater proportion of that very international trade, US popular culture has become the principal vehicle for advertising and legitimating the 'American way' on the world stage.

How, then, should we understand and interpret popular culture and the ways in which it is produced and consumed? Further statistical and economic data suggests we cannot but view it as a motor of American capitalism and a cornerstone of consumer society. Figures for 2002–4 reveal that the American television industry generates about $120 billion in annual revenues, the film industry $46 billion, sports $39.6 billion, radio $14.9 billion, recorded music $11.7 billion, theme parks $10.2 billion, and video and computer games $7 billion. Add the international earnings of US entertainment industries, and the economic significance of American popular culture to contemporary global capitalism becomes even more evident. Moreover, the quintessential industry of consumer capitalism, advertising (the industry that produces nothing but the desire to consume), is almost entirely dependent on popular culture outlets, which account for the greater proportion of the annual US advertising spend of over $266 billion.

For the most part, then, popular culture reaches us in the form of commodities – products designed primarily to generate profits for those who manufacture and market them. And, particularly during the latter part of the twentieth century, a feature of popular culture's inexorable rise has been the concentration of ownership and control into the hands of seven staggeringly powerful corporate behemoths. General Electric owns the NBC, CNBC and Telemundo TV networks; numerous cable TV channels; Universal Pictures and Universal Parks and Resorts; and many other businesses. Time-Warner owns the WB TV network; cable channels CNN, HBO and Cartoon Network; film production companies Warner Bros, New Line Cinema and Castle Rock; music companies WEA and Rhino (representing 15 per cent of the music market); publishers Time-Life Books and DC Comics; online businesses AOL and Netscape; and Atlanta's major league basketball, baseball and hockey teams. The France-based Vivendi-Universal commands 30 per cent of the recorded music market in the United States through such labels as PolyGram, Island Def Jam, Interscope A&M, Motown, MCA, Mercury, DreamWorks and Geffen. It controls Cineplex Odeon Theatres and owns 26.8 million shares of Time-Warner stock. Disney, alongside its eponymous film, cable TV, theme park and merchandising businesses, owns the ABC television network; ten further TV stations; cable channels including ESPN, A&E and the History Channel; over 60 radio stations; the 'independent' film company Miramax; Hyperion Books; and major league baseball and hockey teams. Viacom's holdings include the CBS and UPN television networks; 35 further TV stations; cable channels such as MTV, Showtime, Nickelodeon and Black Entertainment Television; over 175 radio stations; Paramount Pictures; Blockbuster Video; and Simon & Schuster publishing. The German-based media giant Bertelsmann has a powerful US presence through Random House publishing and the BMG, Arista and RCA music groups. Its music businesses, recently merged with Sony, represent 29 per cent of the market. Rupert Murdoch's News Corporation owns the Fox TV network; 34 other TV stations; cable and satellite channels including BSkyB; the Fox film companies; the *New York Post*; HarperCollins Publishers; and the Los Angeles Dodgers baseball team. And on the fringes of the big seven, the Japanese corporation Sony presses its American interests through its music partnership with Bertelsmann; its film businesses, which include MGM pictures and account for 17 per cent of the US market; and its prominence in video and computer games.

Thus American popular culture and globalised big business are now insep-arable. This should be cause for reflection on the meaning of the term 'pop-ular'. Doubtless the products of the entertainment industries are 'popular' in the sense that they appeal to and are enjoyed by broad masses of people, across distinctions of class, race and region, and without the requirement of specialist knowledge or education. Yet they are not 'popular' in the sense suggested by the word's Latin root, *popularis*, meaning 'of or from the people'. They do not emerge directly from experiences or organisations that belong to the mass of ordinary people, but are rather manufactured and distributed according to a 'top-down' model of near-monopoly control. And they are consumed by audi-ences whose influence over what they are given and how they receive it is often limited to the bare right of refusal or a meaningless choice between vir-tually identical products. Moreover, when we consider how the 'synergies' sought by entertainments conglomerates often result in the same company's music and film products being promoted and advertised through its TV, radio and publishing outlets and spun off into further product as merchandising, theme park rides or video games, then it is tempting to see popular culture as the plaything of an unaccountable corporate cabal bent on cynical manipulation and exploitation of the unwitting consumer.

One tendency in the study of popular culture, therefore, stresses its anti- or pseudo-democratic qualities, dwelling upon the corporate domination of the media of public expression or upon the standardised and formulaic nature of the commodities that saturate the marketplace. Analysts of this persua-sion often use terms such as 'mass culture' or 'the culture industry' rather than 'popular culture'. These stress the corporate power behind the world of entertainment, suggesting that its products are often escapist fantasies that function to distract essentially passive audiences from the more unpleasant or unjust aspects of social reality, reconciling them to the status quo.

A more optimistic and accepting attitude towards popular culture would think of it rather as the 'art of democracy'. In this view, America's ever-increasing appetite for mass-produced images, stories and spectacles rep-resents the energy and diversity of a nation in which culture is no longer the preserve of an educated and privileged minority. The commercialisa-tion of culture is thus seen as a strength, for while it might entail a degree of coarsening and vulgarity, it also means that culture is minutely attuned to the concerns, tastes, manners and mores of the population, warts and all. Popular culture is thus understood as a mirror in which ordinary Americans see themselves reflected in all their diversity, even to the extent that marginalised groups can attain a visibility through it that is not so will-ingly afforded by political or economic institutions.

Still another view might stress this latter feature and see popular culture as an avenue through which socially excluded communities can achieve entry into the American mainstream. In staking a claim for respect as 'full' Americans by demonstrating prowess in the field of entertainment, such groups do not simply assimilate but frequently reshape in their own image the very idea of 'Americanness' itself. The clearest instance of this is the profound influence exerted by African Americans in the fields of sport and, especially, music. Since the end of the nineteenth century America's sound has been a black sound, from ragtime to jazz and blues, from swing to rock 'n' roll, from soul and disco to hip hop. Black American music styles are the most influential and most listened-to the world over and have had an equally transformative effect in the realms of fashion, speech and body language. Other examples of the same process would include the role played by immigrant Jews in the development of the Hollywood film industry and the musical theatre, or the way in which show business has been a refuge for homosexual artists and the articulation of gay sensibilities.

However, before dismissing the gloomy 'culture industry' perspective and celebrating popular culture as a democratic arena of 'bottom-up' initiatives and grass-roots expressiveness, we should note that for all their rich contribution to music, sports, fashion, dance and speech, African Americans still remain seriously disadvantaged in social and economic terms. Prominence in the world of entertainment is not directly related to lack of progress in other spheres, but the black presence in popular culture has involved the perpetuation of demeaning stereotypes and racist myths as often as the expression of authentically black identities and voices. Questions of ownership and control remain, as the cultural outlets through which African Americans have most forcefully asserted themselves have generally been in white hands. Black creativity is too often distorted into forms deemed appealing to mass – that is, 'white' – audiences in order to make profits for white owners. Other marginalised groups have made their contributions under similar constraints.

A more nuanced view of popular culture as 'contested terrain' might therefore be appropriate. On one level, struggle revolves around the questions of ownership already raised, for as the corporate hold over popular culture has increased so has resistance to it. Grass-roots subcultures, often the source of innovation in popular culture, contest incorporation by adopting independent and often localised means of production and distribution in order to 'keep it real' according to the hip-hop credo. And dissident audience fractions form self-governing fan networks, such as the internet music file-sharers who have been blamed for the $3 billion decline in industry profits between

1999 and 2004, or the amateur writers of 'slash' fiction whose often porno-
graphic subversions of popular TV shows have discomfited stars, production companies and networks alike.

On another level, struggle is waged around the moral and ideological impact
of popular culture. Moral panics, calls for censorship, and élitist dismissals
have accompanied the growth of commercial entertainments every step of
the way. Conservatives tend to regard popular culture as a Trojan horse for
permissiveness and overly liberal attitudes requiring strict regulation; liberals
seek to protect the vulnerable from its excesses without compromising free-
doms of choice and expression; the left veers between viewing popular culture as a mechanism of capitalist mystification and a site of inchoate
democratic resistance; whilst mandarins of all hues blame it for 'dumbing
down' the national character.

These struggles take place at a micro as well as a macro level, for popular culture is also a constellation of texts – complex acts of signification
loaded with meanings not always obvious to the entertainment-hungry consumer. Events and performers are as much texts in this sense as are books,
films, TV shows or songs – think of the interpretive debates provoked by,
for example, Michael Jackson's private life and physiognomy. And these texts
are invariably contradictory – sometimes incoherent – in their complexity,
for as commodities they are generally designed to appeal to the widest constituency possible, across demographic and ideological lines. The contested
and contradictory nature of popular culture, what we might call its inherent dialectic of domination and subversion, can best be illustrated by
the development of film and music in the twentieth century. But this is
not solely a feature of the electronic, corporate age; it is characteristic too
of the period of commercial popular culture's historical emergence in the
nineteenth century.

From the 'folk' to the 'masses': popular culture in the nineteenth century

'Folk culture' is often invoked as the precursor to, and antithesis of, commercial popular culture. Springing directly from the life-ways of ordinary,
predominantly rural people, rooted in oral traditions, and anonymously
or collectively created, folk forms are produced neither for profit nor
according to the strict division between producer and consumer characteristic of commercial entertainments. The earliest manifestations of a distinctively American popular culture arose out of the folk expressions of the

Anglo-Celtics, Europeans and Africans who arrived in the colonial period. New England settlers' narratives of Indian captivity, the ballads and humorous tales of the non-slaveholding whites of the southern colonies, and the superstitions, work songs and sly comic fables of the slaves provided continuity with the past for these groups whilst registering their adaptation to the New World.

Some of these forms were absorbed into the print culture that quickly established itself in America. In 1682 Mary Rowlandson's pamphlet describing her abduction by Indians achieved universal acclaim. Such captivity narratives subsequently gave way to often apocryphal biographies of heroes of the wilderness, such as Daniel Boone and Davy Crockett, and from there fed into the formulaic Westerns that became a staple of the burgeoning postbellum dime novel industry and, eventually, of Hollywood. The impact of pamphlets, chapbooks and later of popular novels and the press was related to the unusually high levels of literacy fostered by the colonies' educational policies and thereafter by state and federal governments. Tom Paine's anti-British pamphlet 'Common Sense' is reputed to have sold up to half a million copies in 1776, the year of its publication, in a country of only 3 million inhabitants, precipitating the American Revolution. It is estimated that by 1790 over 90 per cent of white Americans were literate.

With the rapid growth of the population to 17 million by 1840, the United States had the largest reading audience in history. Increasingly urban, immigrant and working class in composition, this audience underpinned the rise of a distinctively American popular press during the Jacksonian period of the 1830s, represented by 'penny dailies' such as New York papers the *Sun* and the *Herald*. With their aggressive attacks on élites, their racy coverage of sex and crime, and their exploitation of human interest stories, these precursors of today's tabloids typified the by now resolutely populist character of American popular culture, attracting the ire of respectable commentators for their insubordination and moral laxity. Fractions of this same mass reading audience also supported healthy sales of novels, often organised into genres defined by gender and class – sentimental tales of family and marriage for women, adventure and popular biography for men. The nationwide impact of Harriet Beecher Stowe's anti-slavery novel, *Uncle Tom's Cabin* (1852), was credited by some with precipitating the Civil War. Folk forms also took on print existences. The first collection of American folk songs was published in 1814. It took longer for African American folk culture to be compiled and marketed, though, requiring the abolition of slavery and the mediation of white patrons. Boston minister Thomas Higginson published the first collection of Negro spirituals in 1867, while

Atlanta journalist Joel Chandler Harris's Uncle Remus tales, first published in 1881, marked the début of secular black folk culture in the print marketplace.

But the early form that best demonstrates the translation of folk elements into commercial structures, and highlights the racial heterogeneity of American popular culture with its contradictory logic of domination and subversion, is minstrelsy. This practice, in which white performers donned 'blackface' make-up and amused white audiences with imitations of what were claimed to be 'genuine' Negro song, dance and humour, originated in New York in the late 1820s. By the 1840s it dominated the popular theatres and music halls of the burgeoning cities of the industrialising North. Prominent blackface performers such as T. D. 'Daddy' Rice, inventor of the comic 'darky' persona Jim Crow, became wealthy international celebrities, and soon minstrelsy settled into a formula that was to endure for decades. Appearing usually in troupes and portraying a series of stock characters – Jim Crow, Tambo, Mr Bones, Dinah – minstrels performed humorous sketches that purported to be accurate representations of the carefree lives of black plantation slaves in the South, peppering them with songs that were marketed in bestselling sheet music collections under the label of 'Ethiopian airs' or 'plantation melodies'.

The racial politics of minstrelsy are at once shockingly obvious and elusively complex. It was undoubtedly a form of gross racial stereotyping and ridicule, which enabled white working class audiences to affirm their superiority over blacks in a ritual of laughter and forgetting – laughter at the antics of simple Negroes and forgetting of the brute facts of slavery that were turned into song and dance. The African American political leader and antislavery campaigner Frederick Douglass denounced the form on these grounds. But for Douglass the sin of racist caricature was compounded by the theft and economic exploitation of indigenous black folk culture and identity that it entailed. In an 1847 edition of the abolitionist newspaper *The North Star*, he declared minstrels 'the filthy scum of white society, who have stolen from us a complexion denied to them by nature, in which to make money, and pander to the corrupt taste of their fellow white citizens', voicing an accusation that haunts American popular culture to this day as white stars such as Elvis Presley and Eminem achieve prominence with 'borrowed' black cultural materials.

Yet minstrelsy also represented a peculiar commingling of black and white – an opportunity for whites to show an interest in and affection for African Americans impossible outside the theatre doors. White working-class audiences not only laughed at blackface characters, they identified with them too, particularly when, as was the convention in minstrel shows, they ridiculed the white middle and upper classes. Minstrelsy was thus a form of carnival that overturned the prevailing hierarchies of race and class, permitting collective insubordination and solidarity among the downtrodden, regardless of the colour line. Moreover, the popularity among whites of what was presented as authentic black culture was a tribute to the richness and vitality of African American creativity. Blackface performers were not simply thieves and exploiters; they also expressed a deep sympathy and respect for that which they impersonated as, by their approbation, did their audiences. Minstrel songs and sketches were replete with subversive paeans to blackness and critiques of whiteness, such as that contained in Daddy Rice's song, 'Jump Jim Crow'. Addressing the audience as 'my brother niggers', Rice expressed gratitude for being black and thus blessed with unusual talent in the fields of song, dance, wit and sartorial style. He begged his listeners not to mock too harshly the miserable whites who could not choose their complexions and, if they could, would obviously 'spend every dollar' in order to become 'gentlemen of colour'. The song's bitter irony – only a fool would choose to be black in a racist, slaveholding society – was counterbalanced by its genuine commitment to the superiority of blackness as an identity. Mockery and cultural theft mingled inextricably with affection and respect.

Minstrelsy also enabled genuinely black performers to build reputations with white audiences. Even before emancipation, African American minstrels were not uncommon, though they too masqueraded in blackface, adding another curious layer of simulation to the form: here were blacks imitating the way whites imitated blacks in order to give white spectators a taste of 'authentic' Negro life. This was progress of a kind, as even Frederick Douglass admitted. After attending a show by a black minstrel troupe in 1848 he regretted that Negroes had to black-up to conform to minstrelsy's pantomime of racial exaggeration. But he expressed pride in witnessing members of his race perform before an appreciative white audience, something which he felt could contribute to the lessening of prejudice against African Americans.

In the postbellum era more African Americans joined or established their own minstrel revues, sometimes performing in blackface, sometimes not. The careers of important black blues artists such as Gertrude 'Ma' Rainey, Bessie Smith and Ida Cox began in minstrel shows; the composition and publication of minstrel songs formed the basis of the popular music and show-tune industry; and even early white hillbilly singers such as Jimmie Rogers, the 'Father of Country Music', often performed in blackface. Minstrelsy's complex cross-racial politics thus fed into many other branches of American popular culture, and its tendency to transform subcultural folk elements into mainstream commercial gold definitively blurred the boundaries between what was authentic and what merely commodified pandering. Indeed, its influence on the blues calls into question the sometimes romanticised view of that music as the archetypal 'bottom-up' form of unadulterated folk expression.

Minstrelsy remained an important form of working people's popular entertainment to the end of the nineteenth century, even shaping the medium that was to displace it – moving pictures. America's first important 'art' film, D. W. Griffith's *The Birth of a Nation* (1915), and the first 'talkie', Warner Brothers' *The Jazz Singer* (1927), both revolved around blackface performance and minstrel stereotypes, though to very different effect. The former is an overtly racist historical epic that depicts the noble white South of the 1860s rescued from the depredations of unscrupulous Yankees and freed slaves (portrayed by white actors in blackface) by the heroic Ku Klux Klan. The latter is a drama of assimilation in which blackface performance enables a Jewish singer first to escape the restrictions of his ultra-orthodox father and then to reconcile with him, fashioning a modern, ethnically hybrid identity in the process. Griffith's film suggested that the movies would not be as accommodating to African Americans as the minstrel stage had been, whereas *The Jazz Singer* hinted that African Americans would be a powerful force for social and cultural modernisation and homogenisation as the new century progressed.

Movies: popular culture from the top down

It took 25 years from the unveiling in 1893 of Thomas Edison's kinetoscope – a peep-hole viewer accommodating one customer at a time – for the American film industry to develop the kind of corporate business structures that made it the most profound cultural influence on Americans in the twentieth century. This period saw the exhibition of moving pictures progress from fleeting interludes between vaudeville theatre variety acts, through converted storefront movie houses or 'nickelodeons' (often without seating), to purpose-built cinemas that took seriously the comfort of viewers now lured by properly developed narratives and rising production values. It also saw the manufacture of equipment and the production, distribution and exhibition of films become standardised and centralised. The formation of the Moving Pictures Exhibitors Association in 1908 to resist increasing calls for censorship of films and regulation of exhibition venues, and of the Motion Picture Patents Company in 1909, which restricted the use of equipment and the right to produce films to its ten associate members, were early signs of this tendency.

But the crucial development was the emergence of a new kind of national mass audience. By 1914 about 18,000 theatres nationwide were registering over 7 million daily admissions totalling more than $300 million. Moving pictures appealed particularly to the immigrant, working-class wage labourers, many of them non-literate and without English, who flooded into America's great industrial cities in this period. Indeed, most of the entrepreneurs who pioneered the new entertainment form themselves emerged from this class. William Fox, Jack Warner, Marcus Leow, Louis Mayer, Adolph Zukor and Sam Goldwyn were all European Jews with an intimate understanding of the immigrant experience. Early films often dwelt on or alluded to this experience, featuring working-class, sometimes ethnic characters in recognisably urban settings, frequently dealing with the problems of poverty, cultural adjustment or unsympathetic authority, as in Charlie Chaplin's *The Immigrant* (1917). While usually pressed into generic formulae borrowed from dime novels or the popular stage, and played for laughs, thrills or tears, these productions contained a realism and a subversive populism that perhaps lay behind the increasing alarm expressed by social reformers, clergymen and other middle-class guardians of social order and morality at the new form's possibly malign influence.

Such concerns encouraged the industry to appeal to a more respectable type of customer by gentrifying both film content and theatre premises. From the mid-1910s exhibitors built plush cinemas in suburban locations, while filmmakers turned increasingly to literary and historical subjects, putting more 'money on the screen' and shifting the balance of American cinema decisively towards spectacle and escapism. This also made business sense: admission charges rose and a broader, more mainstream family audience was tapped.

The higher levels of capital investment and technological sophistication required for such productions encouraged film companies to abandon the industrial cities of the North and East and move to California where the climate, landscape and natural light were more propitious for filming and where, above all, real estate was cheap. The courts dismantled the Patents Company in 1917 as an unfair monopoly, and independents led the way in developing a new kind of feature film aimed at a classless, national audience. But the cost of investing in sound technology after 1927 led to the emergence of a new cartel of corporations. The 'big five' studios – Paramount, Fox, Loew's (MGM), Warner Bros, and RKO – also pursued policies of vertical integration by buying up distribution and exhibition networks, thus controlling the film business at every level. They could now force independent exhibitors to 'block book' packages of studio product unseen and months in advance of release, and to surrender a disproportionate slice of box office revenues.

But their economic power could not protect the major studios from growing social and moral criticism. Robert and Helen Lynd's seminal sociological study *Middletown* (1929) reported that movies, and the 'private' but much publicised lives of their stars, had displaced religion, school and family as the most important socialising influence on young Americans, sweeping away the remnants of Victorian morality and installing a recognisably modern one. The Catholic Church campaigned against risqué and immoral content in the movies, and the conviction in 1921 of comedy star Fatty Arbuckle for the sex-related killing of a starlet at a Hollywood 'orgy' provoked alarm in Congress and calls for government intervention. The studios responded by forming the Motion Pictures Producers and Distributors of America (MPPDA) in 1922 to co-ordinate industry self-censorship and forestall regulation from outside. But the commercial rewards of sex and violence were difficult to forego. Amid further outrage sparked by the innuendo-laden films of Mae West and the explosive violence of early gangster films like *The Public Enemy* (1931), the MPPDA introduced a code outlining what could not be shown and said on screen. The Production Code or Hays Code (after the MPPDA's head, William Hays) was made mandatory in 1934, from which point any film seeking a general release had to be passed by the Production Code Administration (PCA), which could impose cuts, re-shootings and fines of up to $25,000 on offending producers.

The American film industry was at its most standardised and centralised in the 1930s and 1940s, signalled by its nickname 'the dream factory'. It was also at its most popular. Mass-produced on an industrial basis, films were 'branded' by their studio identities and star names, organised for ease of consumption into familiar genres, and policed for content by the PCA. They conformed in narrative structure to the 'continuity style': a seamless form of storytelling based on sympathetic, simply delineated, goal-oriented characters; linear cause-and-effect sequences of action; and resolutions in which obstacles are overcome and closure is achieved. This 'classical' form of cinema, as it has been called, provided spectators with trancelike immersion in the story within a reassuringly familiar set of conventions that also permitted great variation and novelty. In 1930 weekly cinema attendance was 80 million people, about 65 per cent of the population. It would never reach this level again, but remained high throughout the Great Depression and the Second World War, indicating that going to the movies provided

Americans with respite from life's tribulations and the closest thing to a commonly shared culture available in a period riven by social crisis, class conflict and war.

Was it purely escapism that audiences sought and the industry offered? *Gone with the Wind* (1939), history's most popular film with 206.4 million admissions, suggests it was. But amongst the sumptuous costumes, spectacular battles, tearful love affairs and exotic southern locations (not to mention the stereotyped black characters), the film is also a tale of spirited female independence achieved against the backdrop of a collapsing aristocratic régime in which inherited privilege gives way to a modern, egalitarian order. Such themes clearly resonated with a Depression-era audience and the spirit of liberal populism inculcated by Roosevelt's New Deal.

Other films of the era illustrate this combination of social critique and conservative reassurance typical of Hollywood products. Warner Bros. was characterised by its commitment to the New Deal and its production of liberal, campaigning films such as the prison-reform movie *I Am a Fugitive from a Chain Gang* (1932). But the studio's comedy musical about the Depression was more ambivalent. *Gold Diggers of 1933* stages class conflict between the spunky, self-reliant, but precariously employed showgirls, and the snobbish, privileged male characters who assume that the girls are no better than prostitutes. The girls thoroughly humiliate the men, but the conflict is ultimately resolved in a series of marriages. This escapist ending is counterbalanced by a second, 'realistic' ending constituted by a musical number from the show in which the girls are appearing. 'My Forgotten Man' presents the Depression as a male tragedy of humiliated breadwinners and neglected war heroes, negating the film's earlier focus on the plight of single women and even confirming the assumptions of the male snobs by implying that girls can always walk the streets for funds when times get tough.

Fox's 1940 film version of John Steinbeck's Depression novel *The Grapes of Wrath* also pulled its punches, but was still attacked for being 'un-American.' Steinbeck's chapters on political economy were omitted in favour of focusing on the human drama of the destitute Joad family; and the novel's dark closing scene was replaced by two more uplifting moments from the story. The first is the 'ideological' ending in which Tom Joad goes underground to fight the injustices of a system loaded in favour of the rich and powerful. The second is the 'humanist' ending in which Ma Joad optimistically proclaims the undying spirit of ordinary Americans in the face of adversity, closing the film on an affirmative and apolitically unifying note.

Hollywood's often contradictory blending of escapism and realism, reconciliation and confrontation, was cleverly addressed by Preston Sturges's film *Sullivan's Travels* (1941). Successful comedy-film director Sullivan vows, to the consternation of studio executives, that his next feature will be a socially relevant realist drama about poverty and inequality called *O Brother Where Art Thou?* However, after going on the tramp to experience poverty first-hand, Sullivan concludes that the best service he can do for humanity, particularly the downtrodden, is make another comedy. The proposed film is rewritten as a screwball caper and *Sullivan's Travels* itself, after its brief detour into social realism and tragedy, rushes towards a reassuring comic and romantic resolution.

The dream factory experienced its first major crisis in 1948 when the Supreme Court issued the 'Paramount decree': an anti-trust measure compelling the major studios to divest themselves of their theatre holdings. The classical era entered its twilight as the market opened up to smaller producers and the number of weekly admissions to cinemas declined sharply. The mass audience turned to home entertainment in the new form of television and fragmented along generational lines with the rise of youth culture. The majors sought to adapt to these trends through technological innovation, enhanced spectacle and developing new subject matter specifically for new types of audience. Technicolor, cinemascope, and stereophonic sound were used to lure viewers away from their TV sets, while storylines featuring troubled adolescents and contemporary pop music appealed to the youth market.

The populist tenor of films of the 1930s and 1940s gave way to a more managerial liberalism in this period, reflecting the nation's increasingly middle-class complexion and the general political commitment to the ideal of consensus. Seminal 'juvenile delinquent' films, *The Blackboard Jungle* and *Rebel without a Cause* (both 1955), illustrate this. Each is concerned with generational conflict but is careful to show that there is fault on both sides. Warring parties must shift their positions to a centre ground defined by reason, willingness to communicate honestly, and consideration of the adversary's point of view. Sympathetic and tolerant authority figures are instrumental in this process, embodying a sensitive but strong patriarchy that is prepared to use force to deal with those who refuse to sign up to the consensus, such as the unstable (and, it is implied, homosexual) Plato of *Rebel*, or the resentful proletarian West of *Jungle*. Interestingly, this carefully crafted message was lost on those young fans of the latter film who, stimulated by the sound of Bill Haley's 'Rock Around the Clock' over its opening credits, took to trashing their seats and insulting distressed theatre managers. All the top-down control in the world could not prevent this audience from seizing upon a fragment of the text, bending it to its peculiar world-view, and putting it to entirely unintended expressive uses.

The same could be said of those marginal genres that sprang up in this period in response to an increasingly differentiated market. Melodrama's moments of intense and excessive emotion destabilised narratives that encouraged their female characters – and viewers – to subordinate their own desires to the greater needs of husband and/or family. Horror's monsters gave form to the Freudian unconscious whose implications lingered long after the ghoul was inevitably dispatched in the denouement. Low-budget thrillers presented crime sprees committed by doomed but alluring characters whose subjugation by the law in the film's final seconds was often so perfunctory as to be a mockery of, rather than compliance with, Production Code morality. And science-fiction films, while articulating a fear of invasion by aliens who could be metaphors for a range of threatening 'others' from communists to feminists, also expressed deep reservations about the militarisation of science and the unaccountability of technical élites in America's atomic age.

Nonetheless audiences continued to decline; the proportion of Americans attending cinemas weekly slumped to 10 per cent by 1966. In desperation, autocratic studio heads ceded control of production to a new wave of younger filmmakers who, they hoped, were more in touch with modern, youthful America. The practice of contracting out film production to quasi-independent companies, with studios acting as backers and distributors, increasingly became the norm. The period of what is often termed the 'Hollywood renaissance' (roughly 1965–80) was thus a consequence of industrial crisis and the failure of long-established business formulae, illustrating that popular culture is often at its most open and creative when the institutions that 'own' and control it are at their least confident. Influenced as much by foreign cinema, the international *avant-garde*, and the countercultural attitudes of the time as by the conventions of classical Hollywood, these filmmakers produced a significant body of work in which genre clichés and the continuity system were often ignored or subverted, neat resolutions and happy endings resisted, anti-authoritarian characters celebrated, and mainstream America presented as corrupt, conformist and life-denying.

The main casualty of this period was the Production Code itself. Regarded as a restrictive anachronism for some time, the new wave effectively killed it off with films like *The Chase* (1965), *Bonnie and Clyde* (1967) and *The Graduate* (1967), making way for the age-based classification system that would replace it in 1968. The other main casualty was the movie ideology of consensus and reconciliation. These films staged – and refused to resolve – social and cultural conflicts that reflected a nation riven by battles over civil rights and black power, the Vietnam War, women's liberation and generational attitudes to sex and drugs. *Bonnie and Clyde*'s romantic rebels are brutally annihilated by a law that serves only the interests of greedy banks. *The Graduate*'s idealistic young couple flee, unmarried, from the hellish prison of suburban family life and middle-class career. *Easy Rider*'s (1969) sex, drugs and rock-'n'-roll loving hipsters are assassinated by fearful and bigoted squares. And, in an allegory of the Vietnam War, *The Wild Bunch*'s (1968) grizzled outlaws side with Mexican (read: Vietnamese) peasant revolutionaries fighting a despotic government that is the puppet of sinister foreign (read: US) military powers.

Other filmmakers, though, simply exploited the Code's demise to lard their narratives with gratuitous nudity, expletives and graphic violence, while the breakdown of consensus meant that uncompromising social criticism came from the authoritarian right as well as the libertarian left. *Coogan's Bluff* (1968) and *Dirty Harry* (1972) were arguments for strict patriarchal (some said fascist) discipline to be imposed on America's unruly countercultures, even if constitutional liberties were infringed. So open was the industry at this time that a black cinema of sorts emerged. African Americans had picketed *The Birth of a Nation* in 1915 and attempted to 'answer' it with a film of their own, *The Birth of a Race* (1918). But despite black film pioneers such as Oscar Micheaux, the levels of capital investment required and the grip exerted by the big studios constituted significant obstacles to black participation in American film beyond tokenistic and stereotyped onscreen appearances. The brief flowering of 'blaxploitation' films in the early 1970s, such as *Shaft* (1971) and *Superfly* (1972), was, then, a breakthrough. It represented the first attempt to cater to black audiences through recognisably black storylines and settings – even if these were still too close to caricature for comfort – and employ African American talent behind the camera as well as in front of it.

This period's perhaps more honest reflection of America's diversity did not, however, alleviate Hollywood's financial woes. That was achieved by a return to a traditional emphasis on narrative continuity, escapism, spectacle, and unambiguous contrasts between good and evil spearheaded, paradoxically, by members of the generation of new-wave iconoclasts. Steven Spielberg's *Jaws* (1975) and George Lucas's *Star Wars* (1977) ushered in the age of the blockbuster or mega-picture by convincing studios that simplistic, action-oriented stories with happy resolutions and expensive special effects could tempt Americans back into cinemas in sufficient numbers to generate immense profits from a single release. *Star Wars*' 197 million admissions yielded $323 million from a modest budget of $13 million.

The link it established between advanced special effects, aggressive promotion and box-office gold drove up the average cost of producing a film from $11.9 million in 1983 to $63.8 million in 2003, while average marketing costs rose from $5.2 million to $39.05 million. Huge amounts were now invested in fewer films (yearly production fell from about 500 features in 1937 to about 100 in the 1980s) in the hope of that one massive pay-off.

This has led some commentators to see the 'new Hollywood,' as it is called, as a closed shop churning out expensive, dumb, identikit special-effects extravaganzas that are light on character and narrative as well as formally and ideologically conservative. Hollywood thus reflects the wider culture's turn to the political right since the end of the 1970s. The patriarchal, macho and frequently xenophobic action films of the 1980s and 1990s, typified by the *Rambo* and *Die Hard* series, go some way to support this view. Yet cinema's most expensive ($200 million) and profitable (over $1 billion in global box office) blockbuster, *Titanic* (1997), rekindled the unifying liberal populism of the classical studio era with its emotive attacks on privilege, materialism and women's oppression. Clichéd though some of its elements are, and while its class-war narrative is subservient to one of personal emotional liberation, *Titanic* enabled millions of film-goers to engage critically with the politics of class, gender and personal morality in a pleasurably escapist shared experience, illustrating the continuing power of movies to provide reassurance and social critique in equal measure.

Despite their susceptibility to such formulae, film audiences remain unpredictable. Hollywood studios cannot therefore rely entirely on expensive, focus-grouped blockbusters for profits but must continue to produce smaller-scale, sometimes independently made films, particularly for niche markets such as teenagers, African Americans and even aficionados of 'art' cinema. This is intensified by the imperative to feed the exploding market for DVD titles, now worth more ($15 billion in 2004) than theatrical box office ($9.4 billion). Thus a lively system of subgenres flourishes in the shadow of the blockbuster, more open to bottom-up initiative – as illustrated by the phenomenon of *The Blair Witch Project* (1999), the 'amateur' horror film financed by credit cards, shot on cheap digital video and marketed via the Internet. Also flourishing is a quasi-independent cinema of 'auteurs': filmmakers with a personal vision and signature style like Martin Scorsese, Spike Lee, David Lynch, the Coen brothers or Woody Allen. Such directors will never produce massive profits, but supporting their work allows the studios to claim that they are in the movies for art's sake as well as money's. Contemporary Hollywood's increasingly top-down structure has not, then, entirely emptied its products of variety, distinctiveness or social relevance.

Music: popular culture from the bottom-up

Unlike movies, the making of music is not dependent on significant financial outlays and sophisticated technology. Everyone has a voice, musical instruments are accessible to most, and recording technology has been for much of its existence relatively cheap as well as portable. Thus popular music has been less constrained by corporate control and standardisation than film and television, and hence fundamentally shaped by the vernacular traditions of groups denied access to those media – African Americans especially. The example of minstrelsy illustrates the appetite of white Americans for black 'folk' styles, however distorted by racist assumptions, and the history of American popular music revolves around the repeated 'crossing over' of such styles into the mainstream. This pervasive black influence has brought significant rewards for many black artists and, some would argue, collective progress for African Americans and greater inter-racial understanding. But black music has rarely crossed over entirely on its own terms, raising questions of cultural power, ownership and recognition that go to the heart of the complex politics of race in America.

Prior to the 1920s the economics of the popular music industry rested on the publication of sheet music. Minstrelsy's popularity provided opportunities for numerous black songwriters, many of whom also controlled their own publishing. Some, such as Ernest Hogan, found success by perpetuating derogatory black stereotypes in the 'coon songs' that were so much the rage between 1880 and 1910. Others, such as the Johnson brothers, specialised in more genteel expressions of Negro themes. Others still, such as W. C. Handy, drew directly on the new forms of working-class black musical expression that emerged in the American South in the aftermath of emancipation – blues and jazz. But when it came to recording the new musics, the white-owned companies preferred to use white imitators. The first jazz and blues records, by the Original Dixieland Jass Band and sometime blackface performer Sophie Tucker were issued by Victor in 1917, quickly becoming million-sellers.

This pattern of black innovation and white popularisation continued throughout the 1920s and 1930s, periods defined in terms of black music as the 'jazz age' and the 'swing era'. African American geniuses such as Louis Armstrong and Duke Ellington did most to push the music forward creatively, but it was the aptly named white bandleader Paul Whiteman who was crowned 'King of Jazz', while Benny Goodman, son of Russian immigrants, was hailed as the 'King of Swing'. Segregation marked the consumption of music in live performance too. New York's Cotton Club was the hub of the period's jazz craze, but though the entertainment was black the audience was exclusively white, except on designated 'coloured nights'. For some African Americans, the white passion for black music was no more than voyeuristic racial slumming, and the commercialisation it bred a threat to the music's integrity. Black writer Langston Hughes dismissed the jazz age as 'show nights for the Nordics', while young black musicians turned away from what they saw as the white-friendly sounds of swing to develop a new, more authentically 'black' jazz they could claim as their own. The new sound, 'be-bop', drew deeply on the blues as the bedrock of African American collective identity. But it was also harmonically and rhythmically complex in order, its creators Charlie Parker and Dizzy Gillespie claimed, that white musicians could not copy it and white audiences not understand it. A statement of cultural ownership and authenticity, be-bop was also self-consciously 'difficult', and its displacement of swing in the 1940s signalled the end of jazz as a pop music with mass appeal. Henceforth jazz would be a minority art music, albeit one deeply rooted in African American vernacular culture.

While the major recording companies of the period, Victor and Columbia, initially used white artists to sell jazz and blues to a white audience, severe loss of revenue with the advent of commercial radio caused them to look to black musicians and consumers for salvation. A number of small, independent labels had proved that such a market existed. Okeh Records sold 75,000 copies of the first blues recorded by a black artist, Mamie Smith's 'Crazy Blues', within a month of its release in 1920, and soon a business in 'race records' flourished. By 1925 African Americans were buying 5–6 million discs per year, prompting Victor to devote over 20 per cent of its catalogue to race titles. Race records were segregated from the wider music market – sold in black neighbourhoods, advertised in the black press and, in the case of the major labels, released on specialist race imprints. Sales were published in a separate 'race music' chart alongside the mainstream 'pop' chart. While this segregation allowed a handful of black-owned record companies to emerge, such as W. C. Handy's Black Swan, difficulties paying for advertising and distribution led to their swift absorption by white-owned businesses.

The eventual desegregation of the music market, and the most significant crossover of black culture into the American mainstream in history, was related to yet another economic crisis in the popular culture industries, this time in radio. During the 1940s over a million African Americans left the South for industrial jobs in the North and West, taking their music with them and contributing to the development of a new urbanised black dance music, rhythm and blues or R&B. By 1949 over 400 new independent record labels had emerged to meet the demand for music the major labels ignored. Moreover, radio stations, haemorrhaging audiences and sponsors to television, began programming rhythm and blues to appeal to African Americans enjoying post-war prosperity, inadvertently reaching white listeners who began to demand that 'their' stations play the music and 'their' neighbourhood stores stock the records. White assimilation of the new style was eased by the record industry's 1949 decision to drop 'race music' in favour of 'rhythm and blues' as the term to denote black music. And the racial associations of the style were further obscured by the adoption of the term 'rock 'n' roll' in the early 1950s when R&B releases such as the Chords' 'Sh-Boom' (1954) began to sell enough to appear high on the mainstream pop chart.

The industry trade magazine *Billboard* declared 1955 'the year R&B took over the pop field'. By 1956 25 of the year's top-selling pop records were R&B releases by black artists on small independent labels. A revolution in public taste had occurred, driven by bottom-up pressure from a combination of black musicians and audiences, white teenage music fans, shoestring record companies and economically vulnerable radio stations. The extent of this revolution is indicated by the extraordinary character of the music that was embraced and by the depth of hostility it provoked in certain quarters. Rock 'n' roll songs not only offered an unbridled energy, joyousness and ribald humour largely absent from the world of 'white' pop, they articulated subversive messages about work, fun, sex, the family and race relations that diametrically opposed white middle-class attitudes. Little Richard's 'Good Golly Miss Molly' (1958) prioritised youthful sex over obedience to parental authority. His 'Tutti Frutti' (1956) celebrated polymorphous multiple couplings, the title hinting that they might well be inter-racial. Chuck Berry's 'Roll Over Beethoven' (1956) narrated the replacement of élite white cultural standards by new criteria based on black music and popular taste. And his 'Brown-Eyed Handsome Man' (1956) defined black masculinity as the physical ideal now preferred by women and aspired to by men of all colours.

Rock 'n' roll's success represented a wave of cultural desegregation that accompanied, perhaps in some respects drove, the movement for social desegregation and black civil rights inaugurated by the Supreme Court's 1954 *Brown v. Board of Education* decision. Both Richard and Berry noted how segregated audiences at their southern shows would spontaneously intermingle to the consternation of club owners, concert organisers and police. In response, white citizens' councils and the Ku Klux Klan organised record burnings and boycotts of radio stations that promoted black music. Such activities made little difference to rock 'n' roll's popularity, but the music only became a truly mainstream phenomenon after it was belatedly taken up by the major record companies and identified with white performers, principally Elvis Presley.

The Radio Corporation of America (RCA) bought Presley's contract from Memphis's tiny Sun Records for $35,000 in 1955. RCA held a monopoly on radio technology, supplied weapons to the defence department, and was deeply invested in television, which by 1957 had penetrated 80 per cent of American homes. Presley became the 'King' of rock 'n' roll by virtue of a string of TV appearances throughout 1956, facilitated by his new label. Anxious not to offend, and thus endanger sponsorship, RCA and the networks compelled Elvis to renounce his 'hepcat' clothes and his famously uninhibited dancing, filming him from the waist-up for additional security on the mass-appeal Steve Allen and Ed Sullivan Shows. A lucrative Hollywood contract propelled Elvis to international stardom in a series of increasingly anodyne features from which rhythm and blues elements were progressively drained. Black music had revolutionised American attitudes and achieved mainstream acceptance but, some argued, at the cost of its racial identity and to the ultimate profit of white performers and business interests.

Black music was similarly pivotal and similarly compromised in the second rock 'n' roll revolution of the 1960s. The oppositional youth culture of that decade defined itself through a version of rhythm and blues repatriated to the United States by British musicians who were aficionados of the authentic sounds of 1950s black America. The Beatles and The Rolling Stones had learned their trade by copying the records of independent black-owned or black-oriented labels such as Motown, Chess and Atlantic, and by touring with black originators like Little Richard and Chuck Berry. And the counterculture that coalesced around their sound was more politically black-identified than the white rock 'n' roll fans of the 1950s. An explicit commitment to black freedom and civil rights – as well as to the anti-war movement and to the critique of corporate capitalism in general – now flowed directly from, and fed into, the passion for 'rock' as it was increasingly called, to differentiate it from what was seen as the politically naïve rock 'n' roll of the 1950s. Yet the rock counterculture's figureheads remained predominantly white – with the exception of Sly Stone and Jimi Hendrix, who both ran integrated bands.

The Woodstock Festival of August 1969 is often cited as the high point of this grass-roots cultural and political rebellion structured around popular music. Half a million people attended the free event, organised largely from within the counterculture itself and climaxing with Hendrix's incendiary and satirical version of 'The Star Spangled Banner'. While Woodstock passed without confrontation with 'straight' America, the US authorities were already engaged in covert surveillance and overt harassment of the rock culture. The FBI placed the White Panther Party – founded by John Sinclair and based on the group he managed, the MC5 – on top of its subversive organisations list. Sinclair himself was set up by undercover agents, receiving a ten-year prison sentence for possessing two marijuana joints. The most politically outspoken Beatle, John Lennon, was also subject to FBI surveillance and prevented from entering the country on a number of occasions. Nonetheless, Woodstock's success confirmed to the major record companies that politically radical rock could be good business. They showered bands with large cash advances, divorcing them from the communities that had nurtured them, and co-opted the language and attitudes of cultural and political rebellion into the discourses of advertising and consumer culture. Columbia Records' 1969 promotional campaign was built around the radical slogans, 'The man can't bust *our* music' and 'The revolutionaries are on Columbia', while corporations such as General Motors paid handsomely to use rock songs to soundtrack their TV and radio commercials.

Despite such corporate absorption, the revolutionary rock of this period succeeded in mobilising a youthful 'guitar army', to use John Sinclair's term, which contributed to real social and cultural change through its critique of materialism, its opposition to American imperialism in Vietnam, and its championing of freedom of expression with regard to sex, drugs and personal comportment. It also established popular music as the fundamental touchstone of identity for young Americans. Henceforth, music would no longer be mere amusement: what you listened to defined who you were. Musicians were not entertainers but artists who were judged according to stringent standards of authenticity: they must write their own material, remain accountable to the fan communities they served as gurus and spokespersons, and above all never 'sell out'.

For African Americans, too, music in this period became more overtly a vehicle for individual and collective self-definition. Black listeners and musicians (though not, significantly, the music industry) rechristened rhythm and blues 'soul', a term that denoted not so much any great stylistic development in the music as a desire to assert ownership of it and pride in it, as it crossed further into the mainstream. Such pride was not incompatible with an openly assimilationist outlook. Detroit label Motown, the most significant of a number of independent black-owned record companies that emerged in the early 1960s, rigorously groomed its artists for white acceptance and success on the pop chart, TV and the cabaret circuit, yet it consistently made powerfully joyous music of recognisable blackness. By 1973 Motown was the biggest black-owned company in America, with sales worth $40 million and 135 employees. Some black critics accused Motown of standardising soul and courting the mainstream too assiduously, but its headline artists acquired the same creative freedom as leading rock acts, producing racially conscious, socially critical and musically complex works such as Marvin Gaye's *What's Going On?* (1971) and Stevie Wonder's *Innervisions* (1973).

Soul also pulled in the other direction – not so much deliberately away from the pop mainstream as more definitely towards African American musical roots in gospel and the blues. Atlantic and Stax, white-owned companies with roots in the South and integrated studio bands, specialised in this funkier, less superficially polished but no less sophisticated sound. So too did James Brown, the veteran R&B star who distilled funky rhythm to its essence, attaching to it assertions of racial and sexual pride in hits such as 'Say It Loud, I'm Black and I'm Proud' (1968) and 'Sex Machine' (1970). Soul's twin tendency to reach out for crossover success on the one hand and to assert black distinctiveness on the other reflected a growing tension between assimilationism and cultural nationalism in African American thinking generally. While many blacks saw their music's crossover appeal as evidence of racial progress and empowerment, others denounced its more commercial manifestations as selling out; black militants even pressed Sly Stone and Jimi Hendrix to fire their white band members and take their music in a more radically 'black' direction. As with rock, the music's success made it more vulnerable to commodification. Motown, Stax and Atlantic were all absorbed by voracious entertainments conglomerates in the 1970s and early 1980s. The biggest music star of this period, Michael Jackson, was a Motown protégé who achieved his greatest success with the major label CBS, acquired in 1988 by Sony. Consciously or not, Jackson personified black music's identity crisis in this corporate universe, becoming progressively more Caucasian in appearance, even titling one of his biggest hits 'Black or White' (1991).

The corporate assimilation of black music caused critic Nelson George to proclaim 'the death of rhythm and blues' in a 1988 book of that title. However, a new and powerfully dissident black musical subculture emerged from the blighted post-industrial landscapes of New York City in the late-1970s in the form of rap – or hip hop, as the wider culture that surrounds it is known. Like jazz, rock 'n' roll and rock before it, rap has bitterly divided Americans into those who denounce it, those who live their lives through it, and those who make a living from it. Its frequently misogynistic and anti-social frankness about sex and violence has prompted censorship campaigns and court battles over First-Amendment rights. Its outspoken political attitudinising has led some African Americans to view it as the only trustworthy media information outlet – 'black people's CNN' in the words of rapper Chuck D. And its popularity has created a generation of black entrepreneurs like Russell Simmons or Sean Combs who see no contradiction between associating with the media giants, spinning their music off into fashion, video or computer game businesses, and using their influence to campaign on black social issues or mobilise the African American vote.

As with earlier black music movements, hip hop is torn between reaching for the mainstream and repudiating it. Unquestionably it has galvanised young Americans across the colour line in a post-civil rights age of increased racial polarisation. Yet in a fashion also curiously reminiscent of jazz and rock 'n' roll, this working-class black music's presiding monarch and biggest seller is a white performer, Eminem, whose scabrous, white-trash, proletarian world-view is shaped by his talented black producer, Dr Dre, and bankrolled by the Universal-Vivendi conglomerate. A song such as 'White America' (2002), with its brazen admission, 'Let's do the math, if I was black I would've sold half', artfully revels in these contradictions, which are emblematic of American popular music today.

Part subculture and part mass culture, hip hop is just the latest in a series of dissident vernacular musics to have revolutionised and refreshed the mainstream at the risk of being obliterated by it. It is unlikely to be the last. Yet while American popular music's irrepressible bottom-up energies and racial heterogeneity persist, they do so in constant tension with increasingly powerful corporate impulses toward standardisation and commodification.

Further reading

Belton, John, *American Cinema/American Culture* (2nd edn, 2005).

Compaine, Benjamin N. and Douglas Gomery, *Who Owns the Media? Competition and Concentration in the Mass Media Industry* (2000).

Chapple, Steve and Reebee Garofalo, *Rock 'n' Roll Is Here to Pay: The History and Politics of the Music Industry* (1977).

Cullen, Jim, *The Art of Democracy: A Concise History of Popular Culture in the United States* (1996).

Cullen, Jim (ed.), *Popular Culture in American History* (2001).

Floyd, Samuel A., *The Power of Black Music: Interpreting its History from Africa to the United States* (1995).

Maltby, Richard, *Hollywood Cinema* (2003).

Marc, David, *Demographic Vistas: Television in American Culture* (1996).

Miller, James, *Flowers in the Dustbin: The Rise of Rock and Roll, 1947–1977* (1999).

Neal, Mark Anthony, *What the Music Said: Black Popular Music and Black Public Culture* (1999).

Perkins, William Eric (ed.), *Droppin' Science: Critical Essays on Rap Music and Hip Hop Culture* (1995).

Schatz, Thomas, *The Genius of the System: Hollywood Filmmaking in the Studio Era* (1996).

Starr, Larry, and Christopher Waterman, *American Popular Music: From Minstrelsy to MTV* (2003).

Storey, John, *Cultural Studies and the Study of Popular Culture: Theories and Methods* (2003).

Websites

Columbia Journalism Review – Who Owns What: www.cjr.org/tools/owners

Hip Hop Summit Action Network: www.hiphopsummitactionnetwork.org

MediaChannel.org – PopCultMedia: www.polarity1.com/popcult.html

Motion Picture Association of America: www.mpaa.org/home.htm

Nielsen Media Research: www.nielsenmedia.com

Recording Industry Association of America: www.riaa.com/default.asp

US Census Bureau: www.census.gov/statab/www

CHAPTER 16

America at the millennium

Richard Crockatt

Whose American century?

At the beginning of the third millennium America was to all appearances supreme. Whether one measured American power by the size and dynamism of its economy, continuing attractiveness to immigrants, the global spread of leading American consumer brands, the ability to project military power and to wield political influence, the use of the English language, the prevalence of American popular culture – in all these categories American power was unmatched. Even the global preoccupation with the theme of anti-Americanism told the same story of American supremacy. Anti-Americanism was simply the other side of the coin of America's global power and success. It was regularly suggested by commentators that American global influence was proportionately larger than that of the great empires of the past – the Greek, Roman, and British. Indeed one of the most popular themes among commentators both outside and inside the United States was 'American empire'. The world was now effectively 'unipolar'. American power might be resented but it was not seriously contested by any other nation or grouping of nations.

Perhaps not surprisingly, as the millennium approached, commentators from all parts of the political spectrum resurrected the notion of an 'American century'. The term had originally been coined in February 1941 by Henry Luce, publisher of *Life* and *Time* magazines, in an effort to encourage Americans to embrace the opportunities and responsibilities that America's rising power offered. America, he asserted, was uniquely placed by virtue of its ideals, history and present power to lift the world out of its pain and suffering. War was raging in Europe, and America was on the side-lines of history. Luce called not for intervention in the war as such but for a shift in America's self-image. His was a call to Americans to put their isolationist heritage behind them and seize the opportunity to imprint America's ideals of 'freedom and justice' on the century. Within a few months, the Japanese attack on Pearl Harbor catapulted Americans firmly into the American century, ensuring that Luce's journalistic slogan would assume a lasting position in the popular consciousness.

Though the American century remained a reference point for some time after the Second World War for discussion of the United States and its role in the world, Luce's confident tones were not always easy to reproduce during the strained years of the Cold War. Indeed from the start some, such as Franklin Roosevelt's vice-president, Henry Wallace, were concerned that the idea of an American century contained an element of hubris. He preferred the idea of the 'century of the common man'. The debate in the 1990s demonstrated more clearly than ever that the American century had always been a politically loaded term rather than a description of reality. Some commentators, especially academics, were highly sceptical of the notion that the whole world could or should be described in such exclusively American terms. Many politicians, however, seized on the notion as a useful means of laying claim to a certain conception of America and its role in the world. In his 1999 State of the Union Address President Bill Clinton implicitly endorsed the original spirit of Luce's pronouncement when he asked Americans to reach for 'the next American century'. Indeed the Clinton administration buzzwords of 'democratic enlargement' and 'constructive engagement', meaning broadly the spread of American influence and ideas, were central themes of the Clinton foreign policy from the beginning of his presidential terms. However, the most potent and politically consequential contribution to this debate came from an organisation whose ideas would become central to the political philosophy and practice of the George W. Bush administration: the Project for a New American Century (PNAC).

The PNAC was formed in 1997 by a group of right-wing politicians and policy intellectuals, many of whom had either served in the Reagan administration (1981–9) or had been influential supporters of it. Indeed, as the PNAC Statement of Principles asserted, the organisation's purpose was explicitly to revive a 'Reaganite' vision of the world as an alternative to the 'incoherent policies of the Clinton administration'. At the core of the PNAC lay a group of so-called 'neo-conservatives' whose position, as far as foreign policy was concerned, rested on a number of convictions: that 'moral clarity' must underpin American foreign policy, that American 'global leadership' was indispensable, that military power was decisive in international relations, and that the principal threats to America derived from the Middle East and global Islam. A new 'strategic vision' must thus be developed, based on American global leadership, American military predominance, and a willingness to intervene decisively to protect and promote American interests. Among those who signed the PNAC's Statement of Principles and an important open letter to President Clinton in 1998 were Dick Cheney, later vice-president to George W. Bush, Donald Rumsfeld, Bush's secretary of defense, and Paul Wolfowitz, Rumsfeld's deputy at the Defense Department. The open letter to Clinton in 1998 had criticised his administration's reliance on inspections as a means of controlling the threat posed by Saddam Hussein and called for the 'removal of Saddam Hussein's régime from power' as the 'only way to protect the United States and its allies from the threat of weapons of mass destruction'.

There was, then, a direct line from the founding of the PNAC to the policies of the Bush administration, and crucially it represented a partisan narrowing, indeed an appropriation, of the idea of an American century. That Clinton could also call for Americans to 'reach for the next American century' indicates the presence of deep divisions in America over political priorities and values. Underneath the rhetoric of unity and consensus, engaged in by all political parties in their never-ending efforts to seize the centre-ground of American politics and to present themselves as the real bearers of America's traditions and values, there lay differences that went as deep as any in recent American history. These extended far beyond foreign policy. In fact, foreign policy was less important as a source of domestic division than were social and moral issues. Disputes over 'guns, gays and family' symbolised the resurgence of the 'culture wars' that in one form or another had raged throughout American history but achieved a new focus during the presidency of George W. Bush. The essence of the culture wars lay in the ever-present conflict between pressures for change and the desire for continuity and tradition. 'Liberals' in America (the quotation marks are necessary because no one now dares lay claim to the label, whatever their political views) generally favoured the flexible adaptation of social values and institutions in line with changing realities, albeit within the framework of America's founding values. Conservatives or traditionalists, and particularly those influenced by the resurgent evangelical Christian churches, favoured a more 'absolutist' conception of moral values and an adherence to a more literal interpretation of America's founding values. Typically conservatives regard liberals as destroyers of true Americanism because they entertain compromise and complexity. In turn, liberals regard conservatives as hopelessly rigid and dangerously archaic in their approach to social and moral problems. Meanwhile, both invoke the principles of freedom, liberty and democracy.

Perhaps the most striking aspect of the culture wars at the turn of the millennium was the prominence of religion as a factor in discussion of practically all aspects of public policy. It has long been the case that Americans attend churches in larger numbers than do the citizens of most other Western countries and that the numbers of Americans professing belief in God is correspondingly high. At the approach of the millennium, however, religion entered public life as a major force to an unprecedented degree. The roots of this development lie in the 1970s with the increase in subscription to evangelical forms of Protestantism and the associated rise of political pressure groups such as the Moral Majority, which had a significant impact on the election of Ronald Reagan in 1980. The Moral Majority declined in the 1980s but gave way to the Christian Coalition and an array of other pressure groups that have expanded their influence via the media, publishing houses, and political organisations. Significantly, these groups weighed in consistently on the 'conservative' side of key public debates about abortion, gay rights (and especially gay marriage), genetic research, and other social and moral issues that have seriously divided Americans. The Republican Party has been the main beneficiary. It is generally agreed, for example, that the electoral chances of the 2004 Democratic Party presidential candidate John Kerry were seriously damaged by the Massachusetts Supreme Court's upholding of a state law permitting same-sex marriage. The timing (February 2004, at the beginning of the election campaign) and the place (Kerry's own state) were bad enough; Kerry's refusal to condemn the decision rendered him especially vulnerable.

In some respects the face-off between the protagonists in the culture wars was a debate about the values of the 1960s. Clinton was the first 'baby-boomer' to become president and hence the first to have come of age during a decade that was popularly remembered as one of drugs, the counterculture and opposition to the Vietnam War, which many conservatives believed had come close to destroying America. Clinton's opposition to the Vietnam War was routinely brought up against him. Significantly too, though John Kerry was a decorated Vietnam veteran, what came over to much of the American public in the 2004 election, once his political opponents had gained control of the message, was that he had thrown away his Purple Hearts (medals), turned against the war, and had in any case (so it was claimed in some highly contentious political advertisements) not been the hero he was made out to be. Besides an impressive capacity to spin the message in the media, conservatives had at their disposal some powerful political weapons, not least Republican majorities in both houses of Congress from 1995 onwards, which only made the battle more open and more savage. At the turn of the millennium America was a deeply divided country, aptly symbolised in the knife-edged presidential election of 2000 and its disputed outcome that brought George W. Bush to power. The result of the 2004 presidential election was less contentious but the divisions in America, following a bruising campaign, were just as obvious. There was no single idea of the American century but rather a struggle to define what America was and what it stood for.

There were many ironies in this situation. While George W. Bush and his administration were strongly associated with religious values, Bill Clinton, as his memoirs amply demonstrate, was at least as devout as Bush, as indeed was Al Gore, Clinton's vice-president and Bush's opponent in the election of 2000. (A similar irony was apparent in the 1980 election when Reagan, the occasional church-goer, was the darling of the Christian right, while Jimmy Carter, who wore his evangelical Christianity on his sleeve, was associated predominantly in conservative minds with 'liberal' causes.) By the same token, in the election of 2004 George W. Bush, who had avoided going to Vietnam in the 1960s, managed to portray himself as the man to rely on in military affairs – and hence the ideal commander-in-chief of the armed forces – while the Democratic candidate, John Kerry, who had served with distinction in Vietnam, was pictured as wobbly on national security.

What these examples demonstrate is that in politics the ability to control public images is often more important than realities, but they also demonstrate two other important truths. The first of these is that, despite intense conflicts between political extremes in America, there are equally powerful pressures towards unity and consensus. Each side seeks to claim the prized national values as its own. Political battles in America reflect this complex interchange between consensual ideologies and conflicting notions about what they mean and how they should be put into practice. No doubt political conflict in all countries share this characteristic to some extent. The distinctive feature of the American case is the combination of the long-standing nature of these consensual ideas – ideas of freedom, justice, liberty, equality, going back at least to the eighteenth century – and the explicitness and intensity with which they are held. Moreover, they have a universalising drive; America has always been a nation with a mission. The question is always: who gets to define the mission?

On the question of religion, for example, it is clear that all candidates for high public office are expected to subscribe to the notion of religious faith; it is part of the American public philosophy, despite the constitutional separation of church and state. In short, religious belief in itself is not the key issue in distinguishing between candidates but rather the particular brand of religious belief and how it is deployed politically. At the millennium (perhaps appropriately, given the symbolism of such turning points in fundamentalist belief systems), and particularly after 11 September 2001, the political running, as we have seen, was being made by evangelicals who injected intense moralism into an American public debate that was already characterised by a concern with moral values. George W. Bush was the political beneficiary of such sentiment, in part out of genuine religious conviction and in part out of a recognition that it spoke to a large political constituency in America that he needed to cultivate. Bush was able to project the idea that his version of the national credo was the one to back because it was consonant with the religious as well as the secular convictions of Americans at that particular moment in history.

On the question of national security and the role of commander-in-chief (a role granted by the US Constitution to the president), once again the public expectation is of the president's identification with the armed forces. However, when it comes to elections, the issue is not whether a candidate for office will back the armed forces or believes in defending the national security of the United States – these must be taken as givens – but how successfully they can project the message that the country's security is safe in their hands – a very different and more subjective judgement. Once again, Bush was able to generate confidence among the American people that he was the one to do the job. This was probably the decisive factor in the election of 2004. Of course, this did not happen overnight. The margin in the election of 2000 was extremely narrow and according to many observers was stolen by the Republicans with the help of the United States Supreme Court, thanks to a decision that checked the progress of the recount in the state of Florida. It was circumstances as much as political convictions or skill that enabled Bush to secure among the American people his identification with America's core values. The chief circumstance was September 11, and this leads us to the second important truth illustrated by the above examples: context is all important.

Which version of America's core values – which idea of the American century – is deemed to be most acceptable or necessary at a particular moment will depend on the needs of the time. The content of the idea of the American century does not remain static. The overwhelming challenge in the first years of the new millennium was supplied by the terrorist attacks of September 11. This event largely dictated the direction of the Bush administration and set the terms for the election of 2004. More importantly, it constituted a great divide in the American and indeed the global experience

September 11 and the war against terrorism

Visions of the American century prior to 11 September 2001 could scarcely have anticipated the turn of the events in the new millennium. Terrorism was on the international and American agenda prior to the attacks on the twin towers and the Pentagon, but as yet it was a worry rather than all-consuming concern. The twin towers of the World Trade Center had been bombed in 1993, but without the catastrophic outcome of the later attacks. The American embassies in Tanzania and Kenya were bombed by terrorists in 1998 with great loss of life, but at a distance from the United States, and the bulk of the casualties were non-American. The Clinton administration retaliated with missile attacks on targets in Afghanistan and Sudan, whose governments were known to be harbouring members of al-Qaeda, the principal suspects in the bombings. Finally, in 2000, towards the end of Clinton's presidency, an American warship in the harbour of Aden was the target of a suicide bombing.

In retrospect, the pattern was unmistakable: under the leadership of Osama bin Laden, already by the late 1990s America's most wanted international criminal, al-Qaeda was conducting a concerted campaign of terror on American and other targets. In 1998 bin Laden had issued a fatwa urging his followers to 'kill Americans and their allies . . . as a matter of individual duty for every Muslim', this aim being supposedly in line with the Quranic injunction to 'fight the pagans all together as they fight you all together . . . and fight them until there is no more tumult or oppression, and there prevail justice and faith in God'.

In retrospect the pattern is blindingly obvious; at the time, such events competed for attention with a mass of other events and concerns. September 11 changed perspectives of the past, the present and the future. The impact of these terrorist attacks was felt at many levels and it will be years before a full evaluation of its significance can be made. For the student of American Studies in the first decade of the new millennium, however, three areas seem of paramount importance. First, there was an overwhelming and novel awareness of America's vulnerability. September 11 established an immediate and violent connection between America and the world 'out there', which exceeded even the impact of Pearl Harbor in important respects. The Japanese attack had taken place on American territory (though not yet a state of the

Union) but at a distance from the mainland; the nature and location of the enemy was clear; and the attack led to war fought with the conventional means of large armies, battleships and bombers. The attacks of September 11 took place at the heart of America's home territory, against buildings and in cities that symbolised American power and achievement. Moreover, while both Pearl Harbor and September 11 came out of the blue – contemporaries referred to the 'sneak attack' on Pearl Harbor – the largely civilian nature of the targets on September 11 put these assaults in a separate category: the category of terrorism. The enemy was, if not always invisible, certainly elusive. The sight of the erasure of a familiar skyline and of ordinary people going about their ordinary business – the horrific immediacy of the television images surely explains part of the impact of these attacks – defied a sense of normality. Interviews with Americans then and since testified to the overwhelming sense of a violation not only of American life and society but the idea of humanity itself. To those who said that terrorism and other comparable acts of barbarism take place with some regularity in many parts of the world, the American could only reply: 'but not here'. Even as the immediacy of the event faded, it remained a marker point of a break in experience, the main outcome of which was the conviction that terrorism was now the chief evil in the world and the top item on the political agenda.

It is important to stress that the overwhelming sense of vulnerability provoked by the terrorist attacks did not imply unanimity on the means of dealing with it. Even on the day itself some of those interviewed on the streets of New York expressed the hope that America's response to the attacks would not mirror the violent motives of the attackers. There was a great deal more diversity of opinion in the United States on how to conduct the newly declared 'war on terror' than either government or much of the media suggested. Nevertheless the all but irresistible pressure on government to make a response that reflected the enormity of the acts ensured that it would be substantial. This imperative indicates a second area in which the impact of September 11 was felt: it supplied a focus for American foreign policy, which since the end of the Cold War had been significantly lacking. Attempts during the 1990s to develop a new 'big idea' comparable with the Cold War priorities of containment and deterrence had had only limited success. President George Bush's 'new world order' scarcely survived the Gulf War of 1990–1. It was a useful slogan around which to rally a coalition to push Saddam Hussein out of Kuwait, but once that was achieved the idea proved to have not enough legs to carry it. It assumed a global consensus on essentials that simply did not exist. Clinton's ideas of democratic enlargement, the expansion of market democracy and constructive engagement were intellectually coherent and fitted some of the foreign policy ventures undertaken by the Clinton administration but were too general in scope. The advantage of the 'war on terrorism' was that it identified a threat around which American foreign policies could coalesce and in this respect it bore comparison with the Cold War in which the communist threat was the energising principle in policy formation.

Not that the idea of a war against terrorism automatically prescribed the means to prosecute it. Indeed, some objected to describing it as a war at all since the enemy was unlike the antagonist in a conventional war. There was no such thing as 'terrorism' in the singular, it was said; only 'terrorisms' with many different sources and objectives. The danger of using the rhetoric of conventional war was that excessive expectations might be raised about the ability to defeat terrorism in general. None of these objections made much impression on government in America. The war on terrorism was a broad-based effort that included war against the governments of certain nations on the grounds that they harboured terrorists or supported their activities – hence the military operations against Afghanistan and then Iraq – as well as a wide range of security measures at home and abroad designed to locate terrorist cells and protect American and other citizens against terrorism. These included new security procedures at airports and numerous other public building and facilities, the granting of new powers to security agencies and the police to investigate suspected terrorists, intergovernmental agreements on the sharing of information and intelligence, new powers to freeze the assets of known terrorist organisations, and numerous other comparable measures. At home these efforts were capped by the establishment of a new Department of Homeland Security. Abroad pressure was placed on governments, most notably that of Pakistan, to proceed vigorously against Islamic militants who supported Osama bin Laden and al-Qaeda. At the American military base of Guantanamo Bay, Cuba, the United States set up a prison for suspected terrorists captured in Afghanistan, raising a furore about the legality of the indefinite internment of prisoners without trial or legal representation.

However, the impact of September 11 went beyond even these particular policies and actions in that it led to a redefinition of the goals and the means of American foreign policy. The priorities were expressed in a number of speeches and documents of the Bush administration, most notably Bush's 2002 State of the Union Address and the National Security Strategy document published in the autumn of the same year. The first of these is best known for its use of the phrase 'the axis of evil', which identified a number of 'rogue states' – Iraq, North Korea, and Iran – associated with the spread of international terrorism and weapons of mass destruction. There was some discussion about whether Iran should be included in the group since there were liberalising forces at work there which might be undermined by its being included under the rubric of evil. But the real motive behind the use of the phrase, according to an influential study of the Bush administration by journalist Bob Woodward (*Plan of Attack*, 2004), was the administration's desire to prepare the public for a policy of waging war on Iraq with the aim of removing Saddam Hussein from power. The National Security Strategy announced in September 2002 was evidently consistent with this goal in introducing the idea of 'pre-emption'. According to this doctrine it was neither wise nor necessary to wait until a threat manifested itself before dealing with it; the old doctrines of containment and deterrence had no relevance in a world plagued by terrorism and the existence of weapons of mass destruction that could be passed on by rogue states to fanatical terrorist groups. America should take the initiative to defend not only itself but the whole civilised world. It is clear, not least from pronouncements of members of the PNAC, that these ideas were in the making before September 11, but it is equally clear that September 11 was the catalyst for their implementation.

The third decisive effect of the terrorist attacks of September 11 was to transform the fortunes of the Bush presidency. After a disputed election and a faltering first few months, during which Bush struggled to present a clear and consistent image at home and abroad, he was able to turn the crisis to his political advantage. September 11 made his presidency in the way that the Falklands War of 1982 made Margaret Thatcher's prime ministership. On the day itself, after initial signs of wobble when he was spirited away for security reasons on a plane to an airforce base well away from Washington, Bush returned to the White House and made a television address to the nation in a clear move to take command of the situation. Even so, for a while it seemed that the mayor of New York, Rudolf Giuliani, was the hero of the hour in his role as the mouthpiece for those who had suffered most directly from the attacks. But in the days after September 11 Bush regained credibility, and even enhanced it in the eyes of many as he put his imprint on the crisis with a series of major speeches and measures to counter terrorism. It would not be too much to say that the Bush presidency was defined by September 11 in the sense that the outlines of many of his policies, both domestic and foreign, were set by the war on terrorism, even if that meant violating some of the hallowed ideas of his party. Traditional Republican fiscal conservatism, for example, went by the board as the costs of fighting terrorism led to the accumulation of large federal budget deficits. In fact the election of 2004 turned to a considerable degree on the issue of which candidate could be trusted to handle the war on terrorism. Though the Democratic Party candidate, John Kerry, managed in the TV debates with President Bush to more than hold his own and crucially to present himself as potentially 'presidential', it is likely that many voters accepted the argument of the Bush camp that it would be foolish to change leaders in a war.

Much as the war on terrorism dominated the foreground of events, however, it was not the whole story of the United States at the beginning of the new millennium. Economic and social changes, which can be collectively summed up in the word 'globalisation', were equally as important in defining the kind of world in which Americans lived. Indeed the wave of terrorism that grew in the 1990s and climaxed in the attacks on the twin towers and the Pentagon in 2001 can be seen as both a reaction to globalisation and an instance of it. It was a reaction in the sense that it pitted religious and tribal fundamentalism against secular capitalism or, in Benjamin Barber's suggestive phrase, 'Jihad v. McWorld'. But the attacks of September 11 were also an instance of globalisation in that the terrorists exploited to the full the technologies and institutions of the society they were attacking.

What was the 'new economy' talked of in the corridors of power in Washington at the millennium? And what changes were taking place in American society? We shall examine these questions in the following sections.

America and the 'new economy'

In an economy as large and complex as that of the United States it is possible to find evidence to illustrate almost any argument. To its critics, the US economy remains dangerously subject to boom and bust cycles; witness the long boom of the 1990s and the recession of 2001–2 triggered by the collapse of high-tech stock values. The US economy is also, its critics point out, increasingly productive of inequality. As British journalist and historian Godfrey Hodgson has noted, 'by 1999 the average CEO [Chief Executive officer] earned a remarkable 107 times more than the average worker, double the ration in 1989 and five times that in 1962'. These figures cover only wages and salaries. When total income – which includes return on investments, shares and so on – is taken into account the disparities are even greater, to say nothing of total wealth, which includes property. Critics of the US economy also argue that such growth in employment as has occurred has come predominantly in low-paid service jobs with high turnover of personnel, which are vulnerable to fluctuations of the economy. In short, in these and other respects, American prosperity is built on shaky foundations.

To admirers of the US economy, the above problems, if they are conceived to be such, are incidental by-products of a highly efficient and flexible machine that essentially does what it is supposed to do, which is to produce and distribute goods and wealth on an unmatched scale and to the benefit of society as a whole. Even the relatively poor in America, the argument goes, are well off by global standards. The key ingredient of success, it is claimed, is the market which, if allowed to function with minimum regulation by government, will continue to generate material benefits and, furthermore, sustain America's core values of freedom and opportunity. The bottom line is that the American economy remains the supreme engine of the global economy, which is a clear vindication of the values that underpin it.

The above viewpoints represent broadly liberal and conservative positions respectively, each selecting out certain elements for emphasis and downplaying others. However, these positions do not translate simply on to the national political level. While it is true that Republicans continue to portray the Democrats as a 'tax and spend' party and the Democrats continue to describe the Republicans as purveyors of 'voodoo economics', these labels tells us little about the actual policies of the parties. In practice there is a high measure of consensus in political circles on what has been called the 'free market creed'. Liberals have conceded much ground to conservatives in this field and the differences are more about means than ends, at least as regards the national political parties. Thoroughgoing critiques of the reigning orthodoxy are to be found outside government rather than between the parties. In this respect there has been a general rightward trend in the United States which, as we shall see later, has been true of other spheres of American life.

In the absence of such a thing as a wholly neutral viewpoint we can nevertheless gain a broader perspective by placing these views in their historical contexts. We can begin with some comparative figures, which are indeed striking. At the turn of the millennium the United States accounted for over a quarter of all the world's output of goods and services, which is to say more than that of Japan, Germany and the UK, its principal competitors, combined. 'In terms of both production and consumption', wrote British historian Niall Ferguson in his bestselling *Colossus: The Price of America's Empire* (2004) 'the United States is already a vastly wealthier empire than Britain ever was'. America's economy was also truly global by virtue of such companies as McDonald's, Coca Cola, Nike and many others. According to Benjamin Barber, such companies were 'more central players in global affairs than nations' – or at least than many smaller nations. Because so many multinational companies have their headquarters in the United States and because the US market is such a magnet for global trade, the United States stands to gain from globalisation. Not that this comes without cost. In a highly interdependent world the United States, like all nations, is vulnerable to global economic fluctuations, but its size and strength enables it to ride out crises that damage less robust economies. In the 1990s the economies of South-East Asia fell into deep recession following a currency crisis in Thailand; in 2002 the Argentinian economy collapsed.

What was striking about the situation in 2000 was the scale of the change in assessments of America's economic health as compared with ten years before. In the late 1980s and early 1990s there was much talk of American 'decline', prompted by Paul Kennedy's *Rise and Fall of the Great Powers* (1987), whose publication coincided with a sharp fall on the New York Stock Exchange, seemingly confirming Kennedy's gloomy forecast of the coming costs of American 'imperial overstretch'. At the same time there was a flurry of books on the rise of the economic challenge from Japan, the most dramatic bearing the title *America's Coming War with Japan*. The 'tiger economies' of East and South-East Asia, with their low labour costs and virtual absence of government regulation, similarly seemed poised to eat away at America's manufacturing base. Ten years on such fears looked like fantasies. Japan became mired in economic stagnation and the tiger economies suffered serious damage from the crisis in Thailand, which affected the whole of Asia. All this coincided with the longest period of sustained growth in America's recent history. As Godfrey Hodgson observed, in the run-up to the 2000 presidential election even George W. Bush did not attempt to deny that the economy was in good shape and he restricted his attacks to the failure (as he saw it) of the Clinton administration to capitalise on this boom.

The fact is that, whether through luck or good management or a combination of both, Clinton handed over a strong economy and low levels of federal debt to George W. Bush. The subsequent recession in 2001–2 and the slow and halting recovery thereafter reflected a number of realities, the first being that the boom of the 1990s had relied heavily on the spectacular rise of new dot-com stocks to unrealistic and unsustainable levels. Another was high consumer spending based on an expansion of credit to unheard-of levels. The sharp downturn in the stockmarkets in 2000–1 brought the boom swiftly to a close, indicating that the prosperity of the

Clinton years had been built on rather less firm foundations than he and his supporters had claimed. Under the Bush administration the national emergency of September 11, coupled with the war on terrorism, further dented business and consumer confidence, while government expenditure on Afghanistan, Iraq and anti-terrorist measures turned the annual budget surpluses of the later Clinton years into large deficits. Bush's strategy for recovery was the classic conservative one of tax cuts, whose effect, it was hoped, would be to release consumer purchasing power to get the economy moving again. In the early months of 2003 the signs were that the strategy was achieving some success, as indicators showed swift growth in the economy as a whole and sharp increases in employment and consumer spending. Stock prices were nowhere near what they had reached in the late 1990s but it was generally agreed that they had been artificially high then. As the 2004 election approached, however, the strong signs of recovery of the previous year were no longer so obvious. The combination of tax cuts and the increasing drain on the economy on account of the administration's expenditure on the war in Iraq threatened the basis of public finances.

The situation was thus not straightforward. The US economy remained the primary determinant of the global economy but that very fact rendered the United States vulnerable to events elsewhere. In a globalising world no nation, whatever its size, was exempt from the effects of interdependence. At the approach of the millennium some claimed that the United States was witnessing the advent of a 'new economy' driven by the technological revolution. A combination of the communications revolution – especially the Internet – and automated production opened out the possibility of new horizons of economic growth by virtue of huge productivity gains. By these means, it was believed, the business cycle itself could be overcome. But while there was much justification for the claim that the US economy – and indeed those of all developed nations – was undergoing a structural shift comparable with the introduction of electric power in the early twentieth century, there was no evidence that this exempted the United States from the inexorable logic of the business cycle. Dependence on oil was a further factor exposing the US and other economies to conditions that lay only partially in their control. The oil market, like the stock market, was a sensitive barometer of international confidence. The atmosphere of crisis provoked by the terrorist attacks of September 11 and their aftermath, not least the war in Iraq, pushed oil prices higher, eventually in the autumn of 2004 to the highest ever levels of over $50 a barrel. (In 1973, prior to the Arab–Israeli or 'Yom Kippur' War and the institution of the oil boycott by Arab producers, the price had been $2.50 a barrel.)

However, there were other reasons for the rise in oil prices, in particular the swiftly growing demand for energy by China, which was engaged in a crash programme of modernisation. One observer expressed the view that 'if the Chinese were to drive as many per capita passenger miles as Americans currently do each year, it would take only five years to use up all the Earth's known energy reserves' (Benjamin Barber, *Jihad v McWorld*, 2001). China's ambitions were shared by many other countries in the developing world. Of course, it is never easy to extrapolate from present trends into the future; over the years many of the forecasts of 'limits to growth' have proved to be either wrong or exaggerated. However, there could be little doubt that the aspiration of the developing world to achieve a standard of living enjoyed by Americans would have an impact on global and hence American resources and conditions. Moreover, it was becoming clear that competition for global resources would have environmental as well as economic implications, for increasing prosperity would place further strains on the delicate balance between human desires and needs on the one hand and the natural environment on the other, with the possibility of global warming and other types of environmental change bringing with them incalculable consequences. Interdependence thus extended far beyond the realm of the economic.

The question was what attitude the United States would adopt towards these and other related developments. On the one hand, America was the arch globaliser – supporter of free trade and minimally regulated markets to the extent that many equated globalisation with Americanisation. In so far as American interests dictated open global markets, then its standpoint could be said to transcend the narrowly national. Yet the United States was a nation among nations intent like others on protecting its own interests, and to that extent its globalism was self-serving and selective. Opposition to the Kyoto Accords on climate change centred on the possible damage to the US economy of the limits on emissions set at Kyoto. Furthermore, along with other developed nations, the United States refused to agree to demands from the developing nations at the Cancun international trade conference in early 2004 for the reduction of government subsidies to agriculture, a move that would have ensured fairer access of goods from developing countries into the United States. In short, globalisation did not mean the disappearance of nationalism, least of all in the United States, which had a greater capacity than any other nation to assert its will. A striking feature of the United States at the turn of the millennium was the persistence of a potent national ideology at a time when it was apparently under threat from two sources: globalisation on the one hand

and increasing demographic diversity at home on the other. It is to the latter issue we now turn.

American society and the American nation

The oldest cliché about America is that it is a nation of immigrants. At the millennium that was more evident than ever. A decisive step had been taken in 1965 by the Johnson administration when it passed legislation whose effect was dramatically to change the composition of the American population. In the 1950s the bulk of immigrants to the United States – around 70 per cent – came from Canada and Europe; in the three decades after the 1965 legislation was passed, Canada and Europe accounted for only 14 per cent of incomers, while the figures for Latin America and the Caribbean were 47.9 per cent (Mexico accounting for 23.7 per cent) and for Asia 35.2 per cent. Demographers call this the 'second great migration', the first having been the surge of immigration between 1890 and 1914. Both phases of immigration decisively changed the ethnic mix of the American population, reducing the proportion of 'old stock' Americans in the population, but the second migration exceeded even the first in numbers. According to the 2000 census the Latino population (a term that includes all those coming from Spanish-speaking countries) now matched that of African Americans at around 35 million or 12 per cent of the total population. Asian Americans stood at 11.6 million or 4 per cent of the population, but like the Latino population was growing fast by virtue of both immigration and natural increase. Meanwhile, the Native American population was growing rapidly too. Estimates varied about when the old stock American population would become a minority, but most believed that moment would come before the end of the twenty-first century.

It is one thing to note the changing facts about American immigration, quite another to gauge their significance. It is clear that to many Americans these figures were disturbing. Some observers saw a growing clash between the emerging ideology of multiculturalism and traditional American ideas of individualism and self-help. The fear was that ethnic and other groupings would become more important than individual citizenship, which is the basis of the American legal system and the panoply of individual rights that are guaranteed by it. These anxieties were most visible in the growing reaction against affirmative action programmes, which to their critics enthroned group rights over those of the individual and thus struck a blow at the foundations of American society and constitutionalism. Affirmative action programmes in the spheres of education and employment were instituted in the Johnson administration and became embedded through US Supreme Court decisions in the 1970s, though they remained controversial. The Supreme Court broadly endorsed affirmative action where it was not blatantly depriving individuals of their rights (for example, by setting fixed quotas for minorities whose effect might be to deprive a member of the majority group of 'equal opportunity'). Since then, however, the Court has applied ever stricter criteria in judging affirmative action cases, and in this the justices are in line with trends in American public opinion. Thus at a time when ethnic diversity is increasing, many Americans are reluctant to concede ground to group interests.

An additional concern is the 'ghettoisation' of the United States – its dissolution into competing groups with a consequent loss of unity, cohesion and even national identity. It has partly to do with geography. In many instances immigrant groups congregate in particular localities, creating subcultures large enough, for example, to sustain the use of languages other than English, most notably Spanish among the Cuban community of Miami in Florida, and Mexican in parts of southern California. Such examples, which can be replicated to a degree in the case of Asian and other recent immigrant communities, raise the spectre of, in Arthur Schlesinger Jr's words, the 'disuniting of America'. It is not so much the immigrant numbers themselves that constitute the threat – the United States has a long history of absorbing immigrants – as the celebration of 'difference', which, it is felt, may disincline immigrants to identify with the nation. After all, during the great migration of the early twentieth century the reigning ideology was of the 'melting pot', which meant integration. The melting pot idea, however, had been long discarded to be replaced by metaphors such as the 'salad bowl', implying the maintenance of separation. In the eyes of critics such as Schlesinger these developments were particularly damaging in the sphere of education, which has been the traditional vehicle for Americanisation. The incipient balkanisation of the population, he believed, undermined the notion of a common national heritage, a common history. Whose story was to be told as America's story? Was a synthesis of American history any longer possible? If a common history was no longer available to which all could appeal, what possible common future could there be? These and other related anxieties were powerfully expressed by the influential scholar and commentator Samuel Huntington, in a book entitled *Who Are We? America's Great Debate* (2004). In the changing composition of the American population, he believed, nothing less than America's national identity was at stake.

Demographic changes on this scale could also have implications for foreign policy. With the old stock European proportion of the population dwindling, would there not be a reorientation of American foreign policy towards Asia? Again geography played a part. The centre of gravity of the 'new economy' of the United States moved to the West and South as the old smoke-stack industries of the Northeast died, and trends in settlement by immigrants and population movement generally have paralleled this shift. Since the United States reached the West Coast in the mid-nineteenth century the country has always looked westward across the Pacific as well as eastward across the Atlantic. Nevertheless, during the twentieth century, when forced to make a choice, for example in deciding on strategy in the Second World and Cold Wars, the United States chose a 'Europe-first' strategy, to the anger of some on the Republican right who felt that America's economic and political destiny lay more with Asia. In the twenty-first century it seemed that America's orientation would be increasingly global, which at the very least is likely to reduce the significance of Europe in its calculations. Experience with what the Bush admninistration described as 'old Europe' during the period leading up to the opening of the Iraq war in March 2003 could be said to have confirmed this trend. France and Germany's opposition to American policy provoked some on the American right to downplay the old Atlantic connections, which in any case were based on now defunct Cold War priorities.

These conclusions about the likely impact of demographic change cannot be taken as foregone, however. The first two points – anxiety about the replacement of individual rights by group rights and fear of disunity by ghettoisation – make the assumption that ethnic groups always and only think of themselves in the light of their group identity, but in many instances this is a false assumption. Though on single issues of relevance to particular groups, opinion may show a marked ethnic character, across the spectrum of issues this is not the case. Returns from the 2000 presidential election, for example, show that support for the two major parties was well represented in the Latino population. 'Hispanics', Godfrey Hodgson has observed, 'may be a cultural block but not a political nation.' The same holds true for the election of 2004. Furthermore, the earlier history of American immigration suggests that over time a process of assimilation takes place, one feature of which is the emergence of more variegated patterns of voting as well as acculturation to the norms of American society. Nor must it be forgotten that the United States has much previous experience of assimilating immigrants who were deemed by some to be unassimilable. It is still the case that as a proportion of total population there were more foreign born in the United States in the first two decades of the twentieth century than there were at the beginning of the twenty-first. Finally, the issue of the United States' foreign policy orientation has never been and never could be a matter of either Europe or Asia. The United States and Europe are deeply intertwined by trading, financial, security, cultural and other considerations and will remain so. Indeed, the European Union remains the United States' single largest trading partner, even if Japan exceeds any single nation of the European Union in this respect. As for American anger with 'Europe' over Iraq, evidently this is not with all of Europe, given that Britain is a close ally and governments of the former communist nations of Eastern Europe are keen to align themselves with America. The goal of the Bush administration was rather to drive a wedge between its opponents and supporters in Europe.

For every fear about the changing social composition of the United States, then, we can find balancing factors that suggest that the changes described above do not all operate in the same direction. Indeed one can argue both that important social changes are under way and that the United States has the capacity, based on a history of adaptation and experience, to deal with them. Even if the changes are on an unprecedented scale they are not of a radically novel sort. Much more difficult to address will be challenges to America's way of life such as are being set by environmental change, in particular global warming. The United States possesses the framework of institutions and values to cope with new populations and issues of individual and group rights; it is not so clear that the United States possesses frameworks for addressing problems whose solutions could require radical lifestyle changes. While the same holds true for most nations of the world, the United States has most to lose by such radical measures as may become necessary in the coming decades since it consumes considerably more energy per capita than any other nation in the world. The idea of setting limits to growth cuts away at arguably the most fundamental of all American values – the right to improve one's condition, to progress in life, to become in all senses of the word richer.

However, even here it cannot be assumed that American ingenuity will be helpless in the face of such apparently intractable problems. New ideas about the disposal of carbon dioxide emissions through a process known as 'carbon sequestration' (which essentially means the storing of carbon in underground spaces vacated by the extraction of fossil fuels) may, along with other technical advances, provide at least a partial solution to the problem of global warming. Would such measures, however, only postpone the day when radical changes in social attitudes and social life will be necessary to safeguard the American way? Such speculations take us beyond what historians and social commentators can reasonably envisage. What is clear is that the United States will need to call on all its resources of technical ingenuity and social innovation to meet the challenges of the near to medium-term future. What are the signs that such resources are available?

The balance sheet

There can be little doubt that the United States displayed an increasing conservatism across the spectrum of social and political issues at the turn of the millennium. This could not be put down only to the effects of September 11 since the signs were unmistakable well before that – in the rise of the religious right, the resurgence of traditionalism in moral and social issues, and the Republican gains in Congress during the 1990s. Some argue that the Republicans now possess the kind of dominance in the political system that Roosevelt and the Democrats gained in the 1930s. The Republicans, on this view, are now the 'sun' around which the Democrats as the 'moon' revolve. In the Roosevelt case, Democratic dominance lasted for over 30 years, effectively institutionalising interventionist 'big government' ideas through legislation and appointments to such key bodies as the Supreme Court of the United States and other parts of the federal judiciary. George W. Bush's re-election in 2004, it is held, may signal the same sort of scenario for the Republicans, representing the ultimate conservative triumph over the legacy of Roosevelt and his successors such as Kennedy and Johnson. In fact, the transition may already have taken place, the 2004 election being the culmination of a process that began with the Reagan presidency in the 1980s. On this view, Clinton's two terms were a temporary aberration, based on Clinton's supreme political skills, the absence of a suitable challenger among the Republicans, and also, crucially, on Clinton's concessions to many of the principles of the conservatives, particularly on economic and social policy.

As yet no definitive answer can be given to the questions raised above. Much depends on whether Republican gains in the Congressional 2004 elections are sustained, on how many judicial appointments Bush is able to make, and on the results of the presidential election of 2008. Answers to these questions in turn depend on the course of events, international and domestic, in the coming years. A long and inconclusive war in Iraq could drain support from the Bush administration just as a success would bolster it, though as always definitions of success and failure will be subject to self-serving political interpretation. Economic problems, not least those that the Iraq war may generate, equally could constrain the agenda of the Bush administration. In 2005 expenditure on defence, although larger by far in absolute terms than in any previous administration at just over $400 billion, as a proportion of gross domestic product was nowhere near the largest in America's 'peacetime' history. In the late 1980s the Reagan administration was spending over 6 per cent of GDP on defence as compared with the 2005 figure of 3.6 per cent. Nevertheless, expenditures on the Iraq war and other ventures have kept on rising and have the potential to undermine the health of the economy, as do very high levels of domestic debt. America's adverse trade balance could also destabilise the American economy since much of America's debt is held overseas, making the United States vulnerable to decisions made by others. Interdependence, as suggested earlier, is a double-edged sword. Nevertheless, the Clinton years demonstrate that, such is the dynamism in the American economy, it is possible to generate positive growth and budget surpluses in a remarkably short period of time.

Finally, one can reflect that at the turn of the millennium America presents the paradox of social and political conservatism coupled with, as always in American history, ceaseless and ruthless innovation in business and technology. Indeed there has always been a radical strain in American conservatism from the industrial leaders and their apologists of the 'gilded age' through the moguls of the 1920s to their present neo-conservative heirs. There has also, however, been another tradition in American history, known as liberalism or progressivism, which tempers the radical individualism of American life with a more communal or co-operative idea of public good. Its present eclipse, then, is not necessarily a sign of its total disappearance.

Further reading

The 9/11 Commission Report: Final Report of the National Commission on Terrorist Attacks Upon the United States (2004).

Barber, Benjamin R., Jihad v. McWorld: Terrorism's Challenge to Democracy (1995).

Daalder, Ivo H. and James M. Lindsay, America Unbound: The Bush Revolution in Foreign Policy (2003).

Hodgson, Godfrey, More Equal Than Others: America From Nixon to the New Century (2004).

Huntington, Samuel, Who Are We? America's Great Debate (2004).

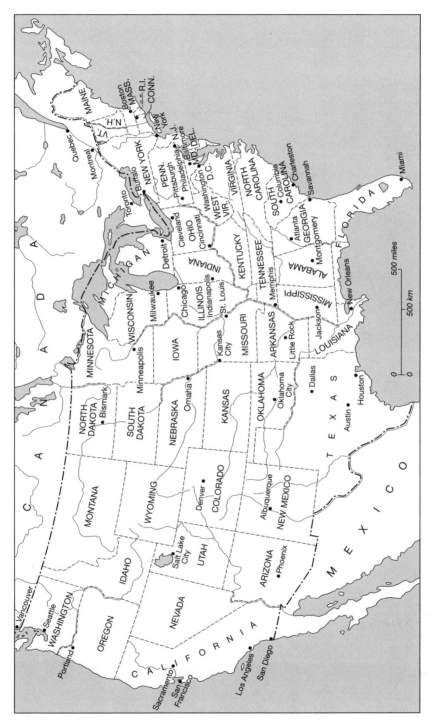

Map 1 The American States.

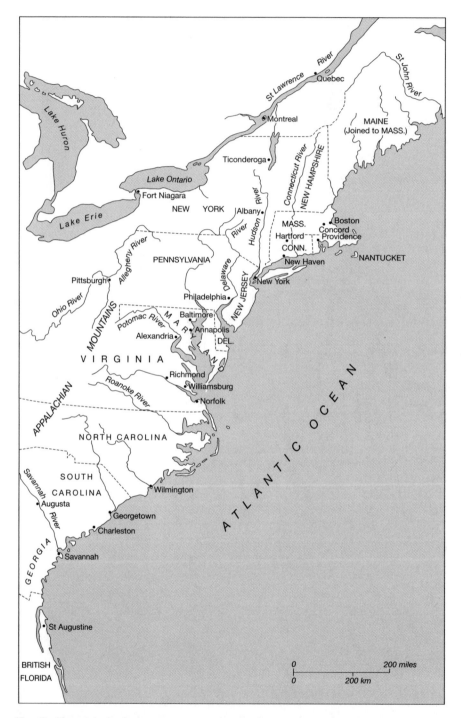

Map 2 The original colonies.

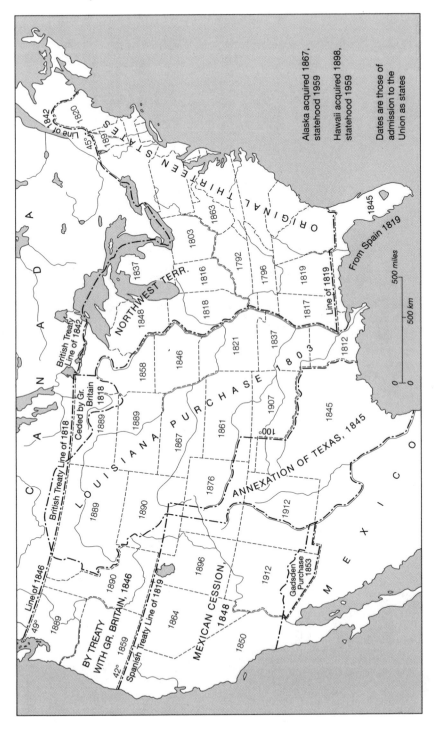

Alaska acquired 1867, statehood 1959

Hawaii acquired 1898, statehood 1959

Dates are those of admission to the Union as states

Map 3 Territorial acquisitions.

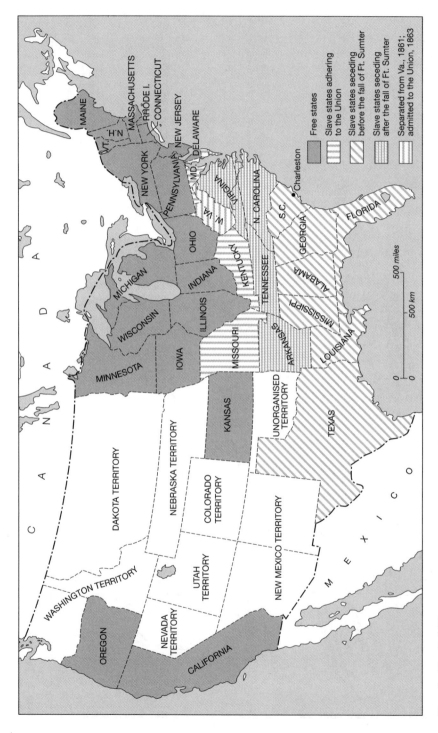

Free states

Slave states adhering
to the Union

Slave states seceding
before the fall of Ft. Sumter

Slave states seceding
after the fall of Ft. Sumter

Separated from Va., 1861;
admitted to the Union, 1863

500 miles

500 km

Charleston

Map 4 The Civil War.

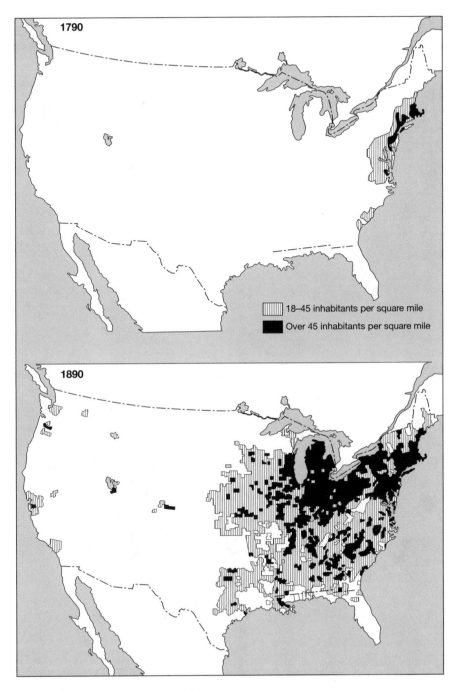

1790

18–45 inhabitants per square mile

Over 45 inhabitants per square mile

1890

Map 5 Population expansion, 1790–1940.

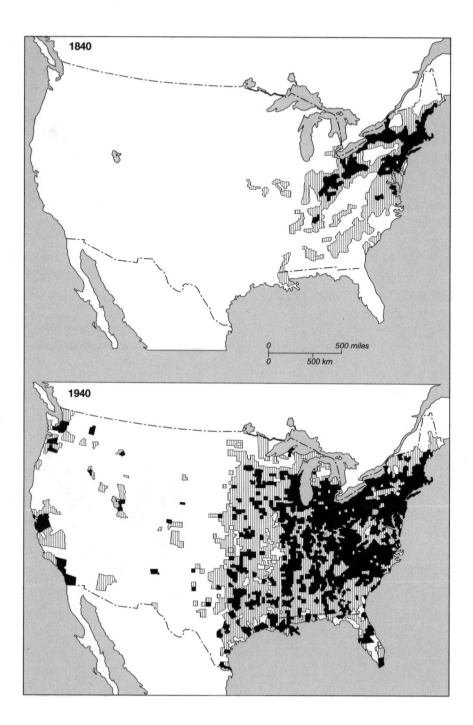

Notes on the contributors

CHRISTOPHER BIGSBY is Professor of American Studies at the University of East Anglia. He has written numerous books on aspects of American culture, including a three-volume *Critical Introduction to 20th Century American Drama* (1982–5), *Modern American Drama, 1940–2000* (2000) and *Arthur Miller: A Critical Study* (2005).

COLIN BONWICK is Professor Emeritus at Keele University. He is the author of *English Radicals and the American Revolution* (1977) and *The American Revolution* (1991), and is the author of numerous articles on aspects of the American colonial period. He is currently writing a political biography of Thomas Jefferson.

ELIZABETH J. CLAPP is Lecturer in American History at the University of Leicester. She is the author of *Mothers of All Children: Women Reformers and the Rise of Juvenile Courts in Progressive Era America* (1998), as well as a number of articles on women in the Progressive era. She is currently working on a study of Anne Royall and the political culture of Jacksonian America.

CHRISTOPHER CLARK is Professor of History at the University of Connecticut. His books include *The Roots of Rural Capitalism* (1990), *The Communitarian Moment* (1995) and (with Nancy Hewitt) *Who Built America?* Vol. 1 (2nd edition, 2000). He is currently completing a short social history of the United States between the 1770s and the 1870s.

PETER COATES is Reader in American and Environmental History at the University of Bristol. He is the author of various books and essays on human relations with the rest of nature, including *The Trans-Alaska Pipeline Controversy* (1991), *In Nature's Defence: Americans and Conservation* (1993), *Nature: Western Attitudes Since Ancient Times* (1998) and (with William

Beinart) *Environment and History: The Taming of Nature in the USA and South Africa* (1995).

RICHARD CROCKATT is Professor of American History at the University of East Anglia. His publications include *The United States and the Cold War* (1989), *The Fifty Years War: The United States and the Soviet Union in World Politics, 1941–1991* (1995) and *America Embattled: September 11, Anti-Americanism and the Global Order* (2003).

NICK HEFFERNAN is Senior Lecturer in American Literature and Popular Culture at University College Northampton. He has published on music, film, popular fiction and cultural theory, and is the author of *Capital, Class and Technology in Contemporary American Culture: Projecting Post-Fordism* (2000).

DANIEL KANE is Lecturer of American Studies at the University of East Anglia. His most recent publications include *All Poets Welcome: The Lower East Side Poetry Scene in the 1960s* (2003) and *What is Poetry: Conversations with the American Avant-Garde* (2003).

GAIL D. MACLEITCH is Lecturer in American Studies at King's College London. She is just completing her first book, which examines Iroquois entanglement in the British Empire in the mid-eighteenth century. In addition, she has published various articles on Indian involvement in the market economy and aspects of imperial–frontier cultural relations.

BRIAN HOLDEN REID is Professor of American History and Military Institutions and Head of the Department of War Studies at King's College London. He has written widely on American military history, and his books include *J. F. C. Fuller: Military Thinker* (1987), *The Origins of the American Civil War* (1996), *Studies in British Military Thought* (1998), *The American Civil War and the Wars of the Industrial Revolution* (1999) and *Robert E Lee: Icon for a Nation* (2005).

AXEL R. SCHÄFER is Lecturer in United States History at Keele University. His main research interests are in US intellectual and political history, with a particular focus on the Progressive era and Cold War America. He is the author of *American Progressives and German Social Reform, 1875–1920* (2000), and is currently completing a book on evangelicals, the Cold War state, and the resurgence of conservatism in the United States, 1942–1990.

ADAM I. P. SMITH is a Lecturer in the History of the United States at University College, London. He is currently completing a book on politics during the American Civil War for Oxford University Press.

ALLAN LLOYD SMITH is Senior Lecturer at the University of East Anglia. His books include *American Gothic Fiction* (2004), *Uncanny American Fiction* (1987), *Eve Tempted: Hawthorne* (1984) and, as co-editor, two collections of essays: *Modern Gothic: A Reader* (1996) and *Gothick: Origins and Innovations* (1994).

HOWARD TEMPERLEY is Emeritus Professor of American History at the University of East Anglia. He is a former editor of the *Journal of American Studies* and a former President of the British Association of American Studies. His most recent books are *After Slavery: Emancipation and its Discontents* (2000) and *Britain and America since Independence* (2002).

MARGARET WALSH is Professor of American Economic and Social History in the School of American and Canadian Studies at the University of Nottingham. Her recent publications include *Motor Transport* (ed.) (1997), *Working Out Gender: Perspectives from Labour History* (ed.) (1999), *Making Connections. The Long-Distance Bus Industry in the United States* (2000) and *The American West: Visions and Revisions* (2005).

JOHN S. WHITLEY is Reader in American Studies at the University of Sussex. He has published books on Golding and F. Scott Fitzgerald, an edition of Poe's stories and a descriptive bibliography of Poe, in addition to a number of essays on American writers.

Index

Abbey, Edward 25
Adams, John 332
affirmative action programmes 391–2
Afghanistan 289, 382, 384
African Americans 19, 26, 33, 39, 52,
    64–5, 76–9, 111, 141, 156, 158,
    231, 251, 253, 264, 268, 339–45,
    355, 358–60, 366–74, 391
agriculture 11–14, 37, 40, 107, 129,
    133–4; *see also* plantation system
Albee, Edward 6, 277, 288–91, 299
Alcott, Bronson 176, 181
Algarín, Miguel 264, 270
al-Qaeda 382, 384
American Civil War 59–60, 66, 93–6,
    179, 191–3, 204–5, 216, 304–5,
    311–12, 317, 320, 337–41, 357
American Philosophical Society 44, 47
American Studies 1–2, 100–1, 110, 123,
    125, 142, 273, 382
American values 57, 60, 63, 380–1, 387,
    391, 394
American War of Independence 78–80,
    96, 274, 332–3
Anderson, Benedict 54
Andrews, Bruce 266–8
anthropology 99, 111
anti-Americanism 303, 376
anti-Semitism 250, 284–5
Apollo missions 23, 212–13
art 16, 143–4, 182
Ashbery, John 247, 257–62
Asian 'tiger' economies 388
Asian Americans 268, 391
assimilation 148, 159–64, 168
Austen, Jane 171–2, 225–6
Auster, Paul 235, 238

Austin, Mary 14, 144, 233
autonomy, individual 68–9, 330–3,
    346–8

Bailyn, Bernard 43, 65
Baldwin, James 232, 291
Baraka, Amiri 257, 260, 268, 291
Barber, Benjamin 66, 386, 388, 390
Barry, Philip 278, 281
Barthes, Roland 266
Beckett, Samuel 277–8, 293–5
Beecher, Catherine 335, 341
Belasco, David 275
Bellow, Saul 230–1
Bercovitch, Sacvan 57–9, 70
Berlin, Ira 38–9
Berrigan, Ted 260–4
Bierce, Ambrose 192
Bierstadt, Albert 16, 143
Bill of Rights 79, 88
bin Laden, Osama 382, 384
Boone, Daniel 357
Boorstin, Daniel 56
Boucicault, Dion 275
Braque, Georges 247
British Americans 46–8
British Empire 302–3
Brook, Peter 286
Brooke, Sir Alan 321
Brown, Capability 16
Brown, Charles Brockden 170–3
Brown, Dee 102–3, 316
buffalo herds 15, 21, 27
Burke Act (1906) 108–9
Bush, George W. 2, 6, 26, 302–3, 315,
    318, 324, 377–81, 384–6, 389,
    393–6

Bush, George snr 383
Bush, Laura 302

Calloway, Colin 118, 120
Canada 17, 19–20, 30–1, 47, 130
capitalism 57–8, 70, 104–5, 120, 129,
    133, 148, 155–6, 165, 168, 193,
    352, 371
Capote, Truman 234
carbon sequestration 394
Carson, Kit 143
Carson, Rachel 23, 26, 213
Carter, Jimmy 21, 116, 380
Cather, Willa 144, 223, 225
Catlin, George 99, 143
Chaplin, Charlie 276, 361
Chaucer, Geoffrey 245
Chávez, César 21, 23
Cheney, Dick 378
Chinese Americans 141, 237, 299
Chopin, Kate 193, 196, 220, 233
Christian Coalition 379
citizenship 45–6, 63–4, 152, 156–62
    passim, 333–4, 339–40, 343,
    347, 391
civil rights 23, 53, 64, 157, 163–4, 232,
    348–9, 365, 371
Clapp, Moses A. 109, 113
Clark, Mark 318
Clinton, Bill 27, 377–84, 388–90, 395–6
Clinton, Hillary 297–8
Cody, William 15, 99, 143–4
Cold War 152, 212–13, 217, 255,
    306–9, 316–17, 322, 347–8,
    377, 383–4, 393
Coleridge, Samuel Taylor 176–7, 182
colonial government 41–3
colonisation 11–13, 29–48, 102–4, 110,
    126, 135, 148, 327–31
Columbus, Christopher 10, 101, 110
communitarianism 67–70, 185
Conrad, Joseph 225
consensus theory of American history
    59–73 passim
conservationism 7, 21, 128, 134, 136
conservatism 61, 356, 378–80, 385–7
Cook, Jig 275–7
Coolidge, Calvin 210

Cooper, James Fenimore 4, 20, 98–9,
    143, 173–5, 178–9
Corso, Gregory 257–9
cotton-growing and the cotton gin
    81–3, 107–8
cowboy stories 144–5
Crane, Stephen 191–5, 220–1
Crèvecoeur, J. Hector St John de 5,
    50–1, 54, 63–4, 162
Crockett, Davy 143, 357
Crosby, Alfred J. 7–8, 10
cultural history 143–5
cultural imperialism 103
culture wars 378–9
cummings, e.e. 242
Cummins, Maria 335
Cunliffe, Marcus 311, 320
Currier, Nathaniel 143
Curtis, Edward 99, 310
Custer, George Armstrong 145

Dances with Wolves 15, 98, 119
Darwinism 99, 193–4
Dawes Allotment Act (1887) 108–9,
    113–14
Dean, James 231
defence expenditure 212, 306, 309,
    322, 396
Defore, Daniel 75
Democratic Party 2, 25, 92–3, 348, 379,
    386–7, 395
demographic change 392–3
Derrida, Jacques 266
Dickens, Charles 173, 229
Dickinson, Emily 180–1, 240–2, 258
Dillingham Commission (1907) 159
disease, effects of 8–10, 30–2, 77, 83,
    102, 129, 157
distribution of income and wealth
    37–40, 183, 386
Doctorow, E.L. 147, 234
Dos Passos, John 222, 228–30
Douglas, Frederick 189, 358–9
drama, 20th-century 273–301
Dreiser, Theodore 191, 195,
    220–3, 279
DuBois, W.E.B. 251, 253
dust bowl conditions 14, 134

ecological imperialism 8, 11
economic activity 33–7, 198, 386–91
Edison, Thomas 209, 360
education 44, 114, 330, 334, 341–2
egalitarianism 62–3, 66, 74
    and liberalism 67–71
Eisenhower, Dwight D. 212, 290,
    313–14, 320, 323
Eliot, T.S. 242–54 *passim*, 263, 289
elite groups 41–6 *passim*, 331
Ellis, Richard 68–72
Ellis Island 157–9
Ellison, Ralph 232, 237–9
Emancipation Proclamation (1863)
    95–6, 251
Emerson, Ralph Waldo 20, 61, 175–87
    passim
Enlightenment thinking 4, 44–5, 52,
    59, 72–3, 79, 154, 156, 171, 177
entertainment industries 352–6
environmental damage 134–7, 390
environmentalism 7, 21–6, 98, 213
Equal Rights Amendments 344, 348
equality, concepts of 46, 69–74
Erdrich, Louise 119, 237, 268–70
ethnic communities 140, 163
ethnicity, concept of 110
ethnogenesis 111
ethnohistory 101
European Union 394
Everglades National Park 18
exceptionalism, American 50–2, 557,
    62, 70–2, 125, 303

Faulkner, William 225–9, 233, 252, 282
Federal Theatre 280–1
Federal Writers' Project 85
feminism 297, 344, 348
Fiedler, Leslie 171, 196
film industry 99, 144, 230, 357, 360–7
First World War 148, 158–9, 191, 211,
    229, 248, 251, 309, 312, 314,
    318, 323
Fitzgerald, F. Scott 3, 6, 7, 221–5,
    228–9, 290
folk culture 356–8
Foner, Eric 63–4, 67–70
Ford, Henry 207, 210–13

foreign policy of the US 304, 307,
    313–14, 319, 377–8, 383–4, 393–4
Foucault, Michel 266
Founding Fathers 53, 59, 66, 72–3,
    78–81, 89–91, 333
Franklin, Benjamin 31, 44, 157,
    198–200
Freud, Sigmund 227, 277
Friedan, Betty 348–9
frontier thesis 124–7, 167, 183–4
Frost, Robert 180, 245–6, 265
Fulbright, J. William 307
Fuller, Margaret 176, 185
fur trade 31, 106–8, 129, 135

Galbraith, John Kenneth 21–2, 320
gambling ventures 120
Gandhi, Mahatma 186
Garland, Hamlin 191, 193
General Electric 209, 353
George, Henry 70
George, Nelson 373
Gettysburg Address 94
'ghettoisation' 392–3
Gilman, Charlotte Perkins 196, 344
Ginsberg, Allen 249, 257–9, 264
Giuliani, Rudolf 385
Glaspell, Susan 275–7, 297
global warming 390, 394
globalisation 216–17, 306, 354, 386,
    388, 390
Golding, William 229, 231
Goldman, Emma 234, 344
Gore, Al 26, 380
gothic fiction 171–2, 175, 190, 195
Gramsci, Antonio 70
Grand Canyon 18
Grant, Ulysses S. 312, 318, 321
Great Awakening 45, 47
Great Depression 14, 210–11, 228–9,
    279, 345, 362–3
Greenpeace 24
Greenstone, J. David 61
Grenada 318
Grey, Zane 144
Griffith, D.W. 360
Group of Seven (painters) 20
growth, economic 33–4, 396

Guthrie, Woody 21
Guthrie-Smith, Herbert 13

Habakkuk, H.J. 202
haiku 244
Haley, Bill 364
Hall, Donald 243, 257
Hamilton, Alexander 200
Handy, W.C. 368–9
'Harlem Renaissance' 251–3
Harmon, Alexandra 110–11
Hartz, Louis 52–73 *passim*
Hawkes, John 229–30, 235
Hawthorne, Nathaniel 4, 171–4, 177–9, 185, 188, 190, 195, 327
Hays Code 362, 365–6
'HD' 242, 244, 248
Heller, Joseph 230
Hellman, Lillian 280, 297
Hemingway, Ernest 223–9, 285
Hendrix, Jimi 371–3
hip hop 374
Hobbes, Thomas 46
Hodgson, Godfrey 386, 388, 393
Hofstadter, Richard 55, 60
Holmes, Oliver Wendell 179–81
Homestead Act (1862) 132
Hoover, Herbert 210
House UnAmerican Activities Committee 279–81, 285–6; *see also* McCarthy, Joseph
Howe, Daniel Walker 59
Howe, Henry 203–4
Howe, Susan 241, 266
Howe, Tina 298
Howells, William Dean 194, 221
Hoxie, Frederick 114
Hudson River School 16, 20
Hughes, Langston 251–3, 369
human rights 78–9, 156
Huntington, Samuel 60, 392
Hussein, Saddam 315, 378, 383, 385

iambic pentameters 240, 245, 255
Ibsen, Henrik 275, 285
'imagined communities' 54
imagism 243–5
immigration 11, 32, 101, 140, 147–69, 193, 204, 217, 391–3

imperialism 5–6, 42, 48, 148, 302–3, 325, 372; *see also* cultural imperialism; ecological imperialism
'Indian', use of term 100
Indian Claims Commission 116
Indian identity 110–14, 117–18
individualism 46, 67–71, 74, 156
industry and technology 198–217
Iraq War (2003) 302, 311, 315, 318–19, 322–4, 384–5, 389, 393–6
Ireland 11, 150, 154–5, 163–4, 204
Irving, Washington 172–3
isolationism 306–7

Jackson, Andrew 69, 107
Jackson, Michael 356, 373
Jacobs, Harriet 189, 336–7
James, Henry 179, 195–6, 220–1
jazz 368–9, 373–4
Jefferson, Thomas 3, 10, 12, 47, 53, 78–9, 84, 94, 130, 166, 171, 198, 304, 308, 310, 313, 333, 337
jeremiads 58–9, 87
Johnson, James W. 231, 251
Johnson, Lady Bird 24
Johnson, Lyndon B. 24, 52–3, 119, 311, 391–2, 395
Johnson, Samuel 64, 78
Jones, LeRoi *see* Baraka, Amiri
Joyce, James 280

Kant, Immanuel 182–3
Kazan, Elia 279, 285–6
Keats, John 225, 228
Kennan, George F. 319–20
Kennedy, Edward 21
Kennedy, John F. 23, 215, 238, 290, 348, 395
Kennedy, Paul 306–7, 388
Kerouac, Jack 22, 233, 257, 259
Kerry, John 21, 379–80, 386
King, Martin Luther 20, 52, 57
Koch, Kenneth 257, 259
Kristeva, Julia 266
Kyoto Accords 390

labour unions 166–8
laissez-faire doctrine 70

land rights 106–9, 114, 128–32
Lewis, Meriwether 26
Lewis, Wyndham 244, 247
liberalism 51–74, 157, 165, 213, 356,
        364, 378–80, 387, 396
    economic 67, 217
    and egalitarianism 67–71
liberty, concepts of 46, 53
Liddell, Hart, Sir Basil 320
Lincoln, Abraham 23, 52, 57, 59, 81,
        91–5, 126, 275, 304, 311, 316
Lipset, Seymour M. 55, 61
literacy 43–4, 330–1, 334–5, 357
literature 143–5, 170–96, 335; see also
        novels; poetry
Locke, John 46, 53–61, 65, 67, 181
Longfellow, Henry Wadsworth 11–12,
        179–80
Lorca, Garcia 293
Louisiana Purchase (1803) 84–5, 92,
        107, 130
Lowell (Mass.) 201–2
Lowell, James Russell 179–80
Lowell, Robert 254–6

MacArthur, Douglas 319
McCarthy, Cormac 144
McCarthy, Joseph 2–3, 256, 259;
        see also House UnAmerican
        Activities Committee
McCarthy, Mary 233, 277
McClure, Michael 257, 259
Ma-con-no-qua 112
Mailer, Norman 230, 234
Mamet, David 293–6
'manifest destiny' doctrine 92, 126,
        130–1, 175, 310
March, William 227, 229, 231
Márquez, Gabriel Garcia 236
Melville, Herman 4, 175, 187–92,
        223, 225
Mencken, H.L. 194, 227–8
Mexico 92, 130, 139–40, 148, 164,
        304–12 passim
Miller, Arthur 230, 274–89
Milton, John 242, 255–6
minstrelsy 358–60, 368
Mitchell, Margaret 226–7
Momaday, F. Scott 119, 144, 237

motherhood, attitudes to 333–7,
        345, 347
multiculturalism 138–42, 148, 165, 264,
        268, 391
Mumford, Lewis 207, 213
music industry 368–74
Myrdal, Gunnar 52–7, 60, 63

Nabokov, Vladimir 235
Nagel, Joanne 117
national identity, American 2–5, 8,
        16–17, 51–8, 63, 73–4, 161–3,
        172, 188, 270, 273, 392
national parks 17–25, 134
nationalism, ethnic and civic 54, 63,
        161–2, 168
Native Americans 5, 8–12, 30–2, 38,
        98–121, 128–9, 135, 138–40,
        145, 172, 237, 268–9, 293, 300,
        310, 391
natural environment, attitudes to and
        relationships with 7–8, 15–16,
        19–22, 25–7, 44, 175, 21516
New Deal policies 21, 116, 211, 213,
        345, 363
New Western Historians 126–7, 131
Nietzsche, Friedrich 173, 194
Nixon, Richard M. 24, 305, 316
Norris, Frank 191, 194–5, 220–1
North Atlantic Treaty Organisation
        (NATO) 314–15
novels 220–39, 273, 357

objectivist poets 249–51
Odets, Clifford 278–9, 285
Olson, Charles 257, 260
O'Neill, Eugene 275–82 passim,
        288–9, 294
Oppen, George 249–51, 271
Oppenheimer, J. Robert 22

Paine, Thomas 69, 357
participation, political 65–6, 71–2, 162,
        168, 333
Patton, George S. 314, 318
Peacock, Thomas Love 171–2
Pearl Harbor 253, 306, 309, 311, 377,
        382–3
Picasso, Pablo 247, 252

plantation system 75, 78, 82–4, 108, 112, 329–31, 337–8
Plath, Sylvia 233, 256–7
Poe, Edgar Allan 171–7 *passim*, 181, 189
poetry 179–81, 185–7, 240–71, 273
popular culture 46, 237–8, 270, 344, 348, 352–74
populism 68, 193, 264–5, 357, 361, 364
postmodernism 143, 199, 215–16, 234
Pound, Ezra 186, 240–53, 258, 263, 271
poverty 120, 157, 193, 342, 361, 387
Powell, Colin 318
Presley, Elvis 20, 358, 371
Project for a New American Century (PNAC) 6, 377–8, 385
Protestant values 58, 61, 63, 68, 72, 156
Puritanism 45, 56–9, 69, 175, 182–3, 215, 227, 329–30, 335
Pynchon, Thomas 234, 238

racism and racial discrimination 52–3, 64, 77–9, 86, 99, 141, 160, 165–8, 269
Reagan, Ronald 25, 303, 305, 309, 316–18, 377–80, 395–6
'realism' in literature 191, 194–5, 220–1, 235–6
religion 42–5, 58–9, 103–4, 164, 181, 190, 329, 335–6, 362, 379–81
Republican Party 2, 93–4, 379–81, 385–7, 393–5
republicanism 45, 65–72, 148, 156, 161–2, 168
Reston, James Jr 316
rock 'n' roll 370, 373–4
Roosevelt, Eleanor 345–8
Roosevelt, Franklin D. 211, 311, 320–4, 345, 363, 395
Roosevelt, Theodore 124
Roth, Philip 230, 235
Rumsfeld, Donald 378
Rushdie, Salman 236

Salinger, J.D. 221, 230–1
Saroyan, William 278
Schlesinger, Arthur J. Jr 60–1, 392
Schulberg, Budd 225, 286
Schuyler, James 257, 262
Schwarzenegger, Arnold 17, 302

Second World War 152, 210–12, 216, 229, 234, 253, 280, 313–14, 318–21, 346, 362, 376–7, 393
September 11th 2001 attacks 2, 303, 309, 381–6, 389, 395
settlement patterns 30–3, 153–5
Shakespeare, William 263, 275, 281
Shelley, Mary 171
Shepard, Sam 291–4
Sherwood, Robert 278
Silko, Leslie Marmon 119, 237
Silliman, Ron 266–7, 270
slavery 3, 5, 19, 33–40, 44, 64, 68, 71, 75–87, 108, 166, 175, 189–90, 193, 329–31, 33740, 357–9
    abolition of 87–96, 186, 204, 336–7, 340
Smiles, Samuel 203
Smith, Henry Nash 142
Smith, Mamie 369
Smith, Rogers M. 63–4
Snyder, Gary 22, 259
social contract theory 53–4
Social Darwinism 193–4, 221
socialism 55, 70, 193
sovereignty 88–9, 96, 304
Soviet Union 55, 280–1, 306, 315–17, 319–24
Spicer, Jack 257, 271
standardisation 210–11
Star Wars (film) 366–7; *see also* Strategic Defense Initiative
Stein, Gertrude 224, 242, 247–8, 252, 258, 261, 263, 266, 270–1
Steinbeck, John 14, 144, 225–9, 363
Stevens, Wallace 242, 245–8, 258, 261, 271
Stone, Sly 371, 373
Stowe, Harriet Beecher 23, 82, 189–90, 336, 357
Strategic Defense Initiative 316–17
Sturges, Preston 363–4

Taylor, Frederick 207
Taylor, Zachary 310
Tennyson, Alfred 240
terrorism 324, 382–3
    war on 383–6, 389
    see also September 11th 2001 attacks

Texas 92, 130, 304, 309–10
Thoreau, Henry David 1, 20, 175–6, 180–1, 184–7
tobacco-growing 30, 37, 82, 328
Tocqueville, Alexis de 1, 5, 20, 50–3, 56–7, 63, 65, 70–4, 318–19, 327
Toomer, Jean 231, 251
transcendentalists 176, 181, 184–9
Truman, Harry S. 309, 319, 322
Turner, Frederick Jackson 99, 123–9, 144
Twain, Mark 4, 174, 193, 220–1, 275

United Nations 90, 315
United States Constitution 3, 73, 81, 112, 348, 381
    1st Amendment 373–4
    13th Amendment 95
    14th Amendment 64, 340
    19th Amendment 343–4
United States Declaration of Independence 29, 52–3, 73, 79, 94, 337
United States Supreme Court 85, 88–90, 94–5, 159, 370, 381, 392, 395
Updike, John 233
Uris, Leon 230

Vidal, Gore 325
Vietnam War 186, 213, 305, 310–12, 315–18, 320, 323–4, 365–6, 372, 379–80
vorticism 243–5
voting rights 64–5, 340, 343–4

Washington, Booker T. 232, 234
Washington, George 41, 47, 78, 80
Weber, Max 57–8
Weinberger, Caspar 317

Weinberger, Eliot 251
Welty, Eudora 225, 227
West, American 123–45, 167
West, Nathanael 225, 229
Westmoreland, William C. 322
Wharton, Edith 196, 220
White, Richard 103, 126
Whitman, Walt 3, 175, 180, 182, 186–7, 240–3, 258, 299
Whitney, Eli 82, 199
Whittier, John Greenleaf 179–80, 240
Wilder, Thornton 279–80
Williams, Tennessee 277, 281–3, 288–9, 292, 299
Williams, William Carlos 180, 242–9 *passim*, 255, 258
Wilson, August 291, 300
Wilson, Woodrow 309, 314, 320, 343
witchcraft allegations 330
Wittgenstein, Ludwig 267
Wolfowitz, Paul 378
Wollstonecraft, Mary 333
women, role and status of 326–50
women's movement 326, 349, 365–6
Wood, Gordon 65, 69
Woodstock Festival 371–2
Woodward, Bob 385
Wordsworth, William 242
Wouk, Herman 221, 230

xenophobia 367

Yellowstone Park 17–18, 27
Young, Alfred F. 41
Young, James P. 61

Zola, Emile 191
Zukofsky, Louis 249–50, 266
Zukor, Adolph 361